The Essential Guide to Forest School and Nature Pedagogy

This book is a complete guide to Forest School provision and Nature Pedagogy and it examines the models, methods, worldviews and values that underpin teaching in nature. Cree and Robb show how a robust Nature Pedagogy can support learning, behaviour, and physical and emotional well-being, and, importantly, a deeper relationship with the natural world. They offer an overview of what a Forest School programme could look like through the year.

The Essential Guide to Forest School and Nature Pedagogy provides 'real-life' examples from a variety of contexts, sample session plans and detailed guidance on using language, crafting and working with the natural world. This accessible resource guides readers along the Forest School path, covering topics such as:

- the history of nature education
- our sensory system in nature
- Forest School ethos and worldview
- playing and crafting in the natural world.

Guiding practitioners through planning for a programme, including taking care of a woodland site and preparing all the essential policies and procedures for working with groups and nature, this book is written by dedicated Forest School and nature education experts and is essential reading for settings, schools, youth groups, families and any practitioner working with children and young people.

Jon Cree is an international trainer for the Institute for Earth Education and Founding Director of the Forest School Association, UK. He worked at Bishops Wood Centre, Worcestershire County Council's award-winning environmental centre, helping establish Forest School nationally. He now works as a self-employed nature-based trainer and educator.

Marina Robb is Founder and Managing Director of Circle of Life Rediscovery CIC (www.circleofliferediscovery.com) and The Outdoor Teacher Ltd (www.theoutdoorteacher.com). She is a leading author and practitioner in the outdoor sector, an international trainer in the design and delivery of nature-based experiences and an advocate for the integration of environmental, education and health and well-being services.

"This book is an inspired, timely and great resource for those who want to help young children love and care for the Earth. *The Essential Guide to Forest School and Nature Pedagogy* contains everything a leader will need to plan and creatively craft life-changing outdoor experiences for young children."

— **Joseph Bharat Cornell, author of *Sharing Nature, Deep Nature Play* and founder of Sharing Nature Worldwide**

"This is a stimulating and important book. It bridges the philosophical and practical and celebrates the importance of connection, play and discovery. Forest Schools are one of the most exciting and dynamic areas of nature connection in the world today and this book will help the movement to blossom further."

— **Tristan Gooley, author of *Natural Navigator***

"I really enjoyed reading this. It is a wonderful mix of all the important things about being a Forest School leader and will make a great handbook. It provides a launch-pad into a myriad of eco-avenues."

— **Sara Knight, Forest School author and lecturer at Anglian Ruskin University, UK**

"A very timely reminder of the importance of engaging with and valuing nature by engaging and enthusing current and future generations through Forest School and Nature Pedagogy approaches. A book to remind us of the vital role of nature in supporting learning and development, and the wonder, awe and interest it can inspire in all of us. Coupled with this are lots of case studies and practical examples and tips to improve understanding and provide ideas for all those who want to learn and improve their practice."

— **Liz O'Brien, Head of Social and Economic Research, Forest Research**

"This book overflows with great ideas and excellent advice. It also offers a thorough pedagogical rationale for the work. Buy it. Read it. Expand your practice. Before long this book will be your go-to source."

— **Alida Gersie, writer and author**

"Marina Robb and Jon Cree are extremely experienced practitioners and two of the foremost teachers of Forest School approaches in the UK. Their book offers a broad overview of the theory and a deep dive into the practical realities of nature-based learning from early years to adulthood. Many practitioners concerned about the health, well-being and development of children will find it both rigorous and relevant: it would be a useful part of the training of any mental health practitioner or therapist working with young people. Interested parents will undoubtedly be inspired too. Robb and Cree show how Forest Schools offer an alternative and a complementary approach not just in education but in health care too, and they offer nuggets of wisdom to the crucial debate about how to equip future generations for a more vital and healthy relationship with the natural world."

– Alan Kellas, consultant psychiatrist and representative for nature approaches,
Royal College of Psychiatrists, UK

"Jon Cree and Marina Robb offer readers a deep, deep dive into the ideas that have shaped their seven decades at the forefront of outdoor learning. Drawing on neuroscience, play theory, dark green ecology and behavioural psychology, the book blends insight, reflection, research and practical advice. The result is full of wisdom and compassion, grounded in a profoundly spiritual conception of our connections with each other and the biosphere."

– Tim Gill, play activist, researcher, author and independent scholar

The Essential Guide to Forest School and Nature Pedagogy

JON CREE AND MARINA ROBB

Routledge
Taylor & Francis Group

LONDON AND NEW YORK

First edition published 2021
by Routledge
2 Park Square, Milton Park, Abingdon, Oxon, OX14 4RN

and by Routledge
605 Third Avenue, New York, NY 10158

Routledge is an imprint of the Taylor & Francis Group, an informa business

British Library Cataloguing-in-Publication Data
A catalogue record for this book is available from the British Library

Library of Congress Cataloging-in-Publication Data
Names: Cree, Jon, author. | Robb, Marina, author.
Title: The essential guide to Forest School and nature pedagogy / Jon Cree and Marina Robb.
Description: Abingdon, Oxon ; New York, NY : Routledge, 2021. | Includes bibliographical
    references and index.
Identifiers: LCCN 2020045049 (print) | LCCN 2020045050 (ebook) |
    ISBN 9780367425593 (hardback) | ISBN 9780367425616 (paperback) |
    ISBN 9780367853440 (ebook)
Subjects: LCSH: Holistic education. | Outdoor education. | Environmental education. |
    Nature study.
Classification: LCC LC990 .C74 2021 (print) | LCC LC990 (ebook) | DDC 370.11—dc23
LC record available at https://lccn.loc.gov/2020045049
LC ebook record available at https://lccn.loc.gov/2020045050

ISBN: 978-0-367-42559-3 (hbk)
ISBN: 978-0-367-42561-6 (pbk)
ISBN: 978-0-367-85344-0 (ebk)

Typeset in Folio
By Apex CoVantage, LLC

Printed in Great Britain by Bell and Bain Ltd, Glasgow

Access the Support Material: www.routledge.com/9780367425616

Contents

Support Material available at www.routledge.com/9780367425616

- chapter appendices with many 'tools' and 'tables'
- bonus online chapter: 'The evidence and green interventions'

Acknowledgements

We would like to acknowledge all the people whom we have sat with around the many fires. We are grateful for all of your natural wisdom and your decision to come play in the woods! Firstly, we thank our families, our partners Geoff and Jude, and our children who have patiently supported us when we disappear to discuss and write, again and again.

As co-authors, we thank each other. Marina for her friendship, really supportive questioning and most importantly for keeping me on track! To Jon, for his enthusiasm and warm-hearted friendship, his depth of knowledge and listening. We have been meeting for quite a few years now and discussing the finer details of what Nature Pedagogy means and both valued our continuous commitment to the unpacking of this huge subject, indeed life's work.

To Jude, who's been there to bounce ideas and insecurities off and what's more has done quite a bit of proofreading. To Tim Robb (Leia's grandfather, Marina's father-in-law), who stepped in and edited our words, I thank wholeheartedly. Their backbone support has been immense.

We see ourselves as hugely privileged, having spent most of our adult lives in the woods and nature, learning on many, many school and informal settings' grounds . . . and all with generally enthusiastic learners and educators. It is to the whole variety of learners, from the disenfranchised teenagers to the enthusiastic tots, that we owe a huge debt of gratitude. We are sure we have learned more from them than they have from us.

And then to the educators and all those who have shared our trainer's journey – we are so lucky to have been part of this community. In this respect Jon would particularly like to honour Steve van Matre, who was the first person to articulate for him everything he had felt about education and ecology and brought these two together so seamlessly and magically, and then his mother, Pat, for exposing him to the natural world and story at such an early age. Jon would also like to pay tribute to Alida Gersie for instilling in him the importance of story, in particular our own story, for making meaning of our relationship to the natural world. For Marina, she would like to honour Malcolm Plant from Nottingham University, her MSc lecturer in environmental education, who provided endless research and thinking about this huge subject, from deep ecology to revolutionary paradigms – even more relevant now 30 years on! She also honours her parents who, though they weren't so nature enthusiastic, provided a childhood where, often left to her own devices, she learned from many different cultures and their worldviews, which was never 'normal'.

acknowledgements

And her supervisor and anchor Richard Cleminson, for his authenticity, care, deep listening and encouragement.

We would both like to say a huge thanks to those who have reviewed the book; the contributors, including Lily Horseman for her unbounding creativity, Caylin Gans for her deep reflections, and Rivkah Cummerson for her key dynamics and forest principle drawings; and all those who have been part of the case studies and photographs that make this type of education real and 'alive'. Finally, we are both indebted to the 'indigenous' – to those communities who across the earth have tended her for safekeeping, who despite continued extermination have continued to sing, dance and have fun! In their honour, we are proudly part of the community to come.

Foreword

Phew! It's been a tough year hasn't it? To echo Dorothy, the Tin Man and the Scarecrow, *Climate change and terrorists and pandemic, oh my!* What are we to do? This book is the 'To Do'. With this book, Jon and Marina have created a potent vision of the *interviability* of children, nature and the community. It's about the world we want to live in and the path to follow to get there. In the United States, when you drive from New Hampshire across the Piscataqua River Bridge into Maine, you're greeted with a sign that says, *Welcome to Maine, The Way Life Should Be*. This book could be titled, *Welcome to Forest School, The Way Education Should Be*.

Or here's another potential title. The publishers of the book originally wanted Jon and Marina to call this book *Nature Pedagogy and Forest School: The Definitive Guide*. They balked at the word *definitive*. Too self-congratulatory, too preachy. Well, even though they decided to excise definitive from the title, as an objective reader I can tell you – this book is definitely definitive. It's a theory-to-practice, soup-to-nuts, pie-in-the-sky to mud-under-your-feet rich compendium of everything you need to know about trundling into the forest safely and productively with children and teens. But before articulating all the specific ways in which this book is powerful, here's the big picture.

Let's start at the end. There's a poignant story in the last pages of this book about a 7-year-old child who returns home from school traumatised by a lesson about the destruction of the Amazon. Almost a million hectares of rainforest burned in the last year, loss of habitat for endangered animals and indigenous people, the lungs of the planet burning – you know the drill. Whether it's children fearful of rainforest burning or the global pandemic, too much of our education system inculcates fear. And fear makes us retreat into ourselves and become incapable of learning. This book is about replacing a culture of fear with a culture of hope. It's about replacing head-centric education with a balanced head-heart-hands education. It's about a vision of education that empowers children and teens with a sense of hopeful resolve, commitment to community and an appreciation of the gift of life on earth.

The Essential Guide to Forest School and Nature Pedagogy comes at an important point in the evolution of environmental education and nature-based education in the last half century or so. Environmental education flourished after the first Earth Day 50 years ago. It came out of the activist orientation to do something about the destruction of ecosystems, the ozone hole, the plundering of elephants for their ivory tusks. Environmental educators argued that if children learn that these bad things are happening, then they'll be motivated to turn off the tap when brushing their teeth, not squish spiders and become protectors of the natural world. Children were taught to identify trees, understand food chains, learn why DDT makes eagles' eggs break in the nest. In order to play with the science big boys – biology, chemistry, physics – environmental education followed the path of curriculum guidelines and science standards. There was a body of knowledge that every child needed to learn to become earth savvy. It became too much like head-centric traditional education. At the same time, it evolved a 'look, don't touch' mentality. Nature is over there, behind the glass. Don't step off the trail, don't pick the flowers – lots of don'ts.

Parallel to this evolution there was a separate branch that was a quieter, more down-and-dirty approach. Innovators like Joseph Cornell and Steve Van Matre advocated for sensory immersion, integrating feeling with thinking, being joyful in nature. One strand of this movement in the last 20 years has been the nature or coyote mentoring movement. Advocates of this approach encourage us to embrace our wild selves and encourage children to play in nature, take appropriate risks, construct shelters, build fires. The approach aligns with the instinctual impulses of children that have existed for millennia. It's about knowing thyself through being in nature. Whereas environmental education lost sight of the 'thyself,' the nature mentoring approach wove children and nature together. This strand has evolved into Nature Pedagogy and Forest Schools where the emphasis is equally inward and outward, becoming a whole person *and* preserving the wholeness of the natural world.

Now, how is this book so definitive? Let me count the ways.

PHILOSOPHY, PSYCHOLOGY, PEDAGOGY AND NEUROPHYSIOLOGY

Nature Pedagogy didn't just spring anew from practitioners in the late 20th century. Instead there are centuries-old streams of thoughts out of which Nature Pedagogy is a recent florescence. There's a separate chapter dedicated to each one of these disciplines and sophisticated articulation of how these disciplines weave together. The awareness of depth psychology and social-emotional learning is what is sometimes missing from environmental education literature. The 'thyself' part of the equation is front and centre here.

THEORY, STORIES AND GRAPHICS

In reflecting a commitment to head, heart and hands, the structure of the book is wonderfully differentiated. There's lots of philosophy and developmental theory for the head. Most of the chapters include evocative, heartfelt stories from Forest School – real-world challenges – that ground the theory. Both of these are complemented with lavish charts, diagrams, and photos of children with their hands full of, and on, the natural world. I like the numerous pictures of outdoor toileting options (in part because I didn't cover that in a recent book of mine). In addition there are unique images of minibeast hotels, the materials you need for building temporary tarp structures, poisonous and edible plants, handmade tools. This makes it all seem do-able.

FORMS AND MORE FORMS

When you're starting a new programme, what you really want is a model letter home to parents about what gear their children need. Or the framework for how to do a risk assessment on your site. Or the checklist of what you need in your first aid kits. And you'll really appreciate the letter to landowners about how you'll be using their land as part of your programme. The book includes more forms than you can shake a stick at. Even forms illustrating how to shake sticks. There's a remarkable chart on all the possible tools you should buy – for use by both adults and children – that is almost worth the price of book itself. You'll appreciate having all these at your fingertips.

FOREST SCHOOL FOR ALL

Nature-based programmes are sometimes criticised for being elite, un-diverse, available only to well-off children. That's not the case here. Jon and Marina want to make it clear that Nature Pedagogy approaches are valuable for children from toddlerhood through the elementary grades to high school to the parents of all those children. Similarly, Nature Pedagogy is valuable for the wide range of differently abled children, for urban and rural children, for children on the spectrum and for black, brown, yellow and white children. No stone is left unturned regarding how Forest School provides learning and healing opportunities for everyone.

Now it's time to have at it. One warning. Don't think you're going to sit down and read this book in a couple of days or a week. This is the kind of book that will benefit from sipping, like nursing a good brandy. Read a chapter here and then a chapter there. Jump right into the Crafting chapter or Journey with Plants and Animals chapter when you're in the midst of planning a fall curriculum. Settle in for a quiet evening to immerse yourself in the neurophysiology of the Brain, Body and Place chapter. When my son was about 10 years old he said, "I'm a good explorer because I really look at all the details, all the little places you can go, all the crannies you can find. I don't just look at it and go, I spend a lot of time on it, make forts and stuff and traps." That's my suggestion to you. Jon and Marina have created a great neighbourhood for you to explore with this book. Don't just look at it and go; spend a lot of time on it. You'll be glad you did.

David Sobel, Professor Emeritus, Antioch University, New England. International Researcher, Author and Expert in environmental education and play

Introduction

It is a sense of community, contentment, challenge, play, creativity and exploration in education communities that we wish to explore in this book – Forest School settings in particular. While the book focuses on Forest School and nature-based practice, it is with the understanding that these pedagogies both complement other 'progressive' forms of education and sit on the shoulders of 'ways of knowing' in relation to learners and the natural world that go far back into our human evolution.

> *One of the sayings in our country is Ubuntu – the essence of being human. Ubuntu speaks particularly about the fact that you can't exist as a human being in isolation. It speaks about our interconnectedness. You can't be human all by yourself, and when you have this quality – Ubuntu – you are known for your generosity. We think of ourselves far too frequently as just individuals, separated from one another, whereas you are connected and what you do affects the whole World. When you do well, it spreads out; it is for the whole of humanity.*
>
> Desmond Tutu

We write this introduction while spending much-needed time away from the screen and electronic connection – although we are now doing this in front of a screen! We feel a sense of disconnection yet connection. Jon started writing this book with Marina while looking over one of the many islands of the Stockholm archipelago, one of the largest in the world with approximately 42,000 islands. He saw the 'human' world as a series of islands disconnected in many ways from what really supports communities on the planet. *Fear* seems to have been the zeitgeist in the past and is certainly present as we write this book, and the quickening effects of climate change herald huge changes. Politicians prey upon our fear of increased numbers of refugees supposedly flooding 'our' communities. There is now a normalisation of mass displacement, with nations of peoples with no community to speak of. As we write, the world has a 'refugee nation' that has the 23rd largest population, a result of war, persecution and climate change. Other ecological fears include the disappearance of the arctic ice flows and the rapid decline of the British songbird population. In fact, in our lifetime we have lost half our UK biodiversity, and butterflies, Jon's childhood obsession, have witnessed great declines in the last 50 years. As we write this, the latest report from Germany shows a 75% decrease in flying insects (McCarthy, 2015; State of Nature Report 2019). Where are those squashed insects on the windscreen we witnessed in our youth? These are just some of the many breakdowns in human and natural communities on our planet.

This book is about the fundamental importance in education of repairing, creating and developing communities of learning that are about working in harmony with humans and the natural world, or as some put it (Abram, 1996), the 'more than human' world. It is also about moving right away from the current climate of fear – from the fear of failure in exams, the fear of punishment for what is seen as inappropriate behaviour and attainment and the fear of disconnection to the paranoid fear of 'other peoples' promulgated by many Western political systems. So yes, we 'feel' that sense of societal disconnection even more today than back in the 1970s when we started exploring a deep connection with the 'more than human' world. It is the more than human world that in some ways we 'feel' even deeper connections with than we did 40 years ago, when we both started out on this vocation in facilitating deeper connections to the natural world and trying to help learners make environmental choices in their lives. Nature offers the much-needed solitude which shows us that aloneness is not the same as loneliness, that the earth and elements are always with us. Are we ever alone? The oak, lime, hazel, pine, birch and sweet chestnut trees in our woodlands are all deeply familiar beings. At sea, 'our blue community' reflects too that we are connected. The salty smell of the sea speaks words that the English language can never emulate. Watching in silence the terns performing their daring dives into the sun-dappled waters touches something deep within our sea-blue souls, and Rachel Carson's book *The Sea Around Us* comes to mind.

> *To stand at the edge of the sea, to sense the ebb and flow of the tides, to feel the breath of a mist moving over a great salt marsh, to watch the flight of shore birds that have swept up and down the surf lines of the continents for untold thousands of years, to see the running of the old eels and the young shad to the sea, is to have knowledge of things that are as nearly eternal as any earthly life can be.*
>
> (Carson, 1961)

Beyond our innate drive towards survival, what do we most value in Forest School and Nature Education for our learners? Is it that sense of connection and being part of a human and more than human community that is much bigger than the self that we get in places such as the Swedish archipelago or the oak woods where we work, play, learn and grow, week in and week out? What are the ingredients for our children's future success? If we want our children to be 'happy', a word overused in common parlance in education and academic circles, or maybe having contentment/well-being are better – how do we support this? The key predictor of happiness (the most approved-of emotion) is satisfying loving relationships and friendships. Beyond a level of income, said to be $75,000, happiness and emotional well-being does not increase (Deaton and Kahnemann, 2010). When our energy is used on survival, on possible danger, our stress levels increase and our capacity for learning and development is significantly reduced. All humans thrive within an emotionally safe environment, full of opportunities for play, risk and challenge. Our brains need information-rich, reciprocal stimulation that other human beings and the living world provide.

So, what does a community of learning not driven by fear but by hope, strong relationships and community, look like? And what is the role of the educator?

In this book we aim to paint a picture of the landscape and of the details – from the overall feel and look of a setting that is moving towards this *shared community focus* through to the specific dialogue and conversations that enable an inclusive learning community. We want a place where adults and young people alike are seen as learners and educators, a place where power over learning is shared and, importantly, hope is engendered, moving away from a fear culture. How do we engender a *playful* approach that encourages creativity and an atmosphere where individual identity is seen as important within a *collaborative* atmosphere? This is where 'play' literally comes into play, working with our fears in a non-judgmental way, and helps us make sense of the world. After all, there are many philosophers and educators, in the past and today, who see play as fundamental to learning – Froebel being a prime theorist in this respect,

Play is the highest expression of human development in childhood, for it alone is the free expression of what is in a child's soul.

(Froebel, 1887)

We will also explore how we learn to empathise and regulate our emotions. How do we reach a point where we can understand that there is no such thing as a 'bad' or 'good' emotion? How can we recognise a safe environment, one where we can learn to realise that all behaviour is a choice?

How do we create positive connections in a world that is connected more than ever before regarding information and conversation – witnessed through Facebook, Twitter, Instagram and the rest – yet is disconnected when it comes to deep meaningful relationships – human and more than human? How can we, as adult educators, rediscover the clear thinking and questions that children and young people so often pose and discuss and explore these *equally* with our learners in a way that builds deeper and positive respectful relationships? It is these clear questions and thinking that Greta Thunberg, for example, has posed over the recent years, presenting challenges that politicians have often shied away from, that have really made the world sit up and start to take action. It is this that has inspired some 'active hope'. To see schools and head teachers supporting their students to take the time to make their voices heard on the school Friday climate change demonstrations in 2019, is heartening, and for us, symptomatic of a respectful relationship.

With the current ecological and systemic changes in society, how do we create learning communities that engender a resilient problem-solving, compassionate ethos? How do we deal with uncertainty in the face of an outcome-based education system still firmly embedded in economic growth and a fixed mindset?

When tackling many of these issues best practice relies on facilitators who are reflective and aware, who know the limitations of their own perceptions and know they are always learning. This approach is embedded within a deep respect for the non-human and human world. The hard skills that require instruction and adult-led facilitation are tools developed from our indigenous roots, and it is these that we will allude to when tackling specific roles in the book. Forest School has been involved with education and connecting communities to the natural world for over 25 years in the UK. We will draw on our environmental and ecological education, Forest School experiences and Forest School training experiences to pull together our own reflections on the big picture and small details that create this sense of community.

The initial chapters will highlight the importance of the natural world to our health and well-being and, in the context of the book, how regular contact with the natural world has always been an intrinsic element in healthy human learning and development. This will be backed by much of the research carried out recently (see the bonus online chapter), particularly into brain/body development and how the outdoor world is one of the important 'glues' for developing good cognition. Forest School principles will be illuminated and discussed. We will also explore the important role that empathy and language play in creating productive and resilient learning communities. When we speak of language, this means all forms of communication – not just words (this book can only go so far!). Further chapters look at the importance of following the learner and the natural world and working with the seasons and the various practical aspects of working with familiar elements of Forest School – handtools, fire, growing, foraging and cooking, craft, story, stewardship of woodland. One of our key threads will be to explore how we work with the natural world in a world dominated by technological advances and build on experiences in the natural world inside our schools and homes.

The Forest School ethos provides a safe and natural setting for people and the living world to form long-lasting relationships where a sense of belonging is fostered. We will explore in more detail the values that underpin this ethos. In this place, we all learn to care for ourselves, others and the natural world, building in reciprocal actions and honouring of everything that makes this web of life. The great news is that we all play to learn, to remember more and to become better at language, less stressed, more socially skilled, empathetic and emotionally regulated – all indictors that we will be successful and happy.

The book includes many 'practical tools' regarding how we plan, dialogue, case studies throughout and pointers to equipment needed. We have also made reference to some useful **online materials** that accompany the book with templates for forms such as risk-benefit analysis and woodland management plans, sample session plans and reflections, as well as sources of further evidence and equipment. Appendices for all the chapters with many 'tools' and 'tables' can be found online at www.routledge.com/9780367425616.

Towards the end of the book we will look at the challenges and changes required in ourselves to move our education system to a more human-scale learning pedagogy. How do we work within an 'industrial-based' education to shift our own practice and influence those around us to be more empathic and 'community based', in order to stimulate our inherent creativity and innovation? And how do we do so such that we can meet the biggest challenge of all in our education system, indeed the world – the diminishment of the natural world and breakdown of its ecological systems?

The role of a creative leader is not to have all the ideas; it's to create a culture where everyone can have ideas and feel that they're valued.

(Ken Robinson, 2011)

Let's see how Forest School and nature-based practices, like many progressive approaches to education, can join up some of the 'islands' in our education system and contribute to a playful, creative and, importantly, *community* approach. We will start by looking at the antecedents of a nature-based education and the values that we feel underpin such a pedagogy.

OVERVIEW

Chapters 1 and 2 look at the values that underpin a Nature Pedagogy and the historical influences.
Chapters 3 and 4, and indeed all the chapters in the book, examine what we mean by a Nature Pedagogy and how we sensitively work with our own ancestral and 'indigenous' cultures in this contemporary world.
Chapters 5, 6, 7, 10, 11, 12 and 13 look at how the ecological underpins learning and development, how to follow the seasons, the Forest School site and how to care for it, and ways of working with plants, animals and the elements.
Chapters 6, 8, 9 and 11 explain how to support the learner-centred community process, risk-taking, holistic learning and development.
Chapter 14 revisits goals of the Nature Pedagogy that we have outlined in this book and emphasises the importance of empathy for ourselves and the human and more than human world, as anticipated by international law.
A bonus chapter and appendices for all the chapters with many 'tools' and 'tables' can be found online at www.routledge.com/9780367425616

BIBLIOGRAPHY

Abram, D (1996) *Spell of Sensuous: Perception and Language in a More-Than-Human World*. New York: Pantheon Books.

Carson, R (1961) *The Sea Around Us*. New York: Oxford University Publishing.

Deaton, A and Kahnemann, D (2010) *High Income Improves Evaluation of Life but Not Emotional Well-Being*. University of Princeton. See www.pnas.org/content/107/38/16489.

Froebel, F (1887) *The Education of Man*. New York, London: D. Appleton Century.

McCarthy, M (2015) *Moth Snowstorm: Nature and Joy*. London: John Murray Publishers.

Robinson, K (2011) *Out of Our Minds: Learning to Be Creative*. Oxford: Capstone.

State of Nature Partnerships (2019) *State of Nature 2019 Report*. See https://nbn.org.uk/wp-content/uploads/2019/09/State-of-Nature-2019-UK-full-report.pdf.

Tutu, D (2000) *No Future without Forgiveness*. London: Random House.

1 Nature Pedagogy, Forest School ethos and valuing nature

As long as I live, I'll hear waterfalls and birds and winds sing. I'll interpret the rocks. Learn the language of the flood, storm and avalanche. I'll acquaint myself with the glaciers and wild gardens, and get as close to the heart of the world as I can. – John Muir (1871)

(via Wolfe, 1945)

It is fundamental to begin this exploration acknowledging that the wider natural world is an essential and necessary part of our learning and development. With the appropriate guidance, there can be a co-development that is immensely informative and draws on the natural intelligence of the living world. This is not just 'in our heads', but rather includes our minds, hearts and bodies and the valuable feedback that is gained from the wider natural world.

Experiencing your development and learning indoors is inherently different from 'being' in the outdoors. The moment you step outside and are receptive, you will receive different answers to questions, an increase in your sensory and inner life, all because the whole field of your experience is now larger and more complex. You are no longer within four walls but a component within a larger biological and ecological system.

'How are we informed by nature?' This question will weave itself throughout this book as we paint a picture of both the theories behind an education-in-nature programme and what it looks like in reality. We propose that the natural world, our 'beloved' earth, does indeed hold a place in our understanding, informing our values and our ego and eco identity. We understand that nature is often the 'invisible' curriculum, secretly developing us and carefully cultivating our pedagogy, and is part of our own true maturation, our sense of who we are and what it means to belong to this world.

In this opening chapter we would like to share the values, ethos and principles that underpin Forest School and nature-based practice, showing the antecedents to the current practice in the UK and the similarities with many other outdoor environmental learning programmes in this country and across the planet. At the same time, we will provide a framework that will be repeated through the book and serve as a signpost to chapters that fill in the detail of what Forest School practice, in particular, looks like, what guides the practice and tools for practitioners. This will range from the specific dialogues that happen in Forest School in a variety of contexts and case studies to the types of experiences that are facilitated in a Forest School/nature education setting.

As John Muir so eloquently espouses in his many writings – learning is living and living is learning. This idea is always at the heart of nature-based learning. We would argue that Forest School is striving to get to the 'heart of the world'! We are feeling beings, and we remember more vividly what we have felt most strongly.

In the last 27 years, one of the largest nature education movements has grown and had quite an impact on mainstream education in the UK . . . Forest School. While we will be looking at the wider nature education movement, we will begin by describing Forest School as it has informed our thoughts and wider nature education practices.

LEARNING IN THE OUTDOORS THROUGH FOREST SCHOOL

We are often asked, "What is Forest School?" and it is a hard thing to define. While there are many books on Forest School and learning in nature, we would like to delve more deeply into what this looks like in practice and the impact of immersing a group in nature.

CASE STUDY: FOREST SCHOOL IN ACTION

Let's begin by painting a Forest School scene (mixed group of 10- to 13-year-olds.)

It's mid-January as I approach the 'Forest School gate' – in fact a rope between two posts. I hear the sounds of delight at the far end of the woodland clearing, a voice shouting from behind a tree, "I'm over here!" and above this a gentle wind blowing through the oaks and birches. There is also a robin singing its heart out despite the exuberant sounds of people – both old and young. I gently lift the rope and walk the muddy path that has obviously had feet splashing everywhere, and I see two planks. Maybe a bridge protecting human feet from a troll? As I approach the 'base camp', there is a small fire surrounded by wooden planks on tree stumps, and next to this a semi-permanent shelter with a basket and trolley. The basket is open and spilling out of it are a camo-net and ropes. Next to that are some stakes and what look like homemade mallets. On one of the benches are two youngsters making a batter – half of which seems to have made its way on to the bench. They are both beating the batter in tandem . . . and they smile at me and ask if I like pancakes . . . "Pancakes with crab apply jelly wot I made". Squeals of delight come from two children and an adult on a rope swing, and the adult near the pancake makers is busy weaving a basket. There is a slightly older girl wandering and talking to herself who seems to be threading something on to a piece of wool as she walks. The four that are running everywhere are completely engrossed in their own hide and seek game. The adult greets me and says, "Just in time for dinner, Jon!" and she turns to one of the pancake makers. "Do you reckon it's lunchtime yet Holly?" Holly replies, "Let's just wait a bit for the first pancake to be ready, then we'll call everyone else over." A minute later both pancake makers make a loud bird-type call. Everyone returns and asks if it is indeed lunchtime, and without hesitation all kick into gear and gather the handwashing materials.

This scene (Figure 1.1) is indicative of what you instinctively feel is a playful learning community that is looking after its own needs, interacting with the woodland in a playful yet respectful way, and where it is tricky to see who is leading whom. It's Forest School underpinned by a certain ethos and values!

Figure 1.1 A Forest School 'scene'

The definition of Forest School in the UK, arrived at after an extensive consultation in 2010 and 2011, is

Forest School is an inspirational process offering ALL learners regular opportunities to achieve and develop confidence and self-esteem through hands-on learning experiences in a woodland or natural environment with trees. Forest School is a specialized learning approach that sits within and complements the wider context of outdoor learning.

(www.forestschoolassociation.org)

FOREST SCHOOL AND NATURE-BASED VALUES

Forest School and indeed many other long-term nature connection education programmes under different names have spawned in various countries in recent times, each sharing common values.

Nature as a teacher

At the heart of Forest School and 'good education' is valuing all learners and the contribution they make to the learning community. This means working with learners' needs, interests, motivations and preferred ways of learning, and alongside this, recognising the intrinsic value of the non-human world. Respect and humility are core values that all Forest School practitioners work with, giving 'power' over to our learners for their own learning – through providing choice, tempered with compassion for the non-human. Nature is the teacher, the pedagogue. We could say, the *relationship* between the person and the natural world is the teacher. It is the *relationship* that is revealing something. Nature is also the therapist and a guide. A person, adult or child, learns something about their lives or themselves through this emerging relationship. This may not always be conscious or 'visible', but at some point their appreciation of the natural world is deepened.

A holistic approach

In a nutshell, this is a holistic form of education creating a vibrant nature-based learning community. 'Holistic' is a term often bandied around in the education world, and we will expand on holistic development in Chapters 3 and 4. We see a holistic approach as an 'integrated' approach to learning which means accepting the 'whole' person – warts and all. It is an approach that works with everyone's needs and sense of self – accepting we are all imperfect, but *we are who we are* and are worthy of love and acceptance. A tall order but very much something that underpins the practice of Forest School, and we have to struggle with it. What we are hoping to develop from these values is the building of resilience, creativity, self-worth, emotional literacy and connection to and caring for the non-human world, so our planet and society thrives. In the end we are trying to create something akin to a 'family full of kinship' with human and non-humans 'being' together – a village of learning and living. The important aspects that make Forest School special are the playful *equal relationships* and the deeply empathic connections that develop.

Intrinsic and extrinsic values

How often do we go ahead and just 'do' stuff in our environmental education work without really unpacking the values that drive the work? Too much, we would say. It is worth spending time trying to understand the community values we bring to our approach. A good place to start is with the 'Common Cause' values, which have compassion at their heart and are based on extensive research on universal values across cultures and countries carried out by a number of environmental organisations and researchers, first published in 2011 (Common Cause Foundation). A number of 'sets' of values were identified and put into two categories: 'intrinsic' and 'extrinsic'.

Intrinsic values are centred on inherently rewarding pursuits such as affiliation to friends and family, connection to nature, creativity, self-acceptance and concern for others, while extrinsic values are centred on external approval and rewards – external image, achievement within the community, prestige, power and status. See Figure 1.2 below for a complete list and the 'sets' where values overlap.

The intrinsic values are very much in line with Forest School principles as outlined later in this chapter. When it comes to a connection with nature, we are as intrinsic to our living world as the rivers and trees, made and woven by the same mind and flows of energy and materials – we can tell nature's stories through our own 'being'.

It has also been shown by researchers and writers in education such as Kohn (2006) that extrinsic values can erode the intrinsic values of universalism, benevolence, self-direction, self-control (agency) and, importantly, community-building and learner-centred values. Offering small specific rewards such as verbal recognition of someone's engagement with the learning and place may help learners to begin with. For example, a practitioner might say in an early session, "I am impressed with the way you looked after that small insect and returned it to its home". This might well encourage the child to come back again – "the Forest School practitioner complimented me" (extrinsic reward chiming with an extrinsic value of public recognition); "I definitely want to come back next week." In the long term, though, we wish to rely on intrinsic motivation based on the intrinsic values of compassion: self-determination and creativity; affiliation with other people and the non-human world; and understanding, respect, tolerance and appreciation of other people and the non-human world. This means that in the end we do not rely on self-aggrandisement

Value surveys and maps

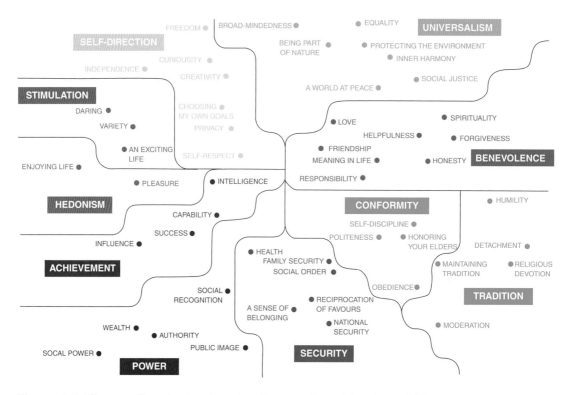

Figure 1.2 'Common Cause' values based on Common Cause Foundation, 2011

and, importantly, have no need to approve a child by saying "I am impressed by . . ." This will be expanded on in Chapters 8 and 9 when looking at behaviour and self-worth.

Conflicting values

This is quite a tall order when the overriding 'values' of our liberal secular society are driven by the self-interest which has seen the accelerating destruction of many ecosystems on our planet in the last half century.

For us, sustainable development never really totally embraced the idea of reciprocity, needing to give back whenever we take from the environment or others in more need. For example, if we cut a tree, even if this enhances the ecology of a site as in coppicing, we need to show gratitude to the tree. It is a frame of mind and heart. Some would say sustainable development has moved on to 'regenerative development', to 'environmental economics' and 'ecosystem services', which seem to be the only 'real' solutions to habitat destruction (McCarthy, 2015).

Take flooding in the UK, where we are now considering watershed management as the solution to flooding based on the ecosystem services that watersheds provide. More tree planting and the simple old techniques of drainage management and non-intensive farming in the watershed, versus building flood defences along rivers and rebuilding after floods, are seen as less expensive (UK Government's Social Value Act 2016 and Well-being of Future Generations Wales Act 2015). In May 1997 the University of Maryland, in publishing the biggest study of all on ecosystem services around the planet (Constanza et al., 2014), showed that these techniques were worth 125 trillion dollars annually, and yet the GDP of the world at the time of the study was 75 trillion dollars. They're a no-brainer in a capital-driven liberal economy.

However, where does that leave the common butterfly, for example, that fed Jon's soul in pre-adolescent times and was part of what helped him become the 'environmentalist' that he is now? Or Marina aged 10 witnessing a poor child on the streets begging in South Korea which left her questioning her privilege and feeling shame? How can you 'value' a brimstone butterfly, and do we really want to commodify nature in this way? How can we intrinsically value one human above another and commodify each other? It is the intrinsic values that are part and parcel of being a Forest School/nature practitioner and, we hope, a human as part of the community to come. In the end it is love of the natural world and humanity that uplifts and becomes what cannot be valued in a monetary way. It is the spiritual communal value of birdsong, for example, along with a giving back, that underpins Forest School and practice within 'natural law'. The familiar song of the robin is part of the Forest School community, and while we value its company, we need to respect its home and take care of the community. This reciprocal feeling with the robin has the comparable worth of a rainforest or coral reef.

Earth-centric values

While the indigenous peoples and Western romantics of the past such as Wordsworth, Thoreau, Muir and Ruskin write eloquent words that communicate the value that every living being has an equal right to life, it is up to the nature educator to help facilitate the poetry of the moment that is in us all. We need to enable close nature connection, not exploitation, which can be proclaimed by all the learners in our own words and remake the value of nature through joy and celebration – appealing to an intrinsic value as defined by the Common Cause Foundation.

Table 1.1 Adapted from 'The Mother Earth vs Western Man: The American confrontation between two opposing value systems' by Faith Justice, American Indian Studies, San Francisco University.

Indigenous way of life – 'harmony with nature'	Western, progress through development way of life – 'domination of nature'
Everything has spiritual value. The spiritual and physical are united.	Everything has monetary value. The spiritual and physical are separated.
The laws of nature are emphasised. Nature reflects the Creator.	The laws of man are emphasised. The Creator is in man's image.
Feelings are important.	Feelings are rationalised.
Society is based on cultural pluralism and the extended family.	Society is based on the nuclear family.
Roots are remembered.	Roots are forgotten.
Cosmology is spatial and timeless.	Cosmology is linear and time-oriented.
Education is experiential. Teachings are from nature and elders.	Education is from mass media and salaried professionals.
Technology serves people and nature.	People and nature serve technology.
Material wealth is shared and given away.	Material wealth is hoarded and consumed.
Behaviour is cooperative.	Behaviour is competitive.
Justice and equality are achieved by cultural form (forms of culture such as theatre, role-play, folklore etc.)	Justice and equality are achieved by legislation.
Society is egalitarian; women and men have equal power.	Society is patriarchal. Women must emulate men.
Leaders put the people above themselves.	Leaders put themselves above the people.
The balance of nature is maintained.	The balance of nature is destroyed.

This can often be difficult when our Western culture is largely reflective of the extrinsic values named in the Common Cause Foundation's work. The values table above is taken from San Francisco University. While fairly stark, somewhat dated in some instances and possibly a somewhat romantic view, it does show how indigenous values are part of intrinsic values versus the values of a Western utilitarian and 'domination of nature' culture that reflect extrinsic values.

> The old Lakota was wise. He knew that man's heart away from nature becomes hard. He knew that lack of respect for growing, living things soon led to a lack of respect for humans too. So he kept his youth close to its softening influence.
>
> (McLuhan, 1971, p. 6)

Throughout the book, we will be looking at how we sensitively work with our own ancestral and 'indigenous' cultures in this contemporary world.

An ambition

The overall goal of Forest School is *to help people develop into resilient, creative compassionate individuals who value the natural world (human and non-human) and care for every living being's welfare.* These goals rely on the intrinsic values that underpin Forest School principles and practice. These values, which we feel need to be constantly revisited, are at the heart of what we do as nature educators and extend to the various aspects of our practice as outlined in the chapters of this book.

FOREST SCHOOL PRINCIPLES

There are six Forest School principles that have been explicitly expressed on the UK Forest School Association website, that are underpinned by the aforementioned values. We have expressed these principles in our words and a Forest School practitioner's pictures to try to encapsulate both the principle and the values that we feel are implicit in the principle:

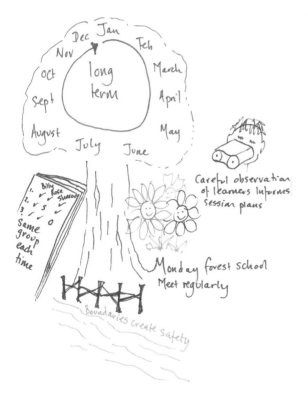

- Developing a relationship between learners and the natural world that features mutuality and compassion.

- Facilitating a long-term programme of regular contact with the natural world that make deeper, caring nature connections.

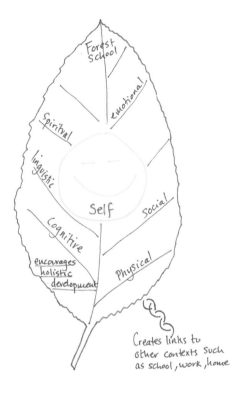

Creates links to other contexts such as school, work, home

- Working in a learner-centred way whereby an 'equal' learning community is developed where there is a combination of autonomous and communal learning, featuring joint decision making regarding the learning. Forest School follows a constructivist approach whereby the learning, in and of, the real natural world and the learners themselves emerges.

- Risk taking in a safe context is encouraged, enabling learners to move into their learning zones where they can manage their own risks, be they emotional, physical, cognitive or social risks.

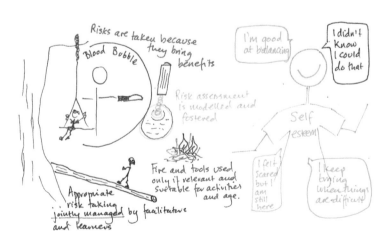

- Developing the whole person, supporting cognitive processes and fostering creative, resilient, physically healthy independent learners.

- Practitioners who are qualified and continually reflect on, question and develop, their own learning and Forest School facilitation.

These principles are key areas that need to be addressed if we want our society to be happy, healthy and protective of our ecology.

This is a multi-disciplined and holistic approach that draws on our 'whole life' experience and relates to the 'whole' of our community health. When we discuss a holistic approach, it includes an internal and external approach – our life within, and our external life with other humans and other non-human life. This thread of the inner and outer life meeting is explored in every chapter. In the end, it means extending our sense of dignity beyond the individual to the wider community and nature.

A PARADIGM SHIFT?

Once you immerse yourself in nature, Forest School and 'nature relationship-based education' can cause a paradigm shift from a utilitarian and rational-based worldview to a kinship, human-in-nature one. This provokes a meaningful change in how we think about education (and beyond) and a desire to participate in an educational model that is regenerative (and ethical) that can sit within nature's capacity.

How we see the world has entertained our thought processes and informed our behaviour for thousands of years. What we value creates the building blocks of learning and subsequent decisions. Peter Gray, professor and researcher in psychology and renowned play specialist, states,

> *What we call knowledge might better be called models, or explanatory concepts, which help people to make sense of the world around them. From this perspective, knowledge is to be judged not so much by its truth or falseness as by its usefulness. A good idea is one that helps a person make sense of some aspect of his or her social or physical world and thereby helps that person to navigate that world.*
>
> (Gray, 2013, p. 86)

A healthy building needs a sound foundation – a healthy human needs 'good' foundations. It is our belief that 'good' essentially needs to include 'good' for the living world, humans and non-humans alike, to create human systems that protect nature's ecosystems. Applying a Forest School approach to the outdoors embodies an experience in which children can experiment, explore, receive nature and intrinsically learn to value the living world. This is a forgotten but essential ingredient for an integrated human-nature relationship. It is unacceptable to be proud of our society if we know that other humans don't have access to 'good' education, 'good' food, 'good' loving carers and appropriate support at the right stage of life. Common sense tells us that wholesome systems can help us to achieve healthy communities. Regardless of our personal position, we must all advocate on behalf of the natural world so that all prosper. We can do this by paying more taxes to support free health care for all, free education (play-based for early years) for all, and making sure through law we can protect the land, an approach commonly seen in the Scandinavian countries.

And what is lovely is to see a developing caring attitude towards each other and nature.
(Deborah Thomas, Forest School leader, West Sussex, 2017)

This 'paradigm shift' is nothing new: it can be witnessed through the ages and is based on many years of theoretical underpinning and praxis from many places around the world. In the next chapter, we

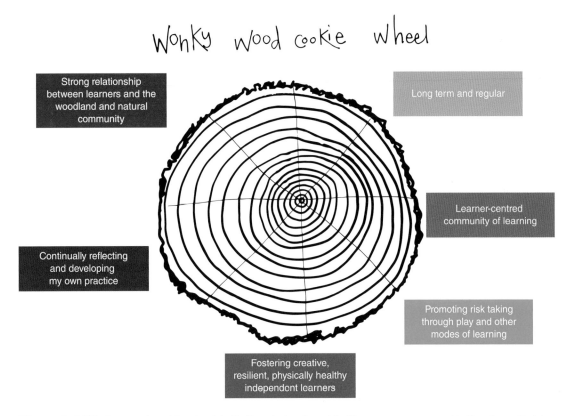

Wonky wood cookie wheel

Strong relationship between learners and the woodland and natural community

Long term and regular

Learner-centred community of learning

Continually reflecting and developing my own practice

Promoting risk taking through play and other modes of learning

Fostering creative, resilient, physically healthy independent learners

Figure 1.4 Wonky wood cookie wheel (with Permission from Lily Horseman, see www.kindlingplayandtraining .co.uk)

will take a look at how we achieved the current upsurge in Forest School and nature connection within our education systems.

QUESTIONS FOR PRACTICE

What values underpin your nature education practice? Can you identify the intrinsic and extrinsic values that chime with you?

Can you trace the origins of your values?

Which Forest School principles do you strongly agree with?

How do these principles translate into your practice?

You may want to use this 'wonky wheel' (Figure 1.4) (L. Horseman – https://kindlingplayandtraining. co.uk/forest-school/wonky-wood-cookie-wheel-reflective-practice/) to map how you apply Forest School principles in your practice, placing on the tree rings how much you are along the way towards embodying that principle in practice – the outside meaning fully and the heartwood meaning only just starting. Then join each up with a line to see where the 'strengths' and 'things to work on' lie.

USEFUL RESOURCES

https://valuesandframes.org/downloads Common Cause resources for looking at values

BIBLIOGRAPHY

Common Cause Foundation (2011) *Common Cause Handbook*. See https://valuesandframes.org/downloads/.

Constanza, R et al. (2014) Changes in the Value of Global Ecosystem Services. *Global Environmental Change* 26: 152–158.

Forest School Association. See www.forestschoolassociation.org/what-is-forest-school/.

Gray, P (2013) *Free to Learn: Why Unleashing the Instinct to Play Will Make Our Children Happier, More Self-Reliant, and Better Students for Life*. New York: Basic Books.

Kohn, A (2006) *Beyond Discipline: From Compliance to Community*. Alexandria, VA: Association for Supervision and Curriculum Development.

McCarthy, M (2015) *The Moth Snowstorm*. London: John Murray.

McLuhan, T C (1971) *Touch the Earth: A Self-Portrait of Indian Existence*. New York: Pocket Books.

Siegal, D (2017) *Mind: A Journey to the Heart of Being Human*. New York: W.W Norton & Co.

Wolfe, L M (1945) *Son of the Wilderness: The Life of John Muir*, p. 144 (from Muir journals undated fragment c. 1871).

2 History of nature education – the influence on nature-based practice

Nature connection has recently become a commonly used term in the environmental education movement – to our minds a sometimes misunderstood concept (see Chapters 3 and 4). Along with this, Forest School is seen as a relatively new phenomenon in the UK. In this chapter we will explore the history of nature education, of which Forest School is just one branch – but one we feel has been an important global movement in this century to date. We will go back to ancient history and then move to the 16th–21st centuries to examine the wisdoms and understandings and sometimes tensions that have been and are still informing today's nature educations. We will finish by looking at the essence of Forest School and how it relates to Nature Pedagogy as we see it, setting the foundation for the Nature Pedagogy models and practices we outline in Chapters 3 and 4.

If you know whence you came, there are absolutely no limitations to where you can go.

(James Arthur Baldwin, 1963)

The term Forest School was formulated in 1993 by a group of nursery nurses at Bridgewater College under the direction of Gordon Woodall, who established and named their own 'Forest School'. This was after a visit to Denmark, led by Jane Williams-Siegfredson, to experience some early years' practices in Denmark. The history of Forest School has been written about in a number of places (see Knight, 2012; Maynard, 2007; Cree and McCree, 2012, 2013; Gans, 2018). It has taken much of its inspiration from the Scandinavian pedagogy, particularly in the early years. Although considered as new, Forest School is based on many years of tradition of outdoor learning pedagogy, developing the 'whole' being and often less acknowledged land-based traditions. It is always good practice to look at the theories and traditions on which this 'modern' nature-based learning is leaning, enabling us to apply some universal principles and build new constructs, as well as validate old ones. One could say play- and community-based pedagogy has been heavily influenced by many native cultures, their learning and observation of young people and the natural world. Witness the growth of modern-day movements like the 'Art of Mentoring', 'School of Lost Borders', 'Forest School Camps' and more. Chinese and Persian philosophers, such as

Lao Tzu and Rumi, and Jain, Buddhist and Yogic traditions, to name but a few of the ancient Indian philosophies, have also had influence. Indeed, the 'Outdoor Schools' movement or 'Gurukula' in India with philosophers and educators such as Rabindranath Tagore and Krishnamurti had an impact on UK 'alternative' outdoor education in the 20th century with the establishment of Dartington Arts College and Brockwood.

PRE-20TH-CENTURY HISTORY OF NATURE EDUCATION

Early cultural relationships to the natural world

The nature educational approach likely began when *Homo sapiens* emerged from the African landmass. In the context of our Western civilisation, much of the ancient classical Greek philosophy, indeed all earth-based cultures/philosophies, are based on 'animism' and have had a huge influence on Forest School/Nature Pedagogy. People with an animistic worldview understood and felt all of life as 'alive' and in relationship with each other. The natural world was held dearly, as part of the 'family'; humans intimately valued different trees, mountains and animals. In the UK we are known to be animal-loving people, and many of us would agree our dogs and cats are part of our family. In our past, this approach and intimate familial relationship was extended to all life because nature (the trees, rivers, animals etc.) was known to us so well that this connection was a real, felt experience.

In many of the Hindu and Greek stories and myths, for example, the meaning of life is based on natural world metaphor wrapped up with gods, titans and other world 'presences'. Drawings and stories help us to understand complex relationships that we are immersed within. Most of us can only begin to understand a fraction of how life works and our place in this web of life. Just take one small Greek myth around how the elixir of gods – ambrosia – came to be. This simple yet compelling story tells of the bee's interaction with Zeus at his wedding, where her honey is seen as the best food provided for the marriage ceremony. In return the solitary bee is given a prize of workers to help her produce more of the ambrosia. To stop others from stealing her sweet nectar, she is given a sting, but if she uses it, she will die (Zeus hated her demands and so granted her a wish with this one proviso!). The bee belongs to the Hymenoptera order of insects – which means 'wedding wings'. This story gives a deeper meaning, shows the multiple relationships of a bee's life, yet is still based on the science of what we know about a bee – it makes the bee 'animate' and meaningful to our own human existence.

For example, the picture on the front of the *Permaculture Manual* (Mollison, 1988; see https://www.permaculturenews.org/permaculture-shop/books/permaculture-designers-manual/), which launched the worldwide permaculture movement in the 1980s, represents the 'egg of life'; the quantity of life is finite within the egg, it cannot be created or destroyed, but from within which all things that live are expressed (the finite egg also representing our ecological limits). The egg is shaped by a coiled rainbow snake – the earth shaper of Australian aboriginal peoples. The tree of life expresses lifeforms – roots in the earth and crown in rain, sunlight and wind. The elemental cosmological matter, the sun and physical forces are external to the egg. This symbol dedicates itself to the complexity of life and is used as an educational tool to show how life works on the planet (Mollison, 1988). A drawing like this provides us with a wider lens through which to work with and care for the natural world and the elements. In our work, this practically informs our entire approach to woodland management and environmental impact assessments!

There has been a rekindling of the effects of thousands of years of living in the natural world and the deep connections that the animistic indigenous cultures have. This has been stimulated, in large part, by evolutionary biologist E O Wilson, who coined the term 'biophilia' in 1984. He argued that all humans, due to our evolution in and with the natural world, have an evolved inclination to affiliate with nature. Wilson stated that we are 'hard-wired' into nature and as such our well-being, indeed our poetry and creativity, is dependent on it. We will explore this further in much of this book.

EARLY CULTURES AND THEIR LEARNING PHILOSOPHIES – SOCRATES TO THE PRESENT DAY

Combine this intertwining with nature with the learning philosophies of thinkers like Socrates and we almost have Forest School! In his 'circles', Socrates propounded dialogue in which learners take the lead in conversations and questioning when making meaning of the world. The role of the teacher is to follow the conversation and 'draw out' the wisdom (expanded further in Chapters 3 and 10). There is a shared power over the learning. After Socrates was Aristotle, who was one of the first philosophers to expand on the concept of self-respect and -esteem, one of the key aspects of Forest School. It is interesting to note that the questioning strategies used in many classrooms today are supposedly based on the Socratic dialogues and yet end up being about what is in the teacher's and curriculum creator's mind rather than the learner's mind. When the questioning doesn't work, is it the learner that is at fault or the curriculum? This, to us, seems inevitable when we live in a society where the education system is based on a behaviourist approach, promotes 'rationalism' over other human aspects, and relies on outcomes and extrinsic (not intrinsic) values as defined by many the decision-makers in our society (see Chapter 1 and bonus online chapter).

17th- to early 20th-century 'pioneers of nature-based education'

We can trace this learner-centred educational thinking forward from the Greeks to other influential European philosophers and thinkers active at the end of the Middle Ages and into the Renaissance period. Notable thinkers included Comenius (early 17th century), who was the forerunner of key theorists such as Pestalozzi, Froebel and Vygotsky. Comenius supported the idea of teachers 'following in the footsteps of nature', meaning that they ought to pay attention to the mind of the child and the way the student learned – working with objects from the natural world and making the acquisition of knowledge pleasurable. While his ideas are simple, he is probably one of the biggest influencers on the shaping of Western education.

Froebel, over 100 years later, devised the kindergarten system and saw 'playing in nature' as key to developing children's creativity, their love for nature and a sense of place and unity in the world. Many would argue that Froebel is probably one of the largest modern influencers on Forest School pedagogy because of his belief in marrying natural world contact and connection with learning and play. Vygotsky, however, added another dimension in the early 20th century, 100 years later – the social and holistic/gestalt nature of true learning. He emphasised the importance of learning with others (community of learners), language cementing learning and more knowledgeable peers and teachers helping learners meet their true potential. Vygotsky's 'more knowledgeable other' (MKO) is an important part of Forest School. Once we see the 'big picture' by integrating all the areas of development, we see another meaning/aspect of learning and development – the gestalt. These aspects are seen as central in Forest School in Canada (Forest School Canada, 2014) where there is much made of the 'emergent' curriculum. New meanings emerge when we use all our faculties, especially when interacting with other human and non-human beings. The recent findings in neuroscience all bear out the interconnection between the emotional brain and the problem-solving brain – or systems 1 and 2 (Kahneman, 2011), as outlined in Chapter 7. All are part of our holistic/gestalt existence.

Maria Montessori and the English pioneers of outdoor 'nature-based' learning like the Macmillan sisters and Susan Isaacs in the early 20th century had a large part to play, particularly in the early years of UK practice. These practices were all about learning in the 'real world' and being led by the child's spirit, as articulated by leading American philosopher and educator of the time John Dewey.

The 19th- and 20th-century *romantics* and *transcendentalists* also have had a large influence on Forest School and nature-based practice in celebrating the natural world – figures such as Muir, Thoreau, Wordsworth, Hardy and Ruskin – author of the famous quote,

Sunshine is delicious, rain is refreshing, wind braces us up, snow is exhilarating; there is really no such thing as bad weather, only different kinds of good weather.

(John Ruskin, 1889)

The main tenet of these writers and thinkers showed how we are inextricably linked to the natural world for our spiritual and cellular existence and, as Froebel stated, "people are 'part of' not 'separate from' the natural world" (Froebel, 1887). He saw nature as the ultimate teacher. Octavia Hill (Hunt), a close friend of Ruskin in the late 19th century, also pioneered the idea that all should have access to green spaces, including woodland, if we are to survive and thrive in the world. She was one of the founders of the National Trust, in 1907, wishing to provide both decent housing with access, particularly to those in poverty, to health, well-being and 'learning spaces'.

Other UK 20th-century influencers of the current Forest School provision that were born out of the world wars were the Scout and Guide movement, Woodcraft Folk, Forest School Camps and Outward Bound movements. In other parts of the world, we see the emergence of various nature education movements in the 20th and the early 21st century in places such as Scandinavia, Germany, Australia, New Zealand, Canada, South Korea and Australia (there are more!). These countries all have nature-based educations that are culturally different – skovbørnehaver, Friluftsliv, Skogsmulle, Metsamoori, Waldkindergarten, Bush Kinder and Te Whāriki, to name but a few of these approaches (McCree, 2015).

CONTEMPORARY HISTORY AND THE PRESENT

This brings us into the late 20th century, the early 21st century and the present day. In the mid-20th century we saw the birth of the modern environmental movement in the so-called developed West. This was arguably catalysed by the publication of Rachel Carson's *Silent Spring* in 1962. She spoke eloquently about the impacts of pesticides and herbicides on the natural world and on humans, emphasising in her books the importance of sensory connections with nature. With a society increasingly disconnected from ecological systems and communities, various nature-based approaches to education emerged. Two key figures in the 1970s and 1980s were Steve Van Matre with the international Institute for Earth Education (Van Matre, 1990) and Joseph Cornell with the 'Sharing Nature' movement (Cornell, 2015). Both published books and programmes that helped practitioners take a more sensory-based, and with earth education, a more ecological conceptual, 'hands-on' approach to learning in nature.

More recently, concern has arisen from the overuse of screens, eloquently talked about in Sue Palmer's *Toxic Childhood* (Palmer, 2006) and *Upstart* (Palmer, 2016).

It seems there has been an upsurge in nature connection initiatives, from organisations such as the National Trust, Royal Society for the Protection of Birds and Wildlife Trusts and others previously mentioned in this chapter. These international 'natural play space pedagogies' and growing dissatisfaction with a crowded industrial, outcome-based UK curriculum saw the Bridgwater Nurses lighting the blue touch paper in 1993 for an incredible growth in 'Forest School' in the UK. Forest School is now seen all over the UK as a part of many schools or run as an informal programme and is growing in many countries (Knight, 2013b; McCree, 2015).

As we write there will be thousands of early years – even pre-tots, primary and secondary school students, special needs groups, families and certain adult groups – experiencing nature education programmes in many different settings and institutions. In the UK, many young people of all ages and backgrounds are now experiencing regular time in nature. Forest School sits within the wider context of nature-based education. Rough statistics estimate conservatively that we had in 2011 (the last count) 13,000 learners accessing regular longer-term Forest School programmes (Wellings, 2012), and in 2015 there were estimated to be 17,000 trained Forest School professionals in the UK at all levels. The last survey carried out at a local authority level where data was available was in Worcestershire in 2013, and it showed there were 350 settings in the county running some sort of Forest School provision. All of these groups will have their theoretical and practical underpinning, to one degree or other, based on practitioners, theorists and pragmatists of history. Often, we are not conscious of these historical influences and hopefully we have brought them to the fore, going back to the early earth-based cultures we started this chapter off with.

Even the UK government has now recognised this as an important 'movement' in having a role in improving the health and well-being of the nation. Forest School is named in its 25-year environmental action plan published in January 2018 (DEFRA, 2018). With the rise in mental health issues in many developed countries, in particular the UK (see mental health statistics and research in Chapters 5, 8 and 14), a nature connection and Forest School approach is increasingly being seen as a 'green intervention' for vulnerable people (see bonus online chapter: 'The evidence and green interventions').

In 2012, as a result of almost 3 years of extensive consultation, the UK established its own Forest School professional body, the Forest School Association (FSA). The six principles, outlined in Chapter 1, were formulated through consultations with almost 2000 practitioners and a final consultation exercise at a national UK Forest School conference in Swindon in 2011 (see Wellings, 2012). It is significant that this conference was addressed by Sue Palmer, who is now spearheading the Upstart movement in Scotland to try to raise the school entry age to 7, as per Scandinavia, and have a more play-based, outdoor curriculum (Palmer, 2016).

There is a certain synergy happening around the world of movements advocating this approach to education – witness the growing international 'Children and Nature Network' started in 2006 as a result of the publication of Richard Louv's *Last Child in the Woods* (2005). Yet despite the phenomenal growth of the use of the term Forest School in the last 25 years, in the UK and across the world, there are many practitioners and 'schools' concerned that it is being paid lip service and not truly following the principles outlined in Chapter 1. In the UK this is often due to a highly crowded and outcome-focused curriculum where there is little room for the *time* and *space* required for developing a Forest School or nature-based curriculum (Sackville-Ford, 2019). There is a mismatch between an education system that is so reliant on 'names and numbers' rather than 'magic and meaning' and is risk averse (Maynard, 2008). In 2018 and late 2019 standards for Forest School (FS) provision and training were announced by the FSA in order to try and advocate for a deeper holistic practice of Forest School (FSA, 2018). It is hoped this will support the delivery of a quality FS programme that meets the relational, emotional, cognitive, physical, psychological and soul needs of young people today, while creating pro-ecological relationships and actions.

A truly holistic programme is lacking within our education system, despite the many well-researched approaches being practised in parts of our education system, such as Carol Dweck's 'growth mindset' (Dweck, 2012), Guy Claxton's 'building learning power' (Claxton, 2002), Anna Craft's 'possibility thinking' (Craft, 2002) and Catriona O'Toole's 'contemplative pedagogies'

(O'Toole, 2019). The recently published research in Yorkshire schools on Professor Robin Alexander's 'dialogic teaching' (Alexander, 2017), which places the student at the centre of their own learning, demonstrates how we have moved away from Socratic dialogue to a teacher-based dialogue and the resultant learning is the poorer for it. All of the five contemporary schools of thought referenced in this section, and the psychological theories and practices from writers like Bowlby, Glasser, Bruner, Jung, Freud, and Maslow, to name but a few, have had recent influence on the practices not just in Forest School but wider nature-based education. This brings us to a wider practice of Nature Pedagogy within which Forest School fits.

Current school systems and nature education

Some countries around the world are attempting to shift their educational system to a more real-world-based holistic/systems-based nature – such as the Scandinavian/Baltic countries. The UK educational system, in particular England, seems currently at odds with the approach we have outlined in the opening chapter. It is interesting to note that Estonia and Finland rank in the top of the most recent Organisation for Economic Co-operation and Development's (OECD's) 'Level 3' countries' PISA (Programme for International Student Assessment) scores in reading, mathematics and science, while the UK ranks in the middle (Schleider, 2019).

At the 2018 Forest School UK festival/conference in Norfolk, some well-informed debates occurred over the tensions that arise from trying to implement a holistic community nature-based programme in an outcome-based, 'instrumental', fragmented UK education system and curriculum, especially in England. One of the most common calls to action and questions voiced was how to influence decision-makers to make this an integral part of a system that is seemingly antagonistic to the Forest School ethos and approach.

The UK system seems to have embraced outdoor learning and Forest School in early years (witness the incredible growth of 'Forest Kindergartens' over the last few years) in both formal and more importantly informal settings (Palmer, 2016). One of the main challenges is trying to integrate Forest School as we move up the education system. At the time of writing, there is a contradiction happening where both government and many parents are wanting children to be 'school ready', ignoring their natural drive to play, and yet more parents and decision-makers see well-being and 'space' as key!

Sue Waite and Alice Goodenough (2018), Plymouth University, outline in their latest study how Forest School can create an 'alternative pedagogy' in the English school system. They recognise Forest School can indeed provide space for a culturally lighter and more inclusive pedagogy but warn how the learner-led and 'light' culture can be superseded –

With the increasing presence of FS within UK schools, higher level structural political influences inevitably impinge on how FS is positioned and enacted in the mainstream arena.

27

The learner-led principle may be superseded by a focus on curriculum objectives when co-located within schooling.

(Waite and Goodenough, 2018)

Yet Forest School and outdoor learning can easily support and complement the more fragmented classroom-based adult-led learning model – indeed, it can bring alive aspects of classroom-based learning through a holistic and 'play-based' approach. This can work *only if* the learner-centred character of the Nature Pedagogy and Forest School is not compromised – and there lies the rub! The rest of this book attempts to show how this can be achieved in a pragmatic yet still integral way.

THE ESSENCE OF FOREST SCHOOL

Having outlined the values, principles and history of Forest School, we would like to finish this chapter by describing what we see as the essence of Forest School in an attempt to answer the question, 'What is Forest School?'

Children are the great teachers of being caught up in the moment. In long-term programmes we often see '**the flow**' within a session where all the children are totally absorbed in what they

Figure 2.1 Children and young person immersed in 'activity'

Figure 2.1 Continued

are doing in the here and now; at these points the practitioner can stand back and observe. The image of a woodland village emerges, as painted in the first page, where everyone is involved in enquiries and activities, together or apart, and the atmosphere is safe, held within the trees and plants. This is a safe space also to explore challenging issues that may range from despair at the loss of natural places to issues that revolve around mental health and relationships. From a practitioner's perspective, **Time** and **Space** are two words that frequently come back to us, words which are both crucial for a deeply reflective and creative learning process. (We are here to look and notice.) **Relationship** is at the heart Forest School.

Throughout this book, we draw on an understanding of how the 'relational' experience of life, moment to moment, affects us. We are affected by our surroundings, by how we are treated (at home and by society), and our perceptions are determined by a multitude of inner and outer factors. We see the world and each other through the lens of relationships and 'connections' or 'disconnections'. One of the often cited disconnects in these contemporary times is the way mobile phones can detract from our full attention to the moment and disrupt an ongoing mindful relationship with the natural world and yet can also be useful tool for creating a greater understanding if used 'wisely' (Mitchell, 2017). We can be triggered by memories of which we are unaware, guided by our values and influenced by where our intention lies at any given moment.

The four key dynamics

The Forest School approach fosters relationships within four key dynamics outlined in the following sections. Whilst a practitioner plans, considers last week's evaluation and assesses risk for all sessions in advance, the day brings its ever-changing surprises! There is a 50–50 principle in which you make a plan for the entire time and then usually drop at least 50% (see Chapters 10 and 11)! In essence, as practitioners we are responding all the time to *ourselves*, *others*, *nature* and the *resources available* to enable a holistic, healthy and 'in the moment' experience.

1 The practitioner

Know thyself. When we work with children or others, we can support others when we feel most centred and experienced. Learning never ends, so a position of humility and openness is often helpful. As the 'leader', the Forest School atmosphere is enabled by you and your own life experiences – what you find easy and interesting, how far beyond your comfort you are prepared to go, when to say 'No', and if you trust others and yourself. Awareness of your inner sensations. How do we read the language and cues that the learners in our community give us (Chapter 5)? How do learners read the response to our cues? Our response can either shut it down and adulterate it or can come in as part of the flow. Who creates the play frame that children are within? The 'ludic' or play process in the outdoors is outlined in more detail in Chapter 6.

As a training, the Forest School qualification doesn't tell us what activities to lead or not. Rather it rests within principles or conducts where we are building a long-term relationship with the land, and ensuring it is looked after for future generations and is based on an in-depth understanding of human development.

(Deborah Thomas, Forest School trainee, 2015)

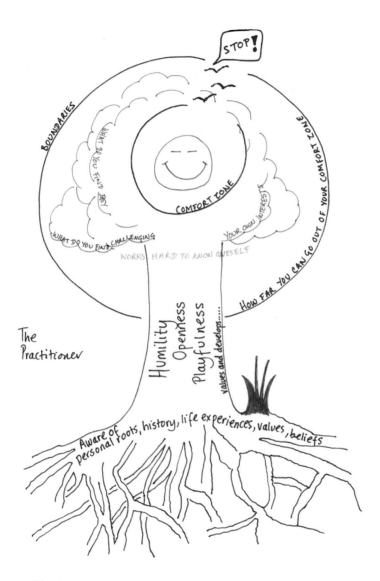

Figure 2.2 The practitioner

Key aspects of the practitioner role

All practitioners will bring their own style, interests, weaknesses and expertise to the woods or green space. You will bring your **communication** and **observation** skills, your determination of risk, your relationships to young people in the group. Your role is to **facilitate a safe and healthy space for the young people to discover their own strengths and aptitudes –**

31

to use your knowledge to direct their own learning, to get out of the way of your own agenda enough to make space for them to show what they are seeking. It is a hugely skilful role. The UK Level 3 Forest School training begins the journey tenderly. We learn as we go, **reflecting** on sessions, seeking other's opinions, co-learning with the children. We look and notice the young people and all of the moving parts of nature. We are within a living film, with its dramas and joys, its highs and lows, its tears and laughter, where all is part of life and welcome. We aim for **authentic connection**.

Ultimately, as the adult we are fully responsible. While we support the children's exploration and are led by their interests, we stop activities when there is significant danger to them, us, nature or the human resources. All our **procedures** are in place, revisited and updated as new things occur (see Chapter 10).

You may be a scientist, musician, artist, forager, or early years or disability expert. You may love mud, using knives or climbing. As practitioners we are interested in who the learner is in front of you. What do they need and want to be?

2 The learner

Forest School groups have a high ratio of staff to learners. We want to get to know the children, young people and adults. With smaller groups it is possible to build those individual relationships and provide tailored pathways for the children.

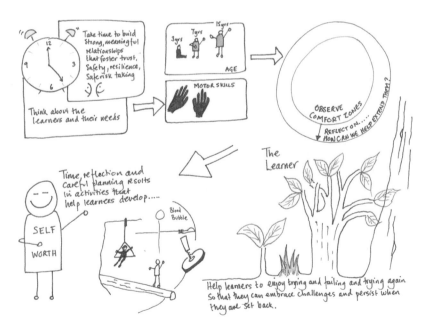

Figure 2.3 The learner

- To know them well enough to trust them to climb a tree that is more than 2 metres high.
- To be able to trust that they are learning and getting what is needed from returning to their shelter on a weekly basis.
- To provide opportunities to talk through difficult group issues, to listen to their solutions and provide your thoughts.

People learn at a different pace with varied capacity. It is now considered important for young people to build resilience by trying and failing, then trying again (Dweck, 2012), for them to internalise the skill of endeavour, rather than deciding without much effort that it is not for them or that they can't do it. Our dopamine-friendly technology makes quick rewards very enticing but means that our young people give up quickly and can ultimately feel useless.

Learner considerations

So who are the learners? How old are they? What do we know about child development that supports us to co-create appropriately challenging and interesting sessions that satisfy these young people and build their self-worth? Where are they comfortable? Where do they resist? Where is there tension? How are they today? What level are their gross or fine motor skills at? Do they seek out familiar activities, and how can we support to extend this? Chapter 3 will dive into child development in a thorough way – seeing each individual for who and what they are.

3 The place and season

One of the great benefits of the outdoors is full sensory immersion: the visuals, smells, surfaces, sounds and tastes. Each day and each season brings something unique to the Forest School session. Nothing is permanent. In the autumn, we may need to make more fires as the weather cools. When bushes are laden with berries, we can hardly pass by the opportunity to make a cordial or some yummy berry pudding. And what are the animals up to in autumn? Can we try to find out? What about experimenting with different natural paints and potions? Or perhaps one child wants to continue with her digging?

One of the most profound experiences at all ages is an embodied knowledge that change is inevitable – the great cycles of life with birth and death at the doorways and exits. Even the youngest child understands this. In Western cultures we are often not taught the life cycle of a nature-made object (e.g. plant or stone) or a human-made object (e.g. where the clothes come from). In so doing, we as humans are removed from these natural cycles.

Some children run outside and get stuck into an idea they have; others may need time alone or given ideas to get them going. Some may find touching the mud disgusting and need gloves;

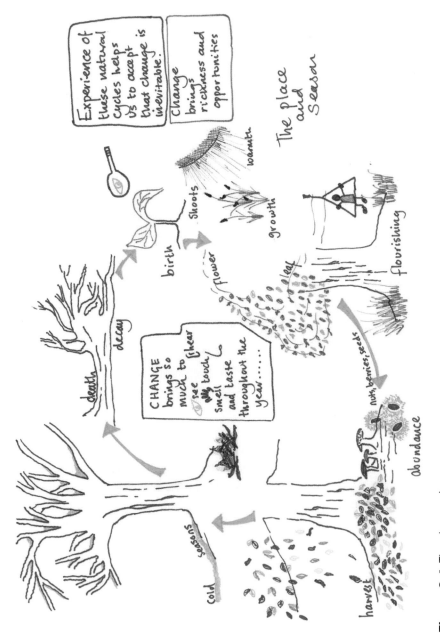

Figure 2.4 The place and seasons

Figure 2.5 Tapping birch in spring and making crab apple jelly and berry paint and oak apple ink in autumn

others may want to put it in their mouths! Does your place have trees? Is there water? Do you need to bring in materials? Do you have to walk there or get transport? (Chapter 10 looks at management planning and Chapter 6 looks at play processes.)

Needless to say, after years of working outdoors, all Forest School (and nature-based) sessions relate in some way to what is occurring in nature at that time – more generally within the seasons in the northern hemisphere. We aim to build this kinship to nature, understanding our interdependence while noticing and adapting what may be happening that day within your session. Later in the book we look at common seasonal activities that are led by a child's interest and supported by adult knowledge and interests.

4 The resources

The fourth and final element is resources. Practitioners often talk about the Forest School kit (see Chapter 10) and the limits, or not, of the place where the sessions are being run. In a most natural and wild setting, Forest Schools are full of the sensations and diversity of nature, and depending on your age group and their interests, nature itself will be your main resource.

We want to involve the whole group as much as possible in carrying what is needed to and from your site. Although not always practical or realistic, being a Forest School practitioner can be physically heavy work, with wheel barrowing water in, equipment, tarps, ropes etc., so we want to make the whole experience as easy as possible.

At the same time, many sites may not have great diversity – from the school field to a little patch of nature. (See Urban Forest School planning in Chapter 10.) In this case we may need to bring in natural materials on a weekly basis, and some 'loose parts' (see 'loose parts' theory in Chapter 6), so that children can choose to use materials in any way to encourage their own creativity and imagination. There are a multitude of possible materials, for example stones, stumps, twigs, carving wood, sand, ropes, buckets, nets, shells, seeds, guide books and tools, that you may decide to include in a session.

The dance of the four 'dynamics' – practitioner, learner, place and resources

In summary, the Forest School session and programme is influenced by the dynamic relationships between you, the practitioner, and other 'helpers', the young person, the place and time of year, and the available resources. Each session aims to be responsive and in relationship to all four elements, so one can never totally pre-determine what may happen and where the session may lead. We have often been distracted and diverted into another track because of something unexpected, for example the remains of a dead mole provoked the teenager in Figure 2.8 and with the resources to hand he made a marked grave. Or the pouring rain, or more cooking because it's so delicious, or hours of den making and creative knots! Remember to leave space for the unexpected!

If this is learner led, then we (the practitioners) wouldn't be there, and it would be 'wild play' (Bob Hughes, 2015). Embodying Forest School involves an internal decision-making

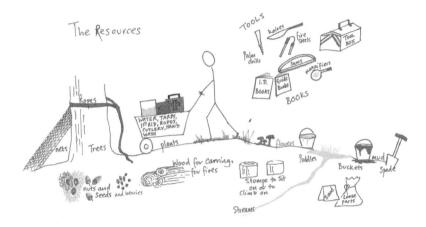

Figure 2.6 The resources

Figure 2.7 Tools and resources

Figure 2.8 Teen burying a mole

dance that is moving with the relationships being created and developed and deciding when it is pure learner led, adult (practitioner led), when it's dictated entirely by the place or by the resources we are using. In most cases it will be a mix of all four and how they relate to each other.

Having explored what has led to today's nature education movements, we will ask the reader, throughout the book, to consider the four elements and to explore how we arrive at a healthy learning community. We also begin the book by remembering that we sit on the shoulders of many people and natural beings across land and cultures who have gone before us. In the next chapter we will look further into the idea of Nature Pedagogy and how in particular our sense of place impacts on the learner, the leader, the place and the resources.

QUESTIONS FOR PRACTICE

Are there any educational thinkers that have particularly affected your nature education practice? If so, in what way?

What specific tensions do you see between a more learner-led, holistic, nature-based approach to education and the education system we experience in schools in the UK today?

Do you consider yourself a reflective practitioner?

USEFUL RESOURCES

Children and Nature Network is an international body which has many resources on the website giving an overview of nature education worldwide. The blog is excellent at keeping you up to date on the international picture. See www.childrenandnature.org

For the history of Forest School in UK up to 2012 see www.forestschoolassociation.org/history-of-forest-school/

BIBLIOGRAPHY

Alexander, R J (2017) *Towards Dialogic Teaching: Rethinking Classroom Talk* (5th edition). Dialogos. See www.robinalexander.org.uk/dialogic-teaching.

Art of Mentoring. See http://8shields.org.

Baldwin, J (1963) *The Fire Next Time*. New York: Penguin.

Carson, R (1962) *Silent Spring*. New York: Houghton Mifflin Company.

Carson, R (1965) *A Sense of Wonder*. New York: Harper.

Child and Nature Alliance of Canada (2014) *Forest and Nature School in Canada: A Head, Heart, Hands Approach to Outdoor Learning*. See http://childnature.ca/wp-content/uploads/2017/10/FSC-Guide-1.pdf.

Claxton, G (2002) *Building Learning Power*. TLO Publishers. See www.buildinglearningpower.com/about.

Cornell, J (2015) *Sharing Nature: Nature Awareness Activities for All Ages*. Nevada City, CA: Crystal Clarity Publishers. See www.sharingnature.com/.

Craft, A (2002) *Creativity and Early Years Education*. Continuum Books.

Cree, J and McCree, M (2012) A Brief History of the Roots of Forest School in the UK (2013) A Brief History of Forest School – Part 2 Horizons 60 and 61, Institute for Outdoor Learning.

DEFRA (2018) *UK Government – A Green Future: Our 25 Year Plan to Improve the Environment* (see p 71). See www.gov.uk/government/uploads/system/uploads/attachment_data/file/693158/25-year-environment-plan.pdf.

Dweck, C (2012) *Mindset: Changing the Way You Think to Fulfill Your Potential*. Robinson.

Forest School Association (FSA) (2018) *Forest School Recognised Providers and Trainers Scheme*. See www.forestschoolassociation.org/membership-options-page.

Forest School Canada (2014) *Forest and Nature School in Canada: A Head, Hearts, Hand Approach to Outdoor Learning*. See https://childnature.ca/wp-content/uploads/2017/10/FSC-Guide-1.pdf.

Froebel, F (1887) *The Education of Man*. New York, London: D. Appleton Century.

Gans, C (2018) *A History of the UK and US Forest School Movement*. See www.forestschooled.com; www.fsc.org.uk/about.htm.

Hughes, B (2015) *Keynote Speech at National Forest School Conference* (October). See www.forestschoolassociation.org/national-conference-2015-condover-hall-shropshire/.

Hunt, T see www.nationaltrust.org.uk/features/octavia-hill – her-life-and-legacy.

Kahneman, D (2011) *Thinking, Fast and Slow*. London: Penguin.

Knight, S (2012) *Forest School for All*. London: Sage.

Knight, S (2013a) *Forest School and Outdoor Learning in Early Years*. London: Sage.

Knight, S (2013b) *International Perspectives on Forest School*. London: Sage.

Louv, R (2005) *Last Child in the Woods*. Algonquin Books.

Maynard, T (2007) Forest Schools in Great Britain: An Initial Exploration. *Contemporary Issues in Early Childhood* 8(4): 320–331.

Maynard, T (2008) Encounters with Forest School and Foucault: A Risky Business. *International Journal of Primary, Elementary and Early Years Education* 35(4): 379–391.

McCree, M (2015) *Forest School and Friends Around the World*. FSA Conference 2015. See www.forestschoolassociation.org/wp-content/uploads/2015/12/Mel-McCree-World-FS-Friends-prez-Oct-2015.pdf.

Mitchell, A (2017) *The Social and Environmental Impact of Mobile Phones*. See https://en.reset.org/knowledge/ecological-impact-mobile-phones.

Mollison, B (1988) *Permaculture: A Designers Manual*. Australia: Tagari Publications.

O'Toole, C (2019, January) Time to Teach the Politics of Mental Health: Implications of the Power Threat Meaning Framework for Teacher Education. *Clinical Psychology Forum* 313.

Palmer, S (2006) *Toxic Childhood: How the Modern World Is Damaging Our Children and What We Can Do About It*. London: Orion House.

Palmer, S (2016) *Upstart: The Case for Raising the School Starting Age and Providing What Under-Sevens Really Need*. Edinburgh: Floris Books.

Sackville-Ford, M and Davenport, H (2019) *Critical Issues in Forest School*. London: Sage.

School of the Lost Borders. See http://schooloflostborders.org/.

Schleider, A (2019) *PISA 2018: Insights and Interpretations*. OECD. See www.oecd.org/pisa/PISA%202018%20Insights%20and%20Interpretations%20FINAL%20PDF.pdf.

Van Matre, S (1990) *Earth Education: A New Beginning*. Institute for Earth Education. See www.eartheducation.org.uk/.

Waite, S and Goodenough, A (2018) What Is Different About Forest School? Creating Space for an Alternative Pedagogy in England. *Journal of Outdoor and Environmental Education* 21(1): 25–44.

Wellings, E (2012) *A Feasibility Study into Establishing a National Professional Association for Forest School in the UK*. Forest School Association. See www.forestschoolassociation.org.

Wilson, E O (1984) *Biophilia*. Cambridge, MA: Harvard University Press.

3 Nature Pedagogy – teaching within a nature-centric worldview

This chapter examines what we mean by a pedagogy for teaching and learning in nature and how it influences our worldview. We will explore how holistic development – the relational view as per O'Brien's quote – the nature play cycle and place-attached practice are part of this pedagogy. Characteristics of Nature Pedagogy will be proposed. The chapter will finish by showing how working and integrating nature into our practice provides a holistic approach to learning and development. We will propose that spiritual development, indigenous ways of learning in and about nature and awareness of 'power dynamics' have relevance to today's nature education practices.

> *Relationships are the heartbeat of pedagogy.*
>
> (Dr Tim O'Brien, 2017)

WHAT IS PEDAGOGY?

The word 'pedagogy' is often used within education. Simply stated, it is the method and practice of teaching. A pedagogue walks alongside us, understanding learners' needs and interests and providing relevant valuable experiences. **Nature Pedagogy is the practice of teaching alongside nature and the learner.** We are endlessly nourished by nature and have an inbuilt 'natural operating manual' that is influenced by external sensory input into our vast internal sensory and electrical systems within the body. This is what E O Wilson's biophilia hypothesis is about – the natural world is essential to human experience and life (1984) (see bonus online chapter: 'The evidence and green interventions').

We are using the word pedagogy for two key reasons:

- Firstly, because it has the potential to raise the value of what is actually happening when a young person or child is in the outdoors – namely that we are learning and educating ourselves. Nature often does this subliminally.

- Secondly, through using our pedagogy practices in the natural world, we learn to develop our expertise and ability to communicate what and how we are learning in the outdoors.

Access to nature is essential for well-being and optimum learning. In practice, it makes a difference what activities and experiences are provided at certain times, in certain places, and how they are facilitated (Higgins et al., 2006). In our experience, with nature as the 'third teacher', the more children access green spaces and wilder spaces, experiencing multiple relationships, the healthier they are throughout their life. A childhood in nature, followed by regular access and connection throughout our lives, provides endless benefits in well-being, health and life-long learning (Twohig-Bennett and Jones, 2018) (see bonus online chapter). What's more, there have been a number of studies showing that regular exposure to the natural world early in life leads to pro-environmental behaviours (see Wells and Lekies, 2006).

Pedagogical blindness

We are coining the term 'pedagogical blindness' as an offshoot of the more well-known 'cultural blindness'. This refers to the lack of essential teaching experience or perspective needed to 'see' with new lenses and understand the learning and development in front of you; for example, to observe and know the value of a child playing in nature or to understand how vital emotional regulation is developed during time outdoors. Many people are not able to see what is actually occurring because they don't have the framework that an experienced practitioner might have. It's common to hear 'they are only playing' when it is far more complex than appears to the untrained eye. Cultural blindness means because of what we are used to, we might unconsciously pay no attention to natural surroundings or specific features, for example a tree, instead just 'seeing green', or we are unaware and don't value another's viewpoint. There is a need to be open-minded and to gain experience and training to value and understand what may be new or unfamiliar. Another culture will value different ways of knowing, pick out unique details, apply different experiences and have different reference points. This is why culturally appropriate training and valuing our teaching professionals and our nature professionals is so important.

We want to enable education and health practitioners and parents to feel confident to organise, safely set up and facilitate outdoor sessions and to fully understand why outdoor play and experience in nature matters. Unless we understand what learning and development processes are happening in the natural world, we will not advocate and include them. Unless we are keenly observing and clarifying what the learner may be making of an experience, we cannot plan and set up further appropriate learning experiences and thus facilitate a meaningful, cumulative learning programme. Deeper understandings of the way we learn and keen observation can literally wipe away our pedagogical blind spots.

In Nature Pedagogy, it is important to distinguish if your practice addresses the nature-based intrinsic values outlined in Chapter 1. These include valuing nature for its own sake and building a teaching and development process that puts the importance of nature at its heart, thereby increasing kinship and ecological understanding of the natural world.

For children in the earlier years of life, the practitioner's role is to observe first, notice the well-being and then, where appropriate, consider the curriculum and relational learning that has been met. Nature Pedagogy follows a play-based approach where there is a flow between the person and their environment. The expert respects this.

(See the useful resources section at the end of this chapter: the Scottish Well-being Audit: GIRFEC.)

Nature Pedagogy is the practice of teaching alongside nature and the learner.

(Robb and Cree)

Key features of Nature Pedagogy

This approach to learning is highly participatory. It supports the agency (self-control) of the child and offers a healthy 'container' (a boundaried, emotionally safe space) that benefits the 'whole' person. Children are listened to and noticed, so that their interests and experiences are valued. In this model, there is always an adult present. The adult remains aware, at times needing to stand back and 'be invisible' and, in other moments, building an empathetic and authentic relationship with the person, holding a 'safe-enough space' and supporting learning in the moment. Knowing when to interact is a key skill. (See Chapter 6 on the nature play cycle and Chapter 11's Language and Communication section). We aim to be compassionate, whilst holding boundaries which are firm, kind to them and to us.

The pedagogue or practitioner is helping the learner feel and understand what our place is in the natural world – to be both an ecological and a social human, with our full range of emotions and needs underpinning the learning and development. The relationship with peers, practitioner, place and resources eventually develops our 'ecological' self. Our sensory systems (see Chapter 5) decipher all the input, and we discover what supports us and what we need to avoid! In a sense, our inner world encompasses everything we feel and experience from the external world; how we are inside deeply influences our experience of the external.

Through developing relationships to nature, others and ourselves, we build our resilience, creativity, self-worth and emotional literacy (see Chapters 8 and 9). We learn how to self-soothe, self-regulate and integrate our senses. We share sustained conversations that nourish our well-being, are restorative and enable positive social dynamics. Nature provokes our language, level of compassion and kindness for 'the other'. We become natural scientists and develop individually, learning to express ourselves and our uniqueness. We hold a space that encourages the inner human landscape to enjoy the feeling of nature, not knowing what may result, and allowing for the mystery to unfold.

> *From birth to death, life enmeshes individuals within a dynamic culture consisting of the natural environment (light, heat, air, land, water, minerals, flora, fauna), the human-made environment (material objects, buildings, roads, machinery, appliances, technology), social arrangements (families, social networks, associations, institutions, economies), and human consciousness (knowledge, beliefs, understanding, skills, traditions). Well-being depends on all the factors that interact within this culture and can be seen as a state of health or sufficiency in all aspects of life.*
>
> (Australian Bureau of Statistics, 2001)

Core aspects of training to become a nature pedagogue

Forest School training for budding practitioners has high standards and follows a rich set of learning outcomes. In many ways the content is universal and can be applied to all learners. As our physical and mental health has deteriorated, the training and practice is increasingly applied to adult and vulnerable groups. However, the vast majority of practitioners are working with young people and children and ideally have had at least 2 years' experience working with young people before starting the training. The training pulls on a multitude of theories and practices that enable us to cater for diverse people, within diverse natural spaces. The Forest School approach is a multi-disciplined, holistic and integrated approach, drawing on observation, connection to and understanding of the natural world. Our direct approach will vary according to the children's ages, needs, where they are playing, whether in a park, field or wood, how long they are out of doors, and the positional power, values and skill level of the practitioner. The nature play cycle on page 50 explores positional power in more detail.

CHARACTERISTICS OF PEDAGOGY

The UK National College for School Leadership (NCSL) carried out extensive research in 2012 to examine and describe successful methods and practices for positive outcomes for young people across school ages. Below are the nine claims of great 'pedagogy', or what it is that 'good' teachers do to promote 'good' learning.

1   Effective pedagogies give serious consideration to pupil voice.
2   Effective pedagogies depend on behaviour (what teachers do), knowledge and understanding (what teachers know) and beliefs (why teachers act as they do).

3   Effective pedagogies involve clear thinking about longer term learning outcomes as well as short-term goals.

4   Effective pedagogies build on pupils' prior learning and experience.

5   Effective pedagogies involve scaffolding pupil learning.

6   Effective pedagogies involve a range of techniques, including whole-class and structured group work, guided learning and individual activity.

7   Effective pedagogies focus on developing higher order thinking and metacognition, and make good use of dialogue and questioning in order to do so.

8   Effective pedagogies embed assessment for learning.

9   Effective pedagogies are inclusive and take the diverse needs of a range of learners, as well as matters of student equity, into account.

(Husbands and Pearce, 2012 © National College for School Leadership)

In addition to these qualities, Nature Pedagogy also includes:

- considering contact with the natural world as essential for learning and development.
- meaningful building of natural world relationship that intrinsically values the nature.

What's more, Nature Pedagogy should be seen as an *informal* process.

Embedded assessment for learning is mentioned in the NCSL characteristics of pedagogy. In Nature Pedagogy we would see this as helping *learners* reflect on an experience by:

- expressing what is happening emotionally, cognitively and physically to themselves.
- how this informs their relationships to the natural world, place and people.
- what learning and experiences they would want to pursue further based on their current and prior experiences.

The observations and evaluations of the learning happening in nature by the *practitioner* are key to further planned experiences, and *planning for future experiences is collaborative*.

THE KEY ELEMENTS OF NATURE PEDAGOGY

As we discussed in Chapter 2, there are four key elements to consider – the practitioner, the learner, the resources and the place and season (see Figure 3.1).

We see the following as key characteristics of a nature pedagogue:

- It is about you the practitioner. We recognise that when you facilitate you have power, and you need to use this wisely. You are 'holding' the place and people, and children look to you. You need to be empathetic and have a reflective, non-judgmental, compassionate approach.

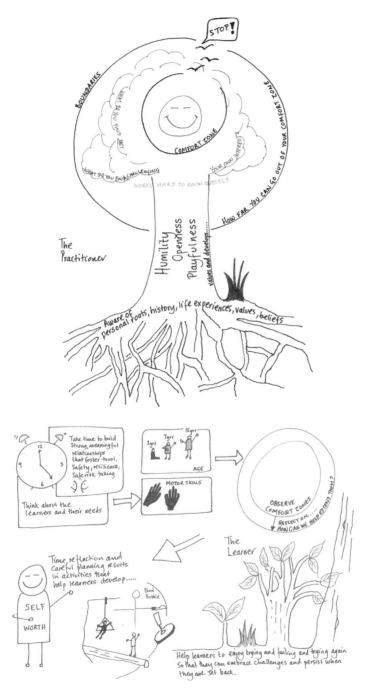

Figure 3.1 Key dynamics

Figure 3.1 Continued

- You are accepting and loving towards the people in your care, accepting them as they are. You may not like what they do, but your role requires an understanding of their needs and yours and the strategies to support the well-being and self-respect of everyone in the community.
- You discover a love of nature. Nature has central importance in well-being. You understand that ecological processes support life.
- You demonstrate caring attitudes and actions with and towards the natural world.
- You adopt a perspective of endless reflective, 'critical' learning.

Within Forest School, the elements that enable great practice and methods include going 'beyond the fence' and demanding that practitioners are reflective and reflexive in their service to the learner. They ask us to think about social justice and equality and employ 'critical pedagogy', thinking that develops ethical worldviews about how we work together and care for and respect plants, animals and ecological communities.

In Dr Sue Elliot's words, we need "pedagogies that challenge our ways of being with nature" (2018).

Nature Pedagogy can be challenging

Educators in early childhood have a history of returning to Froebel and Pestalozzi and those romanticised ideas of "Isn't it lovely that children are in nature and nature will somehow be nice and everything will be nice for children" and suddenly they'll have sustainable worldviews (Early Years Summit, 2018). We'd like to add to this that being with nature isn't necessarily all roses. The natural world can be challenging, wet, cold, 'bitey', messy, even scary. It can also be physically demanding for the group to carry water, tarpaulins and any other resources into the woods, getting set up and so on before the 'play' begins. You have to negotiate with your fellow learners and practitioners and are unable to control your natural surroundings, particularly in mid-winter. It is these types of 'edgy' experiences that can also develop, in the long term, a certain resilience, physically, cognitively and emotionally.

Providing real-life experiences of tuning in then improving natural spaces and examining lifestyle impact creates active participants and citizens who feel empowered. David Sobel eloquently showed that loving and celebrating nature comes first, "If we want children to flourish, to be truly empowered, we must first allow them to love the earth before we ask them to save it" (Sobel, 1996). As we will discover, instilling fear of climate change without providing the skills, emotional support or fundamental love of our earth will, in the end, do our children a huge disservice.

The practice of spending time in nature inevitably informs our worldview. Our worldview is developed from peers, family, culture, education, direct experience, thought and emotional-provoking moments, where our perceptions are extended and irreversibly changed. We want to provide outdoor opportunities in which young people can test themselves, rehearse life in action and discover their capabilities and creative expression. Often in a world where the natural world is seen as alien and 'not my thing', it is challenging for both the learner and the nature educator – it can take time to come to know and love the earth.

As educators we need to tune into what each learner is feeling, thinking and wanting to express – this often requires the keen observation mentioned earlier and expanded on in Chapter 11. Only when we have done this can we introduce activities and experiences that we feel may engage and supportively challenge, without tipping the learner into a panic zone or a place where they want to withdraw (see Chapters 6 and 7). A key question to consider always is, when do we withdraw from the learner's space to allow them to learn for themselves?

THE NATURE PLAY CYCLE

A fundamental aspect of the Forest School approach across the developmental stages is the movement through what we call a nature play cycle. How much of a session is participant/learner/child led, and how much of the session is practitioner/adult led? How much of the child's experience is supported by an adult who is responsive to the child's interest and how much is guided, adult initiated or highly structured or directed?

Each position on the nature play cycle, based on Andrews' play continuum (2012), is outlined in Figure 3.2. The outcomes of the different approaches can vary depending on the context,

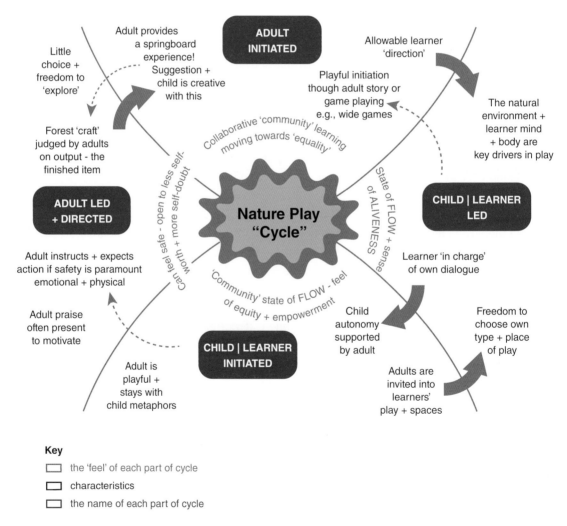

Figure 3.2 The nature play cycle

Table 3.1 The nature play cycle – characteristics of each part of the cycle (see the wheel to see how each part interacts with another in a more cyclical way)

Child/learner led (non-directed)	Child/learner initiated	Adult led (directed)	Adult initiated
Learner displays 'total' interaction with the space and place with little interference from adults. Intensive focused concentration on what the learner is doing at any moment. Loss of awareness of self and others. Being in own body. The learner has a sense of control over own actions and has capacity to respond to any nature-based situations and respond to what comes next. Time is no worry! The end goal is an excuse to experience the process, e.g. making a rope swing is as fulfilling as the swinging! Child/learner has own ideas that they follow through, asking for support when they need it. The educator wears a 'cloak of invisibility'!	The child/learner creates the 'play' frame, i.e. the 'theme', storyline, project or investigation. The cue for an experience or play comes from the learner. The learner initiates the line of curiosity and seeks out the newness of a situation, e.g. What is over behind that tree? Where is that bird going? I am going to find a toilet in the woods! Simple adult involvement – from being a supplier of materials and ideas to encouraging the play that maintains a child/learner-centred approach to nature play. The adult is therefore 'on tap but not on top'. Feel of a joint approach in the imaginative world of the learner.	Adult structures a programme and the activities within the programme, e.g. "Today we are going to go on a minibeast hunt, then have a sit spot followed by some rope course making and then free play then we'll have a review lunch". Instructional approach where the adult demonstrates and the learner then imitates exactly what the adult has demonstrated. Adult dictates the right and wrong ways of doing things, e.g. one way to whittle with a knife. Adult designs and delivers an activity with little input from the learners and sticks to a way of leading from the front while outside. Adult leaves little room for an experience to be directed by learners' own creativity, e.g. leaving little choice to play with ingredients for a stew made over an open fire.	Adult provides a *choice* of materials (preferably natural) and/or resources that are 'real' and 'long lasting' with as low embodied energy as possible. This means they have a minimal environmental impact and are in keeping with the natural environment. The adult works with the learner's energies and needs. Adult shows a sense of appreciation of the learner and the natural world – both perceived and real! There is an honouring of learners' uniqueness.

where the learner is on their learning journey, how independent they are, what type of learning they respond to and relish and so on. Forest School is a child-led approach in which we want to encourage autonomy, self-control and the development of intrinsic motivation and self-worth. This arises out of a learner-led approach supported by an empathetic and skilled adult. Everyday education is commonly skewed to the adult-directive approach with external rewards and outcomes that often take away control and creativity from the learner and fail to show you trust the person.

In training we often split the group with some clay. We offer one group clay and the freedom to create what they want; the other we 'teach' to make a finger pot. The 'free approach' (though we limited the choice to provided clay and a time frame) created an abundant array of clay-based objects – from houses to birds and nothing but a lump! This simple exercise is an embodied experience of how it feels to be directed and goal-oriented versus given the freedom to explore and be creative. Another parallel could be made with the gardener and the carpenter (Gopnick, 2017) – the carpenter has a goal and skills to arrive at what he/she wants to make and does so, whilst the gardener plants many seeds and, with certain conditions, many diverse experiences emerge.

Figure 3.2 and Table 3.1 provide some of the key characteristics of each part of the cycle. The reason we have created a 'cycle' is that in a session we often move from one 'state' to another, hence the arrows. Quite often this is a cycle through all four or between two or three states. The arrows show the common strengths of direction we have observed in this movement from one part of the cycle to another.

Let's make this concrete by looking at a session Jon witnessed at a Forest School one autumn.

Carol, the Forest School leader, was working in a children's centre and the session was the seventh in the programme, mid-November when the trees were still golden. The children were all between 4 and 5 years old. The previous session had involved making small dens for fairies and goblins, climbing trees, making mud pies and dancing; the whole group had devised a woodland whirl . . . their new dance that had started two weeks before, spontaneously mimicking the first falling leaves. Carol had finished the previous session with a storymaking review of what had happened and how the children wanted to continue the story. The session began with a 'dance' into the woods. Carol had suggested they sing into the woods (**adult led**), but she was quickly interrupted by a swirling 4-year-old who said, "No . . . let's do our swirly dance into the woods". Carol replied, "How about we sing and dance?" All the children said, "Let's just dance!" Carol said, "OK, let's show Jon the dance". She had carefully chosen her words here, not our dance or your dance, *the* dance . . . it was a sign to Jon that this was a special dance in which they all had a stake. (After talking to Carol about how the dance came about, Jon concluded the group was on the **child-initiated/adult-supported part of the cycle**.) The group arrived in the copse, a small woodland next to a garden, and Carol put the drink equipment on a wooden table with one child, a couple of children lifted some baskets out of the trolley, two went straight to a tree with a low branch and started climbing, and three got trowels and buckets out. Once all had settled in,

Carol called them all to the circle of stumps and asked them to sit and introduce themselves to the newcomer . . . Jon! She reminded them of the ends of the story from the previous week, and then wove in a story about autumn and eight children who loved to whirl and twirl their way into the sky. It was an enchanting story full of rhyme and child participation that invited their contributions, which were woven in. Carol had taken a traditional tale and shifted it to accommodate the eight children but stayed true to the essence of the story, which focused on the children's relationship with the non-human characters in the story – the elements, animals and plants, some magical, in an enchanted wood. Jon could see this was being used as a stimulus for the session but cleverly weaving in the end of the story from the previous week (**adult led with child collaboration**). The children were then invited to say which parts of the story meant something to them; some voiced their thoughts and feelings, some didn't. Carol then asked the children if they wanted to carry the story on into their own activity in the wood or to explore and carry on with what they wanted to play with in the woods. Two-thirds of the group went straight away to certain places in the copse, some with trowels, some with ropes and some with clay and mud! Three stayed with Carol and the other adult, one sat and watched while the other two asked for more of the story (**child led**)! Through the session there were varying degrees of **child-led exploration and play**, with no adult intervention, and **child-initiated exploration and play supported by the adults** – sometimes offering equipment or ways of creating or just working alongside. The adults were immersed in their own play alongside the children and conscious of keeping the child-initiated and -directed play – mud creatures making rain seemed to be a common motif emerging from the initial story stimulus. These two aspects of the play cycle carried on until it came to the break and end of the session, when Carol called everyone back with a 'singing bowl' (**adult led**). During the break, Carol asked who would like to pour and hand out the drinks and cake, and three willing volunteers then stepped forward and like clockwork took on the drinks and cake job with little support from Carol and her helper. The helper was with the 'refreshment' children while Carol could sit and chat with the others (**a mixture of child led and child initiated supported by adults**). At the end of the session Carol carried on from where the starting story had left off, incorporating some of the moments she had witnessed through the session, with the children chipping in (**adult led**). She then invited the children to finish with highs and lows of the morning, in the language of the twirling, whirling dance (**adult initiated**).

This pattern of the various forms of 'intervention' and 'non-intervention' at different stages through a session seems to be common in Forest School sessions – a nature play cycle. It is this that helps form a community of learning where all, including the natural world, have an equal stake.

BUILDING NATURE CONNECTION AND
A SENSE OF PLACE

Building a relationship with nature, place and community is implicit in one of the six Forest School principles (see Figure 3.3).

The importance of place attachment or knowing a place is often underestimated and key to nature interventions and Forest School.

Our sense of belonging to a place, growing up with nature as friend and ally in modern cultures, is often lost in adulthood. We lose this vital living connection with the land and we develop place attachment difficulties, indeed 'cosmos' dis-attachment! The nature-centric models that underpin the pedagogy of nature are based in a worldwide living relationship with the earth, the seasons, at whatever latitude it can be found in all cultures. There will be differences in interpretations, but essentially they provide maps that include all of life together, showing our relationship to life – from the stone and rocks that absorb the carbon in our atmosphere to the sun and stars – we are the

Figure 3.3 Forest School takes place in a woodland or a natural environment with trees to support the development of a relationship between the learner and the natural world

stars! Those who have lived close to the earth, and those that still do, understand that our lives are intricately woven with each other and know where things originate. Our warm houses and modern accessories are hugely comfortable, but they have taken us far from remembering where everything comes from. An awe and reverence for nature is not only spiritual but intensely practical.

Place attachment often begins with meeting our survival needs for water, shelter, food and fire/warmth, now taken for granted and paid for. However, a fifth essential ingredient is community (belonging), and in the past our connection to place always involved cultural community nature practices, many of which were long term – coppicing, for instance, not only provided 'houses' going back thousands of years, but also was inextricably linked to the trackways that connected communities as well as the seasonal nature of harvesting. This historical influence on our connection to land and place is explored more in other chapters, in particular Chapters 12 and 13.

A place has many characters, present and past, its secrets largely invisible until you have found time to explore it. Patience, determination, curiosity and a quiet mind are required to reveal the attributes of natural features. Rocks, soil, slopes, light, plants, trees, birds and insects reveal stories to us, gently providing meaning and context. A real experience of a stone is entirely different from a photo of a stone or a plastic stone toy. Fostering this relationship arises from direct experience in nature, the stories we tell and share, where the value of nature becomes intrinsically embedded. Significant 'human-nature' stories can provide a context for understanding and connecting to a place.

For example, the centre where Jon worked is called Bishops Wood, which got its name from a 'gospel' oak, a boundary oak tree to the wood – the 'Mitre Oak'. This is where the local priests in Saxon, Roman and mediaeval times would have delivered their sermons. This particular oak was, according to local folklore, the Mitre Oak where St Augustine met the Celtic bishops from across the River Severn to persuade them to embrace the new Roman Catholic Christianity. Before and since that time, the local monks and priests cut the hazel in the wood, kept pigs that would graze in the wood and gathered for prayer and gratitude for the gifts of God. Today the hazel is harvested in the traditional way and used not for sheep and pig fences but mostly for chairs and artefacts made by learners and for cooking and heat. The groups honour this in their own way at the end of each session, voicing their appreciations – one of the appreciations that came out regularly with one of Jon's Forest School groups at the Centre was for the man who built the composting loo – Mick was seen as part and parcel of the place (that group had two learners who spent a lot of time in and down the loo!).

Such stories can and do create a sense of connection and place, honouring the trees and all the non-humans that live in the wood – in the Bishops Wood case, this is often badgers, a robin and the buzzards that nest in or near the Forest School site. We are creating our own sacred meeting place under the trees that has in fact been a meeting place for centuries. Storytelling and storymaking in and of places, human and non-human, is fundamental to creating a sense of place. We take much inspiration from the many sources of stories from various cultures around the world that chime with our own places and relationships to those places. There are many sources, and this is about those stories that chime in our hearts that can create a sense of place (here are just three of Jon's favourites – Gersie, 1992; Galbraith and Wills, 2017; Yolen, 1986).

The foundation of Forest School or any nature-based education concerns re-integrating human behaviour, 'what we do', and our culture within nature, creating systems of education, health and society that make sure we acknowledge and look after the natural spaces and create a sense of identity with the place. The process is a multifaceted one, which brings us to holism.

Nature-centric models of practice and holistic learning

Our current National Curriculum is 'subject based' and follows a Cartesian approach whereby subjects are often reduced down to a molecular level – without seeing the more holistic picture. The English national curriculum aims to 'promote the spiritual, moral, cultural, mental and physical development of all pupils at school and of society' (section 31, Education Act 1996). The balance is seen as this:

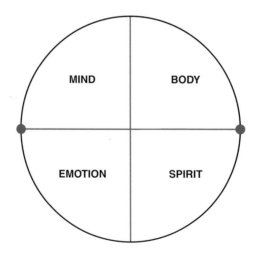

Figure 3.4 We often hear that our schooling addresses the 'whole' of us, yet the direct experience looks more like this:

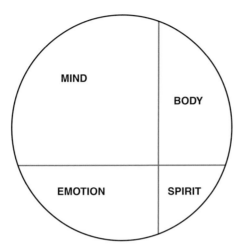

Figure 3.5

For most learners, the experience of school is focusing on what they can learn and remembering facts about what someone else has thought. The Key Stage 1 (ages 5 to 7 years) & Key Stage 2 (ages 7 to 11 years) curriculum is dominated by learning Maths, English and Science, more than other key subjects. The time spent on developing authentic relationships, communicating about difficult feelings, what learners love, enjoy and feel passionate about is not valued equally. The idea of 'spiritual' is rarely developed and is often framed by the major religions. We feel that 'spiritual' is so much more than looking at religious doctrines. At the heart of this, is our connection to the great mysteries of life and death, which really interest children. Coming to terms with death and loss is an essential tool in life and one which we are often underequipped to support in our culture. Children create diverse 'rituals' to express moments of celebration – through making up songs, or 'plays' or something artistic with nature. A trainee recalls marrying his friend in an outdoor ceremony when he was six years old! We bear witness in the outdoors to the ever-changing seasons and weather, reminding us of how things die, change and find life again. It is also hopeful, reassuring and fosters a connection that is 'greater than individual' connections.

As emphasised throughout the book, the holistic approach (our intrinsic intelligences) is at the heart of Nature Pedagogy and Forest School. Indeed, in the opening chapter we referred to a central principle of Forest School – *holistic learning*.

HOLISTIC LEARNING

In this section, we would like to expand what 'holistic' means in a natural world setting.

If you were to ask early years' practitioners currently working in England what is meant by child development, they might respond with the seven areas of learning in the current English 'Early Years Framework' (EYFS Framework 2017 for children aged between 0 to 5 years old):

- communication and language
- physical development
- personal, social and emotional development
- mathematical development
- literacy
- understanding of the world
- expressive arts and design

Within the Early Years Framework, each child is seen to relate to people and things through the 'Characteristics of Effective Learning', which move through all the aforementioned areas of learning. They include:

- playing and exploring – engagement, finding out and exploring, playing with what they know, being willing to 'have a go'.
- active learning – motivation, being involved and concentrating, willing to keep on trying, enjoying achievement.
- creating and thinking critically, having their own ideas, making links, choosing ways to do things.

Take a moment to consider the many ways in which the outdoors and nature provides opportunities to facilitate effective learning. What is challenging for teachers is that these characteristics do not continue to be valued throughout education as a whole. Once a child enters the primary curriculum, this holistic approach is largely diminished. This is in spite of the 'Top 10 Skills' by the World Economic Foundation in 2020 being:

1 Complex Problem Solving
2 Critical Thinking
3 Creativity

Figure 3.6

```
  4  People Management
  5  Coordinating with Others
  6  Emotional Intelligence
  7  Judgment and Decision Making
  8  Service Orientation
  9  Negotiation
 10  Cognitive Flexibility
```

Figure 3.6 Continued

The term 'holistic', when referring to human development, comes from the idea of 'holism' which emerged in the 1970s in educational thinking, that things need to be understood as a whole (though its roots are much older). The *Oxford English Dictionary* defines 'holistic' as "characterized by comprehension of the parts of something as intimately interconnected and explicable only by reference to the whole".

As humans, we naturally learn and develop in a more circular, complex yet integral way. Holistic development is literally doing all seven (and more) areas at once, in a messy interconnected way and in which new learning is made – the gestalt (the sum of the parts makes something bigger than the individual parts). To be wholesome we must remain true to our vulnerable complexity.

Our brain is not a linear thing. Brain scan images demonstrate so well how it connects like a web. Take a look inside any brain, the human body and its surroundings. There would be no way you could visualise just seven separate areas of development as in the early years curriculum. The brain *and* body *and* environment interact (see Chapter 7). For example, we now know through the latest neurological discoveries that we are not just working on mathematical development when sorting sizes of sticks for laying a fire. There is active sensory development, textural and creative development, internal and often external communication, natural world connective development and emotional development!

SPIRITUAL DEVELOPMENT WITH NATURE

In the current English Early Years Framework, there is no mention of spiritual development, and yet it is one important core aim of the National Curriculum. In order to understand ourselves, modern approaches separate different aspects in order to study them when in reality every part of ourselves, and beyond ourselves, is an integrated system dependant on our spiritual development. This is true of ecological or natural systems as well as our human systems. By putting these areas of development in the EYFS framework in bullet points, omitting spiritual development, we have broken up what is really a more complicated and integrated phenomenon.

Figure 3.7 Children in Sheffield exploring an injured pigeon 'feigning death' at Forest School.."where does the pigeon go when it is dead?" "is it dead?"

Our education system has struggled to define and explore spiritual development, particularly as society becomes increasingly secular. It is worth mentioning this, as it is virtually impossible to work in nature with young people and not engage (often profoundly) with the experience of life and death, of immense feelings of connection alongside the humility of knowing so little about the answers for questions that are so easily asked by children, for example, "Why are there so many stars?"

Giesenberg (2007) defines spirituality as

An innate part of a person. It is an awareness or consciousness of the surrounding world, a sense of compassion and love towards this world and anything in it shown through wonder and through activities and relationship with peers and significant adults in the child's life.

As we will discover later in the book (Chapters 8 and 9), our mental well-being is often linked to this emotional and spiritual resilience that provides a foundation in our own and others' dignity and worth.

Pre-21st-century views on holism

A number of views about holistic development have been expressed by philosophers, thinkers and educators over the centuries, in particular the central importance of the 'spiritual'. One of the world-renowned thinkers on education and human development was Krishnamurti (1895–1986). He espoused the individual as one who should see him/herself as an integrated whole and unique, only truly free when we see ourselves as a 'global citizen', as part of the human race. "The highest function of education is to bring about an integrated individual who is capable of dealing with life as a whole" (Krishnamurti, 1964).

He saw love of the world and higher, deeper thinking combined with 'freedom' of the mind as essential to whole human development. He did not expound any philosophy or religion but rather considered the things that concern all of us in our everyday life. He unravelled with great precision the subtle workings of the human mind and pointed to the need for bringing to our daily life a deeply meditative and religious quality. When children are outdoors, the quality of relationships grounded in love and compassion with the non-human and human facilitate huge potential of holistic learning and development. This increases the learner's capacity to navigate and live in a society where violence and disconnection is present.

Many of the Swiss humanitarians, including Johann Pestalozzi; Austrian Rudolf Steiner; American transcendentalists Thoreau, Emerson and Alcott; founders of 'progressive' education Francis Parker and John Dewey; and pioneers such as Maria Montessori (all referred to in Chapter 2) insisted that education should be understood as the art of cultivating the moral, emotional, physical, psychological and spiritual dimensions of the developing child. All saw contact with the 'real', and often the natural world, as something essential to child development. Developing our self-worth, agency, resilience and inner resources is enhanced by adults who can share power and not seek power *over* children or another person. Current thinkers (O'Toole 2019, 2018; Rossi et al., 2018) have offered a place for critical and contemplative pedagogies, where students are given opportunities to consider how their own lives and experiences impact their sense of holistic 'self', placing the learner at the centre of their own learning.

Contemporary and present-day holism

For Ron Miller, a contemporary educationalist, a holistic way of thinking encompasses and integrates multiple layers of meaning and experience rather than defining human possibilities narrowly. Children are more than future employees; their intelligence and abilities more complex than a score on standardised tests. In his book *What Are Schools For?* (1997) integrating the emotional, physical, psychological and cognitive aspects of child development, he demonstrates that holistic education, grounded in a fundamentally different worldview, reflects very different assumptions about education and schooling from the common Western view.

Older cultures and holism

It is interesting that some apparently modern education systems now inform their teachings from older ways which are also holistic. These maps and perspectives are common in many Native American, African and Eastern cultures. Even the supposedly more linear Greek Aristotelean thinking on human development sees more systematic web-like connections between the elements, temperaments and learning development – the Steiner movement has based some of their pedagogy on the Greek ideas of temperament. These older paradigms don't separate us from nature but rather understand that we are nature, both in a physical sense, containing the elements (we are stardust) within us, and in a metaphysical sense, that energy exists beyond what we can see with our naked eye. It is this 'invisible energy' that is a unifying spiritual force behind holism. Quantum physicists now allude to this energy, and they cannot really name it, where you can feel infinite and integrated. Systems scientists call this an emergent phenomenon, where the sum of the parts become something else (Siegel, 2019). We leave you with this question, is this energy of integration the 'spiritual'?

Power and recognising its impact on an integrated learning community – digging into indigenous ways of knowing

The nature play cycle is about who has the power over the learning community at any one time. We would like to finish this chapter introducing Nature Pedagogy by naming this 'elephant in the room'!

In many cultures – in Brazil (Freire, 1970), New Zealand, Canada, Australia, Korea and China, to name but a few, there is recognition of the power dynamic that has been highlighted by years of colonising.

In New Zealand, for example, the early childhood curriculum Te Whāriki (New Zealand Ministry of Education, 1996) is "underpinned by a vision for children who are competent and confident learners and communicators, healthy in mind, body and spirit, secure in their sense of belonging and in the knowledge that they make a valued contribution to society". This framework supports key principles and strands. The personal, social, emotional development (PSED) emphasises a child's willingness, readiness and ability to take an interest, be involved, be resilient and communicate with others. It also highlights the importance of the practitioner's pedagogical approach and how this is influenced by personal values and experiences. This begins to raise a key question, who has the power and how is power used across our cultures, families and classrooms? Our history of colonisation, our enforcement of Western approaches onto other people, often with great violence and oppression, requires us to reflect on and evaluate our practice. This oppression is within all of our cultural and societal systems and affects us all in positive and negative ways (see O'Toole and the Power Threat Meaning Framework, 2018).

The natural world, however, is a great leveller when working with groups outdoors. As adults we have a responsibility to respect children's experiences in developing a close, caring relationship. And of course we are cultivating a community that respects all of our experiences – the adults' too!

We don't last long on our own without human interaction and attachment for basic emotional health, especially in the natural world. For centuries our Western culture has esteemed humans over nature, and has placed the human out of the natural system and cycles from which we evolved. The predominance of westernised ways of knowing have dominated education models that were exported through the British Empire, diminishing a body of knowledge that never separated human, nature and community. The next chapter will summarise some of the key earth-based paradigms that embrace inclusion and integration. We have adapted some of these understandings to create simple pedagogy models that provide nature-centric frameworks that can underpin practice and, in the end, harmony.

QUESTIONS FOR PRACTICE

How much of your practice reflects the principles of Nature Pedagogy – the walking alongside, and with, the natural world and learner, integrating learning, encouraging playfulness and creativity?

Consider the importance of supporting the observed learning and development in your setting – how much learning and development do you miss?

USEFUL RESOURCES

www.naturepedagogy.com/about-us/ This is a new worldwide network looking at Nature Pedagogy for under-8-year-olds with a host of nature education networks that are part of this network. There are some case studies and videos about nature-based practice on the website.

www.childreninpermaculture.com This website is full of ideas for enacting permaculture and nature pedagogic principles/designs. It has a good up-to-date resource list to support nature-based educators.

Understanding Wellbeing (Scottish Well-being Audit _ GIRFEC): www.gov.scot/publications/ getting-right-child-understanding-wellbeing-leaflet/

www.youtube.com/watch?v=T0hQNR5fDK A useful TED Talk by Lora Smothers on the importance of a natural self way of educating. Although not nature based, this talk recognises the importance of the 'indigenous local way of educating' – 'unschooling'.

Juliet Robertson: Creative Star Blog and Website: www.creativestarlearning.co.uk

The Power Threat Meaning Framework (2018) The British Psychological Society. Division of Clinical Psychology. January 2018: www.bps.org.uk/sites/bps.org.uk/files/Policy/Policy%20-%20Files/PTM%20Main.pdf

BIBLIOGRAPHY

Andrews, M (2012) *Exploring Play for Early Childhood Studies*. Sage.

Australian Bureau of Statistics (2001) *Beyond Blue to Green: The Benefits of Contact with Nature for Health and Well-Being*.

Elliot, S (Dr) – Early Years Summit (2018) *Organised by Kathy Brodie*. See www.kathybrodie.com/.

Freire, P (1970) *Pedagogy of the Oppressed*. Penguin.

Galbraith, A and Wills, A (2017) *Dancing with Trees: Eco-tales from the British Isles*. History Press.

Gersie, A (1992) *Earthtales: Storytelling in Times of Change*. Green Print.

Giesenberg, A (2007) *The Phenomenon of Preschool Children's Spirituality* (Thesis at Queensland University of Technology).

Gopnik, A (2017) *The Gardener and the Carpenter: What the New Science of Child Development Tells Us About the Relationship Between Parents and Children*. Penguin.

Higgins, P, Nicol, R and Ross, H (2006) *Teachers' Approaches and Attitudes to Engaging with the Natural Heritage Through the Curriculum*. Perth: Scottish Natural Heritage www.education.ed.ac.uk/outdoored/research/teachers_approaches.pdf (accessed 14/01/07).

Husbands, C and Pearce, J (2012) *What Makes Great Pedagogy? Nine Claims from Research*. National College for School Leadership.

Knight, S (2009) *Forest Schools and Outdoor Learning in the Early Years*. London: Sage.

Krishnamurti, J (1964) *Think on These Things*. New York: Harper and Row.

See Krishnamurti Foundation Trust www.krishnamurticentre.org.uk/teachings.

Miller, R (1997) *What Are Schools For? Holistic Education in American Culture* (3rd edition). Brandon, VT: Holistic Education Press.

Millennium Cohort Study (MCS). University of London, Institute of Education, Centre for Longitudinal Studies (ESRC Funded). https://cls.ucl.ac.uk/cls-studies/millennium-cohort-study/.

O'Brien, T (2017) Psychology and Reflection. In McGill, R M (ed.), *Mark. Plan. Teach 2016*. London: Bloomsbury.

O'Toole, C (2018) Mindfulness, contemplative pedagogy and trauma-informed praxis in education. Poster presented at the Mind and Life European Summer Research Institute, Lake Chiemsee, Germany, 20–26 August.

O'Toole, C (2019) Time to Teach the Politics of Mental Health: Implications of the Power Threat Meaning Framework for Teacher Education. *Clinical Psychology Forum* 313 (January).

Rossi, T, McCuaig, L, Enright, E and Macdonald, D (2018) Who Does Health Work and Health Education in Schools? Teachers Work as an Increasingly Loose Concept. Paper presented at the European Education Research Conference. Bolzano, Italy, 4–7 September.

Siegel, D (2019) *The Science of Psychotherapy*. See www.youtube.com/watch?v=CiUz_UOOm8o.

Sobel, D (1996) *Beyond Ecophobia: Reclaiming the Heart in Nature Education*. Great Barrington, MA: The Orion Society and the Myrin Institute.

Sobel, D (2019) *Beyond Ecophobia: Reclaiming the Heart in Nature Education*. Orion Reader.

Twohig-Bennet, C and Jones, A (2018) The Health Benefits of the Great Outdoors: A Systematic Review and Meta-Analysis of Greenspace Exposure and Health Outcomes. *Environmental Research* 166 (October): 628–637. doi: 10.1016/j.envres.2018.06.030.

Wells, N M and Lekies, K S (2006) Nature and the Life Course: Pathways from Childhood Nature. *White Hutchinson Leisure & Learning Group* Page 11 Experiences to Adult Environmentalism. *Children, Youth and Environments* 16: 1–24.

Wilson, E O (1984) *Biophilia: The Human Bond with Other Species*. Cambridge Press.

Yolen, J (1986) *Favourite Folktales from Around the World*. Pantheon Books.

New Zealand Ministry of Education (1996) See https://www.education.govt.nz/assets/Documents/Early-Childhood/Te-Whariki-1996.pdf.

4 Nature Pedagogy models

Through many oral indigenous and traditional ways of knowing and direct time spent in nature, simplified practical models have been created to chart human life within its wider natural context. Some attempt (and intentionally fail) to describe a wholeness that exists yet is impossible to fully know from a human-centric perspective alone. In this chapter we will outline some of these maps as wheels and show how they relate to a Nature Pedagogy/teaching, from those that look at yearly nature cycles to those at whole life cycles, both physical and psychological. We will go on to examine the importance of play types throughout life. We will finish by making links to permaculture and its models and principles showing how important it is we incorporate these models into an overall Nature Pedagogy.

NATURE CYCLES AND HUMAN DEVELOPMENT

Nature Pedagogy is best framed within nature-centric models that place the human within the **circle of life**. We will now propose some simple models that link our human nature with an integrated place-based philosophy. Circular models help us as practitioners to reclaim this work within a connective, natural system. They provide a template upon which to offer experiences, big perspectives, activities and planning that aim to inspire our learners. These 'maps' give us a helpful foundational worldview upon which all good nature education rests.

Perhaps some of our models don't match what you believe or have experienced. We are only able to provide a stimulus with our approach, and we hope you will bring your own ideas and frameworks that make sense to you. They need to be authentic to you, and sometimes finding different words to express some of the ideas shared here will make a real difference.

Circles, cycles and 'wheels' as models to underpin our Nature Pedagogy

Circles or *wheels* have been used throughout time and across cultures to help us to remember that our life is inextricably linked to all living beings, including the ever-changing cycles of the rocks, plants, earth, sun, moon and wind. Understanding how energy flows through the system is key to knowing how the planet works ecologically. Indeed, earth education sees these understandings as primary for developing a deep relationship with the natural world (Van Matre, 1990).

Although applying indigenous earth-based models to modern education can be problematic, there is much to be learned from these maps which lead us to feel a deeper connection to nature. We will be referring to these throughout the book to show how they underpin practice.

> *From infancy we concentrate happily on ourselves and other organisms. We learn to distinguish life from the inanimate and move towards it like moths to a porch light. To explore and affiliate with life is a deep and complicated process in mental development. To an extent still undervalued in philosophy and religion, our existence depends on this propensity, our spirit is woven from it, hope rises on its current.*
>
> (Wilson, 1984, p. 1)

The sun wheel – earth's yearly rotational cycles around the sun and human growth

The first nature-centric model (Wheel 1) represents our human relationship with the daily sun cycle, and how our earth moves across the solar system creating the seasons. We will expand with more depth on the other references later as we discuss the different cyclical maps.

Wheel 1: universal directional diagram (northern hemisphere and day/night cycle) (see Figure 4.1)

Orange refers to the times of day: sunrise, midday, sunset and midnight and, depending on the time of year, where the sun appears in relation to our perspective from the earth.

Blue refers to the seasons: spring, late spring, summer, late summer, autumn, late autumn, winter and late winter. The perspective is from the northern hemisphere. There are no fixed points; rather, the circle continues to move, passing through key transitions.

Cardinal directions: east, south, west and north are from a northern hemisphere perspective (and can be flipped for the southern hemisphere), where the sun rises from the eastern direction and travels across the sky from east to west, passing through the south at midday. Having an embodied sense of where the directions are, particularly when you are in nature, increases your core place-relationship (attachment). It is our detachment from nature that has meant that many people have no sense that we are living on a planet that is circulating around the sun.

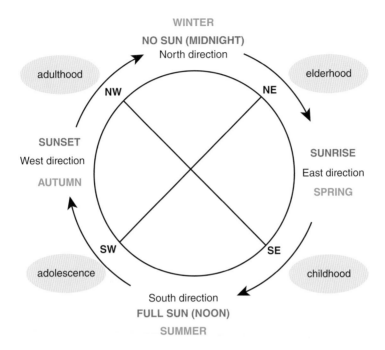

Figure 4.1 Wheel 1

Many children learn about the moon and the sun in geography, but it is a disembodied experience, often book-based, that has little meaning to the experience of a sunrise or the movement of the waters during the tides, all of which affect our moods and our sense of belonging as well as our basic survival needs. We often apply simple, fun exercises and games to build our internal compass and external awareness of the impact of the sun, for example, on the land – the sun's and wind's footprints (e.g. "Close your eyes and point to where you think the sun rose today"). Natural navigation is a modern version of basic tracking in which you have to use your senses to find your way (e.g. two sides of a tree will not feel the same due to the warmth of the sun). Everything you sense is part of a map, too, and builds a story and leaves natural footprints.

Our own creations

During Forest School sessions or trainings, we often create wheels using natural materials (like a mandala, see Figure 4.2) to give us all an experience of co-creating a wheel and applying it to the time of day, season, directions and our ages. Sometimes we do this together and sometimes we do this on our own. This gives us an opportunity to have discussion, reflections, games and activities that link us back into a common nature-based framework.

Figure 4.2 Mandalas made at FS representing cycles and wheels

Wheel 2: human life cycle

In this model we use the metaphor of the daily rotation of the earth and seasons to link to the stages of human life (found in Celtic, Greek, Eastern and Native American cultures, to name a few).

The properties of each direction very much correspond to our 'life stages', the position of the sun in the sky as well as its general position through the seasons corresponding to our development.

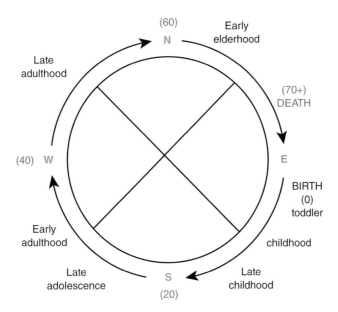

Figure 4.3 Wheel 2: human life cycle

Just like the seasons in Wheel 1, we humans also go through our 'seasons'. Every stage of life, you could say, has a particular quality that relates to a natural flow. The second nature-centric model (Wheel 2) represents the journey from conception to death – with the east to south-east (SE) movement representing birth to springtime/early childhood (0–10/11 years old). The movement from SE to south represents early adolescence (11–12 years old) to late adolescence (20 years old), with movement from south to south-west (SW) representing early adulthood to adulthood (40 years old). Human life from spring to autumn is usually more active and external, just like the seasons. In other traditional understanding, this half of the cycle is known as the solar masculine, where masculine energy is equated with outward giving, 'yang', external power, the exhale and the summerlands.

In Forest School we are generally working with younger people who are in the east to south, or the spring to early summer, time of their lives. What qualities does springtime evoke? This stage is usually full of fast growth, lots of movement and not sitting still. Think of a puppy or kitten. This age group loves to move and is full of fascination, play fighting and fantasy. Young children's consciousness doesn't separate objective and subjective experience; they interact with the world as animate. This all has a developmental purpose. The natural world awakens our developmental capacity as our neurological system expands and is strengthened. We are hard-wired to educate and develop ourselves. The sunrise in the east and start of growth in spring is a time of the early years, 'daily birth of the sun' representing young growth, light and full of discovery and rising energy in childhood. Even as older humans we feel this new energy in spring. In this phase, we make sure there is ample opportunity for children to move and explore, filling themselves with sensory experiences.

> *Children are designed to be messy and unpredictable, playful and imaginative, and to be very different both from their parents and from each other. The variability and flexibility of childhood lets them innovate, create, and survive in an unpredictable world.*
>
> (Gopnik, 2017)

When we reach the highest sun in the south and the hotter summer season, passion and risk-taking are just two of the characteristics seen at the stage of our adolescence. As we incorporate healthy risk-taking into our lives at this age, so this ability to discern when to take risks and when not to into adulthood is formulated. Our ability to move through fear and be courageous increases during this developmental phase.

When the sun reaches the west and the start of autumn, before the leaves have dropped, we reach adulthood. This sees us becoming an independent yet a connected, responsible member of the community, finding our vocation and contributing to decision-making and community building. Here there is a consolidation of learning and 'knowing' where we are in life, in effect 'harvest time', when the 'fruits of our labour' start to manifest. We start to plant the seeds of our knowledge and communicate more deeply with others in our community – the human and non-human world.

Autumn, the west direction, represents the beginning of our journey of letting go of what is not helpful or no longer useful. We need to continue to grow internally, be more focused with our activeness (compared to childhood) as we move towards the north, representing the beginning of elderhood (see more in Chapter 9 on psychology/emotional wheel). The north or winter stage of our life (60 years old) is where we can offer stability to our families and communities and impart the wisdom we have gathered from a life well lived. Midnight and the north direction on the wheel sees us entering elderhood – a time to pass on wisdom and witness the 'seeds of knowledge' grow. The acorn during November already has its shoots in the ground and goes further into the darker cycle of the year. Life is about watching and being vigilant in the world (almost like 'watching the night'). We sense a larger connected world, which includes the cosmos. Caring and letting go characterises the end of this stage. In other traditional understanding, this half of the cycle is known as the lunar feminine, where feminine energy is equated with inward receiving, 'yin', inner power, the inhale and the winterlands.

These simplified wheels or circular maps are not prescriptive but rather offer a bigger perspective that all humans share across cultures. There are many metaphors and reflections through being in nature that are really helpful. A teenager spent a few hours in a 'sit spot' and through watching a spider struggle and not give up, she felt she had understood something more about her challenging situation. It is not unusual to have profound insight or clarity after time spent in nature – Sir Isaac Newton's discovery sitting under an apple tree is one famous example! Nature Pedagogy ideally applies this philosophy through direct experiences, craft-based skills

Figure 4.4 An elder shows learners how to burn a bowl in birch . . . the power of intergenerational exchanges

and a competent guide within our nature-based practice (see Chapters 12 and 13 for inspiration). Creating an intergenerational Forest School, a village-type atmosphere, where we all can look across the ages and enjoy each other's company, is at the heart of a community of learners and people. It also provides role models for your next phase of life. A young person commented once, "You adults look like you are having fun; I have only ever seen adults looking stressed".

If we are ever in doubt what a Forest School looks like, we think of the season of life the young people are in, provide free play opportunities (freedom) and 'choice-based' co-produced activities that link to what is happening around us in nature (see play types and themes in Chapter 6).

WE ARE NATURE

The wheel's depiction of the changing seasons is a metaphor for our transitions in life. Broadly speaking, the winter is the darker time and more internal, while summer is lighter and more external. Every day, we pass through darkness and light which reflects the constant moving and changing we experience in our lives. We all have moments that are inward, and moments that are external. We have emotions that are personal and hidden, and those that are easily shared. (See Chapter 9 for ways of working with these emotions and the emotional and psychological wheel.) There is wisdom in knowing that as we grow up, we are inevitably going to have difficult times that leave scars, yet we can transform challenging emotional memories into the ability to help others, or influence and inform our values and future choices we make. Nature reminds us that everything changes, and nothing stays the same; there is never this same moment again. We are nature. Our evolution and psychology have co-developed with nature.

The task, as we move around the wheel of life, is to grow beyond our self-centredness, *me* and *mine* (and our own family) and move often painfully to a new perspective of *we* and *us* (the wider family and community) – as Daniel Siegel puts it, the *mwe* (see Chapter 7).

The Celtic wheel and story from this land

Our ancestors observed natural cycles and followed natural patterns. What we observe in nature is a movement of receiving and giving, where every organism has a strategy or niche, which in modern terms represents a diverse ecological system. In order to survive and thrive, our ancestors were superb trackers and for the most part respected this reciprocal relationship. China and India, for example, developed profound philosophy centred on the elements, energy cycles and human development. In Europe, our own Celtic ancestral culture was centred on the inextricable link between the external and internal, nature and human as a rich creative and imaginative unifying 'friendship' as manifested in Celtic myth and story. The term Anam Cara, central to Celtic culture, places the soul at the heart of our development rather than the mind. (See Chapter 7 for further exploration of 'mind'.)

The fire has been the heart of our communities for many years, and numerous indigenous communities going back from the Neolithic to the Middle Ages – Norman, Saxon, Roman, Celtic – learned around the fire through storytelling. Indeed today there has been a revival of this oral tradition, and Forest School is a large part of it. There is nothing like telling and listening to stories around the fire both to bring a community together and to listen, talk about and digest the meaning of our place in the world.

We are walking story makers, and to impart and solidify our own meaning making, 'art' of all forms is important in telling our stories. In our traditions, around the world, this can be dance, song, poetry and storytelling around the fire. In the UK the Celtic, Nordic and Gaelic traditions involve immensely powerful story sessions about life and death; our shadow and light; the hero overcoming adversity etc. These can be powerful moments in working through how we are to unify and live in a more holistic way while embracing life's complexities and tensions. Thomas Aquinas (Eco, 1988) in the 13th century said that all great art had three components: *gravitas* (serious tense matters to consider), *levitas* (a lightness or mildness) and *harmony* (some sort of reconciliation or resolution, be it 'good' or 'bad'). It is this trinity among other trinities – beginning, middle and end; life, death and rebirth and so on – that can be found in many stories of the land and nature. While we allude to story in the craft and non-human chapters, this book does not dive deeply into story; a number of resources are provided at the end of Chapters 12 and 13 that point to storytelling and other art forms that are integral to a Nature Pedagogy.

The triskelion

The triskelion (common throughout Gaelic-speaking countries) is an old representation of the trinities mentioned earlier and can be used as another model to relate to when considering a Nature Pedagogy and 'our story'. It represents the elements of earth, air and water; mind, body and spirit; life, death and rebirth; creation, preservation and destruction. It is drawn as a continuous spiral showing the fluid movement of energies within these sets of three realms developing through time . . . at its simplest in Celtic cultures it represented the cycles of air, water and soil and how these linked into our body, mind and spiritual developments.

For many practitioners the Celtic symbolism and representations do chime with a nature-centred way of looking at the world, in particular within our northern hemisphere cultures. You

Figure 4.5 The triskelion

73

see the triskelion in many contexts, including sporting (Irish rugby for one!), and so bringing to the fore its nature/human meanings can make a pedagogy more visually meaningful. These wheels and circles often resonate with something deep within our psyche. We will develop this further by looking at the yearly cycles and putting these into the context of how we work in a nature education way year in, year out.

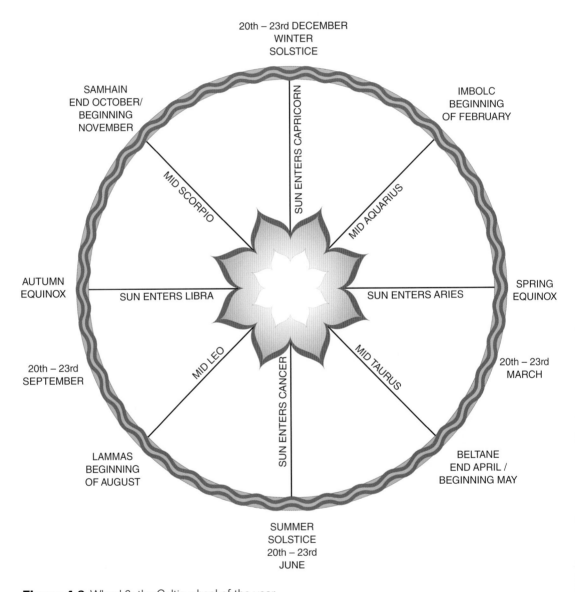

Figure 4.6 Wheel 3: the Celtic wheel of the year

Many of the nature-centric models are based on earlier wheels that celebrate key transition points of change in nature. We are more familiar with terms like 'solstice' or 'equinox'. The equinoxes, March 21st and September 21st, are times when there is equal light and darkness (12 hours each). The solstices, on or around June 21st and December 21st, are times when there is the most sunlight and the least sunlight. The amount of sunlight impacts available warmth, the growth of plants and the availability of food and are times of year marked across cultures through ceremony and ritual that provided deep reverence, respect and connection to land. The Celtic wheel reflects key and solar transitions and provides guidance on how to prepare for different phases, see Figure 4.6.

They are very practical observations and, in our opinion, are complementary to other religious and spiritual understandings found across the world. In the UK, children dance around the maypole on May 1st as a spring dance (this is a Beltane celebration), at the time of year when everything is beginning to grow, and the cold is hopefully behind us. This is a time when all the hawthorns are in bloom! At Forest School, we may make crowns of flowers, or plant perfume. The elderflowers are oozing their sweet smell, perfect for creating elderflower cordial or elderflower pancakes. Birds continue to fledge from the nests. There is a lot going on in the outdoors. Every exploration offers a process of learning. Picking tiny flowers for young children requires fine motor skills. Separating the flowers from the stalks offers an opportunity to sort the different flower parts. Looking at a flower under a magnifying glass enables an in-depth view of what the insects are trying to gather. Making fire, approaching the heat with care, and cooking or heating the fruit or flowers provide insight into how things change and transform, not to mention the medicinal qualities of what they may be preparing.

For the Celts, May 1st, known as Beltane, was when fires were lit and people celebrated spring and fertility. At the opposite time of year, Samhain, at the end of October and beginning of November, was considered a new year, a time when everything around was dying. The natural metaphor and learning here is that all life is born in the presence of death and is sustained and dependent on this (Siddons Heginworth, 2008). All the children gather seeds and carefully replant them to increase the diversity of the trees. Some make paper pots to take them home to grow them and replant when they are ready. "All things begin gently with a seed, an idea, a dream, and this must lay dormant and await its proper time and season before it can grow" (ibid).

At this time of year, we celebrate Halloween, perhaps with pumpkin soup around the fire or apple bobbing! We huddle in together to keep warm and share stories. We make medicines from the berries that help with our colds and coughs, for example rosehip cordial, hawthorn leather, blackberry pancakes!

Our fourth nature-centric model brings our attention to the life cycle of a plant following the same points of reference through the seasons. Our relationship with plants reflects and supports our whole development. They are the source of our food, heat and more, and they also show many similar characteristics to humans.

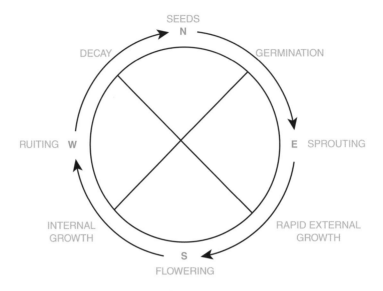

Figure 4.7 Wheel 4: plant cycle. In NW (November time)

The citrus fragrance of the phytoncide (the plant's chemicals) D-limonene is more effective than antidepressants for lifting mood and ensuring emotional well-being in patients with mental-health disorders.

(Dr Qing Li, 2018)

Peter Wohlleben, in his milestone book *The Hidden Life of Trees*, showed that this is actually more than metaphor and that trees literally follow life cycles similar to humans. "When you know that trees experience pain and have memories and that tree parents live together with their children, then you can no longer just chop them down and disrupt their lives with larger machines" (Wohlleben, 2017).

Like humans, plants and trees appear different at each stage. In youth, their external growth is rapid, their inner core is weaker, and they heal faster. In early adulthood the blossoming of sexuality occurs, with the desire to mate, where fruiting may occur. As aging occurs, the inner core strengthens, the outer appearance ages and skin becomes coarser.

Eventually the relationships we have made over our lifetime support us until our time to 'transition' out of life as we know it. In the human cycle, this may be our relatives supporting us in old age, and us looking after our grandchildren. In plant cycles, the root system, fungi and soil work together with the old trees to support the younger generations.

Like all of life, plants and trees have their love of certain places, have particular characters and stages of life. (Chapter 13 on plants gives you a practical and theoretical appreciation of plants and the seasons.) The stages, like the human and sun cycles mentioned earlier, link together, providing a natural flow from germination (conception) through to flowering, fruiting, decay and the seeds that hold the potential of the next generation. We remember too that it is in the compost of the old where life begins again. Nature is regenerative. In the middle of winter, the roots deep within the earth grow, creating stability before they burst through the soil towards the sun.

> Jon worked with a learner at the start of her adolescence who had little language and spent much of her time in Forest School clutching elderflowers. She seemed to need to collect and hold 'posies', which caused her to sing "New York, New York, What a wanderful town.." while walking through the woods. This was a time when she was most herself. After a few weeks of this behaviour when Jon asked what the singing and flowers represented to her, she exclaimed, "This is my New York, my happy place where I feel alive!"

Jon could see that this springtime feeling was probably affirming her 'adolescent' energetic feeling and providing an internal metaphor for where her life had reached. Interestingly, Forest School did have an impact on her language development, singing being a key.

Plants and trees provide a host of ecology and healing services, feeding us, providing all the medicines, furniture, fire, smells and beauty, homes and the air we breathe. We are entirely in their debt for our life and are connected to them. I have seen many adults surprised to taste aspirin from the willow tree at our Forest School site. All these experiences and moments build meaningful relationships when we spend time in nature.

A mature human society needs more mature human individuals, where age with internal personal growth has value. This is also true in the forests where the elder trees provide shelter and nutrients to the young generations.

We have learned that mother trees recognize and talk with their kin, shaping future generations. In addition, injured trees pass their legacies on to their neighbors, affecting gene regulation, defense chemistry, and resilience in the forest community.

(Wohlleben, 2017)

Jon witnessed this with a 14-year-old young man from a special school who struggled with communication, spatial/vestibular development, and 'staying on task'. The group had been putting up a swing for weeks and he had been finding it 'hard', giving up after a few seconds. He had a real issue working alongside the other learners and Jon on some days. Then suddenly he clicked into a shared wavelength, the tree and the rope, Jon and another boy. All together they threw the rope over the branch and he got so lost in the process that you could see something deeper was going on inside. Jon could have surmised from this that he had gained some fine motor skills, increased his ability to work with others, learned a new knot, improved his hand/eye coordination, exercised his larger muscles, learned to communicate more effectively and achieved a task.

However, when the group had their review of the session, in a circle around the tree in question, Jon could see what was more significant than all these areas of development. The learner spoke for the first time in front of the group. This is what he said – "I now feel at one with tree, Forest School, the ground, and you and it's good friendship". Wow! It is the sensory threshold this learner had crossed combined with the 'feeding' from the four elements and meeting of inner and outer worlds that is so prevalent in the outdoors and, in the end, we get 'integration' and 'friendship'.

The value of learning with nature through play

Forest School and other natural play spaces create the foundational experiences that form a life-long kinship with nature and a vital health support system for our well-being. We are facilitating learners of all ages and providing a community where we are valued and respected. Our props become 'playing' or 'quiet time', rather than screens. Nature time is part of life-long preventative medicine.

We need to value the visceral and embodied experience as a basis too for physical and emotional development. David Sobel's research (2008) provides a wonderful nature-centric framework for practitioners to trust in the learning and well-being that occurs through play. Play is particularly important for all ages to experience nature through their bodies.

Figure 4.8 Young people at play

Without any resources, just green spaces, Sobel observed seven universal play motifs or design principles that children will naturally follow when they have safe free time in nature, at any age.

1　Special places (constructing different spaces as dens, finding hidey holes)
2　Acting out fantasies/scenarios (stories, plays, puppets, living ideas)
3　Hunting and gathering (searching, finding, collecting, foraging and using bushcraft skills, treasure hunts, hide and seek games)
4　Creating miniature worlds (fairy houses, gardens, etc.)
5　Forming friendships with animals (empathy with animals and plants, feelings for other creatures)
6　Mapmaking and following paths (shortcuts and secret routes, exploring local geography and maps)
7　Constructing adventures (physical challenges, balancing, not knowing the outcome)

Jan White (2014) considered the work of Sobel, Appleton (1975) and Pelo (2013) and identified further relevant play behaviours or 'pathways'. She proposes 'Make Rituals and give gifts' and 'Gaining prospect' (getting views from high spots), where gifts provide a binding process and small rituals like shaking the leaves are common play experiences. In Chapter 6 on play, we have expanded on these themes that provide a useful and emerging framework to work with when considering play as an integral part of a Nature Pedagogy.

As practitioners, we have to resist providing activities and directing learning. When we let go and trust that children know how to self-direct what they need to learn, we observe how capable they are to self-discover and naturally create self-learning opportunities through their own play.

The nature play cycle described in the previous chapter provides a framework that underpins good practice and leads to resilient, creative and compassionate humans who value nature. We are all limited by our own experience to date (our own cultural blindness). In the beginning it takes considerable effort, confidence and a leap of faith to lay down old habits and allow children to learn through play, learning concepts experientially so that they develop into successful, confident, responsible individuals who are effective contributors.

PHYSICAL DEVELOPMENT AND IMMERSION IN THE NATURAL WORLD

Our physical development is inextricably linked to these natural/outdoor world play types, and this is at the heart of a Nature Pedagogy. The Early Years Framework (2017, s3.57) recognises the importance of outdoor play for children's development. It states that childcare providers for ages 0–5 should offer outdoor activities every day, unless unsafe weather conditions prevent it. However, as children move up the education system, they are less active and more sedentary. There is abundant research that links physical opportunity to health and learning. 'Green gym' also recognises this as an important aspect of healthy body development in adults (see Chapter 14). The following wheel provides numerous examples of how the natural/outdoor world supports our physical development. As educators we are clear that optimum learning arises from a healthy body, mind, emotion and spirit. Our approach to learning must be holistic.

> *Physical development sits at the heart of wellbeing, learning and development – and it creates school readiness.*
>
> (White, 2015)

The wheel in Figure 4.9 and Table 4.1 provide a simple model outlining the multiple ways that outdoor experience contributes to our physical development. Every activity that a child engages with has pedagogical significance. They are not 'just playing' or 'just having fun'! This chapter has provided both a philosophical underpinning of nature education and insight into the learning and development that can occur in nature with the guidance of an experienced facilitator. As part of your reflection practice, take time to consider what areas of learning are occurring during a session. Consider all the holistic aspects, the primary or secondary curriculum outcomes, EYFS framework and social, emotional and psychological aspects – it is all there!

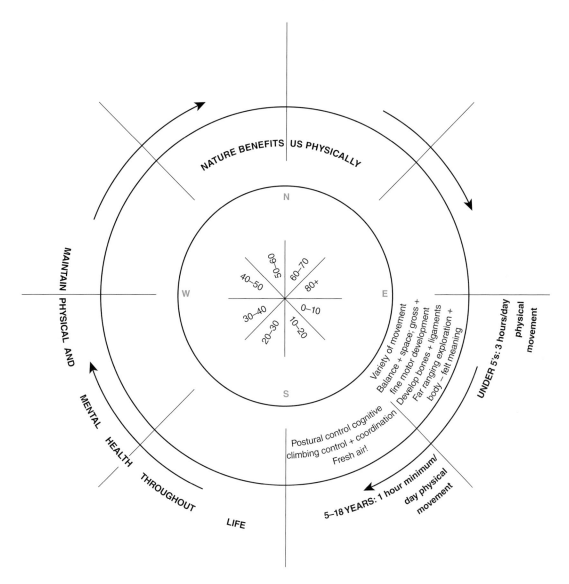

Figure 4.9 Wheel 5: Physical development wheel related to the outdoors/natural world

Table 4.1

Physical wheel	What nature provides	Cumulative benefits
East 0–18 months	Eye and head movement Variety of movements in nature, e.g. leaf falling, branches swaying, grasses and clouds moving, birds flying; colours in nature	Robust sense of self Awareness of self, objects and others in space Control and coordination Feeling good in your body
18 months–4 years	Balance and space Logs, stepping stones, fallen trees, puddles, climbing, wonky steps Gross motor skills Running, rolling, swinging – uneven and spacious Digging, pushing, pulling, dragging, life, large logs, stumps, buckets of water, soil, mud and clay; using pulleys	Secure in your world Sensory integration to combine information and manage effectively Cognitive climbing Develop bones, muscles, ligaments, tendons Cardiovascular functioning – heart, lung, blood circulation Core neurological systems Vestibular and proprioception
2–3 years	Fine motor skills Peeling willow stick and vegetables, cutting twine, first knot tying and wrapping Fine whittling of soft sticks	Depth perception and special awareness Dextrous tool use, focus (pre-writing skills) Join in socially valued activity, sense of belonging Aids attention, memory and learning via brain/body connection Experience body-felt meaning, e.g. weight, shape, size (pre-math skills) Postural control overriding primitive reflexes Breathe clean air Build inner drive for physiological rewards (via dopamine production)
For children aged 5 and under: minimum of 3 hours of physical activity every day		
South-east 4–12	Increased activity, movement, balance Freely available spontaneous and calculated movements in a sensory-rich environment Increasingly complex skills to enable use of ropes for swings, climbing and building Engagement and independent use of tools and creative pursuits	
For children aged 5 to 18 years: minimum of 1 hour of physical activity up to several hours every day		
12–20+	Space and freedom Far-ranging exploration Risk-taking Experiential knowledge of flora and fauna Non-human relationships Calming environment Diverse sensory environment Sounds in nature	Health continues to build on previous experience During puberty, body awareness and physical exercise supports his transition Maintain core strength Remain mentally and physically healthy

Nature Pedagogy and fire

In Forest School, particularly if we are cooking or in need of a warm and welcoming atmosphere, we will make fire! Fire is something that is so visceral and part of being human (more is said about this in Chapter 12). It is mesmerising. We see fire as something that is intrinsic to Nature Pedagogy: it takes us into our origins and is a place where we can feel most at home. This doesn't mean having fires all the time, but we see fire as something that at least should be experienced seasonally, as part of following and celebrating the natural cycles.

To make this concrete, we have taken one specific activity and examined key pedagogical characteristics of firemaking (see also Chapter 12 Appendix online materials for more details on firemaking). This is based on some thinking from Juliet Robertson (see the useful resources section and Chapter 4 online appendix).

How do we enable the learner-centred element of Nature Pedagogy to be part of the 'fire' experience? The age and developmental level of a child or person affects their understanding of fire and the recognition of associated hazards. Fire activities should be meaningful and chosen to be age and stage appropriate, to support progression in the development of skills, responsibilities and competencies. They also need to be part and parcel of the learning and place. In the online appendices, we have shown how firemaking is also related to the age-related wheel.

Fire as a third teacher provides endless knowledge transfer and emotional resilience! The fire always gives us direct feedback and provides ongoing dialogue, in particular listening, non-verbal cues between the young person and this element. There are so many teachable moments, both self-teaching and from the outside, that is, from adults or peers. It can be deeply frustrating and require expression of feelings and vulnerability. Success may be knowing when to stop. Learning what an acceptable edge is and not to go further is great self-awareness and compassion. The long-term principle of Forest School means that they can nearly always have the opportunity to return to an activity. Firemaking provides that wonderful 'I did it!' feeling, building perseverance, resilience and respect for this primal relationship. The sense of achievement and self-esteem is based on doing something for yourself and seeing the results of your efforts.

The physical wheel (Figure 4.9) draws out some ways of how our body is strengthening or developing during possible explorations. There is a wide range of open resources in nature and many ways to gather and use them! Firemaking is a sensory-rich experience that requires fine motor skills and balance and offers many options for solutions. We have yet to meet anyone who always is successful – it is a humbling experience. Fire brings many strands of learning into an experience that has meaning and purpose. It is holistic, involving critical thinking and physical, social, cognitive and emotional development that is all happening simultaneously.

Figure 4.10 Permaculture principles for children (with permission from Charlene Chesnier, https://cchesnier. wixsite.com/charlytamalou. Taken from the Children in Permaculture Manual)

The relevance of permaculture

The study of Nature Pedagogy would not be complete without looking at the field of permaculture, which we introduced on page 22 of Chapter 2. Permaculture enquires deeply into the study and methods of the human and nature relationship and recognises the planet as a self-regulating system. Effective experiential education works with good design, which includes careful planning to create an atmosphere that requires minimum effort and gives maximum effect, creating abundance. This is the same as permaculture – whose principles are also based on deep observations on how natural systems work. Mammals generally only do what is necessary and are masters of conservation – spending only the energy necessary for survival – minimum in, maximum out. Indeed, many earth-based cultures are the same. The book *Affluence without Abundance* (Suzman, 2017) looks at the oldest tribes on the planet in the cradle of civilisation, South Africa. Suzman shows that the 'Khoisan' lead a very affluent life in terms of fulfilment and well-being and yet have plenty of time for relaxation and do not understand the Western concept of work. The Khoisan have for thousands of years lived expending as little energy as possible until these modern times, when the lands they inhabit have been 'squeezed' by the modern world.

Permaculture follows three broad principles which can be easily integrated into a Nature Pedagogy. These are:

Earth Care – working in harmony with nature in order to minimize negative and maximise positive human impact on the natural world

People Care – taking care of others and self. Cooperation, empathy, clear communication, creative expression, wellbeing and inclusive thinking are all encouraged

Fair Share – striving towards equality and equity between people

(Alderslowe et al., 2018)

12 Permaculture principles and pathways

Bill Mollison (1988) and David Holmgren (2002) present 12 permaculture principles and pathways to help us as nature practitioners follow a Nature Pedagogy. Holmgren learned from growing food in nature and provides a number of nature connection exercises or themes that can be embedded within our Forest School and nature education practice (see Alderslowe et al., 2018). The following principles ask us reflective questions to bring us into awareness of place and begin to consider how we may support nature and humans to thrive together best.

- Observe and interact – what can you see, hear, taste and/or feel? What has changed since the last time we were here? Let's look more closely. What curious questions do you have about this?
- Catch and store energy – how do animals, plants, people save food for different times of year? How can we catch the rain, sun or wind? How can we save energy here? How can we fix it?
- Obtain a yield
- Apply self-regulation and accept feedback
- Use and value renewable resources and services
- Produce no waste
- Design from patterns to details
- Integrate rather than segregate
- Use small and slow solutions
- Use and value diversity
- Use edges and value the marginal
- Creatively use and respond to change

The following practices are based on Mollison's 'Attitudinal Principles' (1988):

- Work with nature, rather than against it – what would nature do here? How would you feel if you were that tree, frog, dragonfly or rock? How can we make sure that the things we do are acceptable with nature?

- The problem is the solution (everything works both ways) – what are the causes of the problem? Let's find a way to solve this. What is the good side of the problem?
- Minimum effort for maximum effect
- The yield of a system is theoretically unlimited – things that we can get out of it whether physical, educational or emotional
- Everything 'gardens' (or has an effect on its environment)

(Collado et al., 2015)

When we think about holistic development, we need to consider that wholeness includes nature and natural cycles. These models use nature's cycles as templates for human maturation.

The future of our planet depends on a change of consciousness, in which the people and the resources of the natural world are no longer taken for granted and exploited without considering long term impacts. Supporting children from early childhood to develop a sensitive, compassionate and cooperative relationship with each other and the natural world is a crucial step in generating this new consciousness.

(Alderslowe et al., 2018)

The need for a Nature Pedagogy

It is continually astonishing how our natural creativity and imagination is extended in nature and fulfils our deepest developmental, psychological and physical needs. We need to trust children's inner drive while holding them in an emotionally and physically 'safe' container. Children need to be given autonomy, choice and secure attachment in order to build relationships between each other and the world (see strategies for emotional development in Chapter 8).

Nature Pedagogy is more than embracing the natural world as a living classroom (though this is true), more than a utilitarian worldview. This relationship asks us to foster a harmonious way with nature, not a dominion of nature, and which is extended beyond our education systems to other health, political and economic systems. We desperately need to 'sense' and rediscover how important nature is for our life-long development, health and learning.

This pedagogy places the Forest School practitioner within nature, the external and internal natural cycles. How far we go into a deeper awareness of our own life's meaning and relationship to 'other' is up to us. It has mundane and spiritual implications and lays the foundation of our worldview and how we relate to one another, the children we work with, and the value we place on 'wild nature' and 'wild play'. We must develop our confidence to apply what we know about child/human development, the importance of childhood and free play within our Forest School sessions, and have positive well-being outcomes linked to self-esteem and resilience. We can encourage young people to be stewards of nature. What is true for us is that buying organic food (which is currently not feasible for many) or using less electricity by switching off lights (though helpful) is not going to be enough to get us back on track living within our ecological means.

Radical systemic change

At this point in our history we remain hopeful that we can develop systems – economic, political, environmental, educational – that can live within nature's law. We need to radically change what we are doing locally and globally because we know at multiple levels what to do. Some of this is within our individual capacity and some of this needs larger system support. We need to value and respect our educational, social and health practitioners as experts in their fields. We need to retrain lecturers in education in Nature Pedagogy and the value of nature experiences so that all educators feel confident to take young people outdoors. We need local authorities to provide continued professional development for teachers and other professionals, so this approach becomes a normal part of our daily practice and approach. We need to address the frightening reality of how our current systems continue to reduce life on this planet – the ocean's fish, the land's mammals, the keystone species that balance life on earth and human life. Nature Pedagogy puts humans within the natural system and celebrates all that we receive from the trees, plants, animals and fungi.

Nature Pedagogy is sensory and practical. Being in touch with the elements of water (rain, streams, ponds, mud), air (out in the open and trees), earth (soil and rocks) and fire (sun and wood) feeds this integrated way of learning. We now understand how nature's sensory 'data' inputs and transforms our internal environment, supporting emotional regulation (bottom-up regulation, Chapter 9) and healthy human development. Deep harmony and peace has to do with how living in the moment, 'being and doing' in the moment, can and does integrate all our sensory and cognitive functions. It is this sensory integration and the benefits of the natural world we would like to explore next.

QUESTIONS FOR PRACTICE

Do you embody the previously described wheels in your practice?

How far should we go concerning working with indigenous ways of 'being and doing' in the modern world? Should we? How do you acknowledge ancestral wisdoms?

How much do you consciously integrate the 'elements', 'directions' and 'planetary' influences in your practice?

How can you express some of these ideas in a way that is meaningful and appropriate to your setting?

USEFUL RESOURCES

www.naturepedagogy.com/about-us/ This is a new worldwide network looking at Nature Pedagogy for under-8-year-olds through a host of nature education organisations. There are some case studies and videos about nature-based practice on the website.

www.childreninpaermaculture.com This is a website full of ideas for 'enacting' permaculture and nature pedagogic principles/designs. It has a good up-to-date resource list to support nature-based educators. We highly recommend the Children in Permaculture Manual

www.youtube.com/watch?v=T0hQNR5fDK A useful TED Talk by Lora Smothers on the importance of a natural self way of educating. Although not nature based this talk recognises the importance of the 'indigenous local way of educating' – 'unschooling'.

Juliet Robertson: Creative Star Blog & Website: www.creativestarlearning.co.uk

The Power Threat Meaning Framework (2018) The British Psychological Society. Division of Clinical Psychology. January 2018: www.bps.org.uk/sites/bps.org.uk/files/Policy/Policy%20-%20Files/PTM%20Main.pdf

Deep ecology–based resources: www.shambhala.com/deep-ecology-for-the-twenty-first-century.html

Stephan Harding: www.schumachercollege.org.uk/learning-resources/what-is-deep-ecology

BIBLIOGRAPHY

Alderslowe, L, Amus, G and Devapriya, D (2018) *Earth Care, People Care and Fair Share in Education – the Children in Permaculture Manual*. See www.childreninpermaculture.com.

Appleton, J (1975) *The Experience of Landscape*. New York: John Wiley & Sons.

Collado, S, Corraliza, J, Staats, H and Ruiz, M (2015) Effect of Frequency and Mode of Contact with Nature on Children's Self-Reported Ecological Behaviours. *Journal of Environmental Psychology* 41: 65–73.

Department of Education (2017) *Statutory Framework for the Early Years Foundation Stage: Setting the Standards for Learning, Development and Care for Children Age Birth to Five*. See www.foundation-years.org.uk/files/2017/03/EYFS_STATUTORY_FRAMEWORK_ 2017.pdf.

Eco, U (1988) *The Aesthetics of Thomas Aquinas*. Harvard University Press.

Gopnik, A (2017) *The Gardener and the Carpenter: What the New Science of Child Development Tells Us About the Relationship Between Parents and Children*. Penguin.

Holmgren, D (2002) *Permaculture: Principles and Pathways Beyond Sustainability*. See https://store.holmgren.com.au/product/principles-and-pathways-signed-hardcover-bundle/.

Krishnamurti, J (1964) *Think on These Things*. New York: Harper and Row. Krishnamurti Foundation Trust. www.krishnamurticentre.org.uk/teachings

Loose Parts Toolkit (2016) *This Toolkit Was Produced by Inspiring Scotland in Collaboration with Play Strategy Group and Scottish Government*. https://www.inspiringscotland.org.uk/wp-content/uploads/2017/03/Loose-Parts-Play-web.pdf.

Mollison, B (1988) *Permaculture: The Design Manual*. Tagari Publications.

Millennium Cohort Study (MCS). University of London, Institute of Education, Centre for Longitudinal Studies (ESRC Funded). https://cls.ucl.ac.uk/cls-studies/millennium-cohort-study/.

Pelo, A (2013) *The Goodness of Rain: Developing an Ecological Identity in Young Children*. Redmond: Exchange Press.

Qing Li, Dr (2018) *Shinrin-Yoku: The Art and Science of Forest-Bathing; How Trees Can Help You Find Health and Happiness. Nippon Medical School*. Penguin, Random House U.K.

Siddons Heginworth, I (2008) *Environmental Arts Therapy and the Tree of Life*. Exeter: Spirit's Rest Books.

Sobel, D (2008) *Childhood and Nature: Design Principles for Educators*. Portland, ME: Stenhouse Publishers.

Sobel, D (2019) *Beyond Ecophobia: Reclaiming the Heart in Nature Education*. Orion Reader.

Suzman, J (2017) *Affluence Without Abundance: What We Can Learn from the World's Most Successful Civilisation*. Bloomsbury.

Van Matre, S (1990) *Earth Education, a New Beginning*. Institute for Earth Education.

White, J (2014) Ecological Identity – Values, Principles and Practice. In Duckett, R and Drummond, M J (eds.), *Learning to Learn in Nature*. Newcastle-upon-Tyne: Sightlines Initiative.

White, J (2015) *Every Child a Mover: A Practical Guide to Providing Young Children with the Physical Opportunities They Need*. Early Education: The British Association for Earth Childhood Education.

White, J (2017) *Tides: The Science and Spirit of the Ocean*. Trinity University Press.

Wilson, E O (1984) *Biophilia – the Human Bond with Other Species*. Cambridge Press.

Wohlleben, P (2017) *The Hidden Life of Trees: What They Feel, How They Communicate – Discoveries from a Secret World*. London: William Collins Books.

Young, J, Haas, E and McGown, E (2008) *Coyote's Guide to Connecting with Nature*. Shelton, WA: Owlink Media.

5 Our sensory system – how nature stimulates sensory development and integration

We process everything through our senses via the brain and heart. This chapter will explore how the senses work with our bodies. We will look at why learning in nature is so fundamentally important for sensory human development. Integrating sensory and emotional human attachment is growing increasingly important – the chapter will briefly explore this. Sensory processing disorders and the importance of contact with nature will also be looked at. We will then move on to discover how Nature Pedagogy supports the eight core human senses.

This chapter should be read in conjunction with Chapters 7, 8 and 9, as our sensory system is inextricably linked to our brain, body, mind and behaviour patterns.

> *You go right to the planet and if you become at one with it, you think like the planet works. It touches your senses and all of a sudden you can make sense of your life because of what is sitting in the subconscious – we call it the subconscious because we will not allow it to be conscious.*

(Cohen, 2010)

WHY NATURE CONNECTION IS SO IMPORTANT FOR HUMAN SENSORY DEVELOPMENT

Nature and sensory motivation

Our world is an entirely sensory place. Our bodies have co-evolved in nature, which provides a regulating sensory environment where our natural operating system is most likely to relax. The key recent research into this co-living in nature is expanded on in the online appendix. When we understand why someone may be doing something, it is much easier to support them and provide resources or offerings for their enjoyment, learning and healthy development.

We are sensory beings, and the subliminal multisensory stimulation that happens in the outdoors, particularly natural places, both feeds our well-being and directs our attention. All of us have different ways of responding to the sensory experiences and information we are receiving through our senses.

As with our nature play cycle, all our behaviour is intrinsically and extrinsically motivated, often cyclically, where responses are developed through our sensory systems, as well as our thoughts and emotions. In every moment our senses provide information through our bodies and neural networks from the external world. Our everyday reactions, from liking a taste to craving physical space, show us what our individual sensory system and preferences are, and when we know ourselves, we can learn to regulate and have more satisfying lives. Marina's daughter in pre-teenagerhood loved touching soft, warm materials, squashing play dough and slime. Her whole body was calmed by the experience, and she knew when to seek it out. Some love to play and touch what is to them 'cool' sand, whilst others find it itchy and horrible.

Our brain and heart need to know about everything the body is doing, the heart in particular. The heart's beating patterns, pulse waves and electrical output all influence hormonal functioning and neurochemical release, and the heart is the primary sensory processing organ – working closely with the brain and central nervous system (Buhner, 2004).

Sensory processing system

Our major sensory systems provide feedback that gives us the information and understanding about our surroundings. This makes us feel and act in certain ways. How we make sense of the input is called sensory processing. The calmer and more alert we are, the better able we are to process and organise our senses. The development of healthy sensory systems is closely linked to a *child's physical and psychological well-being*.

Let's take a moment again to feel the sensory feedback from the indoors compared to the outdoors. What is it like sitting inside reading this book? What do you notice? What physical activity do you engage with inside? Now think about going outside and participating in an education programme that follows a nature pedagogical approach as described in Chapters 3 and 4. The big, heavy, awkward tree stumps that need moving to form the circle in the morning. The full experiences of gathering blackberries and eating them! The fascination of minibeasts performing extraordinary physical and technical skills, for example manipulating a spider's web. The extensive storymaking of mini-worlds and unseen lives. The alchemy of mixing soil and water, watching the cause and effect of the decisions we make in our play and activity in the woods. Now consider the differences between the two places.

No doubt you have concluded that there are more sensory opportunities outside and that they are changing and happening all the time in a subliminal, easier way.

Many of our indoor and busy school/work lives are full of information bombarding us. We ask children to concentrate and focus while they are bombarded with bright lights, lots of talking and little space to move. What we can end up with is sensory disorganisation. This occurs when there are too many senses being over-activated at once; our body can't decode the information properly and we often have fight or flight response, going into our sympathetic system outlined in Chapter 7. Time spent in quieter, natural environments really is a tonic for our bodies; the multisensory input is calmer and subliminal for neurotypical brains. In principle, as animals, our biological and sensory systems aim to be as efficient as possible, not wasting energy and enabling us to focus our attention. Nature really is a tonic, a place where we can be at ease and be at our best. Our 'blueprint' developed in nature, and our human development is programmed to play and play when we are young, to learn all the skills needed in an integrated way.

We are aiming for children to have fully integrated sensory systems, with a strong and healthy sense of themselves in their surroundings. Our whole body experiences the world and over time builds internal systems that support us to learn, process and integrate information and generate appropriate responses to the sensory information in our environment. Whilst some young people have sensory processing disorders that need expert support, most of us will have stronger or weaker sensory systems that will affect our everyday experience in different ways. We all have the ability to improve and develop our systems. This enables us to regulate ourselves and feel an inner confidence and gives us the ability to listen and respond to our sensory feedback.

Jon had a young man who was labelled with ADHD and supposedly couldn't focus on anything, particularly the 'detail of anything'. He was indeed a little 'erratic' on the first session, not settling on anything and seemingly jumping from one thing to another. However, a question on the first session provided a way into his energetic pathway. On the way to the site he asked Jon, "Will we be hunting animals?" Jon answered, "Depends what you mean by hunting, Will." Before Jon finished his sentence, Will said, "I go out shooting with my dad." To cut a long story short, eventually Will showed an interest in visiting badger setts and became completely absorbed in animal smells and signs. He became a keen observer and engrossed in the detail of the natural world – there was no sign of ADHD!

What this story shows is that the small details in nature, if we find our energetic neural pathway, can indeed focus attention.

Sensory integration

The term 'sensory integration' defines the brain's process of integrating the many sources of information, but it also describes a clinical theory and treatment model developed by Dr A. Jean Ayres in 1989, an occupational therapist with advanced training in neuroscience and educational psychology.

She defined sensory integration as

> *the neurological process that organises sensations from one's own body and from the environment and makes it possible to use the body effectively within the environment . . . The brain must select, enhance, inhibit, compare and associate the sensory information in a flexible, constantly changing pattern: in other words the brain must integrate it.*
>
> (Ayres, 1989, p. 11)

Most of our behaviours are moderate and don't stand out, but if you work with people who have learning disabilities (see green care/interventions in Chapters 8, 9 and 14), you are able to see how atypical behaviours are often accompanied by intense sensory processing difficulties.

New research is teasing out the different issues our children and young people (and adults) may be experiencing, helping us as practitioners to respond in the most effective ways and applying sensory modulation to change how children feel (see Chapters 8 and 9 on behaviour strategies and the use of functional senses for emotional regulation). For some, our difficulties may be in processing our senses, for others it may be related to early attachment-based issues. Certainly, for all of us, we can be best supported when our behaviours are understood as communication. Furthermore, this provides us with other therapeutic interventions and coping strategies that help us to provide a safer community learning environment.

At Forest School we have endless opportunities to explore and develop our sensory systems. Most of our senses are underused and somewhat atrophied. Entering this natural world provides the time and space for young people to explore, absorb and interact with the sensory information around them. The latest research from Stockholm University (Guisti et al., 2018), which pulled together research from 22 different countries across the ages (0–18 years), found that engagement with the senses in nature was the most effective way of enabling people to value nature. The study claimed that the sensory 'valuing' effected an emotional connection to the *whole* learning community. What was also significant was that increasing positive nature values was linked to a child-centred approach to education – something we have shown in the first three chapters that is an essential element of nature and Forest School pedagogy.

OUR SENSES

Most professionals working with sensory integration have identified eight senses which are now in common parlance and which we will look at in the remainder of this chapter – describing them and how nature education can support them.

The eight senses

We have three functional sensory systems: proprioceptive, vestibular and interoception, and five survival sensory systems: visual, auditory, tactile, olfactory and gustatory. (Our online appendix summarizes all eight sensory systems.)

> *The brain constantly selects which information it attends to, enhances, and inhibits, to enable us to function. How we process this information determines our behaviour and affects our capacity to engage with others.*
>
> (Bhreathnach, 2018)

NATURE PEDAGOGY, AND HOW IT SUPPORTS THE EIGHT SENSES

Functional senses: the body-centred senses

Proprioceptive system

This sensory feedback system, often referred to as the sixth sense, helps us to coordinate the movement of our arms and legs in an efficient manner so that we can move and play without having to look. This mechanism helps keep the body oriented, so that our brain can send out immediate and unconscious adjustments to our muscles and joints. The system uses proprioceptors in the muscles that monitor parts of our body that are being stretched (in your joints, muscles, ligaments, connective tissue) and relay this information. It regulates how much force you need to complete a task and is developed through series of pushes, stretches and pulls, for example picking up a stick, carrying heavy objects, pulling a wagon, playing in sand. It helps children regulate how hard they touch or hit. It helps them to judge distances and not bump into things.

Figure 5.1 Stimulating the proprioceptive and vestibular senses

Figure 5.2 Climbing is good for proprioceptive and vestibular feedback

Children with good healthy proprioceptive feedback can write with a pencil without pushing it so hard that they break the tip, or pick up delicate things without crushing them. A functioning proprioceptive system allows children to move, play and explore in a smoothly coordinated and efficient way – not too gently, not too roughly. At Forest School, the practitioner and nature provide children with a variety of opportunities for developing this sense, including more heavy work, free play, climbing, using ropes and swings and stretching and pulling games.

Figure 5.3 Ropes are good for stretching and swinging – vestibular, proprioceptive and muscular sensing

Interoceptive system

Our interoceptive system gives us the ability to *feel* what is happening inside our body and provides awareness of the deep connection between our body and our mind. Recent research has highlighted its role in self-awareness and the 'embodied self' (Seth, 2013):

> *It is the body-to-brain axis of signals originating from the internal body and visceral organs (gastrointestinal, respiratory, hormonal and circulatory systems).*
>
> (Tsakiris and De Preester, 2019)

It is known as the 'hidden sense' or eighth sensory system and refers to our body's ability to identify internal sensations – whether we feel cold, tired, hungry, needing the toilet or sexually aroused. We have special nerve receptors all over our body, internal organs and skin. The interoceptive system is also responsible for allowing us to feel our emotions. It gives us our ability to read our own physical signals and directly relates to how well we can identify and regulate our own and others' emotional states. Being in connection with our inner world enables us to listen to ourselves and look after ourselves. It allows us to be in contact with our emotional and physical responses that can direct us to behaviours that support us and reduce stressful and toxic lifestyles.

Healthy interoception enables us to respond to and interpret our inner sensations. It keeps us in contact with what we are feeling internally, knowing when we feel safe or not, and listening and acting upon our internal cues. It goes deeper than physical sensations and is linked with our sense of well-being, mood and emotional regulation. Awareness of what is going on for us internally is hugely beneficial. Learning to regulate and change our internal environment, through

Figure 5.4 Net and Hammock – good self-soothing bits of kit!

use of our breath or mindfulness techniques or repetitive balancing and rhythmic activities (swaying or rocking), for example, can improve self-regulation (see Chapter 9). If we can satisfy and appropriately respond to our hunger, pain and level of energy, then we can be confident in our bodies. If we know we are okay we can go on at ease. Children and adults can be over-responsive to internal cues, for example feel like they need the toilet all day, or under-responsive, for example don't feel pain or work till exhausted. This can all be very distracting, be emotionally difficult and lead to negative behaviours for no apparent reasons.

At Forest School children can seek out deep pressure (sitting in a hammock) or physically holding. Combining physical opportunities with clear language and communication (see Chapter 9), Forest Schools provide helpful strategies that support healthy relationships to self, other and nature. We know that when children's physical development is robust, then healthy cognitive development follows.

Vestibular system

The vestibular system tells our brain about balance, moving against gravity, speed, size and head position. We have vestibular organs located deep inside our ears. When we move our heads, the fluid in these organs move and shift, constantly providing us with information about the position of our heads and bodies in space (spatial awareness). This sense provides us with the confidence that we can maintain a position without falling. It allows us to move smoothly and efficiently. Children needs lots and lots of balance practice.

'Boing' – up and down movements

'Whoosh' – to and from movements

'Roly poly' – movement where body rotates

When our vestibular sense is fully functioning, we are secure and organised enough in our bodies to be able to attend and respond to all of the other senses we encounter daily. It is central to the integration of the other sensory systems. A child with a well-developed vestibular sense feels confident and safe during movement activities, even if his feet are off the ground. He is able to start and stop movement activities calmly and with control. He is comfortable with climbing, swinging, somersaulting and jumping – knowing that his body will adapt and that he will be able to maintain his balance and keep himself from falling or getting hurt. Many outdoor and creative activities increase this sensory input.

When a child's vestibular system is not functioning well, this may display a need to move or be frightened of movement. An unbalanced child may feel insecure and appear uncoordinated or clumsy, fall easily, and have poor posture. Vision is also closely related to the vestibular system. Difficulty with tasks that require the eyes to move left to right (e.g. reading) or up and down repeatedly (e.g. copying information from the board) may be signs of an underdeveloped or troubled vestibular system.

Figure 5.5 Swinging is a good balancing action

There are plenty of opportunities to strengthen the vestibular system through play and movement in the outdoors. Swinging from front to back, side to side or round and round, hanging upside down from trees, spinning and jumping, climbing across trees and under natural objects all support the vestibular system.

It is considered one of the 3 power sensations (the other two being proprioception and touch). This means it can be considered one of the strongest options for calming and regulating emotions, and to help a person feel more grounded and safe.

(Sullivan and Fitzgibbon, 2018)

Here is an example of a Forest School intervention for integrating senses, in particular auditory, proprioceptive and vestibular.

CASE STUDY FOR GREEN INTERVENTION (CIRCLE OF LIFE REDISCOVERY CIC AND EAST SUSSEX CHILD AND ADOLESCENT MENTAL HEALTH SERVICES/LEARN DISABILITY/FAMILY INTENSIVE SERVICE PARTNERSHIP PROJECT):

Boy, 8-year-old Joseph (not his real name)

a   Your role in the service

I work as a specialist speech and language therapist. My role involves supporting families with a child or young person with additional needs. I support where there is challenging behaviour or emotional or psychological needs, especially where these needs are amplified by a difficulty in communication. For example, difficultly in understanding, recognising and regulating emotion, difficulty making oneself understood by any means of communication. Means of communication can include speech, but for a lot of the children and young people I work with their primary means of communicating their needs is through alternative methods, such as using printed symbols on cards.

b   Background of family and why they were referred

Joseph was originally referred to our support service because of near continuous vocal stimming (making vocal noises) and poor sleep pattern. This was in July 2014, when Joseph was 4 years old. He is now 8 years old. Joseph does not use speech to communicate. He uses photos and symbols to make requests and, when he is less anxious and therefore more able to communicate, to make comments. His understanding is also supported by visual aids to verbal communication.

c   What are the presenting problems or difficulties?

Joseph is a highly anxious boy. He has diagnoses of severe/high level autistic spectrum disorder (ASD) and severe learning disability. He requires a very high level of support in all areas and struggles to leave the house at all – he does not attend school currently due to the level of his anxiety. Joseph also has very challenging behaviours, including hitting and hair pulling, and also self-injurious behaviour, including scratching at his head. At times this has resulted in wounds and infection which have required antibiotics and also hospitalisation for the physical care of the wounds. One of the main behaviours which persists across different settings is his difficulty leaving places or people and his need to hold an adult's hands. This appears to correlate with when he is most anxious, i.e. when most anxious he grasps tightly with both his hands to an adult's hands. If a hand is removed this is likely to result in hitting, hair pulling and self-injuring behaviour as described above.

d   What is the focus(es) of the work, in particular for the woodland days?

The work focus is:

- To support the family owing to the demands of the high level of care Joseph requires in a way that supports them to provide this care to the best of their ability. This can involve a high level of emotional support and helping Joseph's mother to look after herself, including thinking about her own health needs, both physical and mental.
- To engage with the family in functional assessment of Joseph's challenging behaviours, including analysis of why and when behaviours occur and formulation of support plans to limit the behaviours.
- To support an increase in communication – Joseph's ability to both understand and express his needs and teaching and support to parents to know and understand how best to communicate with Joseph.

e   What has gone well within this intervention?

Being in the woods is a unique place where Joseph's anxiety levels noticeably reduce to the point that he will relax and let go of hand holding. He is more relaxed there than anywhere else. His tension visibly disappears as he arrives, even after a difficult morning or journey to the woods. He has managed to engage in activities such as playing on a suspended cargo net, running through the woods, skipping, exploring the environment and tickling from his father. In order to do this, he is able to let go of hands and also to be away from his parents and trust other adults.

Clinicians have been able to practise communication techniques with him, demonstrating these to his parents and teaching them to Joseph, for example, using a visual system to show that an activity has started, is nearly finished and is finished. This is particularly supportive for Joseph because of difficulty moving from one activity to another, which is related to ASD. Clinicians have also been able to model offering an elbow instead of handholding, which is one of the strategies that has been agreed to support Joseph and his family. This is largely because, due to a pain condition, it is very painful, in addition to the other obvious difficulties, for Joseph's mother to hold his hands a lot.

The Woodland Project also supports our focus and hugely increases our ability for providing emotional well-being support for Joseph's parents.

f   What feedback have you had from the family?

The family have said that the Woodland Family Days are Joseph's happy place. They have seen him giggling and being happy there and have commented that they have not seen him like that, other than at the Woodland Family Days, in a long time. They find the Woodland Family Days invaluable. Joseph's mother also loves to attend Woodland Parent/Carer Days and finds these invaluable for her own mental health. She has commented on the noticeable difference to how she is feeling at the start of a day as compared to at the end of one of these days.

Our survival senses: external stimulated senses

Tactile system

The tactile system helps us process information we receive from receptors in our skin. When we touch an object, our nervous system sends this information to our brain, which interprets various tactile qualities, including texture, friction, temperature, pressure, and if there is any pain, in order that we know what we are feeling. All our sensory experiences are associated with emotions, and memories are formed. This sense is known to be the first to develop in the womb, and the skin is the largest sensory organ of the body. We are always actively or passively touching something – from wind to a hard floor.

> *Touch is also important for safety, understanding, communication, and can increase feelings of connection to ourselves and others.*
>
> (Sullivan and Fitzgibbon, 2018)

When the tactile sense is fully functioning, children are able to filter out which tactile information is important and which isn't so important. Their memory and experience of touch allows for safe touch with others and new objects, for curiosity and for carrying out daily activities like washing hands, whilst not trying to touch everything. In the outdoors, touch is greatly enhanced, and some children may struggle with all the new tactile experiences, for example mud and clay. We sometimes offer 'first aid' gloves as an option if a person seems hypersensitive. Some children may not be able to distinguish between objects that might be dangerous, so knowing this in advance or observing a craving or seeking excessive touch needs to be part of our reflection and risk assessment. Reduction in anxiety is associated with touch processing, and many young people benefit from being in tight spaces, for example a hammock, and enjoy the feeling of being held in and physically squeezed.

At Forest School we may utilise sensory areas. These include having available sand, stones, leaves and water. Providing opportunities for hide and find, cups for scooping, digging and loose parts such as sponges in water, watering cans, dough, clay, and finger paint. Thinking about providing moments for barefoot walking and exposing children to surfaces and objects of different textures such as smooth, rough, soft and hard all add to creating healthy tactile systems.

Figure 5.6 Tactile sensory stimulation through interaction with natural materials

Figure 5.6 Continued

Auditory system

This sensory system enables a child's sense of hearing to be processed by the brain. It involves the ears, with their complex sensory organs, that interpret every sound, integrate every sensation and move us appropriately into action. The outdoors, and in particular wilder spaces, offer the range of nature-based sounds for us to immerse ourselves within. Playing outdoors provides an abundance of listening opportunities for children to naturally practice auditory discrimination skills. Learning to be quiet and listen to bird song, for example, is deeply rewarding.

A healthy auditory system enables children to follow and locate sounds and map a 'sound scape'. A functioning auditory system provides the ability to filter out sounds that are not important or desired, such as road noise, whilst allowing a child to direct their focus where they choose. This system builds a healthy awareness of our surroundings, allowing us to respond appropriately and develop listening skills, communication and social skills.

Auditory processing refers to the ability to discriminate between similar sounds, tune into a speaker and pick up on pertinent information, and understand information presented verbally. Two more common examples of difficulties with the auditory system are hypersensitivity (overwhelmed by sensory input, possibly resulting in avoiding noisy spaces or being distracted) and hyposensitivity (appearing to not hear input, always talking or humming).

Figure 5.7 The 'drum stalk' stimulates the Auditory system.

In Forest School, we play sound games, create rhymes, sing songs, discover natural sounds by tapping or creating instruments and listen to or create stories. Young people learn to discriminate sounds and communicate clearly, all through a rich experience of sound-based activities. Learning songs helps develop auditory memory, as songs provide long sequences of sound, like language. We may make body sounds like snapping and clapping. Using tools, we may build instruments together, including whistles, castanets, rattles, wood chimes and rain makers.

Visual system

The visual system's main organ is of course the eye. The communication between the eye and the brain via light rays, which are interpreted in the visual cortex, gives us what we see! Our sense of sight is known to be one of the most dominant senses in the human. We use this sense all the time, and along with our other senses like smell and touch, we process the information and take action.

Moving regularly improves the vestibular system, which helps to support the eye muscles. In nature, we develop our visual skills to successfully distinguish colours, depth perception and patterns. Activities like tracking increase our observation skills. When the visual system is underdeveloped, lots of visual stimuli may be very distracting, or at the other end, a child will barely notice their surroundings. As practitioners we may need to establish good eye contact to keep the child's focus and attention.

Children are reported to have a decline in safety awareness and trouble seeing things from a distance. Eye muscles are not working in unison, so some children have difficulty scanning a room to find an object or read a book. In recent years across the world, there has been an increase in 'the myopia boom'. This has been directly attributed to children in countries who spend more time reading or sitting in front of a computer or screen device.

After studying more than 4000 children at Sydney primary and secondary schools for three years, researchers found that children who spent less time outside were at greater risk of developing myopia (E. Dolgin, 2015). More and more, studies suggest that increasing the amount of time children spend outside actually reduces the incidence of myopia. A report last year from the OECD showed that the average 15-year-old in Shanghai now spends 14 hours per week on homework, compared with 5 hours in the United Kingdom. In East Asia, where the population is perhaps slightly ahead in hours in front of screen, an unprecedented rise in myopia research shows:

Sixty years ago, 10–20% of the Chinese population was short-sighted. Today, up to 90% of teenagers and young adults are. In Seoul, a whopping 96.5% of 19-year-old men are short-sighted.
(Dolgin, 2015)

At Forest School and other long-term nature-based programmes, the children unconsciously develop their visual skills, exploring the natural environment. We can extend this through natural scavenger hunts, playing camouflage games, hiding objects or people, collecting a variety of leaves

Figure 5.8 Fox walking stimulates visual and auditory senses and when done barefoot the tactile sense

or seeds, and using mirrors to walk under the tree canopy. As they play, their sensory systems are activated and encouraged to work at their optimum level.

Olfactory system

Our sense of smell helps us receive information about the world around us. The sensory receptors in the nose pick up information that allows us to distinguish all the possible smells that are around us. This sense keeps us safe, letting us know if something doesn't smell right, both physically like a food and emotionally when something doesn't 'smell' right. Smells bring us good and bad memories and are closely related to our limbic system (see Chapter 7 on the brain). Some people have called our sensory system that connects us to plants and their medicines 'floral consciousness'! It is also associated with our sense of taste, together giving us the different flavours. Smells can affect our sympathetic or parasympathetic system (see Chapter 7) and calm us or frighten us.

Nature provides us with an abundance of possible smells and tastes, some of the most delicious and wondrous (honeysuckle) and the most disgusting too (mushroom – stink horn!). Smelling flowers, wood and soil is always interesting and sometimes wonderful. There is a safety element to our smell ability too, and over time it has been critical to the success of a species. Animals, dogs for example, have developed an olfactory part of the brain that is 40 times greater than ours – meaning that their ability to smell is a lot better than ours!

Experiencing a diverse range of smells (and tastes) growing up enables us to enjoy food, eat well and distinguish between safe and dangerous (chemicals) smells. Children with sensory processing issues may be hypersensitive (overly sensitive) to smells. As with all the sensory systems, a hypersensitivity means that children are distracted by smells and unable to stay focused when they want or need to.

In the outdoors, young people will naturally explore the smells of the flora and fauna, woods and fire! We sometimes play sensory smelling games by setting smell trails or making perfume potions, which involves lots of mixing and experimentation (see Figure 5.9).

Oral/gustatory sensory system

The sensory receptors in our mouths allow us to perceive temperature, texture and taste (e.g. sweet, salty, bitter, sour). Our lips and fingers have the most concentration of touch receptors in the body, sending lots of useful information to our brain.

The muscles used for sucking, blowing, speaking, making sounds, chewing, swallowing, biting and breathing are the same muscles that help with good posture. Postural control needs strong neck, chest, stomach and back muscles. This in turn assists a child to be alert and attentive.

Children with healthy oral sensory processing can eat a range of foods, tastes and textures. They are not typically fussy eaters and don't exhibit extreme emotional reactions around food and meal times.

Figure 5.9 The olfactory system – connecting to our 'floral consciousness'

Away from the home and school environment, children often get a chance to be different and show different strengths and aptitudes. In a group of peers, children will often experiment more widely with different foods because their friends are having a go. In our experience, if you pick the food directly from the earth, children are more likely to have a taste. Marina's daughter will happily eat nettle and potato soup at Forest School, for instance! Using a peeler to peel carrots, getting the children involved in hands-on food-making experiences gives them another reason to taste and explore new oral sensations. We love to forage for seasonal plants and berries (see wild food risk assessment examples in the online appendix), play plant sensory-based games, and make crafts and paints using what we find – the endless possibilities of the outdoors.

We can get caught up in making sure all eight senses are being stimulated in the outdoors, and if learners are hypersensitive to certain senses we may need to minimise this or if hyposensitive we may need to stimulate the focus on senses more. Jane Ayres believed (1989) that if we let children follow their inner drive, they will usually do what is best for their nervous system.

The brain is designed to give itself the experiences that are necessary for its own development.

(Ayres, 1989, p. 140)

It is, however, useful to know if learners have a sensory processing disorder (SPD), attachment 'diagnoses' or a 'sensory profile'. We can then integrate diet and sensory input (see Bhreathnach, 2018).

The following is a good example of a child with a sensory profile that was particularly complex. He was attending an Afterschool Forest School provision at Hackney Forest School. This story is related by Lauren, the Forest School leader.

Figure 5.10 Cooking and eating satisfies the gustatory, olfactory and proprioceptive senses and 'sense of community'

X has been diagnosed with Moebius syndrome, which affects the nerves, primarily the cranial nerves, which do not develop properly. This means that X has limited control over a range of muscles and sensations around his face in particular. X has been walking independently since 2015 for short distances (200 metres) and sometimes uses a wheelchair for respite.

At the FS site as we explored, X took my hand to guide his parents around. Every now and then he would check in on his dad to make sure he was close by.

Taking part in activities was a challenge for X. He was strong-minded and would insist in watching instead of taking part unless he initiated it. Activities involving tactile experiences with textures were a challenge, especially when he was playing with mud. With great determination, X sat down on the floor with me and mud printed using a small log, dipping it into the mud with support and stamping it on to the material. At this moment I felt proud that he had demonstrated a can-do attitude whilst with me.

X also loved dancing, especially doing funny dancing. For a moment we danced to the sound of sticks being hit together by another colleague. X mumbled a rhythm and clapped his hands.

There was a moment when we sat on a log listening to the sounds around us. During that moment, X pushed me gently so I decided to pretend to fall off the log. X began to laugh out loud, and this made me laugh. I sat back down next to him and he repeated this action. We laughed and laughed for several moments as we continued with this game. This was the point at which I felt a deeper connection with X as we were beginning to share more fun moments with each other, as our relationship grew.

Another magical moment was during the treasure hunt for pine cones. X requested that he should watch from the log with me, sitting down. He said, "The clues", implying we should give them clues to help them find the pine cones. What a great idea!

So I mentioned, "some may be high and some may be low," and X added, "some may be this way, that way, that way." This made me smile. He told me to repeat it and he joined in this time making it into a whole phrase.

"Some may be high, some may be low, some may be this way, that way, that way."

He loved this phrase, laughing and using his hand to point left, right, up and down as we repeated it. Collaborating together was another special moment for me, that we had just come up with a phrase together and this would always stick with me when I hear the words "Can you give me a clue?" Even now as I type, this makes me smile.

X's parents commented:

He really engaged with Forest School and was keen to put down his digital devices and get his jacket on to arrive on time. He loved helping to organise, so assisting getting the trolley over the bridge and to the forest site was part of the excitement. He developed a strong desire to spend his time with Lauren, who played games aligned to his unique sense of humour and needs. As a result he tolerated things like getting his hands dirty, without realising it was happening, while confidently chatting with Lauren (and the team) about his week as if she were a long-lost friend. After the mandatory game of hide and seek, he was always sad to find out it was time for home.

The case study above, from Hackney Forest School, shows how effective the integration of complex sensory needs combined with a secure 'empathic' attachment to a skilled Forest School leader can greatly benefit learners.

Hopefully, this chapter has given some pointers to working with sensory integration.

We have devoted a whole chapter to sensory development as we feel with the growing 'disorders' in the Western world much of this can be traced to lack of contact with the natural world. One of the key aspects in all of this is the regular exposure to the natural world at an early age through allowing more play in the natural world. Not only are there many opportunities for free creative play in the natural world, especially woodlands, but also the chance to stimulate all our senses at an early age. However, play is a life-long friend and should be integral to all our lives, especially in education. The next chapter will look at what play is in more detail and how we facilitate play in the natural world.

QUESTIONS FOR PRACTICE

Are you aware of the sensory stimulus that your practice provides, and if so, have you observed how this supports learning and development?

Have you noticed any sensory processing issues in your learners? These may be associated with other diagnoses such as autism.

Has this chapter stimulated any thoughts on how you may observe learning in your setting and how you evaluate certain behaviours?

USEFUL RESOURCES

www.sensory-processing-disorder.com for identifying SPD, excellent case studies, ways of working out 'sensory diets' and pointing to other excellent resources.

'The Scared Gang' by Eadaoin Bhreathnach. An excellent set of books based on the Mr Men explaining how children with SPD feel and can work with sensory modulation. Eadaoin's website (www.sensoryattachmentintervention.com) is also a good resource for understanding sensory attachment.

Forest School and Autism. A practical guide by Michael James. Jessica Kingsley, London, 2018.

Phoebe Caldwell's resources: see https://phoebecaldwell.co.uk/ and http://thecaldwellautismfoundation.org.uk/index.php/responsive-communication-the-films/

BIBLIOGRAPHY

Atchley, R A et al (2012) *Creativity in the Wild: Improving Creative Reasoning Through Immersion in Natural Settings*.

Ayres, J (1989) *Sensory Integration and Praxis Tests*. Los Angeles, CA: Western Psychological Services.

Bhreathnach, E (2018) Sensory Information, Sensory Integration and Strategic Functioning. The International Association for the Study of Attachment, paper at 10th Anniversary International Conference, Florence.

Bratman, G N et al. (2015) Nature Experience Reduces Rumination and Subgenual Prefrontal Cortex Activation. *Proceedings of the National Academy of Sciences of the United States of America* 112(28): 8567–8572.

Buhner, S H (2004) *The Secret Teachings of Plants: The Intelligence of the Heart in Direct Experience of Nature*. Bear and Company.

Cohen, M (2007) Reconnecting with Nature – Finding Wellness Through Restoring Your Bond with the Earth. Eco Press. See www.ecopsych.com/insight53senses.html.

Cohen, M (2010) The Eco-Psychology Interview. *Ecopsychology Journal* 2(2): 53–75.

Dolgin, E (2015) The Myopia Boom; Short Shightedness Is Reaching Epidemic Proportions. Some Scientists Think They Have Found a Reason Why. *Nature – International Journal of Science* 519(7543). See https://www.nature.com/news/the-myopia-boom-1.17120.

Dunn, W (2009) *Living Sensationally Understanding Your Senses*. Jessica Kingsley Publishers.

Guisti, M et al (2018) *A Framework to Assess Where and How Children Connect to Nature*. Stockholm: Stockholm Resilience Centre, Stockholm University. Frontiers in Psychology ed Jan 4th.

Morita, E, Fukuda, S, Nagano, J, Hamajima, N, Yamamoto, H, Iwai, Y, Nakashima, T, Ohira, H and Shirakawa, T (2007) Psychological Effects of Forest Environments on Healthy Adults: Shinrin-yoku (Forest-Air Bathing, Walking) as a Possible Method of Stress Reduction. *Public Health* 121(1): 54–63. doi:10.1016/j.puhe.2006.05.024. Epub 2006 Oct 20.

Mountain, J (2017) *Outdoors and Active: Resources from a Recent Action Research Project led by the London Borough of Newham*. Early Education: The British Association for Early Childhood Education.

Park, B J et al. (2010) The physiological effects of Shinrin-yoku (taking in the forest atmosphere or forest bathing): Evidence from field experiments in 24 forests across Japan. *Environmental Health and Preventive Medicine* 15(1): 18–26. doi: 10.1007/s12199-009-0086-9.

Seth, A (2013) Interoceptive Inference, Emotion, and the Embodied Self. *Trends in Cognitive Sciences* 17(11): 565–573.

Sullivan, J O and Fitzgibbon, C (2018) *Sensory Modulation. Resource Manual*. Brisbane: Sensory Modulation.

Tsakiris, M and De Preester, H (2019) *The Interoceptive Mind*. Oxford: Oxford University Press.

6 Play and nature – the ludic process and risky play

When a child enters the woodland, she brings with her a crowd of people and creatures from her ancestral past. The hunter-gatherers, primates, other mammals, anteaters and reptiles. Eventually, the woods are filled with this menagerie, each member of which has a right to be listened to, and if possible, to have her play needs fulfilled.

(Bob Hughes Keynote Speech, National Forest School Conference, Condover 2015)

In this chapter we further explore play – what it is and why it is so important in a natural setting, and we examine risky play, revisit the nature play cycle and how this interacts with the 'ludic process' (ludic means play), and expand on the attributes of a nature play facilitator.

INTRODUCTION

We introduced the state of 'flow' (Csikszentmihalyi, 1990) to achieve integrated holistic learning and development in Chapter 3. This state of flow is most often found when we are in a state of 'pure play', which has been seen by many as when we are our own directors of play and so immersed in it that nothing else matters – be it playing with ideas or physically wrapped up in an experience. Johan Huizinga (1949) saw play as an essential part of humanity that does *more* than serve our evolutionary survival (see Gray, 2011) – in fact, it helps integrate our 'humanness'. Huizinga was so bold as to see humans as '*Homo ludens*' – 'ludic' meaning 'play' from the Latin etymology, man the player. The ultimate experience happens when in flow – this is something that goes beyond education and dare we say it . . . subsumes education! Einstein, for example, was the product of his play in which his education 'fitted' – he constantly played with ideas. Joseph Cornell expands on flow by formulating a process he calls 'flow learning' (see Chapter 10), which he expands upon in his most recent book about deep nature play (2017). Let's see if we can define play.

What is play?

In play we take on roles and ideas and try them out. We can play out feelings and make sense of experiences. Through playing we become. In fact, Huizinga boldly claimed that through play we enact metaphor, myth and ritual and so society 'became' through play.

> *Now in myth and ritual the great instinctive forces of civilized life have their origin: law and order, commerce and profit, craft and art, poetry, wisdom and science. All are rooted in the primaeval soil of play.*
>
> (Huizinga, 1949)

He described play as something that was a borderline between 'jest' and 'earnestness'.

Play is often defined in terms of children – indeed as cited in Hughes (2001), many have referred to 'play as child's work'. Play is the way children learn and is their dominant activity – free play, with a lack of external rules (and adult direction), and the desire to play is initiated by the person themselves. The common definition says play is 'freely chosen, intrinsically motivated and personally directed'. However, look more closely and definitions of play can be hard and often difficult to grab hold of, particularly for adults where play can sometimes descend into whimsical language. This was recognised intensely by Huizinga and more contemporary play theorists and practitioners – notably Hughes, Sturrock, Else and Burghardt. Burghardt (2005) describes the numerous claims made for the benefits of play, citing over 30 functions attributed. He also shows how hard it is to define them!

> *The problem of defining play and its role is one of the greatest challenges facing neuroscience, behavioural biology, psychology, education and the social sciences generally. Alas, it is rarely recognized as such. In a very real sense, only when we understand the nature of play will we be able to understand how to better shape the destinies of human societies in a mutually dependent world, the future of our species, and perhaps even the fate of the biosphere itself.*
>
> (Burghardt, 2005, p. 117)

Furthermore, play researcher and professor Peter Gray, author of *Free to Learn* (2015), shows we have an innate drive to educate ourselves through play and that we have an instinctual need to play . . . indeed, it is 'in our DNA' to play in the natural world. He states we have four natural 'drives', particularly when we are young, that are linked to our survival – *curiosity, playfulness, sociability* and *planfulness*. He eloquently shows how the natural world is the place to develop and nurture these drives.

PLAY TYPES

Writer and educator David Sobel observed seven universal play 'motifs' or design principles (2008) after many years of watching and witnessing children's outdoor play, which help us with the concept of playfulness. Regardless of socioeconomic status, ethnicity or ecosystem, children play in similar ways when they have safe free time in nature.

Starting from a young age, Sobel recommends place-based education programmes that connect children and the curriculum to the natural world on their doorstep, however urban, using these seven motifs, which are outlined in Chapter 4.

In order to create environmentally responsible behaviour, Sobel goes on to say, "educators can structure learning experiences that provide powerful vehicles for curricular knowledge and court the possibility of transcendental experiences."

As stated in Chapter 4, Jan White (Robertson and Casey, 2016 and White, 2014) proposed that the themes could be merged to provide a framework of reference. This framework can help adults to understand how children play, to develop children's attachment to nature and place and to provide engaging environments for playing with loose parts.

- Becoming at home
- Playing hunting and gathering games
- Anthropomorphising non-humans
- Constructing adventures
- Imaginative narratives
- Pathways and journeys, which includes the need to gain 'prospect' or height
- Making rituals and giving gifts

These 'behaviours' can help us to understand how play can develop children's attachment to nature and place. (Our online appendix provides more detailed information on eight play themes.)

The last play type mentioned is a strength of nature or wild play. Indeed, this has been named by Bob Hughes as 'recapitulative play', where players dig into our ancestral rituals and processes, which are inextricably tied into the natural world.

In his book *A Playworker's Taxonomy of Play Types* (2002), Hughes proposed 16 types of play that could be observed when children are at play. These can sometimes be useful as descriptive observational tools in Forest School and Nature Pedagogy, see Figure 6.1.

Perry Else goes on to define ten characteristics of play in his very useful book *Making Sense of Play* (2014):

- Play is a process, not a specific action
- Play is self-chosen, with a willingness to participate
- Active engagement, attentive response to feedback

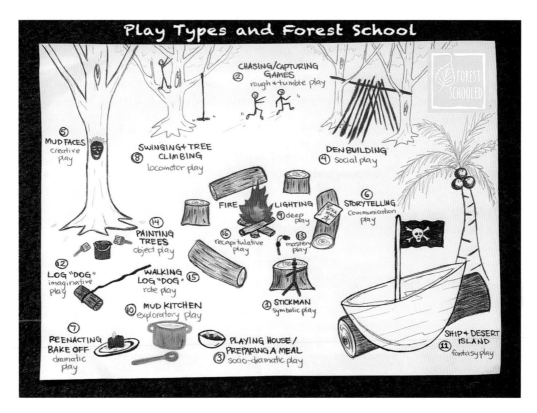

Figure 6.1 Hughes' 16 play types

Source: © Caylin Gans (www.forestschooled.com)

- Sufficiently safe, physically and psychologically
- A whole body/mind experience
- Play has a timeless, lost-in-the-moment quality
- Play is curiosity – it attracts us to newness or new experiences
- Play is pleasurable
- Play is different for each person
- Satisfaction is self-defined, with no extrinsic goals

We find these characteristics go a good way to explaining what play is and looks like, which is useful when integrating into the concept of Nature Pedagogy.

Why play?

Many have pointed out that play is the purest form of learning, as stated in the seminal text *Magical Child* by Joseph Pearce (1977).

In 2012, Pearce stated,

in education there is something like 3–5% retention of information learnt in the first few years of a child's life, however if something is truly experienced with all parts of the child's being (as in imagination and play) then there is 95% retention. That which is learnt in a state of play is literally built in as a permanent neural pathway in the brain.

Play is about 'becoming', rather than about learning facts, and is essential to our learning and development. Play, or lack of it, can define who we are as people. Children who have good play experiences have greater choices in life, as "play lays the foundations for all later forms of intelligence" (Pearce, 2012). As we open up, we explore the outer world and are able to build and imagine a world within, a safe place in which to try out thoughts and ideas.

Without an adult in the lead role, often providing a judgment-laden context, the world is open to us. Children who have their play experiences thwarted are more likely to struggle with their confidence and be less secure in the world, perhaps left reacting to any circumstances they find themselves in, yet feeling powerless to do anything but lash out at the things that seem to be causing it.

Figure 6.2 Becoming a community through play

Play deprivation creates an increased vulnerability to various childhood pathologies – anxiety, depression, helplessness, narcissism and suicide (Gray, 2011). Extreme play deprivation symptoms include aggression, misery and psychopathologies (Brown, 1998; Huttenmoser and Degan-Zimmerman, 1995).

While it is hard to pinpoint the main factors contributing to the recent rise in child and adolescent mental health issues, lack of access to wild play spaces is definitely one cause cited in many studies (see Upstart in Scotland www.upstart.scot/the-evidence/ and Myles Richardson from University of Derby https://findingnature.org.uk/).

Peter Gray (2011) argues that play deprivation can contribute to a reduced sense of personal control, reduced ability to control emotions, increased social isolation and reduced happiness, all of which are associated with anxiety and/or depression.

Affordances, loose parts and compound flexibility – play, creativity and confidence

Play provides the child with opportunities to try and test things out and see what happens if we start 'playing' with things – both human and non-human, made and natural. If there are these opportunities available, we are less likely to display the behaviours named in the previous paragraph as a result of play deprivation. Here is an excerpt from Lily Horseman's blog that eloquently explains the theory of affordances and loose parts:

> The psychologist James J. Gibson called these opportunities 'affordances'. In his 1979 book "The Theory of Affordances", he defined affordances as "action possibilities latent in the environment.

What the outdoors offers, in particular woods and trees, is a diverse ecosystem that presents a milieu of play places, experiences and opportunities. Children 'naturally' interact with natural environments; Forest School is, in effect, their 'home' in evolutionary terms. Try to imagine the invitations that children experience as they walk onto a Forest School site: a gap in the nettles just next to a shallow beach in the stream, a pile of sticks and logs, a tree with branches at just the right height, places to hide, places to run.

Nicholson first propounded the theory of 'loose parts' in his article 'How Not to Cheat Children – the Theory of Loose Parts' (1971). In this he said:

> In any environment, both the degree of inventiveness and creativity, and the possibility of discovery, are directly proportional to the number and kind of variables in it.

The article had a profound effect on the professions of education and play. He saw the potential for creativity and innovation in playing with many loose parts, in particular those that can be found in natural places with lots of diversity, such as the beach or woods. This theory was first brought together in the play profession by Fraser Brown, who extrapolated Nicholson's theory. Brown called it 'compound flexibility':

> This is not a simple interaction but a complex process wherein, flexibility in the play environment leads to increased flexibility in the child. That child is then better able to make use of the flexible environment and so on. There is massive child development potential in a play setting.
>
> (Brown, 2003, p. 56)

The woods are such a flexible environment. But what is meant by a flexible environment?

A 'loose part' environment includes everything from the branched trees of a woodland to the cones, stones, mud and twigs that lie within. Nicholson suggests that a beach is a good example of such an environment. The sand for shaping, the sea ever changing, the rock pools whose life and form shifts with the tide. The flotsam and the jetsam. An environment full of things that fulfil many different roles and functions. A place that can be adapted to our needs and ideas. This environment also needs the flexibility of the adults in it if children are to be allowed to explore the potential.

This permission for exploration leads to experimentation. A wide array of elements means that children have the opportunity to combine things in different ways and find the space or material they require to fulfil the need and further the line of enquiry. Children develop by responding to a rich environment. The fewer elements there are to explore, the slower or more restricted the development. The more stimuli, the broader the development.

One of the key factors in the compound flexibility process is that the child feels in control. This is why self-directed play is so essential for a child's development.

This combination of control and challenge is also what gives us good feelings! We try something, we find the resources we need to be successful. The people around us give us the time and space to work things out for ourselves, which gives ownership to the success. There are things around us that suggest ideas to us. These are the perfect conditions for feeling really good about ourselves.

These good feelings are critical to a child's development. These good feelings mean a child is likely to take a risk and try something else. They are the sort of feelings that govern self-acceptance. They are the feelings that contribute to self-confidence. Good feelings will keep someone involved, interested and focused in a way no amount of cajoling, bribery or threat can manage. The child is at the centre of the process and wants to be there because it feels good.

Self-confidence also means that a child will try to solve problems when they arise. Self-confidence is a desire to keep experimenting even when something goes wrong, the belief that you are able to work things out when things get tricky. This is what we often describe as resilience.

This is where the cycle connects. The exterior becomes interior and the flexibility becomes part of the child's way of being. The successful experiments suggest new ideas. The problem solving suggests a new goal. The experience they have just encountered is added to the toolbox

Figure 6.3 Flexible thinking promoted by a flexible environment and responsive facilitator

Source: © Lily Horseman (see www.kindlingplayandtraining.co.uk)

of the child's mind. The compounding aspect of this is that the more flexible the child is, the more they see the flexibility in the environment.

Conversely, a restricting attitude of the adult can shut down that extraordinary potential found in a flexible environment. The compound flexibility process can stagnate if conditions are unsuitable. Children who have little control over their world inevitably have fewer positive experiences, which in turn slows the development of their self-confidence. Children who lack confidence are less likely to take risks or try out different solutions to the problems they encounter. This makes them less flexible and responsive (Horseman, 2015).

Play and a sense of place and belonging

Hart's (1979) detailed study of children's experience of place and Moore's (1986) exploration of children's playful use of their local environments stand as key texts and have had considerable impact on methods and concepts in studying children's relationship with the natural world. Tuan's (1974) exploration of the human attachment to place, referred to as 'topophilia', established an important framework for more recent approaches. These studies and *Special Places, Special People* from Wendy Titman, looking at school grounds in 1994, chime with the need for regular contact with local natural spaces to build a relationship with that place – something Forest School has at its heart (see Chapter 1).

Hughes (2001), placing play firmly in an evolutionary frame, proposes that play enables children to fit themselves into their complex environments, to 'ground themselves physically and psychologically' in the here and now. Another significant theme is the intimate connection between the children and their environment which is eloquently expressed through the work of Edith Cobb (1977) in *The Ecology of Imagination in Childhood*. This work has laid foundations in exploring the child's interdependence with their surroundings that resonates with the emerging field of environmental psychology and behaviour.

Outdoor play has a much higher profile now in many areas of play strategy, as recognised in all the aforementioned contemporary writings. Many projects are burgeoning – from Nature Kindergartens to 'wild play'. As we write this, a new term is being adopted throughout the Western world – the concept of 'rewilding', which goes hand in hand with 'regeneration', given that so many ecosystems are breaking down. This is not only rewilding the land but also ourselves – through play. Jay Griffiths, in her book *Kith: The Riddle of Childscape* (2013), eloquently shows how 'native' cultures can show us a rewilding of childhood and its attendant benefits, and sees Forest School as something that can support this. Brene Brown (2019) bases her book *Braving the Wilderness* on the importance of 'true belonging', belonging thoroughly to ourselves and connected to one another, a core element of self-confidence and self-worth.

The importance of risk in outdoor play and Forest School

'If you want to feel secure
Do what you already know how to do.
But if you want to grow...
Go to the cutting edge of your competence,
Which means a temporary loss of security.
So, whenever you don't quite know
What you are doing
Know that you are growing...'
(Viscott, 2003)

Unintentional injuries are a leading cause of death and hospitalisation for children worldwide, one million per year (Peden et al., 2008), but not at Forest School, we might add! As parents we really want our children and loved ones to be safe, yet the older we become the more it is our own fear of loss or of difficult consequences (the pain we hope to avoid) that is driving us all to take

Figure 6.4 Fire play – emotional and elemental risky play

children's safety to another 'risk-averse' level. We don't want to suffer. Nevertheless, the tension between safety (e.g. wearing seat belts) and taking risk exists, each fulfilling a human need.

Here is a reflection from Marina on her thoughts about risky play and her childhood experiences.

I learned that I have to confront my own fears of risk when thinking about assessing risk as a practitioner. I sometimes have to stop myself to do my own dynamic risk assessment. What if? is a great question. What if she climbs up too high? What if she gets totally soaking wet? What if he and his friends carry a huge log around? What if they start poking fire sticks at each other? I have to take a moment, take a deep breath and figure out if the benefits outweigh the risks, and how likely they may happen, and if they do happen, what's the worst that could happen.

She climbs really confidently; it's a warm day so she won't get too cold; they may trip over . . . are all thoughts that might go through my head as the group walks to a site. As they look over for approval for their activity, I may ask what they think, or smile! For sure, if I had stopped the activities, the confidence and development opportunities would have been thwarted.

It was only a few decades ago that children could roam freely, without the glare of adults, and I remember getting away with a lot! I can recall a sense of freedom and expansion that still influences me today. I remember disappearing to the 'wreck' – 1970s' playgrounds, negotiating 'dangerous' equipment and strangers, spinning like crazy on the 'witches hat', making sure I didn't rip my clothes on the loose railings. I was 7 or 8 years old. All the conversations and freedom tested out my sense of self, my growing sense of independence, to get out of there when it no longer felt safe.

Safety and risky play are both critical for healthy development. The capacity to feel emotionally safe and to bounce back from negative experiences builds a greater internal risk bandwidth that promotes curiosity, thinking out of the box, experimenting and creativity.

> Play which taps into our ability to experience curiosity, competence and reciprocity and makes it possible for us to exercise outcomes, mastery and a sense of purpose offers some of the most engaging play of all.
>
> (Gauntlett, 2011)

When risks are removed from play and restrictions are too high, a child is more likely to suffer problems such as obesity, mental health concerns, lack of independence and a decrease in learning, perception and judgment skills (Eager and Little, 2011). When we restrict children's risky play, as they get older they fear taking risks, which impacts having enough courage and self-trust to become increasingly independent. We need to trust young people and believe in their ability to manage and assess risks and safety, thereby building their own regulatory systems. As outlined in Chapter 1, one of the Forest School principles is about taking supported risks in order to learn to manage risk-taking;

The criteria for this Forest School principle are:

- FS opportunities are designed to build on an individual's innate motivation, positive attitudes and/or interests

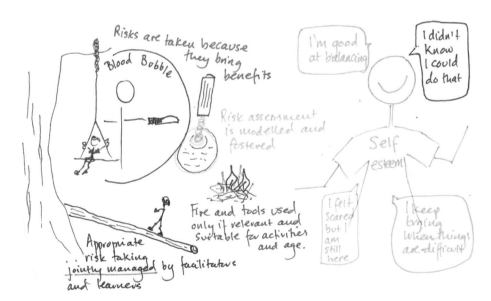

Figure 6.5 Forest School Risk Principle states, 'Forest School offers learners the opportunity to take supported risks appropriate to the environment and themselves'

- FS uses tools and fires only where deemed appropriate to the learners and is dependent on completion of a baseline risk assessment
- Any FS experience follows a risk-benefit process managed jointly by the practitioner and learner that is tailored to the developmental stage of the learner

In addition, Playwork Principle 8 says:

Playworkers choose an intervention style that enables children and young people to extend their play. All playworker intervention must balance risk with the developmental benefit and well-being of children.

We want children to confidently take chances, assess their own skills realistically, be able to ask for help when needed; for example, 'this feels really scary, I am getting down now' or 'this game is getting too rough, stop now'. This, amongst other key future life skills, builds healthy boundaries and 'belonging' to self (described by Brene Brown, 2019). Children are able to bounce back when things don't work out, and will try again and again in a risky situation until they are satisfied. In play that is supported by the practitioner, there is always a dilemma about how much we as practitioners should intervene, since true play is deemed as that where there is no adult present. However, in an educational programme, adults are always there! There is always the balance between practitioner, participant, environment and resources – this four-way dance, outlined in Chapter 3, is always moving through the practitioner's mind, and the distance between the four elements varies depending on who is leading and who is in the dance.

Figure 6.6 Learning zones

Source: www.thempra.org.uk/social-pedagogy/key-concepts-in-social-pedagogy/the-learning-zone-model/

The learning zone model – zones of play, from comfort to panic

The learning zone model was developed by the German adventure pedagogue Tom Senninger (2015) as a social learning model, and is helpful in illustrating how we as practitioners can create rich learning situations that require risk.

In order to learn, we have to explore and venture out into the unknown. We already know our immediate surroundings, which form our 'comfort zone'. In the comfort zone, things are familiar to us; we feel comfortable and don't have to take any risks. The comfort zone is important, because it gives us a place to return to, to reflect and make sense of things – a safe haven.

Although it is cosy to stay in our comfort zone, we have to leave it in order to get to know the unknown. We need to explore our 'learning zone', which lies just outside of our secure environment. Only in the learning zone can we grow and learn, live out our curiosity and make new discoveries, and thus slowly expand our comfort zone by becoming more familiar with more things. Going into our learning zone is a borderline experience, a risky place to be – we feel we're exploring the edge of our abilities, taking risks and pushing our limits. How far dare we stray into the 'risky zone', away from our comfort zone?

Beyond our 'risky' learning zone lies our panic zone, wherein learning is impossible, as it is blocked by a sense of fear and the sympathetic autonomic system which can kick in (see the next chapter). Any learning connected with negative emotions is memorised in a part of the human brain that we can access only in similar emotional situations. Experiences of being in our panic zone are frequently traumatic, and any sense of curiosity is shut down by a need to escape. Therefore, we should aim to get close to, but not into, our panic zone.

In the transition from comfort zone to learning zone we need to be careful when taking risks that we don't go too far out of our comfort zone – beyond the learning zone and into the panic zone, where all our energy is used up for managing/controlling our anxiety and no energy can flow into learning and getting into higher-order thinking. Consider the teacher or parent who believes that pushing a child into a genuinely scary situation is 'good for them' . . . often it means we shut down and are not learning.

Importantly, these three zones are different for different situations and different for each person – we all have our own unique comfort zone, learning zone and panic zone. For example, for a child who has grown up in chaotic family circumstances, drinking out of a dirty cup might be perfectly normal and within their comfort zone, whereas sitting down for a meal together might be far out of their comfort zone to begin with. For children with different experiences, this might be the other way around. Where one zone ends and the other starts is very often not as clearly visible as in the previous illustration. All we can do is invite others to leave their comfort zone, value their decision, take them seriously and give them support so they won't enter their panic zone. Play is key to moving into the more edgy risk zone; it is where the learning really happens, with the proviso that the player can return to the comfort zone.

As we grow older, and hope to live a healthy and happy life, we all need to find enough compassion for ourselves, courage and vulnerability to try things that are not necessarily easy, hopefully believing we are worthy of love and belonging. All of us learn strategies (see Chapters 8 and 9) that help us to navigate into the learning zone, and return when needed into our comfort zone. The comfort zone is really a cultivated inner state, where you can retreat to, and is not reliant on external verification or rewards and is a place where you know you are good enough, no matter

Figure 6.7 Taking a supported risk!

what. Our role as practitioners is to give support where needed to enable learners to take risks that mean learning is optimal.

SMALL STEPS AND A SAFE COMFORT ZONE TO RETREAT TO

At Forest School, through observation and long-term relationship, we get to know the young people/children in our care and together figure out the best ways forward for the individual. We create a safe enough 'container' that is always there, the comfort zone from which to take risks, and provide achievable tasks and risky enough environments for the young people to experiment and learn to enjoy the learning zone, retreating where necessary. The group may start climbing on low ropes before climbing a tree, or sit near to the fire before exploring the edges of the boundaries, or start with a shelter on their own before wanting to share this with others.

By giving choice, allowing for small steps and to self-determine challenges, young people can expand their risk-taking and increase their confidence, resilience and desire to learn.

It can be useful, as a practitioner, to recognise what the risk zone is and what the risky play types are when we are in a natural environment, from which learners and we can retreat to the comfort zone, if needed.

RISKY PLAY TYPES

Ellen Sandseter (2009a), after many years of observing children's risky play, named six categories of risky physical play which has formed a framework plan for kindergartens in Norway and may inform some of what you may find at Forest School. We have also added emotional and social risk. These risky play types are observable and can provide a frame for practitioners to recognise the risk, or learning, zone.

Risky play, as defined by Sandseter (2009a), is thrilling and exciting forms of play that involve a risk of physical injury. Risky play primarily takes place outdoors, often as challenging and adventurous physical activities, children attempting something they have never done before, skirting the borderline of the feeling of being out of control (often because of height or speed) and overcoming fear.

These are:

- *Great heights*. Children climb trees and other structures to scary heights, from which they gain a bird's-eye view of the world and the thrilling feeling of *I did it!*
- *Rapid speeds*. Children swing on vines, ropes, or playground swings; slide on sleds, skis, skates, or playground slides; shoot down rapids on logs or boats; and ride bikes, skateboards, and other devices fast enough to produce the thrill of almost but not quite losing control.

Figure 6.8 Heights

Figure 6.9 Speed from a high swing

- *Dangerous tools*. Depending on the culture, children play with knives, bows and arrows, farm machinery (where work and play combine), or other tools known to be potentially dangerous. There is, of course, great satisfaction in being trusted to handle such tools, but there is also thrill in controlling them, knowing that a mistake could hurt.
- *Dangerous elements*. Children love to play with fire, or in and around deep bodies of water, either of which poses some danger.
- *Rough and tumble*. Children everywhere chase one another around and fight playfully, and they typically prefer being in the most vulnerable position – the one being chased or the one underneath in wrestling – the position that involves the most risk of being hurt and requires the most skill to overcome. For a good case study on this, see the Hackney Forest School website (www.hackneyforestschool.co.uk/web/the_wonders_of_stick_play/332755).
- *Disappearing/getting lost*. Little children play hide and seek and experience the thrill of temporary, scary separation from their companions. Older ones venture off, on their own, away from adults, into territories that to them are new and filled with imagined dangers, including the danger of getting lost.

Figure 6.10 A 4-year-old with dangerous tools

Figure 6.11 Dangerous elements – two children with fire

Figure 6.12 Getting lost in a low den and in the wood

Figure 6.13 Taking an emotional risk – blindfolds can be threatening

We would like to add to Sandseter's list of risky play types;

Taking emotional risks. These determine the quality of our relationships and in some ways underpin the ability to engage with the other risky play types.

It's risky to ask for help, to show you are vulnerable, to show you are also scared, that you don't know or feel good enough, perhaps feel unloved and ashamed at times. As practitioners, as we become more comfortable and courageous in how we feel, we are also more empathetic and can support the young people in our care to build empathy and sharing their feelings. Taking up different roles in play enables young people to express difficult feelings and positive feelings.

The quality of relationships and taking the risk to enter into relationships can often be aided through play; it can be a lifesaver and improve well-being. Risk perception is like a muscle that needs to be developed and flexed. Forest School and nature play is full of these risky play opportunities.

BENEFITS OF TAKING RISKS

The Health and Safety Executive (2012) recognises the benefits of outdoor play:

Play is great for children's wellbeing and development. When planning and providing play opportunities the goal is not to eliminate risk, but to weigh up the risks and benefits. No child will learn about risk if they are wrapped up in cotton wool.

The Play Safety Forum promotes the idea of keeping children *as safe as necessary, not as safe as possible*. When we prepare our risk-benefit assessments (RBAs), we may want to eliminate the hazards that are not obvious to the child, for example a broken tree branch, but not eliminate all the risks, involving the child in the assessment (see online appendix for sample RBAs).

The role of nature practitioner and staff is to work out the main physical and environmental risks and take steps to reduce them if necessary. You need to balance the risks against the benefits and make children the main focus of the risk-benefit assessment process.

The Care Inspectorate in Scotland (2016, p. 10) recommends:

- Know each child as an individual. This means you can help enable them to access an environment safely, so that most activities are within their capabilities but some will challenge them to develop their physical skills and confidence further.
- Consider children's potential to learn and benefit by taking risks. As children and young people develop they need to try new things and learn new skills. They need to work out risks for themselves as part of their learning process.
- Involve children in the risk-benefit assessment process so they can develop their knowledge and self-awareness and contribute more of their ideas and learning. By including children in the risk assessment process, you can empower them to make safe decisions.

Bad risks and hazards are those that are difficult or impossible for children to assess for themselves, and that have no obvious benefits. These might include sharp edges or points on equipment, weak structures that may collapse, and items that include traps for heads or fingers.
(Play England, 2008)

The following is an example of a learner-centred risk-benefit process in action:

A manager at a nursery service in Stirling, Scotland (extract from My World Outdoors (Care Inspectorate, Dundee, 2016, p. 10)), during circle time asked the children, 'How high is too high when you are outside exploring the hills and trees?'

This is some of what the children replied:

"When you can't see your friends anymore."
"Only really high up is too high!"
"When you get stuck."

"When you get scared."

"You can only go really high if you are really brave."

"Just the top."

The manager spoke with the children about how everyone has a different idea of what is too high and that everyone should set their own limits so that they always feel safe.

When they went outside, they had a code phrase, "Do you feel safe?" This became the guide for children as they set their own levels and managed their own risk.

Children made comments about keeping safe when helping each other at the ditch such as: "I had to help with a big branch and had to pull up." "We had to hold on tight and be careful." "I was helping my friend with a stick – he's pulling me out." "We had to be careful. We didn't want our friends to be hurt. We jumped down and climbed up something high and jumped down it."

A US longitudinal study provides compelling evidence of the importance of free 'risky' play on healthy development (Weikart, 1998). Comparing pre-school children who had 21% of free play with those who had 2%, when tested at 15 years old, the latter participated less and had greater misconduct at school; at 23 years old, they were more likely to be arrested and have difficulty at work.

This section has shown many reasons that nature play is important for learning and development, and there is much evidence to support this (also see the bonus online chapter), which includes our own risk-benefit assessments. Increasingly, larger institutions, such as the Health and Safety Executive (HSE) in the UK, support play in natural outdoor environments.

The ludic process and the nature play cycle

We have stated so far in this chapter that in many cases adults may need to support or stimulate play and at other times just get out of the learner's hair! To describe these different intervention styles and the impact this has on the play process, we will now revisit the nature play cycle and introduce the ludic process.

THE NATURE PLAY CYCLE

We have taken the play continuum proposed by Mandy Andrews in 2012 and extended this to a nature play cycle, which we introduced in Chapter 3. We see the continuum as a more cyclical phenomenon rather than a clear linear process. The arrows in pic 1 in Figure 6.14 represent the flows from one type of 'initiated'/'led' play to another, the dashed flows not being as strong as the solid ones – all based on our own experience of play in a woodland setting.

Our overall aim is to enable a learner to take control of their own learning and be 'on tap' rather than 'on top' to maintain the play process. These different types of interaction, which often follow the pattern of a cycle in a session, particularly at the start of a programme (adult led – adult initiated – child led – child initiated/supported by adult – adult led), can be explained further by looking at the nature of the interactions. Else and Sturrock's play process, presented in 1998, famously known as 'the Colorado Paper', goes a long way to explaining these interactions.

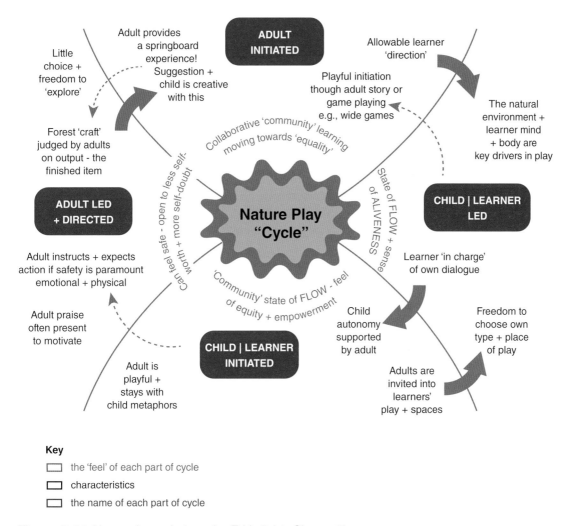

Key

☐ the 'feel' of each part of cycle

☐ characteristics

☐ the name of each part of cycle

Figure 6.14 Nature play cycle (see also Table 3.1 in Chapter 3)

THE LUDIC CYCLE

Else and Sturrock defined the play or 'ludic' cycle in the 'Colorado Paper' – a paper for Play in a Changing Society: Research, Design, Application at the IPA/USA Triennial National Conference in June 1998 and outlined in Else (2014). We can use this to understand play better and how we can support play in Forest School.

The ludic cycle (see Figure 6.15) is an ingeniously simple and yet deeply intriguing way of depicting the child's play process. It is like describing a universal expressive language that children use when they play. As with all languages we can learn the simpler aspects quite easily, but it takes time and practice to become fluent and really understand its meanings. Here are some brief definitions of aspects of the ludic cycle.

Metaludes: inner reverie or contemplation that precedes play (our experience thinking about and of play). Do we have thoughtful, stimulating spaces, objects or images that will spark metaludes?

Frames: this is the 'frame' or 'theme' of the play that is initiated by the child to provide the context, the enclosure. It is the stage that contains and constrains the play. It is organic and can change in shape and size.

Factors that can dictate shape and size include:

Physical elements: stones, rope, hedge, structure, designated area, fence, den, tree etc.

Narrative: storyline, music, rules and so forth

Feelings: a frame can explore a particular feeling. The props, the action, the place and the story can keep changing, but it's the experience of the feeling that holds it all together.

Cues: a lure or an invite to a person, to something in the environment, to another part of self. Play cues can be by a look, gesture, verbal invitation, provocation, testing out, facial or bodily display, presentation of an object or an action.

Return: the response by a child, by a practitioner by the environment or by oneself to a play cue.

Flow: when there's a response and a frame is maintained and develops a 'flow' (see Csikszentmihalyi, 1990) and can last seconds or a week. The players are literally totally immersed in the play and everything flows.

Annihilation: child chooses to end and move on.

Adulteration: practitioner stops/changes the play and play frame is destroyed, the children/players do not go with it – we all do it in multiple ways. Wanting to rescue, educate, improve, make better, control, play ourselves (unplayed-out material) and so forth.

Decay: breakdown of the play over time – a 'fizzling out'.

Dysplay: not to be confused with ordinary lack of return. The speedy misfiring of cues due to having got used to a pattern of non-responses.

Intervention: there are various levels of facilitator intervention:

Play maintenance: play is self-contained

Simple involvement: adult acts as a resource for the play.

Medial involvement: practitioner becomes involved (invited but temporary).

Complex involvement: direct and extended overlap between child and practitioner need to keep frame intact.

Integrity: practitioner may be involved in disputed or conflicting frames (witness position).

Forest School practitioners need to look for play cues and reflect on how to help establish and maintain state of play flow. See Chapter 11 for ways of observing and planning for interventions.

The following example of a Forest School exchange on a primary school site illustrates how this process helps us understand play at Forest School.

Boy A was sitting in his shelter by the fallen tree looking at the branches. He looked around and caught the eye of another boy and nodded (**play cue**); he moved to the fallen tree. The other boy (who was there for the first time that day) came shyly up to the fallen tree and nodded (**play return**). Boy A picked up two sticks (**metalude**) and started tapping the fallen tree, and Boy B also picked up a stick and started tapping (**play return**). They got a background bass rhythm going (**establishing a play frame**). One of the Forest School leaders started dancing nearby (**play return and cue**).

One of the boys looked round and laughed and several other children whooped and cheered (**play returns**). Within a couple of minutes, a line of children had formed doing the conga around the space, which swelled and moved outside and back in through another space (**more returns and cues**). The boys on the fallen tree drum were delighted and decided to keep drumming (**flow**). After about 5 minutes, the line broke up and individual children danced back before involving themselves with something else. The boys on the tree petered out their playing but seemed happy to do so (**decay**). The Forest School leader clapped and said "that was great!" and the two boys spontaneously stood up, bowed, threw the drum sticks down and both ran to the first boys' shelter (**annihilation and moving to another play frame**).

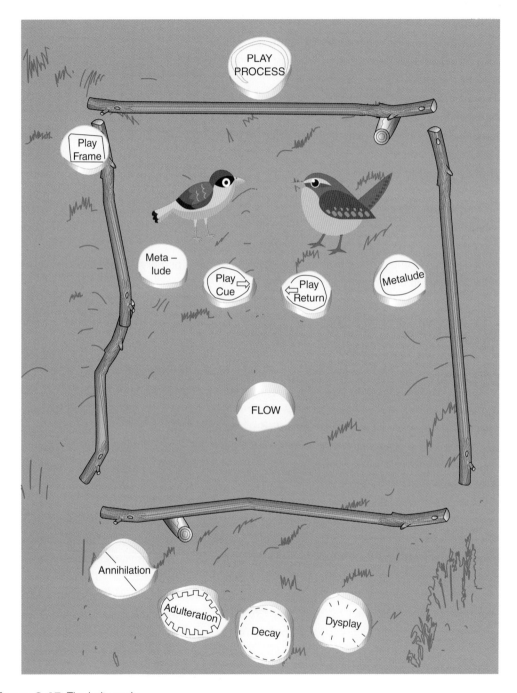

Figure 6.15 The ludic cycle

CONCLUSIONS

Interventions that chime with the learner-/community-centred principles of Forest School (as outlined in Chapter 1) need to be mindful of the play process. If an intervention is complex, as with the previous example, practitioners need to be playful, allow choice for the learners and look to take themselves out of the play in order to maintain the play on the players' terms. This is easier said than done, as we practitioners can get wrapped into the play and get into the flow state. We then have to pinch ourselves, as we can start influencing the frame and, if not careful, take over and subliminally start adulterating the play.

By denying choice, play can be inhibited and the cycle will be incomplete. The play drive will try to compensate in ways that are more urgent or aberrant perhaps causing conflict with the environment or others around them.

The natural world is a rich play environment. We as adults and practitioners are conscious of children's need to play for the sake of playing, not for some external reward, without interference to truly connect to a place and the play frame or play type/motif.

The play drive is a *seeking* to interact with the Forest School environment, materials and resources and the adults/practitioners, often with an unknown higher purpose – it's the four-way 'dance' outlined in Chapter 3.

The 'seeking' part of the brain is key to understanding the importance of brain development and inextricably linked to the 'play' brain systems. In play we now know we access our higher order thinking, empathy, social skills, curiosity and creativity. In effect, we are building relationship between brain, body and environment – the internal and external links talked about throughout the book. The next chapter will examine brain, body development and how we are 'wired to connect' (Banks, 2015) to build relationship. After all, play is largely about building relationship.

QUESTIONS FOR PRACTICE

What role do you tend to gravitate to with regard to the nature play cycle?
What aptitudes does a nature pedagogue need to facilitate wild play?
How often do you engage in play?
Have you observed how play might contribute to a sense of place?

USEFUL RESOURCES

Robertson, J and Casey, T (2016) Loose Parts Play – A Toolkit. Inspiring Scotland; www.inspiringscotland. org.uk/wp-content/uploads/2017/03/Loose-Parts-Play-web.pdf

Care Inspectorate, Dundee (2016) My World Outdoors – early years' good practice. Published by Communication; www.careinspectorate.com/images/documents/3091/My_world_outdoors_-_early_years_good_practice_2016.pdf

Bristol Scrapstore's PlayPods project; www.playpods.co.uk

Play England's 'Play, Naturally' project; www.playengland.org.uk/media/130593/play-naturally.pdf

Play Safety Forum. Managing Risk in Play Provision: Implementation Guide (D Ball, T Gill and B Spiegal, 2013); www.playengland.org.uk/media/172644/managing-risk-in-play-provision.pdf

Fundamental Facts about Mental Health (2015), Mental Health Foundation, London; www.mentalhealth.org.uk/sites/default/files/fundamental-facts-15.pdf

Dweck, C (2000) 'Self-theories: Their Role in Motivation, Personality and Development'

Gill, T (2007) 'No Fear: Growing Up in a Risk Averse Society'

Play Wales (2008) 'A Playworker's Guide to Risk'; download from www.playwales.org.uk/login/uploaded/documents/INFORMATION%20SHEETS/playworkers%20guide%20to%20risk.pdf

BIBLIOGRAPHY

Andrews, M (2012) *Exploring Play for Early Childhood Studies*. Sage.

Appleton, J (1975) *The Experience of Landscape*. New York: John Wiley & Sons.

Banks, A (2015) *Wired to Connect: The Surprising Link Between Brain Science and Strong Healthy Relationships*. New York: Penguin.

Brown, B (2019) *Braving the Wilderness: The Quest for True Belonging and the Courage to Stand Alone*. New York: Random House.

Brown, F (2003) *Playwork: Theory and Practice*. Buckingham: Open University Press.

Brown, S L (1998) Play as an Organising Principle: Clinical Evidence and Personal Observations. In Bekoff, M and Byers, J A (eds.), *Animal Play: Evolutionary, Comparative and Ethological Perspectives*. Cambridge: Cambridge University Press.

Burghardt, G (2005) *The Genesis of Animal Play: Testing the Limits*. Cambridge: MIT Press.

Cobb, E (1977) *The Ecology of Imagination in Childhood*. New York: Columbia University Press.

Cornell, J (2017) *Deep Nature Play*. Crystal Clarity Publishers.

Csikszentmihalyi, M (1990) *Flow: The Psychology of Optimal Experience*. New York: Harper.

Eager, D and Little, H (2011) Risk Deficit Disorder. Proceeding of IPWEA International Public Works Conference, Canberra, Australia, 21–24 August.

Else, P (2009) *The Value of Play*. Continuum Pub.

Else, P (2014) *Making Sense of Play*. Open University.

Gauntlett, D (2011) *Making Is Connecting: The Social Meaning of Creativity, from DIY and Knitting to YouTube and Web 2.0*. Cambridge: Polity Press.

Gibson, J (1979) *The Theory of Affordances. The Ecological Approach to Visual Perception*. Boston: Houghton Mifflin.

Gibson, J (1986) *The Ecological Approach to Visual Perception*. Hillsdale, NJ: Laurence Erlbaum.

Gray, P (2011) The Decline of Play and the Rise of Psychopathology in Children and Adolescents. *The American Journal of Play* 3: 443–463.

Gray, P (2015) *Free to Learn: Why Unleashing the Instinct to Play Will Make Our Children Happier, More Self-Reliant, and Better Students for Life*. New York: Basic Books.

Griffiths, J (2013) *Kith: The Riddle of Childscape*. Hamish Hamilton.

Hart, R (1979) *Children's Experience of Place*. New York: Irvington.

Health and Safety Executive (2012) *Children's Play and Leisure – Promoting a Balanced Approach*. Health and Safety.

Horseman, L (2015) *Compound Flexibility*. See https://kindlingplayandtraining.co.uk/forest-school/compound-flexibility/#more-1487.

Hughes, B (2001) *Evolutionary Playwork and Reflective Analytical Practice*. London: Routledge.

Hughes, B (2002) *A Playworker's Taxonomy of Play Types* (2nd edition). London: PlayLink.

Hughes, B (2003) *Insights and Understandings: Developments in Playwork Theory*. Cornwall: PLAY- ADD.

Huizinga, J (1949) *Homo Ludens – A Study of the Play-Element in Culture*. London: Routledge and Kegan.

Huttenmoser, M and Degan-Zimmermann, D (1995) *Lebenstraume fur Kinder*. Zurich: Swiss Science Foundation.

Kaplan, R and Kaplan, S (1989) *The Experience of Nature: A Psychological Perspective*. New York: Cambridge University Press.

Mental Health Foundation (2015) *Fundamental Facts About UK Mental Health*. See www.mentalhealth.org.uk/publications/fundamental-facts-about-mental-health-2015.

Moore, R (1986) *Childhood's Domain*. London: Croom Helm.

Nicholson, S (1971) How Not to Cheat Children – the Theory of Loose Parts. *Landscape Architecture Journal*, University of Wisconsin. See https://media.kaboom.org/docs/documents/pdf/ip/Imagination-Playground-Theory-of-Loose-Parts-Simon-Nicholson.pdf.

Pearce, J C (1977) *Magical Child*. Plume Publishing.

Pearce, J C (2012) *Heart-Mind Matrix: How the Heart Can Teach the Mind New Ways to Think*. Rochester, VT: Park Street Press.

Peden, M et al. (2008) *In World Report on Child Injury Prevention*. Geneva, Switzerland: World Health Organization Press.

Pelo, A (2013) *The Goodness of Rain: Developing an Ecological Identity in Young Children*. Redmond: Exchange Press.

Play England (2008) *National Play Strategy*. See https://www.playengland.org.uk/resource/national-play-policy/.

Robertson, J and Casey, T (2016) *Loose Parts Play – A Toolkit*. Inspiring Scotland. See www.inspiringscotland.org.uk/wp-content/uploads/2017/03/Loose-Parts-Play-web.pdf.

Sandseter, E B H (2009a) Characteristics of risky play. *Journal of Adventure Education and Outdoor Learning* 9(1): 3–21.

Sandseter, E B H (2009b) Children's Expressions of Exhilaration and Fear in Risky Play. *Contemporary Issues in Early Childhood* 10: 92–106.

Senninger, T (2015) *The Learning Zone Model*. See www.thempra.org.uk/social-pedagogy/key-concepts-in-social-pedagogy/the-learning-zone-model/.

Sobel, D (2008) *Children and Nature-Design Principles for Educators*. Stenhouse Publishers.

Sturrock, G and Else, P (1998) *The Colorado Paper – The Playground as Therapeutic Space: Playwork as Healing*. The Playground as Therapeutic Space: Playwork as Healing. A Paper for Play in a Changing Society: Research, Design, Application at the IPA/USA Triennial National Conference, June 1998. See https://ipaewni.files.wordpress.com/2016/05/colorado-paper.pdf.

Titman, W (1994) *Special Places, Special People*. London: Southgate.

Tuan, Y (1974) *Topophilia: A Study of Environmental Perception, Attitudes and Values*. New York: Columbia University Press.

Viscott, D (2003) *Finding Your Strength in Difficult Times*.

Weikart, D P (1998) Changing Early Childhood Development Through Educational Intervention. *Preventive Medicine* 27(2): 233–237.

White, J (2014) Ecological Identity – Values, Principles and Practice. In Duckett, R and Drummond, M J (eds.), *Learning to Learn in Nature*. Newcastle-upon-Tyne: Sightlines Initiative.

7 The brain, body and place

FS supports an increase in our well-being, prosocial behavior and deeper thinking, it fosters problem solving which creates resilient, creative, adaptive, 'learning', prosocial and inter-relational humans who see the bigger picture and realize connections, cause and effects.

(Robb and Cree, 2019)

This chapter will examine how the human brain interacts and is part of the body and environment we work in. We will look at the structure of the brain, how it interacts with our nervous system and heart, and how Forest School and natural world connection can support prosocial and pro-ecological pathways and learning. We will briefly look at how the brain cell operates, our instinctual and deep slower thought processes and how all the parts of the brain work together. In particular we will explore the emotional brain interactions and how important a Nature Pedagogy is for soothing in our stressful 21st century. One of the key aspects of how we behave and interact with the world is the nature of mind; the chapter will briefly explore the interaction between mind and brain. We will examine the four CARE neural pathways (Banks, 2015):

Calm (pathway governed by the smart vagus nerve)
Accepted (ruled by the dorsal anterior cingulate cortex – our pain centre)
Resonant (mirroring system)
Energetic (dopamine reward pathway)

Finally, we relate the latest neuroscience to some of the noted pedagogical schools of thought outlined in Chapter 2, and what this means for our understandings of learning in and through nature.

It is worth stating we have inevitably missed on some of the detail as we are not neuroscientists!

THE NEURON AND SYNAPSE

The brain is a remarkable thing in the way it connects with everything, even the farthest reaches of the universe – yes, our nervous system reaches out to the moon and beyond. It is interesting that we are born with about 86 billion neurons (Herculano, 2009), the cells that are the basis of our thinking and nervous system – almost the number of stars in our galaxy!

When neurons (see Figure 7.1) are 'wired' together through the synapse, making electrical circuitry in our brains, hearts and bodies, they make our bodies work. These are neural pathways, connecting brain, heart, gut and body and making meaning of the world. The synaptic 'leap' is aided by neurotransmitters (chemical messengers), many of which are hormones, important for emotional and behavioural regulation as well as meaning making.

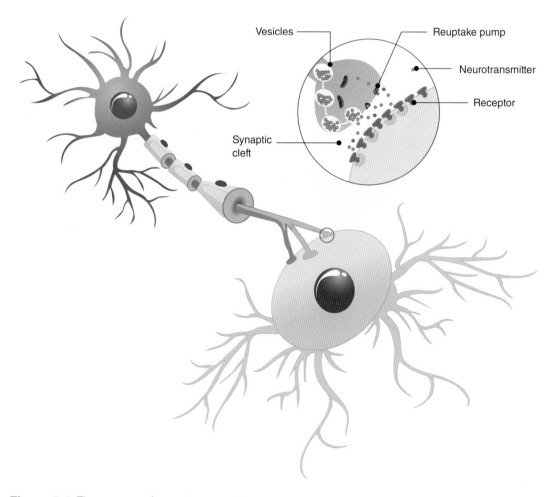

Figure 7.1 The neuron and synaptic connection

As educators, it is essential for outdoor learning and Forest School facilitators to have a basic understanding of how the brain and body works and know of some of the developments in recent neuroscience. This is the seat of learning. Some neuroscientists estimate our brain has the potential to make one million billion synaptic connections when it reaches maturity (some neurons can potentially make up to 15,000 connections). Whenever we touch a tree, make friends, walk, switch on the phone and learn a new skill, millions of neurons in our brains, hearts and guts are communicating using neurotransmitters, which are triggered by brain, body and environment interactions. Not surprisingly, we still know relatively little about the neural workings of our bodies, and most of what we do know has been found out in the last 40 years with the introduction of magnetic resonance scanning.

Whole body thinking

When we say neural workings of our bodies, we mean that – our whole body thinks, not just our brains. In particular we have neural systems in our hearts and guts.

Neurologist Dr Andrew Armour from Nova Scotia in Canada discovered a sophisticated collection of neurons in the heart that organised into a small, complex nervous system. The heart's nervous system contains around 40,000 neurons called sensory neurites that communicate with the brain. Dr Armour dubbed this discovery as the "Little Brain in the Heart" (Armour, 1991). More recently, Professor Patterson at University of Oxford has shown that the heart neurons on the right ventricle do indeed 'think' independently, enabling the heart to beat at different rates depending on what impulses are coming from our nervous system (Paterson et al., 2016 – cited in Learning Mind and film *Of Hearts and Minds* by David Malone, see https://topdocumentaryfilms.com/of-hearts-minds/). The heart does communicate strongly with the brain via the nervous system, especially the vagal nerve – the two work in tandem (see later in this chapter).

The human gut has been referred to by scientists as the 'enteric nervous system' and our 'second brain'. It also has its own independent nervous system, a sophisticated network of 100 million neurons embedded in the gut wall and our gastrointestinal tract from the oesophagus to the rectum.

The gut's multifaceted ability to communicate with the brain, along with its crucial role in defending the body against the perils of the outside world, leads gastroenterologist Emeran Mayer, MD, director of the Center for Neurobiology of Stress at the University of California, to believe that "it is unthinkable to think that the gut is not playing a critical role in our mind states" (Carpenter, 2012).

Further to these extra neural networks, Candace Pert (1997) showed that neurons also interacted with other organs in our bodies through the 'peptide' network. She states, "The mind and body communicate with each other through chemicals known as peptides." Peptides are found in the brain as well as in the stomach, in muscles and in all of our major organs. Dr Pert believed that memory could be accessed anywhere in the peptide receptor network. For example, a memory associated with food can be linked to the pancreas or liver, and such associations can be transplanted from one person to another, hence the terms 'gut feeling', 'tingling in my toes' etc.

This chapter is by no means a definitive picture of how neural circuitry works and connects, and some generalisations are made. We have taken studies done by some of the well-known thinkers and researchers into neural science and tried to synthesise the key aspects applicable to Forest School and nature education.

System 1 and system 2 thinking

In October, Jon visited a Forest School session in the lea of the South Downs hills watching a mixed group of 2017 children, some Year 4s, sharing a session with reception and nursery children. The session started with slight chaos, and some children clearly were not settled and were making some poor decisions in terms of language and the common 'good' of the group – reacting to each other's comments without any thought of the type of language being used. Meanwhile, others were clearly frustrated and impatient, some sat patiently, perhaps bemused . . . waiting. The leader sat down and rather than saying "No", she patiently waited for calm to return. One of the more active boys was shouting across the circle, clearly in a hypervigilant state, and the leader calmly but firmly said "Yes Daniel, let's see what the others want to do so we can all hear what we as a group *need* this morning." She could have taken a different approach and to everyone said, "Stop talking! We aren't going to do anything until I have silence!"

She had quickly, but gently, with a 'yes' brain mode, moved to enable all to engage in what they wanted.

It suddenly struck Jon that some of the group were clearly in 'system 1' mind, responding to each other instinctively without deeper thinking, and some were in 'system 2' mind, patiently waiting and thinking (Kahneman, 2011). This was probably because of what previously happened that morning/ in their own lives – a glimpse of 'yes'/reflective/slower (2) or 'no'/reactive/instinctive/faster (1) brain states.

In his best-selling book *Thinking Fast and Slow*, Kahneman (2011) frames our whole culture around System 1 thinking – thinking fast which is automatic and quick with little effort, and System 2 thinking – which demands effort and is associated with concentration, agency and making choices.

What Jon saw develop during the session in the case study above was a compassionate, engaged group where the older children, incidentally mostly the 'loud' ones at the start of the

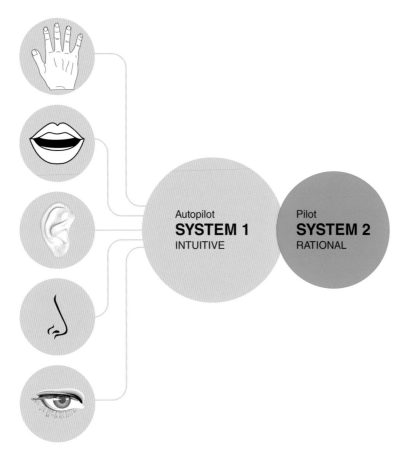

Figure 7.2 Systems 1 and 2 thinking – fast and slow

session, played compassionately and with empathy with the younger ones. Jon realised exactly what the "manifesto for a green mind" put forward by University of Essex in March 2017 (Pretty, 2017) was saying; it is the coming together of, and balance between, the fast and slow mind, aided by a calm outdoor setting that creates a green mind.

This section is about how our brains work and ways of cultivating the green mind – the mind that connects, through neural circuitry, and reconciles system 1 and system 2, bringing balance to our overall system. This increases deeper thinking and problem solving, resulting in prosocial behaviour and a state of well-being. There is no coincidence it is referred to as the 'green mind', as the natural world acts as a great balancer and leveler in getting us into higher order system 2 thinking that is required for a fulfilled and healthy life (see evidence and green interventions online appendices online appendix for more research on these benefits).

Mind and brain

The brain is the organ in our heads, approximately 3 lbs of grey and white matter connected to our bodies through the nervous system. Mind is not the brain. Neurologists deal with brain, whereas educators and therapists deal with the interrelational aspect of the whole body and the environment. The brain and the judgments we make about the way we behave and respond to stimulus (social and natural) is the stuff of the mind. Daniel Siegel and Bryson (2018) refer to this as the 'between-ness'. For us the mind works with the relational experiences that are embodied in the inner felt senses, thinking, attitudes, hopes, dreams and intentions which are a result of the interactions between brain, heart, body, environment and other beings – including humans. In this book we don't just want to look at the brain but also how nature-based and Forest School experiences relate to brain, body and the ways we behave – that is, the resultant mind development.

> When any neurological tissue in the brain or the body is activated, it creates mind. Consequently, from a neuroscientific understanding, mind is the brain in action.
>
> (Dr Joe Dispenza, 2017)

We have previously talked about the benefits of nature to health and well-being and how this is linked in with the 'sympathetic' and 'parasympathetic' systems in our brain/body interaction, which is dependent on our nervous system and neurotransmitter hormones. In order to comprehend these systems, we need to look at the neuroscience behind this. This is a simplified explanation, and we have inevitably picked out the key aspects of the brain that relate to what Forest School and Nature Pedagogy both do and what their aims are. For more detailed explanations, we suggest you look at Panksepp, Sunderland, Banks, Van der Kolk, or Barrett (see the bibliography at the end of this chapter).

Brain structure

The human brain is the result of millions of years of evolution, and we often refer to the triune brain, as named by the neuroscientists in the late 1960s (Maclean, 1990). This comprises three evolutionary parts – the reptilian brain (over 300 million years old), the mammalian/limbic brain (approximately 200 million years old) and the neocortex, the most recent part of this being the prefrontal cortex where we do all our deeper 'thinking' (approximately 200 thousand years old).

The pre frontal lobes, part of the six-layered neocortex, are often referred to as *Homo sapiens*' 'crowning glory'. This is the part of the brain where reasoning, creativity, reflection and deeper processing of emotions happens. It is also the 'problem solving' and 'thinking about thinking' (metacognition) part of the brain. This area is important for learning and development, particularly in the creation of resilient, creative, adaptive, 'learning', prosocial and interrelational humans who see the bigger picture and realise connections, causes and effects etc.

Figure 7.3 The triune brain

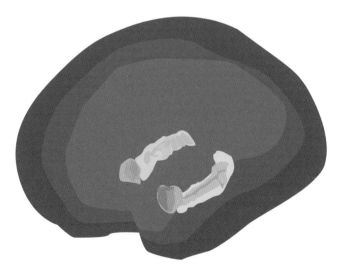

Figure 7.4 The human amygdala

The limbic or pro-mammalian system is seen as the emotional and long-term 'memory' centre of the brain and has a number of structures with distinct sets of neurons that are key to our understanding of the way the brain works – the amygdala (see Figure 7.4) where our significant emotional memories are stored, especially those associated with fear, and the hippocampus, which is responsible for our episodic memory and is seen as the system that is the seat of our memories and responsible for spatial sense. These two systems talk to each other all the time, not only loosely fitting with the limbic system but also the rest of the brain (Phelps, 2004).

The reptilian complex or primitive brain is responsible for our survival, our instincts – fight, flight, freeze and feign actions and basic functions to keep the body going – heart rate, breathing, body temperature, digestion etc.

Maclean (1990) propounded that these brains with the three distinct sets of functions have had a huge influence on the way we see the brain.

Since Maclean's analysis, neuroscientists, psychologists, psychotherapists, educators and many other writers, however, have described the brain as having two systems, which we outlined at the start of this section – higher order thinking (upstairs thinking) and lower order thinking (downstairs thinking), with the emotional limbic system being at the heart of a functioning brain.

We know that threats to survival are first addressed by the primitive brain – as illustrated in 'peripheral shut-down', where blood vessels are constricted on the periphery of the body in anticipation of physical trauma – and take precedence over other brain functions. We also know the limbic system can mediate and make stronger links with the prefrontal cortex if the 'threats' to our survival are minimised and a 'slower', more reflective state is present.

In fact, evolution did not 'layer' the brain. What has happened over time was that core circuits of the whole brain have reorganised, with certain circuits and regions expanding and becoming more complex. Even reptiles have cortex-like structures, just smaller and less complex. While it is true that the reptilian brain is sometimes in competition for the more modern circuits within the cortex regions of the brain, with the limbic systems at the core of brain, there are direct links between the cortex and more primitive areas of the brain.

The whole brain can only work because all parts of the brain are linked in one way or another. What often happens is when a skill or 'awareness' is practised time and time again, it can become instinctive and uses less energy. It is our system 1 lower brain, linking in with the prefrontal cortex, and system 2 upper brain, which ends up storing that learning.

A balanced brain is where the sympathetic, parasympathetic and all the other relational neural pathways are in 'healthy' order.

All of this recent research shows the brain to be relational; all three evolutionary parts and the fast and slow thinking work together. In addition to its own parts, the brain works closely with the body, in particular the heart.

Heart

We now know that up to 25% of the heart's cells are neurons and are our primary receptors of the **sensory inputs** to our body system. The heart and brain are interdependent. For example, the core of the amygdala is dependent on the input from the aortic depressor – the heart's external pump that links into the vagal nerve and up to the amygdala in the brain. In essence, the heart and brain decide together what actions to take – both are in neural dialogue (Buhner, 2004). This nicely echoes many cultures' encouragement to listen to both your heart and your head. Let's look at the role of the amygdala in the sympathetic and parasympathetic pathways.

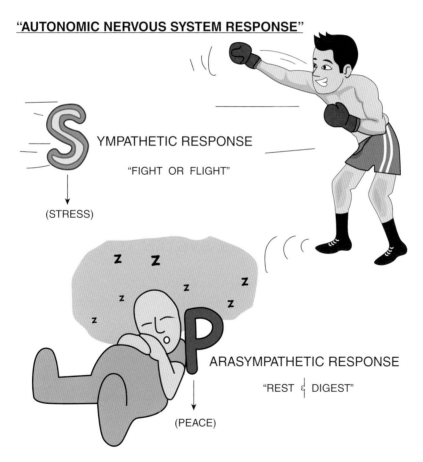

Figure 7.5 The sympathetic and parasympathetic nervous systems and associated behavioural responses

Source: https://efchealth.com/sympathetic-vs-parasympathetic-matter/

151

The sympathetic and parasympathetic

One of the key components of the brain that enables brain/body connection is the **autonomic** nervous system that links into our organs, particularly the heart, which regulates our body automatically. There are two parts to this system – the sympathetic and parasympathetic. If these two are in balance and working together, we can expect to get into the prefrontal cortex and system 2 thinking which is what we, as educators, are striving for – not forgetting that system 1 also has its function.

Our autonomic nervous system regulates three fundamental physiological states. Our level of safety determines which one of these is activated at any one time (Van der Kolk, 2014). These systems have huge implications for how our behaviour is self-regulated (see Chapters 8 and 9 on behaviour).

1   First level: Social engagement system is activated as we seek human relationship to soothe us. Studies of disaster have shown that social support is the most powerful protection against becoming overwhelmed by stress and trauma.
2   Second level: Activation Sytem. As lack of safety increases, our fight or flight system is activated. Our limbic system protects us from shutting down and we become energised.
3   Third level: Immobilization System. If we cannot escape, we shut down, freeze or collapse.

   • *Sympathetic nervous system*: stimulates functions associated with the stress response
   • *Parasympathetic nervous system*: stimulates the relaxation response in the body

OUR SYMPATHETIC NERVOUS SYSTEM (SNS)

The hypothalamus, located in the limbic system, is where our sympathetic nervous system plugs the brain into the glands that produce hormones. These act as neurotransmitters and control things like blood flow and our stress responses.

The **h**ypothalamus communicates with the **p**ituitary gland, often called the 'master' gland, located just behind the bridge of the nose, which then sends messages to the **a**drenal gland, just above the kidneys, which releases three key stress hormones – adrenalin, norepinephrine and cortisol – the **HPA** axis (see Figure 7.6). The reason this is called **sympathetic system** is because its prime function is to look after the body – to survive in times of extreme stress. In a moment we can shut down pain centres and the digestive system, increase blood flow to our muscles, including the heart, and become super vigilant – the *'fast fight or flight' reactive system 1* is activated; a few minutes later the real 'stress' chemical is released, cortisol. What cortisol does is prolong the effects of adrenalin and norepinephrine and feedback into the brain to shut down pathways

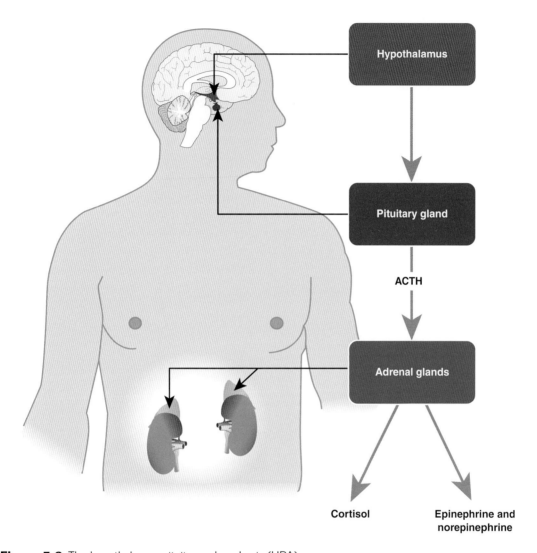

Figure 7.6 The hypothalamus pituitary adrenal axis (HPA)

Source: https://cranemedicine.wordpress.com/2015/05/11/the-biology-of-depression-stress-pt-2-cortisol/

to system 2 or higher order thinking – hence the term 'red mist' – we literally can't think; it all becomes a fog.

Cortisol helps to maintain fluid balance and blood pressure, while regulating some body functions that aren't crucial in the moment, like reproductive drive, immunity, digestion and growth. This was an evolutionary mechanism for the brain to control the body when we either had to kill the sabre tooth tiger, run away from it or freeze and feign death. What happened in the process of dealing with highly stressful life-threatening events and a fight for survival response is that the adrenalin, norepinephrine and cortisol were literally 'exercised' out of our systems and, once these short events were over, we could get back to system 2 thinking. However, our brains have not kept up with human cultural development, and this 'older brain' still deals with stressful situations in the same way. Being outdoors can physically work cortisol out of the system; sitting at the screen just doesn't cut it! This is often called 'discharge' after a stressful event and has implications for much behavioural issues inside our classrooms where ther is no way of 'discharging' in a physeical way.

There is now more constant stress in society and, in the case of education, the constant 'threat' of judgment and in some cases, abuse, can mean cortisol hangs around for longer and we end up being hypervigilant – our stress bucket literally overflows. We see more eating disorders, weaker immune systems and more mental health issues. We have witnessed many situations where a seemingly small trigger has engaged the amygdala in speaking to the hypothalamus and it means we either lash out, withdraw or just shut down completely, and in that moment there is nothing we as educators can do except keep the people in our care physically safe.

The Figure 7.7 shows how this 'stress bucket' can be made bigger to reduce the volume of stress.

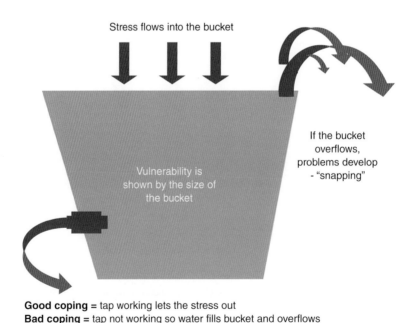

Stress flows into the bucket

Vulnerability is shown by the size of the bucket

If the bucket overflows, problems develop - "snapping"

Good coping = tap working lets the stress out
Bad coping = tap not working so water fills bucket and overflows

Figure 7.7 The stress bucket

CASE STUDY

Just last week Jon could see the sympathetic system provoking an "I won't do that" response to an invitation to walk to the Forest School site with a learner we will call Gina, who mostly is first to the site and first to the swing (the swing is her soothing higher order reasoning and reflective 'thing'). He could see as Gina came off the bus she was in a sensitive vigilant state – Jon's mirror neurons were firing. The thing is, she shows these traits in school all the time, yet at Forest School it is occasional. Something had obviously happened that morning. She wasn't responding or listening to the educator's instructions, she was stuck to the spot, red faced and shaking – in a state of anxiety – the sympathetic system had kicked in and, because of her background and school environment, she finds it hard to literally step out of her cortisol-fuelled body. It's not a matter of 'won't move', it is literally 'can't move'.

As neurologists often say, 'states become traits', and yet quite often Gina finds her true self at Forest School and the 'traits' more often witnessed in school seem to disappear, not completely, but for much of the time. You can see she is in higher order thinking mode, more balanced and 'regulated for reason' – she seems to be in the prefrontal cortex.

Gina started shouting. Jon calmly talked to the teaching assistant in charge, Laura, and a plan was hatched. Jon took the rest of the group to the toilets and Laura walked fast with Gina to the site; she got to the site and went straight to the swing, which luckily had been left up from the previous day's session. Laura had a calm, reassuring, yet assertive, presence. This caring atmosphere with the fast walking and swinging meant that by the time the group arrived at the site, Gina had calmed down and returned to higher order thinking.

OUR PARASYMPATHETIC NERVOUS AND POLYVAGAL SYSTEM (PNS)

The **parasympathetic system** is also a survival system in which the 'freeze' response kicks in and you literally freeze and feign death (Van der Kolk's third level of body response). This is especially switched on when you feel you have no chance of fighting the perceived threat – the body literally shuts down all non-essential organs, sometimes to the detriment of the body in the end . . . some mammals can die if there is too much 'freeze'.

Mammals, luckily, have what is called the **smart vagus nervous system** (sometimes referred to as **PNS**), which also acts on the HPA axis, running alongside (the meaning of 'para') the sympathetic nerves in the spinal cord and inhibiting the sympathetic's activity; it 'interacts' with the parasympathetic and sympathetic. These systems are co-dependent; we like to think of them as the fire and earth of the nervous system – or Holmes and Watson! The main neurotransmitter released by the PNS is acetylcholine, a major destressing hormone, which also stimulates signals to parts of the body – importantly the heart, gut and eyes. What it also does is slow the heart rate and cool the body, allowing it to function properly, regulating sweating, salivation, tear movements, digestion and sexual activity; it is often referred to as the slowing 'rest and digest' or 'rest and recovery' system.

The PNS is also involved in emotional regulation – it is in fact the sympathetic system's fear and rage modulator. The polyvagal theory of emotional regulation is backed by the science behind the PNS system (Porgers, 2011). The key part of this system is the interaction of the vagal nerve with the autonomic nervous system. This is when our parasympathetic system is activated with the vagal nerve and we literally 'feel' our emotions and become aware of them – that is, we get into higher order or prefrontal cortex thinking. We can 'feel' relaxed, hungry or tired, as well as 'feel' emotions – serene, sad, afraid, anxious etc. It is no surprise that this is stimulated by social soothing – the reason mammals have fewer offspring is that they are more reliant on the nurturing and soothing of parents; reptiles, however, produce more eggs and are on their own at birth – they have no vagal nerve, therefore produce more offspring in order to survive.

What does the PNS have to do with the brain? Our **hippocampus**, remember! – the area of the brain that is used for spatial learning and memory, including emotional memories, tries to turn off our physiologic sympathetic stress responses – fight or flight mode. The hippocampus needs our **prefrontal cortex** to be able to turn off the sympathetic response. It does so by activating the PNS and making connections into the vagal nerve to balance out the physiologic stress response, which comes from the sympathetic nervous system.

When the PNS is activated in this way, our brains produce short-term and long-term benefits. The short-term benefits can be a release of destressing hormones like endorphin, prolactin, oxytocin, dopamine, serotonin, vasopressin, and acetylcholine, which can literally counter the cortisol feedback system the sympathetic system initiates.

Interestingly, gut bacteria produce hundreds of neurochemicals that the brain uses to regulate basic physiological processes as well as cognitive functions such as learning, memory and mood. For example, gut bacteria manufactures about 95% of the serotonin in our body, which influences both mood via the PNS as well as gastrointestinal activity (Hadhazy, 2010). Research is still early, but our guess is that exposure to soil bacteria is a key part of this mechanism.

Our brains get a chance to relax and feel more at peace. This gives our brains time to process better. Our prefrontal cortex can continue to regulate, as it is the main processing centre for our short-term memories and links back into the hippocampus in the limbic system. "So what?" I hear you all ask. "What has this to do with Forest School?" The swing, in Gina's case (Figure 7.8), was part of her PNS and stimulates the so-called Happy DOSE chemicals (Figure 7.9), so she can interact with the group and woods in a positive way. What also aids Gina in becoming more prosocial and pro-ecological is the balance that the forest environment, the movement in the forest and the playful and caring way the practitioners interact with her support her 'emotional' limbic system.

Figure 7.8 Motion, in many cases a swing or hammock, can be a form of self-soothing and regulating

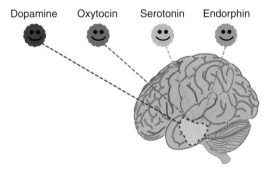

Meet Your Happy Chemicals

Dopamine   Oxytocin   Serotonin   Endorphin

Figure 7.9 DOSE: the chemicals and neurotransmitting hormones released in PNS to maintain a balance of adrenalin and cortisol

The emotional brain

There was a breakthrough in neuroscience in the late 1990s led by the neuroscientist Jaak Panksepp, and since this time neuroscientists all over the world have been working with the ancient mammalian part of our brain. Seven key neurological 'genetically ingrained' systems were found in the limbic (mammalian) system – RAGE, FEAR, GRIEF/PANIC, CARE (attachment), PLAY, SEEKING and LUST (see Figure 7.10).

If these are in balance, they can enable more linking of the hippocampus and the vagal nerve. These systems are written in capital letters to distinguish them from the common meaning of these words – although they are associated with common emotions and actions, they are more than this in terms of the neurological pathways. PLAY is associated with joy, CARE with love and nurturing, RAGE – anger, FEAR – anxiety, GRIEF – panic, LUST – sex and SEEKING – meaning making. Panksepp often refers to the last one as the 'grandparent of all'.

The SEEKING system is a system of desire, curiosity, spontaneity, passion and excitement in embracing the fruits of human existence. An excellent description of these systems and how they apply to the early years can be found in Margot Sunderland's book *The Science of Parenting* (2016).

Figure 7.10 Panksepp's seven 'emotional' limbic systems

While these are compelling and much evidence supports Panksepp's theories, there is still doubt that these systems can be clearly defined, as every individual being has a highly integrated and somewhat contextualised brain, so a general functional view of the brain cannot necessarily be consistent. Every human is faced with unique situations, and our brains act in slightly different 'constructed' ways, depending on our own history and the context in which the brain is operating in that moment (see Barrett, 2017). Barrett, a renowned professor in psychology, also takes issue with the 'functional' way of looking at brain parts and makes a good case for seeing the brain as an integrated whole – which indeed it is. Nevertheless, it can sometimes be useful to look at how all the functional units connect. We do know that the PNS is stimulated by nurturing, curiosity, freedom from threat and a chance to play with ideas as well as play for play's sake, as outlined in Chapter 6.

THE THERAPEUTIC AND LEARNING BENEFITS OF NATURE PLAY AND EMPATHIC COMMUNICATION

Having discovered how the brain/body system works and the interplay between the sympathetic and parasympathetic systems, more therapeutic approaches have been configured to utilise this understanding. One of the most well known in psychotherapeutic circles is PACE. **Playfulness** brings enjoyment to relationship. **Acceptance** creates psychological safety. When we **Curiously** explore within a relationship, we express a desire to know the other more deeply. **Empathy** communicates our curiosity and acceptance, as we recognise and respond to the other's emotional experience.

It is obvious how these all chime with Panksepp's theories. We will come back to this later when looking at the role of mirror neurons in a Forest School setting.

All of the 'PNS systems' (CARE, PLAY, SEEKING) are potentially stimulated by both the 'soothing' and 'diverse and fascinating' environment of Forest School as well as a 'community' approach facilitated by the Forest School practitioner. This brings into balance the hormones and neurotransmitters being produced by the brain's interconnected and, yes, complex circuitry. If we are in a state of flow in play where we merge with our environment, then serotonin, dopamine and certain opioids are produced by the PNS which can interrupt the release of the stress hormone, cortisol, and enable us to be in the higher order thinking mode. It is interesting to note that studies have shown people in natural settings can restore attention more quickly than in other environments (see the research in the online evidence and benefits appendices for further evidence of nature stimulating the PNS). It has been reported in a number of studies that children and young people attending Forest School sessions show more cognition and attentive behaviour in the classroom on the days Forest School happens (Roe and Aspinall, 2009).

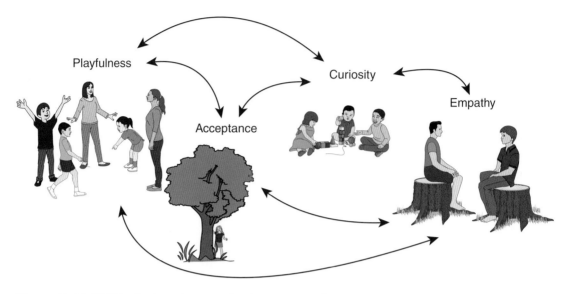

Figure 7.11 PACE – the four elements of a therapeutic circle

Other exciting recent studies (Cryan and Dinan, 2018) have shown that that the PNS highway through the vagus nerve – connecting gut to brain – have shown that the anti-depressant drug, serotonin, can be released from the gut and literally 'feed' the brain. Serotonin can be released through not only a happy, nurturing, calming environment but also via the gut neurons if fed the right bacteria. Yes, you guessed it! Natural bacteria both in our foods and the environment, woodlands in particular, can feed back up via the vagal nerve to the brain – wow! This is something we have intuitively known since the 4th century when the Chinese used 'gut medicine' – faeces – to cure depression!

EMPATHY

The so-called CARE system also correlates with the hormonal release when empathy is present. Empathy is initiated in our mirror neurons. These are situated largely in the inferior frontal gyrus, at the rear of the prefrontal cortex, and are responsible for understanding intentions; inferior frontal gyrus is a key area for mirror neurons, and sensory cortex areas – the visual, brocas (language), temporal (auditory) and motor areas. We are literally soft-wired to experience another's plight and pleasure as though we are experiencing it ourselves. The mirror neurons are the brain cells that are our 'interdependent' cells (Iacoboni, 2009, p. 265).

Let's take a moment to examine the definitions of **sympathy** and **empathy**.

Sympathy is an emotional reaction, immediate and uncontrolled, which inundates when one person imagines him- or herself in the position someone else is. That is why it can lead to suspension of care or alleviate ethical actions. Empathy, on the other hand, is a skill learned or an attitude of life, which can be used to try to come into contact with someone, to communicate and understand others' experiences or feelings (Halpern, 2003). To empathise is also to enter in the situation of 'the other' to take some responsibility for association with other people and beings. The more we activate the PNS through understanding others' emotions and trying to visualise and 'feel' what it is 'like' and co-problem solve a way through tricky situations, the more we can bring balance to our autonomic system and get into the more reflective state. This means activating our mirror neurons by not 'judging', by 'feeling' and then communicating in a congruent way that acts with the 'other's' neurons.

Here is an example of how these nervous systems apply to Forest School, and practice can stimulate the mirror neurons, activating the parasympathetic system.

Two years ago Jon was working with two young adolescents, whom we will call Jeff and Bill. Their brains were starting another phase of development (see later). The 'risk' part of their brains was coming 'online' but was still at least 10 years from being fully developed, and a growth spurt was happening in certain parts of their prefrontal cortex, particularly the 'self-awareness' and non-verbal reasoning parts (Blakemore, 2018). He had been with these two and a teaching assistant (TA) for about 6 months for a minimum of 2 days a week. Relationships were being built and trust was starting to bed in. The two boys had certain traits – Jeff had sensory attachment issues (see Chapter 4 and later for the effects on brain development) and was delayed in some of his sensory development. He had both proprioception (how our limbs position themselves in space and respond to how hard we push and pull against objects and gravity) and vestibular (spatial sense) sensory processing difficulties (see Chapter 5; he couldn't run properly, for example), while Bill had impulse and attention difficulties and liked to fight a lot in school. Jeff was seemingly quite articulate and had a handle on 'knowledge', but he had issues with emotional regulation. We now know there is a strong link between the pro-prioceptive bottom-up part of the nervous system and the limbic system, which accounts for some of Jeff's struggles with emotional regulation (see Chapters 8 and 9). He also definitely had emotion-al-attachment issues.

With Bill, it was the other way around. He knew very well what he was feeling and what triggered certain behaviours. At school his issue was how to control these behaviours, and one of the roots of his aggression was down to attachment issues with caregivers (see Bowlby, 1980). This is often seen as a top-down issue, where the triggers are not necessarily related to sensory and physical inputs but to verbal and human interactions. Much of the fighting was related to wanting to be 'positively held' – he even talked about the staff he 'liked' to be held by and those he didn't.

It was a surprisingly incident-free programme regarding how these two young males interacted. Jeff found that the physical act of swinging really did regulate his proprioception and vestibular systems, producing a smile every time and resulting in prosocial behaviour.

During nesting season, Jeff often would calm himself by spending a good amount of time on the swing – it was the one place he would smile and play. After the swing, he would rest attentively watching the blue tits for many minutes going in and out of the bird box feeding the youngsters. The swing was stimulating his PNS and satisfying his proprioceptive (muscular) and vestibular (balance and place) sense and he could concentrate and 'be with' us, the blue tits and the wood. Meanwhile, Bill found solace in animals, in particular newts and grass snakes – it seems their unconditional acceptance was part of this 'connection'. The reptiles were going about their own lives without any reference to Bill. This, combined with a fascination with reptiles and amphibians, had a calming effect; he would want to know about these creatures. The seeking system was being activated in something he was emotionally invested in, and, we suspect, his very soul; somehow, he identified himself with these animals. He was mostly at home just watching the corrugated metal vivarium where we knew there was a female grass snake waiting to give birth to young, or watching a small puddle and logs next to the pond where great crested newts lived. It seems when the seeking system is activated there is an inherent reward generated in the form of dopamine, and we get pleasure from opening up new knowledge and horizons – thereby activating the parasympathetic system and reducing stress.

There was, however, one incident at about 6 months into their programme where Jeff had started to 'jibe' Bill too much, so Bill, not like before, started getting aggressive and stood up to posture round the fire . . . something had triggered – possibly it had started earlier in the morning at home. Instead of either his 'taking the mick' banter or walking off to his beloved reptile place, his eyes dilated and his fists curled, and he started moving aggressively towards Jeff . . . the sympathetic system had kicked in. The TA immediately jumped between the two and Jon stood next to Jeff, requesting him to talk in a different way and move away. If Jon had not gotten hold of Jeff, he would have pummelled Bill! Then, a dance around the fire (which the TA had put out immediately) started, whereby Jon was jumping this way and that, making fun of himself, as was the TA. This physical mirroring of Bill's movements along with making gentle eye contact and almost mirroring his expressions saw Bill starting to dance and eventually laugh – the mirror neurons, Jon's and his, were bouncing off each other, and the slightly droll facial expressions eventually led to laughter and the cortisol-fuelled atmosphere changed to a serotonin-fuelled situation, whereby the serotonin was acting as a suppressant to the cortisol. Sometimes it can fuel the sympathetic system, but in this case Bill lapsed into banter and calmly took himself off with a clear request from Jon – "Bill, let's go and see what the grass snake is up to".

Figure 7.12 Play can stimulate oxytocin and serotonin

Afterwards, Jon realised this was a classic incident of mirroring and these neurons connecting with the parasympathetic system and just maybe the GRIEF or RAGE systems moving into PLAY and CARE. Empathic dialogue and clear requests enabled clear neural pathways – restoring balance (see Chapters 8 and 9).

OK, so that's some of the brain science. What made the executive decision, in Bill's case, to behave and engage in certain ways that are prosocial and 'mature', that is, to talk in a reasoned way and withdraw himself from a potentially fiery situation? It may have had severe consequences for the friendships that had been built in this group over the last 6 months and maybe even jeopardised his future attendance to something he clearly valued. This is where the **mind** kicks in, sometimes referred to as the 'monkey' and 'elephant' parts of brain – the prefrontal and neocortex, including the limbic amongst this (see Figure 7.13).

All of the values, history, environment, people and 'beings' who are significant to us and our context influence the connections these two parts of the brain make with the internal and external world of our bodies, which bring about the decisions we make at any point in time. Jules Pretty (2017) felt that the 'green mind' is one that over the millennia we have developed – whereby what he calls the red brain (system 1) and blue brain (system 2) can be brought into balance to make for a healthy, purposeful and joyful life.

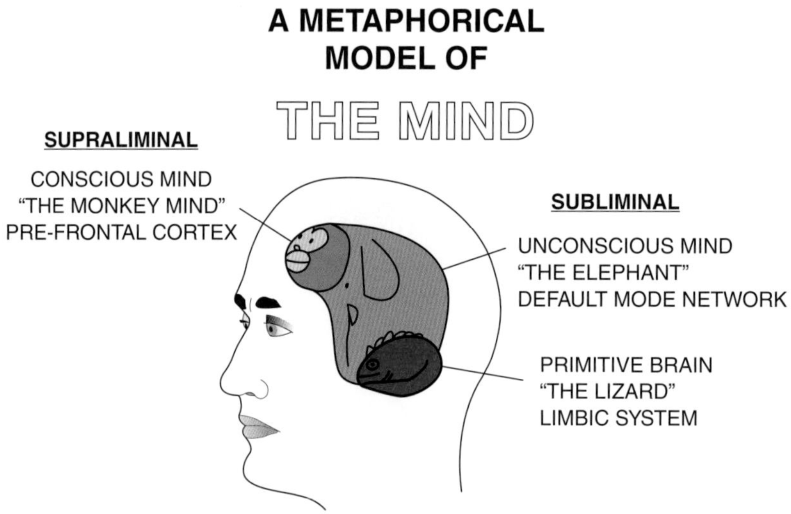

A METAPHORICAL MODEL OF

THE MIND

SUPRALIMINAL

CONSCIOUS MIND
"THE MONKEY MIND"
PRE-FRONTAL CORTEX

SUBLIMINAL

UNCONSCIOUS MIND
"THE ELEPHANT"
DEFAULT MODE NETWORK

PRIMITIVE BRAIN
"THE LIZARD"
LIMBIC SYSTEM

Figure 7.13 The monkey, elephant and lizard mind
Source: *Medium digest*, Dave Gray, March 25th 2016

> *Our minds are built from experiences, and we use the term 'green mind' to indicate that there is an optimal daily mix of mainly PNS-blue, some mild SNS-red for interest and excitement, and occasional spikes of SNS-red when alarmed. Blue and red is best for health and happiness; too much red is bad for health.*
>
> (Pretty, 2017)

Our hunch is that Bill, because of the relationship he had with the small group in Forest School, particularly the adults, the site and his passion for the other beings on the site, *which don't judge*, his green mind kicked in, the mediator between the blue (rational) and red (instinctive). Although there was a spike in his sympathetic nervous system – he came out of this episode all the more prosocial and ecological; he had 'read' our minds – even if he didn't realise it in his monkey/prefrontal brain.

Having sat with Bill after this incident, by the corrugated vivarium, there was a certain 'energy' between Jon and Bill, what this was we cannot be sure, but there was empathy in that moment of silence – a mutual understanding and warm glow emerged – the oxytocin was working its magic. They came back to the circle calm and managed to talk about the incident and facilitate a mature conversation about what was behind the behaviours displayed. After this incident in the following weeks there was a more coherent 'feel' to our sessions – it was definitely more MWE as opposed to ME.

The more you can perceive the internal signals of the body, called interoception, the more insights you have, the more empathy you have, the more capacity for self-regulation.

(Siegel and Bryson 2018)

Neuroscientists are showing that in child and human development, mirror neurons and other neural pathways are demonstrating we are not soft-wired for aggression, violence and self-interest but for sociability, attachment, affection and companionship, and our first drive is the need for belonging. This is what Bill was striving for all along, and the natural world is an important part of the belonging jigsaw!

Our main message from this simple example of FS practice is that there are a number of brain processes at work here, and it is the interrelatedness of the areas of the brain that is developing a 'system of thinking, feeling, being and doing'. Rather than "I think therefore I am", we prefer "I feel, therefore I am", which brings us much more into the brain, body, environment interaction.

The four CARE neural pathways

What this means for practice is that we need to provide a safe, non-threatening, accepting environment, or as Amy Banks (2015) articulates so well in her book, to ensure that the four neural pathways are supported:

Calm – by being calm ourselves we can encourage calm in our learners and move away from chaos and a state of hypervigilance – strengthening our 'smart vagus' and PNS.

Accepted – by ensuring all are part of the learning community and accepted by the leader without judgment. The physical pain part of the frontal cortex processing has been shown to light up in exactly the same place (the dorsal anterior cingulate part of the cortex) when socially excluded, often through judgmental statements – being accepted and not excluded are key to supporting a strong link between the limbic and prefrontal cortex.

Resonant – when leaders show empathy by mirroring and reflecting back (but not too much – see next chapter), we are 'wiring' together and strengthening each other's nervous systems. This is the 'connecting' practice we all strive for.

Energetic – when we tap into other people's motivations and work together on meaning making, using learner-centred dialogue (see Language and Communication at FS – The Art of Dialogue, a Listening Conversation section in Chapter 11). When this system is working, when we get those light bulb moments and feel good about our learning, especially in the company of others (social learning), dopamine is released. One of the pathways that can be stimulated is the meso-limbic – from brain stem to amygdala, thalamus to orbitomedial prefrontal cortex (decision-making), looping back to brain stem to modulate dopamine production. One of the keys to strengthening this pathway is to support the seeking system that the amygdala links into – giving choice, tuning in, 'playing with', giving genuine acknowledgement and 'taking joy' in participating in learning all stimulate this pathway. The amount of contact with the leader will vary from learner to learner depending on their developmental age (see later) and need for adult interaction, but an energetic interest and certain amount of 'playing with' is needed to maintain this pathway.

Use it or lose it

One of big advantages Forest School and true Nature Pedagogy has over other nature-based educations is the long-term and regular nature of the programme. What this means in terms of brain development is that the myelination of the pathways is stronger. It is literally 'use it or lose it' and we can, in the longer term, change our brains. What is myelination? Myelin is a whitish material made up of protein and fats that surrounds the brain cells in sheaths, like a form of insulation. The more we repeat an action or interaction, the thicker the sheath becomes and more resilient the neural pathway. It has been shown a variable rate of reinforcement – doing the same thing but in different ways and applying the same task/interaction in different contexts – results in a thicker myelin sheath. So, for example, when we perform a simple whittling task on a piece of wood then use it to make something more complicated and keep repeating this, we will eventually lay down the 'action' more permanently, laying down more myelin. This applies equally to emotional, communication and relationship building pathways as to certain physical development, 'hard' skills and 'reasoning' pathways. This happens throughout life. There are periods when myelination is more active in neurotypical brains, notably before 7 years old and in early adolescence, but with the first studies done in the late 1990s, neuroscientists discovered that adult brains can also make neurons and myelinise. The brain can, throughout its life, make new pathways through repetition and myelination. Experience that is repetitive, patterned and consistent will be represented by strong neural connections (Spitzer et al., 2003).

This is good news for any educator, and it means that nature education can reignite the pathways that we inherited over the years through the 'natural intuitive' connections and understandings we made while living in the natural world. As stated in Chapters 2 and 3, these theories were espoused by evolutionary biologist E O Wilson (1984) with his theories on biophilia, something now being applied to therapeutic green interventions See.

Brain development

So far, we have referred to some of the developments in the brain as we grow – for 'typical' brain development. To finish up this chapter, we felt it useful to distinguish some of the key brain developments in age and that can be related to the 'human' development phases outlined earlier and the development of our SELF/SOUL.

The hand model of the brain, (see Figure 7.14) developed by Dan Siegel, is a simple, accessible way to explain the brain and some of its functions to children as young as 5 or 6. Using appropriate language for the age group, and becoming a little dramatic, can make understanding the brain for young children really fun! I have heard children as young as 2 years old being able to reflect that their 'amygdala' is really fired up!

All experience (cognitive, emotional, social, physical) allows the brain to create an internal representation of the external world. The development of maps of representations in particular areas of the brain will depend on an individual's experience. The wheel in Figure 7.15 gives a broad and generalised understanding of stages of brain development.

Closing comments

We have tried to simplify the current brain/mind thinking and realise we have probably done the field an injustice in trying to show how this relates to Nature Pedagogy. In the Chapter 9 online appendix, we have shown how it fits with established pedagogies, and through the case studies shown how methods of educating in a Forest School way link to brain and body development. There is a current tide looking at emotional well-being and the brain/body 'balance', which is the basis for prefrontal lobal innovative and purposeful thinking. This understanding is desperately needed if we are to have well-being and soulful, prosocial and pro-environmental minds. Even as we write, OFSTED, the English school inspection body, is now recognising this as something they need to look at more closely in schools.

To sum up, we have a lot in common with Jules Pretty's 'Manifesto for the Green Mind'. Pretty states that he feels there are three types of 'integrated' engagement to cultivate a green mind, which is so important for ecological/human balance:

- Nature engagement
- Social engagement
- Craft engagement

All three are key elements of Forest School. Chapters 12 and 13 go on to show how these nature and craft engagements can be integrated and woven into a Forest School programme, while the next chapter will look at how prosocial engagement can be facilitated in a natural world/ Forest School context.

WHOLE-BRAIN KIDS: Teach Your Kids About Their Downstairs and Upstairs Brain

YOUR DOWNSTAIRS BRAIN AND YOUR UPSTAIRS BRAIN

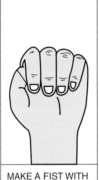

MAKE A FIST WITH YOUR HAND, THIS IS WHAT WE CALL A HAND MODEL OF YOUR BRAIN. RE-MEMBER HOW YOU HAVE A LFFT SIDE TO YOUR BRAIN? WELL YOU ALSO HAVE AN UPSTAIRS AND A DOWN-STAIRS PART OF YOUR BRAIN.

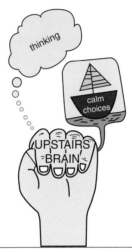

THE UPSTAIRS BRAIN IS WHERE YOU MAKE GOOD DECISIONS AND DO THE RIGHT THING, EVEN WHEN YOU ARE FEELING REALLY UPSET.

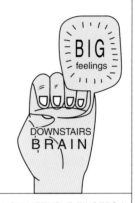

NOW LIFT YOUR FINGERS A LITILE BIT. SEE WHERE YOUR THUMB IS? THAT'S PART OF YOUR DOWN-STAIRS BRAIN, AND IT'S WHERE YOUR REALLY BIG FEELINGS COME FROM. IT LETS YOU CARE ABOUT OTHER PEOPLE AND FEEL LOVE. IT ALSO LETS YOU FEEL UPSET, LIKE WHEN YOU'RE MAD OR FRUS-TRATED.

THERE'S NOTHING WRONG WITH FEELING UPSET; THAT'S NORM AL, ESPECIALLY WHEN YOUR UPSTAIRS BRAIN HELPS YOU CALM DOWN. FOR EXAMPLE, CLOSE YOUR FINGERS AGAIN. SEE HOW THE UPSTAIRS THINKING PART OF YOUR BRAIN IS TOUCHING YOUR THUMB, SO IT CAN HELP YOUR DOWNSTAIRS BRAIN EXPRESS YOUR FEELINGS CALMLY?

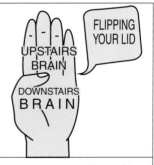

SOMETIMES WHEN WE GET REALLY UPSET, WE CAN FLIP OUR LID. RAISE YOUR FINGERS LIKE THIS. SEE HOW YOUR UPSTAIRS BRAIN IS NO LONGER TOUCHING YOUR DOWNSTAIRS BRAIN? THAT MEANS IT CAN'T HELP IT STAY CALM.

Figure 7.14 Hand model of the brain

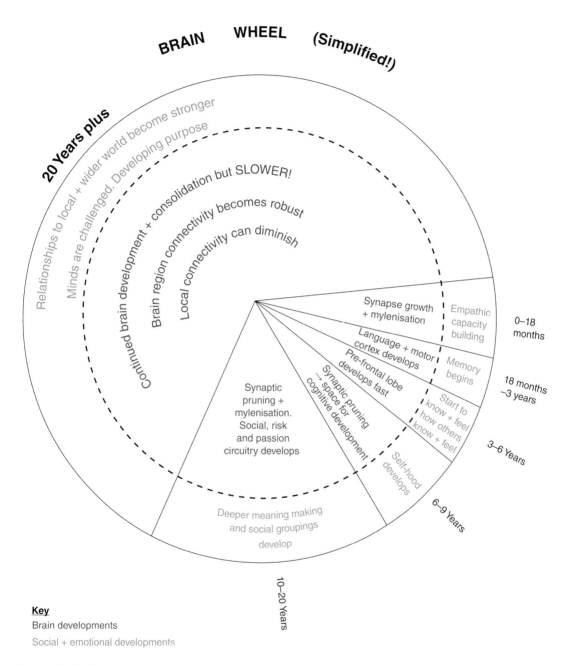

Figure 7.15 Simplified brain development wheel (see also social/emotional/psychological and physical wheels across lifetime in Chapter 4)

QUESTIONS FOR PRACTICE

Do you ever help children learn to think, that is, realise their own metacognition, by working with them to understand their brain/body/environment relationships?

How do you, as a practitioner, work with the slow forms of thinking to support the more instinctual/ belief systems that you may hold?

With a better understanding of the parasympathetic and sympathetic systems, how do you help yourself to self-regulate and self-soothe in order to come into 'balance'?

How do you facilitate the CARE pathways with the learners you are working with in a nature setting?

USEFUL RESOURCES

Mind Your Head by Heather Thompson and Sean McGuire (NEELB). A useful simple guide to brain physiology easy to use with young children, lots of good pictures.

Wired to Connect: The Surprising Link between Brain Science and Strong, Healthy Relationships by Amy Banks (2015, Penguin). A really good read with some useful 'brain-based' models for practice.

The Science of Parenting – How Today's Brain Research Can Help You Raise Happy, Emotionally Balanced Children by Margot Sunderland (2016, Dorling Kindersley). A well-illustrated book on brain development in the early years in particular.

All of these Dan Siegel film clips give a good insight into the brain-mind-body relationships and how we can support healthy human emotional and social development;

Dan Siegel 2 min version: www.youtube.com/watch?v=gm9ClJ74Oxw

Dan Siegel 8 min version: www.youtube.com/watch?v=f-m2YcdMdFw

Longer written description: www.psychalive.org/minding-the-brain-by-daniel-siegel-m-d-2/

Also see Daniel Siegel's blog: www.drdansiegel.com/blog/

Teenage brain understandings and resources:

The Teenage Brain by Daniel Siegel (2014): https://youtu.be/TLULtUPyhog; this is found at Dalai Lama Center for Peace and Education. See https://dalailamacenter.org/learn/daniel-siegel-teenage-brain.

Sarah-Jayne Blakemore: "The Mysterious Workings of the Adolescent Brain" (2012) TED, https://youtube/6zVS8HIPUng

The following books all give a good understanding of the adolescent brain in an accessible way:

Blame My Brain: The Amazing Teenage Brain Revealed by Nicola Morgan (Walker Books, 2013).

Brainstorm by Daniel Siegel (Scribe Publications, 2014).

The Teenage Brain: A Neuroscientist's Survival Guide To Raising Teenagers And Young Adults by Frances Jensen (HarperCollins, 2015).

BIBLIOGRAPHY

Alexander, R J (2017) *Towards Dialogic Teaching: Rethinking Classroom Talk* (5th edition). Dialogos. See www.robinalexander.org.uk/dialogic-teaching.

Armour, J (1991) Intrinsic Cardiac Neurons. *Journal of Cardiovascular Electrophysiology* 2(4): 331–341.

Banks, A (2015) *Wired to Connect: The Surprising Link between Brain Science and Strong, Healthy Relationships*. Penguin.

Barrett, L F (2017) *How Emotions Are Made: The Secret Life of the Brain*. New York: Pan Books.

Biel, L (2014) *Sensory Processing Challenges: Effective Clinical Work with Kids & Teens*. New York: Norton Professional Book.

Blakemore, S J (2018) *Inventing Ourselves: The Secret Life of the Teenage Brain*. Penguin.

Bowlby, J (1980) *Attachment and Loss*, Vol 3. New York: Basic Books.

Buhner, S H (2004) *Secret Teachings of Plants: The Intelligence of the Heart in the Direct Perception of Nature*. Rochester, VT: Bear and Company.

Carpenter, S (2012) That Gut Feeling. *American Psychological Association Monitor Journal* 43(8). See www.apa.org/monitor/2012/09/gut-feeling.

Claxton, G (1997) *Hare-Brain and Tortoise-Mind – How Intelligence Increases When You Think Less*. London: Fourth Estate.

Cryan, J and Dinan, T (2018) *The Psychobiotic Revolution*. National Geographic.

DeFelipe, J (2011) The evolution of the brain, the human nature of cortical circuits, and intellectual creativity. Frontiers in human anatomy

Hadhazy, A (2010) Think Twice: How the Gut's "Second Brain" Influences Mood and Well-Being. *Scientific American* (February 12). See https://www.scientificamerican.com/article/gut-second-brain/.

Halpern, J (2003) What Is Clinical Empathy? *Journal of General Internal Medicine* 18: 670–674.

Herculano-Houzel, S (2009) The Human Brain in Numbers: A Linearly Scaled-Up Primate Brain. *Frontiers in Human Neuroscience Journal*. See www.frontiersin.org/articles/10.3389/neuro.09.031.2009/full.

Iacoboni, M (2009) *Mirroring People: The Science of Empathy and How We Connect with Others*. Picador.

Kahneman, D (2011) *Thinking, Fast and Slow*. Penguin.

Learning – Mind see www.learning-mind.com/the-human-heart-mind/.

Maclean, P (1990) *The Triune Brain in Evolution*. Springer.

Panksepp, J and Bevin, L (2012) *The Archaeology of Mind: Neuroevolutionary Origins of Human Emotions*. New York: W.W Norton & Co.

Pert, C (1997) *Molecules of Emotion. Why You Feel the Way You Feel*. Scribner.

Phelps, E (2004) Human Emotion and Memory: Interactions of the Amygdala and Hippocampal Complex. *Science Direct* 14: 198–202.

Porgers, S (2011) *The Pocket Guide to the Polyvagal Theory: The Transformative Power of Feeling Safe*. W.W Norton & Co.

Pretty, J (2017) Manifesto for the Green Mind. *Resurgence and Ecologist* (March–April).

Roe, J and Aspinall, P (2009) *Forest School: Evidence for Restorative Health Benefits in Young People*. Forest Commission Scotland.

Siegel, D and Bryson, T (2018) *The Yes Brain: How to Cultivate Courage, Curiosity, and Resilience in Your Child*. New York: Random House Books.

Spitzer et al. (2003, February) Emotional Context Modulates Subsequent Memory Effect. *Neuroimage* 18(2): 439–447.

Sunderland, M (2016) *The Science of Parenting: How Today's Brain Research Can Help You Raise Happy, Emotionally Balanced Children*. Dorling Kindersley.

Van der Kolk, B (2014) *The Body Keeps the Score. Mind, Brain and Body in the Transformation of Trauma*. Penguin.

Wilson, E O (1984) *Biophilia*. Cambridge: Cambridge University Press.

8 Behavioural theories – the underpinning of a healthy problem-solving community

This chapter will look in more detail at how working with feelings and the brain-mind-body relationship in the natural world can help us move to a healthy prosocial and ecological community. In order to do that we will explore

- 'behavioural' constructs – behaviourist and constructivist needs-based theories and practice.
- the role of empathy in our practice.
- how to get to the 'energetic' pathway where everyone is realising their own learning – the growth mindset and self-worth.
- how we work with everyone's needs and emotional literacy, including our own as practitioners, as we move through life.
- what working with some special needs looks like.

> When emotional intelligence merges with spiritual intelligence, human nature is transformed.
>
> (Deepak Chopra, 1997)

COMPONENTS OF TOTAL BEHAVIOUR – THE IMPORTANCE OF FEELINGS

Within the Forest School approach, we return again and again to the human being as a holistic, integrated person (see Chapter 3). In this most simple understanding we have four key parts to our experience – our thoughts (head), our feelings (our heart), our actions (our body) and our physiology (body) – these components are what make our total behaviour (Glasser, 1998). In addition, our direct experience of life moves between the relationship with our masculine and feminine sides, our yang and yin, the doing and being sides, the thinking and feeling sides. The inevitable tensions between these aspects of life influence our behaviour and mind, brain, body and environment relationships.

At the earlier stages of life, we experience life in our bodies, full of feeling and present-centredness. As our brains develop, we learn to articulate and emotionally regulate, thinking before reacting, consciously applying our thoughts to our feelings. This is expanded on with the emotional and social development wheel in the next chapter building on the brain development outlined in the previous chapter. In Western culture, we have valued our rational capacities over and above our heart/feelings, in many cases leaving us entirely disconnected from our feelings. However, it is our feelings that are our best compass in life, and our head and thought systems are best when working on behalf of our heart, as shown in the previous chapter. Often as adults it is our distractions and addictions that keep us away from our feelings. The way back to health and well-being is through our feelings.

BEHAVIOUR CONSTRUCTS

Behaviour is a form of communication

Jon remembers the head teacher of a junior school he was working with back in the early 1980s who accepted all behaviour with such graciousness and non-judgment. Her mantra was "remember . . . all behaviour is a form of communication of needs and feelings – not positive or negative, it just *is*".

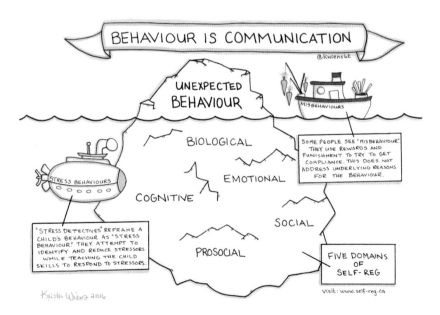

Figure 8.1 Behaviour is always trying to communicate something – all behaviour is communication!
Source: www.self-reg.ca

We all have feelings and whatever comes up is OK; we cannot deny an individual's feelings and it is OK to be fearful, anxious, dismayed, upset, joyous, delighted, disgusted, cranky, infuriated etc. – it is what makes us human. What matters is how we react to this 'humanness' and how these feelings are expressed through our actions – some would say this is a *humanist* perspective. As there are many ways of responding to another person's behaviour, this often depends on the ways we frame behaviour. We are going to concentrate here on two broad 'frames' that have pervaded our Western education systems as to how we react to behaviour. These frames relate to how our values, outlined in Chapter 1, are enacted.

BEHAVIOURISM

Much of the attitudes towards behaviour presented in UK schools is based on behaviourism, as originally espoused by many psychologists and educators in the 20th century. B F Skinner (1972) was one of the most influential psychologists of the mid-20th century when it comes to education. The basic tenet of behaviourism is that behaviour can be 'managed' and 'conditioned' externally, largely through a reward and punishment system. Skinner's theories on behaviour were mostly about rewarding for the behaviour you wish for. 'Operant conditioning' as proposed by Skinner said you do something deemed 'good' because you are rewarded for it and the variable rate of reinforcement, through rewards, is more effective than the regular 'constant'. Let's put this into a Forest School context.

A few years ago, Jon was mentoring a Forest School leader who loved heaping praise on her learners. In the first session he observed a number of statements she made with the Year 1 group she was running the programme with, along the lines of "Good stick carrying Josh", "What a wonderful mud pie", "I was impressed by the way you all stayed within the boundaries" . . . and many more. It seemed the way she operated in the classroom had moved outside. The behaviour developed by the group was operant on her 'reward' system of praise – operant conditioning.

Jon observed this and just fed back his observations on what he'd heard.

She said, "Yes, this is how I was trained and see no harm in it; indeed the children respond well to praise. I was using this in this session to 'train' them in the ways of Forest School to help them feel safe".

Jon asked, "Do you use any form of punishment at school?"

"I feel that extreme punishment, such as exclusion and isolation, is counterproductive and more damaging, as it definitely doesn't meet their needs to belong."

Jon agreed with her, and she continued, "I really have thought about this since the training, Jon."

So Jon asked, "What will you do when they don't comply to the agreements (her word) made at Forest School?"

She said, "If this happens regularly, I would start with some gentle reminders of what to do, rather than not what to do" – an often used and effective strategy of working with the positive rather than negative actions and dialogue, congruent with Carol Dweck's growth mindset. . . . "If this still doesn't work I would have to admonish the child and work through with them how to behave appropriately."

Jon asked, "What sort of admonishment works then?"

"Well, in the class we express our disappointment and state it is not acceptable and you may want to apologise to the other(s) for your inappropriate behaviour."

Jon felt he had moved the conversation into a judgmental arena, so he restated, "So the way this works in school, you are saying you intend to get the behaviour you reward for?"

Short silence. . . "Yes."

"Do you have any other reward systems?"

"Yes," she replied. "We have stars which build up to eventually become something that may aid their learning, like a book or something that they would like that relates to learning – last year a pupil had a pair of binoculars. I'm not sure how healthy that was for the rest of the class."

This is a common approach to working with and responding to appropriate and inappropriate behaviours in our school system, and we must say the binocular reward seems a sensitive, purposeful way of working with rewards. There are 'degrees' of Skinnerism manifested in many of our schools, and we have witnessed its extreme application in Forest School settings. The ultimate punishment being to exclude, causing physical pain (see the accepting pathway in the previous chapter), or even worse being used as a reward, the reward being you can attend if you behave at school. Interestingly, when you delve into what Skinner was proposing about operant conditioning, he never really promoted punishment as a way of 'controlling behaviour'. Skinner actually also stated that when we act meanly, we feel meanly, not vice versa; he didn't see children as natural subverters of the system – guilt does kick in. What is dangerous is when the guilt turns into shame and someone feels that they are a bad person.

Reframing behaviourism

Often inappropriate behaviour is displayed not because a person won't 'behave', but because they can't.

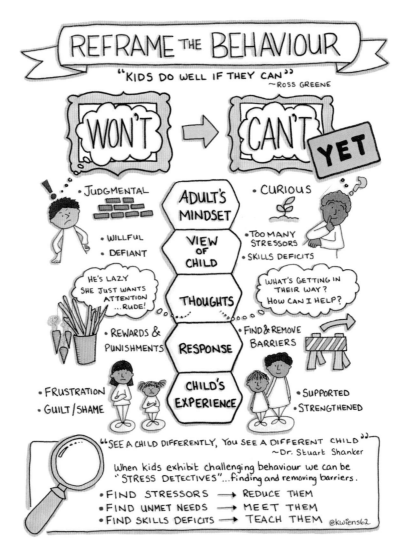

Figure 8.2 Reframing behaviours can change the way we understand the communication and our responses to certain inappropriate behaviours

Source: www.self-reg.com

What Skinner was saying is that we do have a reward system in our brains and bodies that can influence our behaviour and that responds to cues in our environment. This is borne out by all the neuroscience.

What happens, however, when the reward becomes the motivator – right down to "I know I am pleasing the Forest School leader because she is complimenting me"; what happens when that reward is removed completely? Should the reward not be the joy of learning and achieving for its own sake? It is a hard call, especially when we look at that energetic neural pathway. We do revel in focused specific praise and 'working with another', especially when we know that the praise and compliment comes from the other's heart, when it is not the formulaic type of praise often witnessed in the school system (see Banks' energetic pathway in previous chapter, page 165). This can definitely work in the short run in terms of learning and 'behaving' in the moment, but is it a long-term solution to non-prosocial and non-ecological behaviour? Ironically, Skinner's experiments showed a gradual extinction of the desired behaviour when rewards were eventually eliminated. Hall and Jackson (1988) showed that constant praise, smiles and 'pats on the back' with a boy who was highly disruptive and on task for only 25% in the school day showed that eventually he was on task for 70% of the day. The teacher then withdrew the reinforcement and the child's behaviour deteriorated.

The extreme end of behaviourism is where you know punishment/withdrawal of external rewards is seen as *the consequence* if you don't comply to a certain set of controls; public

Table 8.1 The dangers of external controlling of behaviour

Danger to self-confidence	Autonomy is a fundamental need which gives people the confidence to make decisions about their own lives. When taken away, it can have a negative impact on mental health.
Danger to self-esteem	Rewards and punishments are based on an adult's judgment of how good or bad a child's behaviour is. This can lead to the child thinking that another's opinion of them counts more than their own.
Danger to motivation for learning	Rewards and punishments are extrinsically rather than intrinsically motivated, meaning the child is behaving in a way to get a reward or to avoid punishment rather than for the sake of learning.
Danger to creativity and resilience	Rewards and punishments can make children fear making mistakes, so they are less likely to try something new.
Danger to self-regulation	When rewards and punishments are given out, children are not taught to monitor and regulate their own behaviour, but rather come to believe this is the responsibility of an adult or other authority figure.
Danger to social and emotional intelligence	Rewards and punishments focus children's minds on what will happen to *them* if they exhibit inconsiderate behaviour. If the reward or punishment is removed, how will a child choose to behave? Surely, we should be teaching children that considerate behaviour requires thinking about *others*.
Danger to development of problem-solving skills	Rewards and punishments teach learners that they must obey, do as they are told and not question rather than problem solve and think critically about behaviour.
Danger to vulnerability	Rewards and punishments teach children to comply with directions given by an adult or figure of authority. This can make children more susceptible to abuse as they'll be less likely to protest or object to it when it comes from a person of authority.

Source: Louise Porter (2003)

humiliation, corporal punishment or exclusion being the manifestation of this. The ultimate punishment, in our case, would probably be withdrawal from a nature-based programme, or being told to 'sit away' as a form of punishment, in order to 'control', rather than using a voluntary strategy to help the individual work through a way of coping with a stressful situation. Sometimes punishment can be effective in the short term, but at what cost?

The real consequence of much inappropriate behaviour was so pointedly stated in Jon's earlier conversation with the new Forest School practitioner – *it exacerbates an unmet need of wanting to belong*.

We need to respond to the uniqueness of every group and facilitator. As a bottom line, we need to feel safe enough to 'hold' a group's process, and sometimes we don't have enough resources to help many individuals manage their behaviours that are challenging. This means we might eventually have to remove someone from a group, ideally offering a more suitable programme with higher ratios and/or experienced staff.

So if this approach can be so damaging, why is it so prevalent? What we are saying is we need to be aware of extremes of any approach, and in the end we are trying to enable children to take responsibility and have power over their own learning and to develop meaningful purpose, resilience and agency in their lives.

Modelling

Bandura is another behaviourist who bridged to a more intrinsic 'frame' with his social learning theory but still relied on an external influence to change learners' behaviours. He propounded the modelling theory of external influence (1997), made famous by his Bobo doll experiments in which students imitated other students' treatments of said dolls. Modelling, mirroring and attuning to people are incredibly skilful strategies for supporting emotional regulation and building supportive relationships. In nature education and Forest School, this 'theory' can be seen in action all the time when teaching hard skills.

Example of modelling

"I am going to demonstrate how to use a saw to cut a pole from a hazel tree."

By **demonstrating** the safe carrying of the saw, selection of the pole, making the area safe, checking escape routes, showing the correct safe position and then technique, taking the pole out carefully so as not to injure others, showing gratitude to the tree and then showing a safe way to drag to avoid tripping or hitting others and to make it easy on oneself, *we hope the learner will in effect copy all that behaviour to stay safe and effective in the task*.

Figure 8.3 A trainee modelling coppicing to another trainee

According to Bandura, there are four key elements to his social learning theory for this type of modelling to be effective:

- Attention
- Retention
- Reproduction
- Motivation

These are outlined in this chapter's online appendix.

It is the motivational element that is key if modelling is to be effective, activating the energetic neural pathway through the release of oxytocin and dopamine.

Whenever working with behaviours and social/nature interactions, we always should have in mind, whatever our approach, the universal rights of a child from the United Nations (UN) and the basic human needs (and this includes all learners . . . not just the majority). Article 29, in particular, concerns education:

Education must develop every child's personality, talents and abilities to the full. It must encourage the child's respect for human rights, as well as respect for their parents, their own and other cultures, and the environment.

(UNICEF UK, 2019)

When you boil this and other universal rights down and look at the detail, this includes three important rights;

- a right to respect
- a right to learn
- a right to feel safe

Using a sensitive modelling approach, you can see that we are starting to hand the task itself and power over the learning of the task to the learner through giving choice and keeping out of their hair! Which leads us on to the second common behavioural frame in our education systems – constructivism.

CONSTRUCTIVISM

If we believe that the only person who can ultimately control and manage our own behaviour is ourselves, then we often move to a more constructivist view of behaviour and learning. Here, we value the ability of the learner to problem solve through stressful situations, rather than having to be controlled by other people's actions.

Learners continuously test their own meaning making through social interaction and negotiation, and interaction with the physical environment. Each person has a different interpretation and construction of knowledge process. The learner is not a blank slate (*tabula rasa*) but brings past experiences and cultural factors to a situation and is influenced by the cues of the environment. Vygotsky (Mooney, 2012) is probably one of the most prominent social development constructivists. While there is always external influence, a constructivist approach to behaviour is based very much on our own internal feelings and needs and being able to think about feelings and control our own actions *with* others and the external environment.

Choice theory – a needs-based approach to behaviour

Glasser (1998) is one of the major influential constructivists of the 20th century with his work on 'choice theory' and reality therapy in the classroom. He stated that we behave through expression of five basic categories of needs that may in any moment be met or unmet. There are many more needs articulated by other constructivists and psychologists, however we feel that the following can encompass others in broad terms, so let's stick with these for the moment:

- Power
- Survival (basic physical needs)
- Love and belonging
- Freedom
- Fun and play

Think about it now as you read this – what needs are being met to keep you a fulfilled human being, especially in the sphere of learning?

No doubt **power** (self-control) over your own learning will be one of them. Can I learn in a way that suits me best? Can I *ask* to learn in a way that makes sense and *control* this? Can I make my own choices? Does reading this book help me understand this approach or do I need to go out and try it out for myself? Make no mistake, the very fact that you have made your own choice to buy this book means you have made a decision that in some way these words are helping, but only by applying this stuff in your own way will it make sense!

Learning in lots of different places in a woodland with different people might mean I have a desire for **freedom** – would you prefer at this moment to be reading this outside?!

I may be less willing to take risks in my learning and always looking for the correct answer as not wanting to be seen to fail might mean I need to **survive**.

Desiring my own time and space to experiment with ideas and to also game play with the group – laugh and challenge – might mean I have a high need for **fun and play**.

I much prefer working out things with other people, like putting up a rope swing with friends, which might mean I look for **belonging and love**.

In choice theory, seven caring habits are offered to replace external control and the behaviourist view, which Glasser associates with seven deadly habits (see Table 8.2).

Glasser also stated that we are constantly striving for our own goals to achieve our 'total quality world'. By giving choice, we are more likely to take control of our own behaviour. While we cannot control the behaviours of others, we can control our responses to others' behaviours by the choices we make. In terms of our own behavioural traits, these often reflect our striving for what we desire – satisfying our own innermost motivations. In order to do this we often are conflicted by different needs and need to look for balance in terms of the goal at that particular time – be it to finish a tree planting project, to be with a particular group etc. If we are to get what

Table 8.2 Seven caring and seven deadly habits

Seven caring habits	Seven deadly habits
1 Supporting	1 Criticising
2 Encouraging	2 Blaming
3 Listening	3 Complaining
4 Accepting	4 Nagging
5 Trusting	5 Threatening
6 Respecting	6 Punishing
7 Negotiating differences	7 Bribing, rewarding to control

Source: Glasser, 1998

we need and display prosocial behaviour, we need to be able to understand our feelings that arise as a result of needs met or unmet and what the feelings are when we particularly identify conflicting needs.

Alfie Kohn, author of *Beyond Discipline* (2006), proposes there are three Cs to facilitate a more constructivist approach to self-management of behaviour in order to meet needs in an educational setting:

Choice – giving learners choice over their learning goals and approaches
Content – ensuring the content of the learning is meaningful to the life of the learner – this is where motivation and goals and the total quality world concept comes in
Community – ensuring the whole community is enabled through a problem-solving approach to understand how group interaction can promote prosocial behaviour

WORKING IN AN EMPATHIC WAY WITH BEHAVIOUR

To facilitate this constructive community, an open, accepting (empathic) and soothing calm environment is seen as key. To ensure this happens, the four CARE neural pathways need to be engaged (see page 165).

Establishing the way a community works together in a problem-solving way

How do we establish a community problem-solving approach to behaviour? How will we *be* together in a nature programme that supports *calm, accepting, resonating* and *energetic* relationships and reflects the values outlined in Chapters 1 and 3?

Many FS practitioners use another set of three Cs as cues:

Care for self
Care for each other
Care for the woods

We wonder how meaningful these are and whether this is really a problem-solving community-based approach. We need to encourage the learners to articulate what the these guiding principles might resemble, by being specific about what caring for ourselves really looks like – can we paint a picture or show through our bodies and behaviour what this means? (Notice there is no mention of *rules* – they are there to be broken even if made by the group!) Is it not much better to get the group to communicate what they 'need' and even start from their universal rights? The trick is how to do this in a meaningful way so there is a sharing of power but that it also follows the 'energetic' principles of a learner-focused nature pedagogic way, as outlined in Chapter 3. The dilemmas this presents and ways of working with this approach over time are illustrated by this start of a Forest School programme run by Caylin Gans.

As I gathered the group together in our final 20 minutes of the session, Jeffrey remained on his platform in the tree while everyone else came and sat down in our circle. He asked me if he could stay in the tree for our group meeting since it was right next to everyone anyway.

In an effort to include everyone in making this decision democratically, I passed on his question to the group. I asked, "How does everyone feel about Jeffrey staying in the tree during group meeting?" Immediately several of the children expressed they felt it wasn't fair. They wanted to be in a tree too, but there wasn't any room in Jeffrey's tree and there were no other trees nearby that were climbable. However, some kids said they didn't mind Jeffrey being in the tree and it wasn't a problem . . . How were we to make a decision when views were so divided?

Then a 7-year-old girl named Maggie shouted, "I have an idea!! We can do a vote! If more people vote it's ok for Jeffrey to stay in the tree, then he can stay. If more say he shouldn't, then he can come down." I looked to the group and all seemed to agree, including Jeffrey.

So I double checked this with Jeffrey, "Okay Jeffrey, so are you agreeing that if more people vote for you to come down from the tree then you'll be ok with that and you'll come down?"

Jeffrey thought about that for a moment and then said, "No! I don't want to come down. I'm not that far from everyone, so it's fine that I just stay in the tree."

Reluctantly, I told everyone we'd run out of time and needed to pack up and go. Democracy over. Jeffrey came down from the tree and we made our way out of the woods.

What I did decide to do is to try to find a way to address what had transpired the next time we met for continuity and closure. So, during the group meeting at the very beginning of the next session, I asked the group, "We have our main group agreements to look after ourselves, each other, and the forest, and I'm wondering whether anyone would like to add to or adjust these agreements in any way?"

There was a spattering of suggestions that included things like respecting each other's shelters (a previous source of conflict), always sitting in the same seat during group meetings, and . . . everyone sitting together either on a bench or on the ground (not up a tree) during group meetings.

I introduced a simple voting mechanism: thumbs up for agree, thumbs down for disagree, and thumbs sideways for neutral. One by one, we voted with our thumbs on each of the measures. We provided space for all to share their views and then adjusted our proposed agreement based on what people said until we came to consensus. In about 15 minutes we had new agreements:

- *We would take care of and respect other people's built work (e.g. a shelter or other project)*
- *We could sit in the same seat each time during group meetings if we wanted to, but didn't have to*
- *All would sit together on a bench or on the ground (not up a tree) during group meetings. Even Jeffrey agreed to that last one!*

In our experience, initially, the professional 'expert' will often be seen as the leader of a community group. It is essential, therefore, that early in the life of the group, people are given an opportunity to challenge the expert role so that the group can progress to a more collaborative and cohesive stage. It is also important that professionals react positively to such a challenge. It's important to be open to feedback (regardless of its validity or the eloquence with which it is phrased) and encourage further constructive and negative feedback.

(Sarkissian, 2009)

If we take an empathic approach to understanding learners' and our own needs, as outlined in the previous chapter with the story about Bill and the above case study, we are more likely to be seen as 'human' and willing to try to walk in other shoes.

To understand others in our community, especially those who may find the natural world threatening and unsafe – without the certainty of four walls and a container of rules – is to park our own experiences and judgments of others' insecurities. We need to try and 'be' with that feeling and express this by mirroring language – body and spoken, as shown in the following example. In this way both can feel a bond and have that "aha, they do understand what is happening for me" moment.

The group arrived and while they were from a school that had regularly been following Forest School with Jon's setting, this group was different. The teacher had sent in the baseline assessments and all but two of the learners lacked confidence and communication skills. They seemingly were tentative, and a couple of the group were hypervigilant. Jon attuned to this as soon as they got off the bus . . . it had taken a number of minutes to cajole a couple out of their seats. The class TA showed plenty of empathy and once all were off she said, "It's a bit different from school eh? I remember the first time I came here I was so nervous about meeting new people and I had no idea about going outside, I didn't even know any of the trees . . . I was scared in a shaky sort of way . . . this is Jon who helped me through that and now I know how exciting it can be in the end." She gave the group space and time to just be and really 'held' in that scary moment . . . she was very nervous when she first came to the training at the setting. Then she got down to their level and literally mimicked some of the body messages (we know that cells in our bodies pick up the brain messages hence we feel, see Pert, 1997) easing them into a warm smile and open stance that seemed to move the group from a shaky hunched state to a more shoulder lifted state. Jon was impressed with the 'I' statements she used and the energetic empathic sharing she showed. Jon could not help but join in sharing some of his 'butterflies' and then explaining how he eventually made them fly in formation so that inside feeling was warm and anticipatory at the same time.

Jon could also sense a feeling of shame that this group, in contrast to previous groups from the school, was nervous about coming into the woods and probably feeling the lesser for it. The problem with shame is that if we don't acknowledge it and remain silent and secretive about it, it just feeds on itself, whereas empathy and acknowledgement can reduce it (Brown, 2012).

We have talked about finding what makes a person 'tick' and what motivates them to realise their 'quality world' as a key to much of this prosocial behaviour, so we will now look at growth mindset and self-worth.

GROWTH MINDSET AND SELF-WORTH

> *We cannot tell what may happen to us in the strange medley of life. But we can decide what happens in us. How we can take it, what we do with it – and that is what really counts in the end.*

(Joseph Fort Newton, 1922)

There has been much said about the self-esteem movement and how it doesn't necessarily indicate particular prosocial or pro-ecological behaviours in the context of a compassionate caring society (see Elmer, 2001; Craig, 2009). In the last part of this chapter, we look at self-worth in light of the values outlined in Chapter 1 and growth mindset (Dweck, 2017).

Self-worth

Carl Rogers, well-known founder of the more humanist approach to 'person-centred' therapy and who rejected many of the tenets of behaviourism, believed each individual has the capacity to self-heal and behaves because of the way we perceive situations. He stated that our confidence in our own worth or abilities relates closely to

- sense of worth in a community,
- sense of belonging and
- sense of competence/power.

(Rogers, 1961)

Let's start with *sense of competence and power*. In 'promoting the holistic development of all those involved, fostering resilient, confident, independent and creative learners' (FS principle), we as practitioners often need to start with what our learners are motivated by. Very simply, offering a choice of experiences and new experiences can suddenly help learners realise, "this is something I have not done and I like it or am quite good at it". This also provides a new relationship that is built on mutual trust and agency. If you know their interests, you can work immediately with something that is going to be a motivator and tap into that sense of competence and power, if it is framed as a choice.

14-year-old Lisa was loud and throwing around what from the outside would seem as abusive words at people, but they were like water off the duck's back within this group. Lisa's baseline assessment stated that she liked makeup and tattoos! We had planned in the first session to offer dyeing with plants, playing with ropes and string, some running/tracking type games, as well as the usual 'home making' and cooking over a fire for lunch (if this was appropriate). Lisa immediately wanted to paint her skin, so once we were at the Forest School site we played a painting game to establish physical boundaries. She spent the rest of the morning arm painting and seemingly was not as loud as she normally was back in school, except with the tug of war towards the end of the session. She was fully engaged with the game and got very loud with a few choice words thrown in, but in an enthusiastic (not the normally abusive) way! Power and competence were being fed, and from Lisa's perspective she was being prosocial. Jon reflected back to Lisa on the walk back what he had observed and acknowledged how 'concentrated' she seemed in the morning and the 'joi de vivre' she showed in the tug of war . . . she replied, "joi de f*** what!" Jon stated that it meant the energy and zest and loud yet enthusiastic language, not mentioning the language he heard in the morning. The conversation continued, and during it Jon had acknowledged her and given his impression of her image and place in the group.

This is an important part of helping build *self-worth* and impressions of where the learners are at . . . trying also to build, from the start, a *sense of belonging* by reflecting a self-image.

Our job is to help children get a better self-image; create a realistic and attainable ideal self – not reinforce feelings of failure; to work with new skills in small achievable ways, eventually enabling learners to use those skills independently (see the tools section in Chapter 12); and to deal with knock-backs along the way. Maines and Robinson stated, "a sense of self and worth provides a child with the confidence to attempt difficult things without an incapacitating fear of failure" (Maines and Robinson, 1998). This inevitably creates a 'can do' growth mindset rather than a fixed mindset that nothing can change in terms of abilities and traits (Dweck, 2017).

Take a moment to consider your own sense of self and whether you feel you are worthy of love and belonging.

Can you:

1   Tell the story of who you are, with the courage to be imperfect (sense of courage)?
2   Are you kind to yourself first, before others (sense of compassion)?
3   Are you authentic, willing to let go of who you think you should be, to be who you are (sense of connection)?
4   Are you willing to say things like I love you or to ask for help, to be imperfect, to be seen (sense of vulnerability)?

According to Brene Brown (2017), your real sense of worthiness relates to these core four *sense qualities*.

The UK Forest School definition is:

Forest School is an inspirational process, that offers children and young people opportunities to achieve, develop confidence and self-esteem, through hands on learning experiences in a local woodland environment.

We feel that the self-esteem element needs to be a more explicit statement that relates more to this growth mindset, a willingness to be vulnerable and *self-worth*.

As educators, we have spent our careers hearing about the importance of self-esteem for young people, yet as we write the nation's mental health is deteriorating, with one in four young people suffering mental health difficulties, and this is increasing across the globe (Mental Health Foundation, 2015). Two of the key indicators and precursors to mental health are loneliness and not feeling worthy. We should be talking about self-worth rather than self-esteem, which is so often just equated with self-confidence. How well are we as educators, parents and leaders equipped to be vulnerable, be courageous, listen to our needs, and be in contact with what *we* feel and our worth to the community? Mental health starts with us.

Being able to express ourselves and regulate

In the Western world, indeed in most modern contexts, the importance of emotional literacy has not been well understood, and the repercussions of this contribute to a lack of well-being. Alongside developing a language around emotions, we also need to find our way to be comfortable with the expression of emotions. It is through expression that we release our anger, sadness and fear. Within these expressions of anger, hate, fear etc. we need to develop strategies to regulate ourselves and bring us back into our 'window of tolerance', the place between 'flipping our lid' and 'shutting down', and even extend it (described by D. Siegel, 2010).

Within this window, we need to be able to appropriately express and release our feelings. We are social beings, and our sense of self is formed by the careful interaction of our key carers from an early age, the important relationships (non-human and human) that give us feedback that we are essentially okay, loved and belong, and it is okay to have 'dark' feelings, but only if we can grow from them.

This development of relationship is likely to take longer if we are to accept that we all have dark feelings; it is more messy and does not necessarily lead to the outcomes we expect! It is 'emotional labour' (Hochschild, 2012); it takes work and energy.

What do we do when a young boy, let's call him Sam, is really popular and doesn't want to let a young girl, Helen, play with him at Forest School? Sam goes even further by saying that Helen can't come to his party (even though his party is in 6 months).

Sam appears to be mean and at the same time really popular! Poor Helen; she appears to feel sad and left out. What shall we do as the FS facilitator? Shall we take over? Is it okay for Sam to ask and get what he wants? Does he need to control everything? If so, why? Can Helen manage this on her own? Does she need help to communicate what she needs? Are you as the adult providing choices for her? Does this make you anxious or angry? Are you rescuing her from feeling sad or angry? Is there a problem to be solved? Does Helen need us to fix it?

As educators, this situation is a tricky one as we inevitably judge Sam and may want to 'rescue' Helen. We almost need to embrace what we see as a dark side of Sam and what this might trigger in ourselves. Well-known psychologist Carl Jung and wilderness therapist Bill Plotkin talk about the 'shadow and the unconscious'. They state we all have our shadows that, particularly as we get older, we need to embrace and explore in order to realise our full potential, motivating forces and self-worth. This is emotional labour and leads us to examine the drama triangle.

THE GROWTH MINDSET AND DRAMA TRIANGLE

Dr Stephan Karpman (1968) in his 'drama triangle' helps us to understand our power dynamics with other people and places. It is a dynamic model of social interaction and conflict that Karpman developed when he was a student of Eric Berne, MD, from transactional analysis. Ultimately, we are hoping to have healthy and resilient relationships.

> *Definition of a victim: a person to whom life happens.*
>
> (Peter McWilliams, source unknown)

In reality, we all play different roles within the triangle (see Figure 8.4). Often without realising we remain in the familiar positions, more comfortable in the role of persecutor, victim or rescuer, and blaming others for what they are doing to us, rather than taking ownership of our feelings. We all attempt to meet our personal (often unconscious) needs, rather than taking responsibility for our part in keeping the triangle going. The following is a summary of the different positions we play in the triangle.

Victim: Likes to be taken care of and feels helpless, sees others as the perpetrators of problems, and tends to be under-responsible, denying our own problem-solving abilities and potential for operating from our own generated power. We need to take responsibility for our own feelings and assume responsibility for ourselves and learn to take care of ourselves.

Rescuer: Gets to feel good by caretaking; we want to 'fix it or you' and are over-responsible. We don't often look at our own life. It's difficult for us to feel our worth beyond what we do

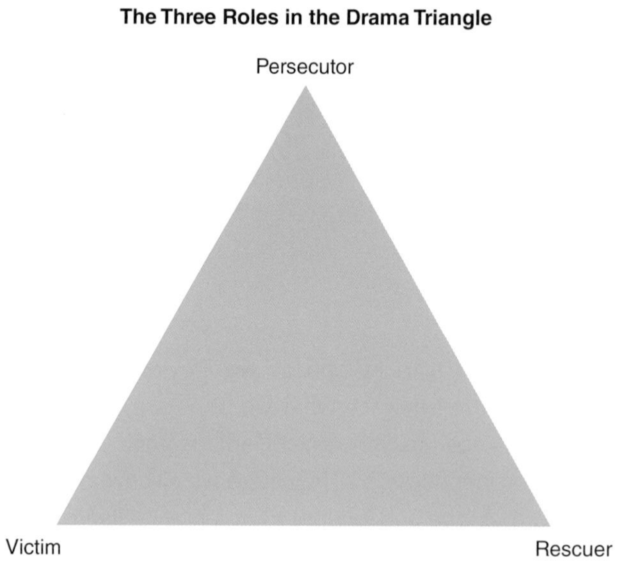

The Three Roles in the Drama Triangle

Persecutor

Victim   Rescuer

Figure 8.4 The drama triangle

for others, and this protects us from the fear of being alone. Rescuers need to learn to empower others to fix things themselves and encourage self-responsibility rather than promote dependency.

Persecutor: Likes to feel superior and self-righteous and fears loss of control – we overcome our sense of helplessness and shame by dominating others. We need to learn to express our own vulnerability and be self-accountable.

How do we get out of this unhealthy dynamic? We need to promote problem-solving and asking questions and support young people to ask for what they want (moving out of the victim role). We need to support and encourage the person to identify solutions themselves and solve it themselves to adopt a growth mindset (let's get round this problem attitude). Questions like, What would you like to see happen? What do you think you can do to change this?

These help the learner and facilitator move out of the victim and rescuer roles, encouraging a growth mindset. We need to be a challenger and be firm but fair, creating boundaries, and to show our feelings and ask if learners really need our help. All of us can learn to get our needs met without becoming a victim, persecutor or rescuer. We need to become self-directed and grow into adults who achieve their needs.

The only way to 'escape' the drama triangle is to function as an 'adult' and not to participate in the game.

(Goulet, source unknown)

These constructs are saying that it is not just the nice feelings we want to promote at Forest School. Is Forest School always a 'happy place'? Can we hold a space that supports young people (and adults) to communicate effectively, so that it is acceptable to have angry, sad and content feelings about ourselves? We need to be comfortable with our not-so-nice feelings, recognise them and show resilience to be able to work *with* them but not be overwhelmed by them.

How do we as practitioners interact with the Helen/Sam scenario? The first thing to say is this approach entails having a good relationship with the community, which takes time. We need to become the adult (not rescuer) and own our own feelings about the scenario.

First, we need to *check in with ourselves to discover what feelings these types of interactions generate in ourselves and what needs are being met/unmet in ourselves.* Is this my problem or Helen's and Sam's or the rest of the group's? If you feel there is a call for help from Helen, then you may intervene using the non-violent approach that encourages problem solving and treats the people involved as responsible listening humans – this process is outlined in the next chapter (Rosenburg, 2003).

At Forest School, we aim to provide a long-term educational programme. This is essential, as young people attending a short-term programme just start to build relationships and then leave! Initially, our aim is to become significant others to each student. Once this is established we can continue our work through observations of young people in varying situations. This relationship-building process can take as little as 6 weeks, but in other cases we might never establish a relationship. Without this significant relationship we cannot begin our work, and then we need to break away.

Breaking away

Context: A year-long woodland-based programme for young people experiencing mental health challenges.

X (with his back to me): *Fuck off!*

W: *I didn't like you saying that. I normally feel respected by you but I felt disrespected then. It sounds like I upset you by saying that. I would like to understand what happened.*

X: *Sorry.*

W: *Thank you. I wonder if it's difficult to think about leaving?*

X (turning to face me and shouting): *Yes, of course it is. It's fantastic here!*

For young people who have developed self-worth through working with significant others, there needs to be a definite plan for them to maintain this self-worth independently. This is achieved at Forest School by

- empowering young people to use skills independently.
- empowering young people by helping them to understand how they learn and act and to intro-duce strategies to cope with difficult situations (such as in the Jake story in the next chapter.)
- offering young people tasks with more responsibility.
- withdrawing slowly and sensitively as a significant other.

Working with neurodiversity and those with autistic spectrum condition

When you have met one autistic person, you have met one autistic person. This is a mantra we stick by, having worked with many autistic people; all have been different, some with an ability to 'read' emotions in a neurotypical way and others who have their own systems for dealing with social situations – and this includes sensory modulation systems, as outlined in the next section. Much of this chapter has referred to the neurotypical ways of working with feelings and behaviour, and we hope that in showing examples of practice some of the principles are similar to those when working with autistic people. The key is to see everybody as an individual with unique ways of working with feelings and communication. We, as practitioners, need to get to know the learner, their sensory preferences (see chapter 5 online appendix), ways of communicating and 'systemising' ways of behaving so they can contribute to the community in a comfortable way that is satisfying their needs.

For example, Jon worked with an autistic boy, called Caleb, who had little language. English was a second language. Every time he got off the bus he would take Jon's hat off his head and have to wear it for the whole session. It was his 'communication' saying, *I am going to Forest School*. Jon would let him take it and then he would back off. Every time just before he got on the bus going back to school, Caleb would put the hat back on Jon's head. The first time Jon was not there Caleb was completely withdrawn, partly because Jon was not there, but also because the hat was not there. Jon discovered that if he left his hat in the toolbox the next time he couldn't be there, that Caleb was OK as the hat was there! This was his Forest School 'system'.

Another autistic girl, Lydia, could not sit round the fire circle at the start of her programme – a routine that is fairly essential for creating this 'family' of learning. It took Jon and the other adults, who knew Lydia much better, a few weeks to realise she had to walk the site before she could sit down. She went off to walk and sing – this was part of her system. We adapted and would have a few min-utes of looking for sticks, putting up swings, doing things, before we got together. For the rest of that year we would follow this routine and always sing a song to start the session. Lydia engaged! Jon had to get to know her story.

One of the most well-known autistic stories is that of Temple Grandin, the compassionate animal scientist and whose book *Thinking in Pictures* was the first inside narrative of an autistic person. She showed how a person with autism is 'differently abled', not disabled. Her 'systems' are arranged around 'pictures'; her brain is 'visually indexed'. Many autistic people will say I am what I do, not necessarily what I feel, as the first port of call. The point is that we all have our own motivations in what makes us ourselves, and one of the key aspects of Forest School is the tapping into one of Glasser's fundamental needs – that of *freedom* to be who we are and find our skills and motivations. The label of autism, while sometimes helpful, does have this negative connotation, and yet without it we probably wouldn't have discovered quantum theory, have the infinite pleasure of listening to a Mozart requiem or indeed have more compassionate animal farming.

See the resources section at the end of the chapter for more detail on working with autism. We refer you to Michael James' book *Forest School and Autism* and the resources he is developing for Forest School, and Phoebe Caldwell's responsive communication methods.

Sensory modulation

The natural world has been shown to stimulate the 54 senses identified by Michael Cohen. He demonstrated that these 54 senses can strengthen our bonds with the non-human and human, and in the end with the planet (Cohen, 2007). We do not have enough space to dedicate to all these senses and recommend you visit the website cited in the bibliography at the end of this chapter. However, using the eight key sense systems (Ayres, 1972) as described in Chapter 5, we will now look at some practices nature educators can use to support processing disorders in order to achieve sensory integration.

These eight systems have been categorised into proximal and distal senses. The proximal senses (tactile, proprioception, vestibular, gustatory and interoception) inform us what is happening internally and immediately externally to our bodies. The distal systems (olfactory, auditory and visual) inform us about the wider environment we are in, enabling us to plan our responses as opposed to simply reacting when a stimulus affects the body. For example, if we are in the woods and we hear a scream nearby (it could be a human scream or an animal's distress call), we automatically check to see where it is. Based on our interpretation of that information, we then decide whether we need to stay put because everything is OK, or move to avoid being attacked, or go and find the source of the noise. In other words, our auditory and visual systems link in with our proximal senses to enable us to take anticipatory action. If we experience some sort of sensory processing disorder (SPD), our senses do not necessarily lead to this type of integration, and in order to cope we may withdraw or react in a seemingly extreme form of behaviour in order to regulate. Sensory integration theory suggests observations of these behaviours indicate that neural modulation of sensory information is faulty (Bundy et al., 2002).

It seems with many SPD instances, working with the proprioceptive sensory system helps us to calm. This is what the natural world has in its favour, as there are so many opportunities to exercise this sense from digging to climbing, swinging, jumping, balancing, running, lifting sticks and tools, pulling branches, pushing wheel barrows and trolleys (we know that one!), throwing sticks, playing tug of war, playing hide and seek, and crawling through mud, along branches and on grass – the list is endless. The very nature of the background subliminal stimulation of all our senses can support more integration and modulation of senses, and with long-term immersion

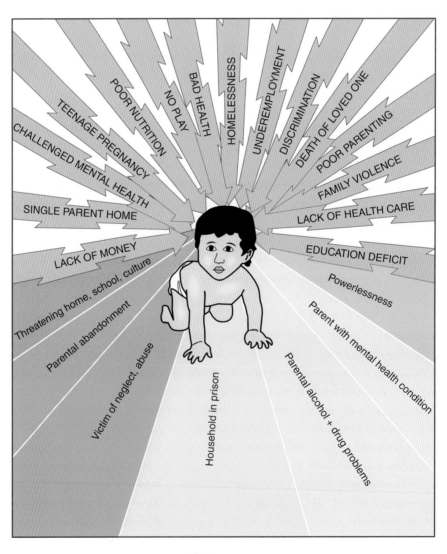

Figure 8.5 Adverse childhood experiences (ACE)

in a wood, in particular, it is felt that this can really boost mental health in people with SPD – the research into this is still young.

Beware! Those who are prone to aggressive behaviour may become more aggressive if engaged in 'fast' movement. For example, a hide and seek game that involves running can mirror fight and flight patterns and escalate aggression. It is also important to differentiate whether the child is triggered by the sensory experience or by an attachment experience. Children may tolerate everyday touch experiences but become frozen or aggressive if nurturing touch is provided, owing to their previous experiences of abuse (Bhreathnach, 2018).

Also, if you know there is a need to positively handle a learner, we highly recommend getting some training. One training provider that many organisations use is 'Team Teach' (see https://www.teamteach.co.uk/), which specialises in positive behaviour management; see the Bernard Allen books recommended in the useful resource section at the end of this chapter. This is a sensitive issue particularly for those children and young people who have had adverse childhood experiences.

Our early experiences have a huge effect on our ability to cope with stress and on the development of our emotional and sensory processing systems. Traumatised children struggle to self-regulate across environments and find it difficult to trust and feel safe with adults. These children tend to experience the world through a 'fear lens' (Perry, 2005).

High cortisol levels during the vulnerable years of 0–3 increase activity in the brain structures that are involved in hypervigilance and arousal. For such a child, the slightest stress unleashes a new surge of stress hormones, causing hyperactivity, anxiety and impulsive behaviour (Early Intervention, The next steps Jan 2011, Graham Allen MP).

The ACE (adverse childhood experiences) Study is the largest study of its kind, with 17,337 participants examined to research the impact *in adults* of adverse childhood experiences (see Figure 8.5). It examined how ACEs affect our minds and bodies and have long-term impact on physical health and well-being without support. Over a person's lifespan, the negative medical, social and economic consequences are in no doubt, as illustrated by the ACE pyramid in Figure 8.6. The consequence of not supporting these children, young people and adults results in the widespread crisis in physical illnesses and rise in mental health issues like teenage suicide. The results show that 28% of children suffer physical abuse. This result alone has huge significance for the potential support that the children we meet in schools or in the doctor's surgery might need. When children and teenagers experience high arousal states of emotional intensity, they react with fight or flight or freeze behaviour, resulting in high anxiety or very challenging behaviour. Some young people and children continue to be punished for this, when they are experiencing an incapacity to emotionally regulate. They have yet to learn how to gain mastery over their internal sensations and emotions and release trauma.

With traumatised children, their sensory systems have become so sensitive to the possibility of danger that they become 'sensory defensive'. Children lash out from sensory overload but are punished for 'bad behaviour'. You are not able to learn if you can't regulate. Building a relationship

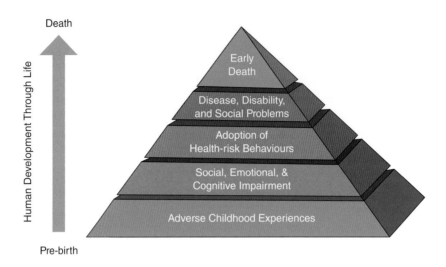

Figure 8.6 The ACE pyramid adapted

with a young person and observing young people help us to understand their sensory needs profile. We become aware of our child/adult bias. We all have the experience of feeling triggered and challenged to not react. Our perspectives are totally different when we are back in the present and calm, safe and grounded.

Many of the young people at Forest School will have experienced a range of challenging life situations as well as many positive relationships. Several will have experienced a range of ACEs, and some come to us with deep human attachment issues. It is also worth noting, too, that many will have already had many positive relationships. When working with particular developmental needs, the key is to get to know the person and their preferences and to show some acceptance of the individual. What they bring is often a gift in insights and new ways of doing and seeing the world. Chapter 5 has outlined some of the sensory understanding in more detail.

We highly recommend the resources and practices promoted by deep thinkers and practitioners such as Phoebe Caldwell and Forest School practitioner Michael James.

Hopefully, you can see that we lean towards a more constructivist, humanistic approach to support the intrinsic values and motivations outlined in Chapters 1 and 3. This is often a tricky line to follow when we operate in a more behaviourist system that relies on extrinsic motivations and sees punishments and rewards as consequences of certain types of behaviour. The final chapter goes into more detail about how we operate in the world where paradigms can be very different.

Chapter 9 moves on to look in more detail at strategies and ways of working with behaviour and building positive prosocial and ecological relationships, especially when facing our own challenges and the challenge of learners with special needs.

QUESTIONS FOR PRACTICE

What really challenges me in my practice and what do I need to work on?

Do I recognise when I take the role of a victim, rescuer and persecutor in our practice? Do I recognise this in group dynamics? How can I support children?

How do I feel when on the receiving end of the seven caring and seven deadly habits?

How do I work with colleagues who take a more behaviourist approach to judgment with consequences being punishments and external rewards, whilst I see a more community problem-solving approach based on maintaining relationship as key?

USEFUL RESOURCES

Allen B (2008) *Persuasive Scripts*. Steaming Publishing. This book is full of useful ways of working with 'scripts' and communication to promote prosocial behaviour. Bernard Allen is a world expert in working with learning disability and behaviour management.

Brene Brown on Empathy – www.youtube.com/watch?v=1Evwgu369Jw RSA

www.sensory-processing-disorder.com This website provides help for identifying SPD, excellent case studies and ways of working out 'sensory diets' and points to other excellent resources.

'The Scared Gang' by Eadaoin Bhreathnach. An excellent set of books based on the Mr Men explaining how children with SPD feel and can work with sensory modulation. Eadaoin's website (www.sensoryattach-mentintervention.com) is also a good resource for understanding sensory attachment.

'Forest School and Autism. A practical guide' by Michael James. Jessica Kingsley, London, 2018.

Phoebe Caldwell's resources: see https://phoebecaldwell.co.uk/ and http://thecaldwellautismfoundation.org.uk/index.php/responsive-communication-the-films/

Video links

https://youngminds.org.uk/resources/ A youth based organisation that has many resources related to working with mental health issues.

www.adversechildhoodexperiences.co.uk/ This is the 'go to' site for information about ACE.

Russell Brand & Brene Brown: Under the Skin Podcast (Vulnerability and Power Brene Brown & Russell Brand June 2019) www.youtube.com/watch?v=SM1ckkGwqZI

BIBLIOGRAPHY

Allen, G (2011) *Early Intervention: The Next Steps*. HM Gov. See https://assets.publishing.service.gov.uk/government/uploads/system/uploads/attachment_data/file/284086/early-intervention-next-steps2.pdf.

Allen, J (1903) *As Man Thinketh*. Creative Space Independent Publishing, 2006.

Apter, T (1997) *The Confident Child: Raising Children to Believe in Themselves*. W.W Norton & Co.

Armour, A (1991, March) The Little Brain on the Heart. *Cleveland Clinic Journal of Medicine* 74(Suppl. 1): 2007.

Ayres, A J (1972) *Sensory Integration and the Child*. Los Angeles, CA: Western Psychological Services.

Bandura, A (1997) *Self-Efficacy: The Exercise of Control*. New York: W.H. Freeman.

Banks, A (2015) *Wired to Connect: The Surprising Link between Brain Science and Strong, Healthy Relationships*. Penguin.

Bhreathnach, E (2018) *Sensory Information, Sensory Integration and Strategic Functioning*. See www.sensoryattachmentintervention.com.

Brown, B (2012) *Listening to Shame – TED Talk*. See www.ted.com/talks/brene_brown_listening_to_shame.

Brown, B (2017) *Braving the Wilderness: The Quest for True Belonging and the Courage to Stand Alone*. Penguin.

Brummelmann, E et al (2014) On Feeding Those Hungry for Praise: Person Praise Backfires in Children with Low Self-Esteem. *Journal of Experimental Psychology*. See www.apa.org/pubs/journals/releases/xge-ofp-brummelman.pdf (accessed 1/12/13).

Bundy, A C, Lane, S J and Murray, E A (2002) *Sensory Integration: Theory and Practice* (2nd edition). Philadelphia, PA: FA Davis Company.

Chopra, D (1997) *Perfect Digestion: The Key to Balanced Living*. Perfect Health Library.

Clark, C and Walberg, H (1968) The Influence of Massive Rewards on Reading Achievement in Potential Urban School Dropouts. *American Educational Research Journal* 5(5): 305–310.

Cohen, M (2007) *Reconnecting with Nature – Finding Wellness Through Restoring Your Bond with the Earth*. Eco Press. See www.ecopsych.com/88-2/.

Craig, C (2009) *Well-Being in Schools: The Curious Case of the Tail Wagging the Dog? Centre for Confidence and Well-Being*. See www.centreforconfidence.co.uk/projects.php?p=cGlkPTU2JmlkPTYzMw.

Dispenza, J (2017) *What Does the Spike in the Schumann Resonance Mean?* Joe Dispenza Blog. See https://blog.drjoedispenza.com/blog/consciousness/what-does-the-spike-in-the-schumann-resonance-mean.

Dweck, C (2017) *Mindset: Changing the Way You Think to Fulfill Your Potential*. Robinson.

Elmer, N (2001) *The Costs and Causes of Low Self Worth*. Joseph Rowntree Foundation. See www.jrf.org.uk/publications/self-esteem-costs-and-causes-low- self-worth.

Felitti, V J, Anda, R F, Nordenberg, D, Williamson, D F, Spitz, A M, Edwards, V and Marks, J S (1998) Relationship of Childhood Abuse and Household Dysfunction to Many of the Leading Causes of Death in Adults: The Adverse Childhood Experiences (ACE) Study. *American Journal of Preventive Medicine* 14(4): 245–258.

Gans, C (2019) *Forest Schooled – The Book*. See www.forestschooled.com.

Glasser, W (1998) *Choice Theory: A New Psychology of Personal Freedom*. Harper Perennial.

Goulet, J MFT see www.johngouletmft.com/Breaking_The_Drama_Triangle_Newest.pdf.

Hall, R V, Lund, D and Jackson, D (1968) Effects of Teacher Attention on Study Behaviour. *Journal of Applied Behaviour Analysis* 1: 1–12.

Hastings, P D, McShane, K E, Parker, R and Ladha, F (2007) Ready to Make Nice: Parental Socialization of Young Sons' and Daughters' Prosocial Behaviors with Peers. *The Journal of Genetic Psychology* 168(2): 177–200.

Hochschild, A (2012) *The Managed Heart – the Commercialisation of Human Feelings*. University of California Press.

Iacoboni, M (2009) *Mirroring People: The Science of Empathy and How We Connect with Others*. Picador.

Karpman, S (1968) Fairy Tales and Script Drama Analysis. *Transactional Analysis Bulletin* 7(26): 39–43.

Kohn, A (2006) *Beyond Discipline: From Compliance to Community*. ASCD.

Maines, B and Robinson, G (1998) *You Can You Know You Can: A Self Concept Approach*. Lucky Duck Publishing.

Mental Health Foundation (2015) *Fundamental Facts About UK Mental Health*. See www.mentalhealth.org.uk/publications/fundamental-facts-about-mental-health-2015.

Mooney, C G (2012) *Theories of Childhood: An Introduction to Dewey, Montessori, Erikson, Piaget and Vygotsky*. Redleaf Professional Library.

Newton, J F (1922) *Preaching in London: A Diary of Anglo-American Friendship*. New York: Doran.

Perry, B D (2005) *Maltreatment and the Developing Child: How Early Childhood Experience Shapes Child and Culture*. London: The Margaret McCain Lecture Series.

Pert, C (1997) *Molecules of Emotion: Why You Feel the Way You Feel*. Scribner.

Plotkin, B (2003) *Soulcraft: Crossing into the Mysteries of Nature and Psyche*. New World Library.

Porter, L (2003) *Young Children's Behaviour* (2nd edition). London: Paul Chapman Publishing.

Rifkin, J (2009) *The Empathic Civilisation: The Race to Global Consciousness in a World in Crisis*. Polity Press.

Rogers, C R (1961) *On Becoming a Person: A Psychotherapists View of Psychotherapy*. Houghton Mifflin.

Rosenburg, M (2003) *Nonviolent Communication: A Language of Life*. Puddle Dancer Press.

Sarkissian, W (2009) *Kitchen Table Sustainability: Practical Recipes for Community Engagement with Sustainability*. London: Earthscan.

Siegel, Daniel J (2010) *The Mindful Therapist: A Clinician's Guide to Mindsight and Neural Integration*. W.W Norton & Co.

Skinner, B F (1972) *Beyond Freedom and Dignity*. New York: Vintage Books.

UNICEF UK (2019) *A Summary of the Unconvention on the Rights of the Child*. See https://www.unicef.org.uk/wp-content/uploads/2019/10/UNCRC_summary-1_1.pdf.

9 Strategies for creating a healthy problem-solving community

In this chapter we will now look at how the natural world supports the more needs-based theory of emotional regulation outlined in the previous chapter. How do we approach what really motivates young people and gives them self-worth and power within a community in order to find their voice and tackle tricky, often sticky, relational issues?

> *When you avoid conflict to make peace, you start a war with them.*
> (Brene Brown in conversation with Russell Brand, 2019)

This chapter will start by looking at the value of an outdoor/nature-based education for regulating behaviour. We will move on to look at emotional and social development and how each stage of human development can be supported through feelings and needs-based strategies. Then, we will look at the importance of looking at ourselves and our own challenges. We will explore how we co-create 'boundaries' and a container in which learners can feel safe to express feelings and manage their own behaviour. We will then move into the capacities and skills required for a prosocial problem-solving community by working with the language of feelings, non-violent communication and empathic communication. We will finish with a short exploration of adverse childhood experiences (ACE) and traumatised learners and how to work alongside professional agencies working with learners who face challenges.

THE VALUE OF NATURE-BASED EXPERIENCES FOR REGULATING BEHAVIOUR

Nature provides an unlimited palette to represent our feelings: a hawthorn twig may be spikey and angry whilst soft and protective, digging in mud may be dirty and slimy yet soothing and able to hide things. Nature offers a multitude of relationships that give sensory and relational feedback. In the growing child's world, their imaginative abilities enable a world full of situations where there is no difficulty in talking to a tree or seeing dinosaurs. This interplay between our external and internal world is completely natural and enables us to place our inner feelings onto a benevolent natural world. This skill of imagination grows exponentially in the outdoors, providing the capacity to problem solve and be creative. Working in and with nature as a metaphor can literally help rewire our neural pathways and understandings of how our needs and feelings drive actions.

The natural cycles and seasons that we have drawn on throughout this book give endless examples of our inner experience of life. The most striking is that everything changes. In nature we can see this every day, in almost every moment. There is loss and death in every moment, alongside life, renewal and hope. Marina remembers a young man in his early 20s going through a very difficult time, questioning life and feeling scared of the changes in his life. After spending time in the woods at her setting, he was soothed by the realisation that life always changed and that it was fine to let go. You could say, in this instance, that nature offered him a way of understanding himself and life from a mental perspective that then soothed his feelings. 'E-motion' indicates the need for movement of emotions to happen – the more we are able to allow our emotions to move internally, the less stuck we will feel, change inevitably occurs, and we are restored back to safety and physical equilibrium. Nature supported this young man to regulate his feelings and provide a new perspective. In the field of emotional regulation we could call this top-down regulation (head-based) – where rational thinking processes helped him 'make sense' of feelings. What is often not understood is the importance of the body in emotional regulation. Nature as a therapeutic tool provides endless sensory experiences that regulate the body from the bottom up (body-based) (see the table in online appendix). Science already provides evidence that our cortisol (stress) levels are lowered in natural spaces after 20 minutes outdoors, which also results in a lower heart rate and improved immunity.

Our behaviour is always worsened and heart rate is escalated when we are stressed and feel unsafe. Nature can successfully support us to be calm enough to rebuild, or build for the first time, memories and networks that have the capacity to cope with our more extreme feelings (Siegel, 2018), without tipping us into the 'red' (anger, flight) or 'blue' (freeze, collapse) zone (see Figure 9.4). Playing in nature helps us to process all the feelings we have in our body that we can't necessarily verbalise. Play is how we learn, but it is also how we metabolise difficult feelings. We can make loud noises and dig until we are tired. We can cry by a tree or play fight with another person. We can express ourselves, whilst being held in a safe and non-judgmental group.

Human beings are story-based creatures who look for meaning. We have a capacity to create images or shapes stimulated by the natural world – a cloud becomes a face, a tree can mirror to us how we are feeling. Imagination allows our minds to play, and our mental flexibility enables imagination and creativity. This is often underestimated; when we work with these metaphors we understand our feelings and behaviours.

Imagination is absolutely critical to the quality of our lives. Our imagination enables us to leave our routine everyday existence by fantasizing about travel, food, sex, falling in love, or having the last word – all the things that make life interesting. Imagination gives us the opportunity to envision new possibilities – it is an essential launchpad for making our hopes come true. It fires our creativity, relieves our boredom, alleviates our pain, enhances our pleasure, and enriches our most intimate relationships. . . . without imagination there is no hope, no chance to envision a better future, no place to go, no goal to reach.

(Van der Kolk, 2014)

Let's look at emotional and social development and how this increased meaning making changes through our lifetime.

Emotional and social development: the psychosocial emotional wheel

The following summary of emotional and social development is influenced particularly by the writings of Erikson (1950) and Plotkin (2003), two significant psychologists/psychotherapists.

The psychosocial and emotional wheel (see Figure 9.1 and Table 9.1) represents an individual moving through different stages of life. According to Erikson, if a child has more trust than mistrust as they enter a new stage – for example, from baby into toddler – they are able to carry the virtue of hope into the remaining stages. Although we attribute a general age to development or virtues, the stages are not necessarily sequential. As with all learning, sometimes we need assistance and support as we move towards mastery. All these processes occur throughout our lifetime, though are perhaps more poignant at particular times.

FEELINGS AND NEEDS

From this wheel you can see that various stages of development may require different strategies for working with the behaviours that are communicating a need, as outlined by Glasser in the previous chapter. Our primary container for our work creates a safe foundation for working with needs. It enables all the wonderful, creative opportunities for working with feelings and memories that occur at Forest School and relating these to needs. We will concentrate on the middle to early adult years here.

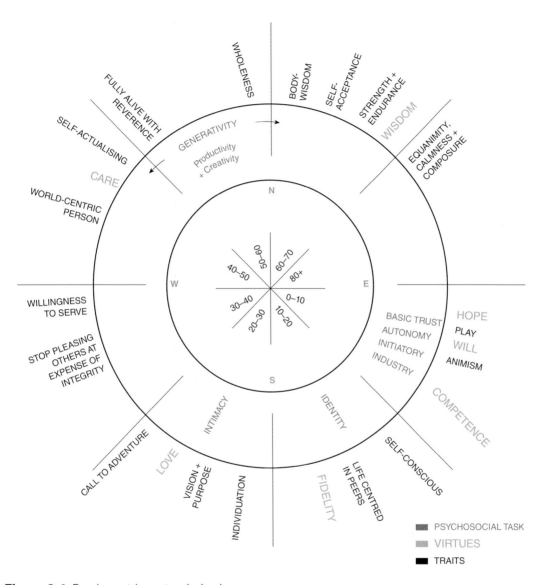

Figure 9.1 Psychosocial emotional wheel

Table 9.1 Psychosocial emotional wheel

Psychosocial emotional wheel				
Approximate age and significant relationship	Virtue	Psychosocial crisis	Qualities	Unfavourable outcomes
Under 2 years Mother/caregiver Can I trust?	Hope	Trust vs. mistrust	Innocence Present centredness Wonder Imagination Joy of existence Inner happiness Trust of self, parents, village, world, belonging to nature Somatic experiences of emotions Ego formation	Anxiety Mistrust Insecurity Lack of hope Neglect Suspicion Fear of future events
Toddlers 2–4 years Parents/carer Is it okay to be me?	Will	Autonomy vs. shame/doubt	Saying "no" Learning autonomy Initiating own activities Newfound control Proud Discovering the natural world Developing beginnings of empathy, understanding right and wrong Learning cultural ways First autographical memory 'I', conscious of own experiences Explorer mind 'mine'	Feelings of shame Self-doubt Afraid of risk Anxious with challenge Learns to attend only to what others expect – submissive and compliant Distrust and fearing oneself
Early childhood 5–8 years Family Is it okay for me to do, move and act?	Purpose	Initiative vs. guilt	Learning initiative Fantasy Active play – exploring nature Interpersonal skills Imagination Able to lead and follow Instinctive animistic response to the world Developing common sense Aliveness and agility	Immobilised by guilt Guilt at being a nuisance Inadequacy to be on one's own Fearful Hangs on fringes of groups Play and imagination restricted

Psychosocial emotional wheel

Approximate age and significant relationship	Virtue	Psychosocial crisis	Qualities	Unfavourable outcomes
Middle childhood 9–12 years *Neighbours and schools* *Can I make it in the world of people and things?*	Competence	Industry vs. inferiority	Competency that is valued by society Ability to achieve goals Learning how things work, to understand and to organise Growing sensitivity of others, can see the difference between one's perspective and others' – individual differences Self-esteem Sense of pride in achievements Free play to structured by more formal teamwork Can be critical of oneself, can consciously hide or deny emotion	A sense of inferiority at organising and understanding Anger Doubting abilities Incapable of meeting people's expectations Lack of motivation, low self-esteem
Adolescence 13–19 years *Peers and role models* *Who am I? Who can I be?*	Fidelity	Identity vs. role confusion	Life centred on peer groups, sexuality and society Commitment to self, on the basis of accepting others, even when there are differences Seeing oneself as a unique and integrated person Freely experimenting and exploring Coherent self-concept Authentic social self Self-consciousness about physical appearance Exploring one's body, imagination and dreams	Role confusion – who and what are they? Mixed ideas and feelings about the ways they fit in Reluctance to commit Isolation

(Continued)

Table 9.1 Continued

Psychosocial emotional wheel

Approximate age and significant relationship	Virtue	Psychosocial crisis	Qualities	Unfavourable outcomes
			Hormonal changes Examination of others' beliefs Inquisitive focus, seeking mentors Developing capacity for the abstract world of possibilities Feeling worthwhile Re-establishing boundaries for oneself	
Early adulthood 20–39 years *Friends and partners* *Can I love?*	Love	Intimacy vs. isolation	Call to adventure Intimacy Ability to make commitments to others Ability to love Exploring the mystery Able to get things done, self-actualising Allowing space for intuition to guide World-centric person Vision and purpose Excitement for life Empathy for life Being proud of accomplishments of self and mate Letting go of roles and relationships that don't feel authentic Task of individuation and developing the capacity to be socially acceptable Developing executive function Independent thinking	Isolation Inability to form affectionate relationships Depression Hopelessness Bitterness
Early/late adulthood 40–59 years *Household and workmates* *Can I make life matter?*	Care	Generativity vs. stagnation	Feeling of concern for family and society in general Guiding the next generation	Stagnation Concern only for self – one's own well-being and prosperity Emptiness

Psychosocial emotional wheel

Approximate age and significant relationship	Virtue	Psychosocial crisis	Qualities	Unfavourable outcomes
			Fully alive in awe and reverence Balanced work for the good, not for success Innovation Sharing power Strength and endurance Taking full responsibility Life-affirming attitude Balancing intellectual thought with grounded body wisdom	
Early/late elderhood 60+ *Humankind and wider nature* *Is it okay to have been me?*	Wisdom	Ego integrity vs. despair	A sense of integrity and fulfilment Caring for more than human world Presence and creativity Fully responsive Retrospection Feelings of contentment Achieved goals Quiet mind Willingness to face death Returning to trust	Despair Dissatisfaction with life Loneliness Despair over prospect of death Fear into death Loss of status and role

Source: Adapted from Erik Ericson's stages of psychosocial development

The recently developed Power Threat Framework, worked on by a group of psychologists and clinicians in the UK, is showing that

> *The power threat framework can be used as a way of helping people to create more hopeful narratives or stories about their lives and the difficulties they have faced or are still facing, instead of seeing themselves as blameworthy, weak, deficient or 'mentally ill'.*
> (Johnstone & Boyle in Power Threat Meaning Framework, British Psychological Society, 2018)

THE POWER-THREAT FRAMEWORK

This works with what has happened to us regarding our needs and how we respond. The needs highlighted in the framework, expanding on Glasser's five, are

- to experience a sense of justice and fairness in the wider community.
- to have a sense of security and belonging in family and social group.
- to be safe, valued, accepted and loved in earliest relationships with caregivers.
- to form basic physical and material needs for themselves and dependents.
- to form intimate relationships and partnerships.
- to feel valued and effective in family and social roles.
- to experience and manage a range of emotions.
- to be able to contribute, achieve and meet goals.
- to be able to exercise agency and control in lives.
- to have a sense of hope, belief, meaning and purpose in their lives.

We feel these are useful in helping nature practitioners and adults/carers understand further the conditions needed for secure, accepting relationships.

From birth to Early Years - east south

As practitioners we can enable some of these needs to be met through providing a caring, emotionally supportive atmosphere, supporting a community of learners in the natural world. The underlying message says, "I'm here, I value you", remaining in the 'adult' role. We welcome a range of feelings and support appropriate ways to express them safely. Marina has set up target ranges in which a group of children can safely express their loud, angry voices. We have created objects that make loud sounds and made loud sounds together. We want to nurture the child's spirit – if they need to be physically active then we provide for that. If they are working in a very imaginary realm, we enter into the metaphor. This stimulates, particularly, the CARE and PLAY limbic systems.

Middle childhood – south-east

In this stage, the child seeks heroes and explores the natural world through metaphor. Family at this stage is at the centre of the human world. A practitioner needs to be aware that wonder and fascination with how things work and mixing reality and fantasy are two key motivations. The natural world provides an ideal place to explore this! What is more fascinating than the fact that sugars are made inside leaves which end up in our chocolate or how wood can change into charcoal by boiling off its gases and moisture in a tin? At the same time, working on friendships and the need for family is important. Creating a 'family' – "we're all in this together" – is pretty fundamental.

Early adolescence – south-west

Moving into adolescence, lust comes online! The social group is key. Working with peers and the fire circle in the outdoors can be a powerful way of meeting the need to start exploring the *intellectual* and seeking meaning in life. Some of the best conversations both Jon and Marina have had, around the fire, are with this age group, as the brain is growing rapidly and wanting to explore meaning and the way society should be. The revolutionary zeal of youth is important to acknowledge as the risk processing in the limbic brain is coming online, and while early adolescents can be hyposensitive to risk, this can also be moderated through sensitive guidance while accepting the need to take risks. As we write this, we see most of the young people's strikes around climate change being supported by early and late adolescents, and our conversations involve the valuing of biodiversity for its intrinsic sake. Our support for this fresh look and revolutionary zeal, while encouraging different perspective taking, is important. Nature education and Forest School in particular can satisfy this need through more risk-taking such as tree climbing, cooking complicated foods over the fire and solo/independent explorations in the woods and with projects. Choice becomes even more important.

Late adolescence and early adulthood – west

When we move into early adulthood, decision-making and autonomy become even more important – exploring our own agency and forming loving relationship are key. As facilitators we need to allow time and space for their own decisions and appreciate that people are making their own impact on society – creating and living their own purposeful lives.

WORKING ON OURSELVES AS PRACTITIONERS

First, we need to apply strategies for ourselves as practitioners and provide experiences that support our emotions and personal story, which can mean regularly following the earlier mentioned practices. Emotions are chemicals that arise from experiences that change our inner world of thoughts and feelings. We all need the positive chemicals to feel good.

When we feel centred and know our boundaries, we have a greater capacity to provide strategies and experiences that support children and young people in our nature-based practice.

According to Bessel Van der Kolk (2015), there are three fundamental avenues to feeling fully alive and well in the present.

1   Head-based: verbal (talking) – by reconnecting with others and allowing ourselves to know and understand what is going on with us, while processing the memories, sometimes memories of traumatic experiences.

2   Body-based: non-verbal – by allowing the body to have experiences that deeply and viscerally (internally) contradict the helplessness, rage or collapse that results from trauma. Just walking can help.

3   By taking medicines that shut down inappropriate alarm reactions or employing other technologies that change the way the brain organises information.

In nature-based experiences we try to work with the first two; indeed, being in nature can release our own internal medicines (see bonus online chapter).

Physical sensations in the body, for example butterflies in your gut, are 'sensed' first. Feelings that you later name or label as emotions don't always have a bodily sensation (as far as we are conscious). They cover a huge range of feelings, for example from envy and anger to joy and awe. Over our lifetime, we are provided with diverse sensory information as well as human-to-human experiences that lay down neural pathways in different parts of the brain (and body) and 'cue' or 'trigger' us to feel safe and familiar or initiate our fight and flight response.

Feeling safe is essential to well-being and learning. As practitioners, if feelings arise that upset our balance and trigger us, taking a *deep* breath is the first 'port of call'. We may need to walk and talk the feeling or literally verbalise to our body what is happening (preferably not in front of our group!). We have on occasions taken our 'talk' to a tree or stream! If a group's interactions are challenging, then by even taking a breath and making a conscious sign to another supporting adult may be enough to bring us into the present and acknowledge our feelings of challenge. The job then to make the space 'safe' is easier. We literally have to try to make the butterflies fly in formation.

One of the key aspects of being a practitioner is having others to support us, debrief and listen, as well as spending our own time in the natural world – see later in this chapter for 'help' scripts.

What capacities, skills and attributes do we want our children to develop and have as adults?

Creating boundaries

What did most compassionate people have in common? They had boundaries of steel . . . They are clear about what is okay and not okay . . . 'I don't subject myself to the abuse of others'.

(Brand & Brown June 2019)

Whilst it is completely natural and appropriate to have a functional fear system – our most fundamental survival system intact – it is not healthy to be in constant survival mode in our homes, schools and workplaces. It takes enormous energy, or numbing substances, to just cope and survive. To be healthy we need to know how to both soothe and take care of ourselves and to know there is a container in which to be held. As practitioners we need to look after ourselves as well as the group and to have healthy boundaries of what is acceptable and what isn't, what you can hold and when you need to rest, what you can provide and what you can't. You are modelling behaviour, and learners need you to be present for them.

As practitioners we need to establish our bottom line – our core boundaries. Our intact boundaries will not allow someone to be abusive. This is not a defensive position but rather a deeply loving and clear position. In older groups, we establish agreements at the beginning. We agree to not hurt ourselves, others and resources and to confidentiality.

QUICK THINGS TO REMEMBER:

- My job is to keep you and the group safe.
- My job is to keep the place/equipment safe.
- My job is to keep me safe.

We ask, what does this group need to feel safe, to meet their needs, including their learning needs, and to have a good time? We let the group come up with their agreements or guiding principles first, then supplement if a core detail is not mentioned and help the group articulate what the agreements look like – be specific. For example, what does 'respect' look and sound like? As stated in Chapter 8, pages 182–183, boundaries need to be both meaningful and dynamic. Our primary job is to help the group feel emotionally and physically safe. When we hurt ourselves or others and things, we need to be able to facilitate a process where feelings are discussed openly. It's not a good idea to avoid bringing up difficult issues, as we will be tested!

One of the most common dynamics we have found in relationships of all kinds is avoiding conflict, usually because we are not comfortable with saying how we really feel and fear imagined consequences. However, avoiding conflict brings us closer to conflict. It is a good idea to either wait until there is a more relaxed time to have a circle and talk or remind the group of any difficulties and vulnerabilities at the beginning of the next group. This is not judging or blaming, rather acknowledging how difficult it can be to have strong feelings and to give options and strategies in how to manage them (see later). Agreements often evolve over time, and behavioural dynamics are dealt with when they come up. For example, use of tools will only really be discussed when tools are gotten out. If something does happen that goes counter to the agreements, then this needs to be approached with either the individual or the group, and the agreements may need to be reviewed. Boundaries are movable, and we need to have a flexible strategy, as illustrated by the story from Forest School practitioner Caylin Gans on page 182 in Chapter 8.

At some point, a child or young person needs to make a choice to follow the agreements, and if they do not, there is a consequence. In most cases, the consequence is a breakdown of relationship, often through people feeling unsafe.

The ultimate consequence may mean not coming to Forest School until there is a plan agreed through a problem-solving approach. The behaviour may be too dangerous or the staff or resource may need to be put in place. Usually the higher the need, the higher the staff ratio and experience needed. In over 20 years of working specifically with 'challenging' groups, we have only had to 'exclude' three people – in two cases this was a staff resource issue. In one of these we had a 1:2 adult to young person ratio, and the person in need required a 1:1 ratio, as they could not stay in the agreed physical boundaries. This is not a punishment, though it may have felt like one. It's a health and safety decision.

WORKING WITH EMPATHY

Whilst we may want our children and teenagers to be well-adjusted to society, we do need to work with where they are and not be battling over issues that are not important, for example wearing a uniform, or always listening to you, or having to do what you say – in the jargon this is called tactical ignoring, often related to things that don't really trigger us as practitioners. This means we have to feel comfortable in 'our space' so we can listen to 'another's space'.

A Forest School training (dealt with further in green interventions online appendix) doesn't train you to be an 'expert' in any of the fields it draws on but rather a 'dilettante'. When working with young people and children, particularly more vulnerable groups, we need to be comfortable with our humanness, which means our feeling self. This speaks to your capacity for empathy and compassion, not rescuing, often listening and offering choices of 'where to go' with a tricky feeling. It means that we learn to have the capacity to tolerate uncomfortable feelings and not rush in to fix or judge them. We can't avoid our judgment as such, but when we have experienced our fear, shame, anger etc., we have empathy and connection with another. Using 'I' statements can really help us own our own feelings without judging another's.

Our role is to be empathic. When people share feelings, we recognise it and feel a connection. We don't try to change it or make it better. We are not trying to be therapists, though we do want to have the awareness and skills to normalise a 'typical' range of feelings, including distress. We need to know when to signpost children and young people to other services that can support a more serious issue. As in first aid, we need look after ourselves first before trying to help someone else. We can only support groups in which we feel confident enough to hold a range of children and young people's needs or establish partnerships with people and organisations that have specialist expertise. Emotional responses are healthy, and you are not going to make it worse. Being both boundaried and caring is really helpful. This means not reacting to what is being shared, rather actively listening and sometimes helping them to name emotions and legitimising their experience; for example, "It sounds like you are feeling sad."

The Forest School approach is child led, supporting the child to take the lead. This applies equally to supporting both emotional needs and development and physical needs and development. We are trying to create a cooperative and empowering atmosphere, not a directive and authoritarian one. Being a good listener and observer and providing a safe space with healthy emotional expression is the container from within which we can all thrive.

THE LANGUAGE OF FEELINGS

Most adults, let alone children, are often challenged to describe their feelings in words. In the early years, describing physical sensations, "a tight tummy . . . just about to go twang", is a much more appropriate way of talking about feelings. This increases awareness of the data your body is sending you. You need to have this data to make decisions that support your well-being. As we get older, we can learn to articulate common feelings like fear, guilt, anger, sadness and love with more accurate descriptions of the noun, aided by a natural world metaphor! This takes experience and courage.

It is not a weakness to name our feelings. As practitioners, we clearly need to be able to do this for ourselves before we can comfortably support another person to be at ease with uncomfortable feelings. Our communicated message is only 7% in our words. Humans are primed to respond to body language and tone of voice. We are an animal, after all. Emotions are the source of motivation to initiate action and are primarily expressed through muscles in the face and body. Our brains have 'mirror neurons' that can pick up anomalies in what people say and what their bodies are saying. This is really important, as we need to be congruent with our body (sensations), feelings (emotions) and thoughts (words) to be essentially trusted. Working with young people with severe learning disabilities amplifies the importance of physical signals and listening to what is being communicated – metaphor alone might not be appropriate. Overwhelming experiences affect our ability to appropriately read our sensations, as outlined in the brain/body chapter. The relationship we build with each other and the natural world provides opportunities for health and care and the recovery of a form of ecology for our lives.

Our own experience is that our culture, at least in the U.K, is very uncomfortable with challenging feelings such as anger, disgust, shame, fear and sadness, and we would rather bypass them in the body and emotion in favour of the rational self, who comes up with stories about what is happening. The problem with not feeling and appropriately expressing what our body is telling us is that we are cutting ourselves off from a natural communication, processing and release that keeps us safe and well and helps us to search out people and places where we are accepted, valued and listened to. The alternative is isolation and often loneliness.

According to O'Toole (2017),

Students are now faced with frequent exhortations to be upbeat, to persist in the face of challenges, to display a growth mindset, to be enterprising and resilient, all of which can, over time, give rise to an atmosphere of toxic positivity, particularly for those whose experiences don't easily lend themselves to feelings of cheery enthusiasm.

Accepting all our feelings is the key. We have discussed in direct and indirect ways how our work with children and their psychological and emotional well-being is tied up with outside influences beyond their control. In understanding why people show emotional distress, we need to be critical about power structures that manipulate, for example, our self-image, or how what we believe and feel is linked to inequality and adversity (see Power Threat Meaning Framework, 2018 in the useful resources section).

We are forced to recognize that behaviours arise in response to adversities and injustices, and this in turn reorients us towards more compassionate, open-hearted encounters with students.

(O'Toole, 2017)

It is usually the adult, parent and culture that expects the child to be a certain way and despite best intentions repeats what they believe worked for them. We are now living in a different time to our own childhoods and, as historian and philosopher Yuval Harari (2018) said,

Many pedagogical experts argue that schools should switch to teaching the 'four C's: critical thinking, communication, collaboration and creativity'. More important will be the ability to deal with change, learn new things, and to preserve your mental balance in unfamiliar situations. By 2050, you will need not merely to invent new ideas and products – you will above all need to reinvent yourself again and again.

All thinking and memory is based on feelings which need to be taken into account if we are to work with the above 'four Cs'. The long-term model of working in nature is essential because working with feelings and relationship building with the human and non-human takes time. It takes time and positive experiences for someone to trust the situation. This trust provides confidence for a person to question and think critically, communicate openly, collaborate and create. The long-term relationships mean you know them (and nature) well enough to notice when something changes or when a person isn't themselves, for example.

CRITICAL THINKING AND COMMUNICATION

It is possible to group together lots of feelings into main categories of feelings, in order to understand, empathise and collaborate. However, happy, for example, is such a catch-all so it is

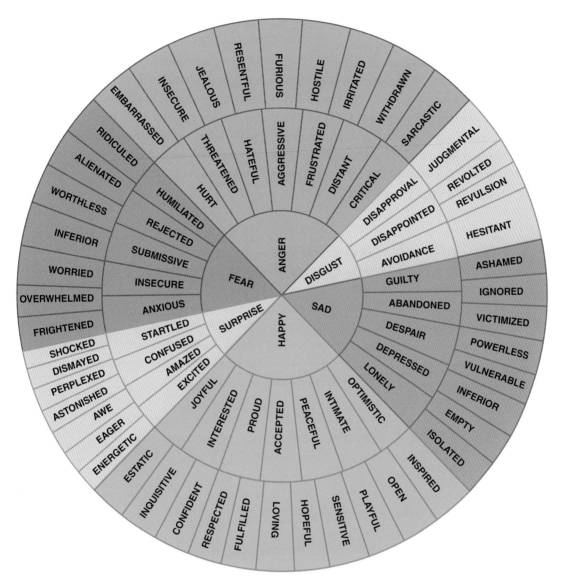

Figure 9.2 Kaitlin Robbs' emotional wheel of feelings

Source: https://brotherpeteshistory.blogspot.com/2015/11/the-best-and-most-beautiful-things-in.html

worth trying to pinpoint the language of the feeling. Kaitlin Robbs created a wheel of emotions can help articulate and name a range of what we experience (see Figure 9.2).

You can see how these emotions can be fitted into the six core emotions as a simple way to navigate what may be going on for you as a practitioner. Awareness of your own feelings and your met or unmet needs, and practising strategies for you yourself, is unavoidable. This has an impact on the learners we are with, both through the modelling of a clearer language, as espoused by Bandura (see Chapter 8), and through building relationship with our learners. Often the specific words and actions can help learners express their feelings. The joy of working in the natural world is that these feelings can be expressed also through movement, as we have space, the natural world can act as metaphor and tell a story, or we can use natural spaces and materials to literally sculpt or draw how we feel.

The following is a story about a 15-year-old learner, we will call him Jake, whom Jon worked with at Forest School, illustrating how metaphor, sculpting, the woodland space and resources helped him to manage his own anger. In the end, Jake recognised and articulated his need for control and what he perceived as survival but realised this was about the need to belong and show worth to the community he was part of.

Jon: "Jake, can we chat about the picnic table going into the pond thing that happened two days ago, so I can understand what was going on and see if we can work through this together?" Pause for about 20 seconds, then Jake nodded.

Jon: "When you threw the table into the pond I was at first gobsmacked at your strength (a wee bit of humour can ease a tricky situation), and then I saw the school group walking on the other side of the pond and I felt a mixture of anxiousness, tightness in chest, knottiness in stomach, infuriation that a student from another school could harm others, and nervousness and guilt that I hadn't managed to help you stop yourself from throwing the picnic table."

A few seconds of silence.

Jake: "I am not sure what was going on. I feel this anger and just wanted to throw something and then didn't even know I was throwing the table apart from hearing a splash."

Jon: "You said you feel anger. Do you know what happens just before you feel anger?"

Even more seconds of silence.

Jake: "Not sure, Jon, sometimes it's what the others are like, but I do like Bishops Wood."

Jon waited, and there was silence for quite a time.

Jake: "So can I come?"

Jon: "I need to know it's safe and that the others aren't going to get hurt, so that means not throwing picnic tables in the pond and injuring the ducks and others, and trying to respond to the others in a way that means they feel safe and won't be injured, including me."

At this point the head teacher said, "Do you want to think about this, Jake, and we can get back to Jon on the phone?" Jake nodded.

Jon thought this was an a pretty articulate exchange. He wanted to understand what Jake was feeling at the time. What Jon got was "I am not sure what I was feeling" (understandable, as the sympathetic system was definitely up and running on all four cylinders; see previous chapter). Jake then said he felt out of control and got even tighter and felt stronger.

NON-VIOLENT COMMUNICATION

Jon was taking the non-violent communication (NVC) process (see Rosenburg, 2003) to the dialogue with Jake using 'I' statements about his own feelings without judging Jake's actions and feelings, in an attempt to take the threat out of the situation. In a nutshell, NVC states that each of the parties in conflict situations follow this four-stage process, providing that the place and time is conducive to system 2 prefrontal cortex thinking:

- State their **observations** of what is happening without judgment; for example, "when you threw the picnic table there was a group on the other side of the pond".
- Express their **feelings**, that is, the sensation, using the language of feelings (not the emotion!); for example, "knottiness in the stomach".
- State their **needs**, for example, "to know the other people are physically safe".
- Make clear **requests for action** and **negotiate** a way forward to promote prosocial relationship building; for example, "responding to others so they know they won't be injured".

EMPATHIC COMMUNICATION

To continue with Jake, Jon went on to tell a Greek myth in one of the Forest School sessions a few weeks later. This was about anger and greed and the impact of this on a King Eryscython and his kingdom – a classic Greek environmental myth. Empathy was shown through the story and interactions through the following weeks. When Jake decided to sculpt his interpretation of the story, there developed a joint understanding of his feelings and actions (see Figure 9.3).

This story displayed what Teresa Wiseman calls the four qualities of empathy (1996):

- Perspective taking – to be able to see the world as others see it, and in order to do this we must understand our own perspectives; self-awareness is key.
- Staying out of judgment; self-awareness is also key here!
- Recognising emotion – trying to understand the other's feelings.
- Communicating emotion – to be able to communicate the understanding of that person's feelings.

The last of these four qualities is where our own, others' and many traditional stories are the 'holders' of metaphor in a non-threatening way such that deeper understandings of ourselves and our feelings can be gained through the oral telling of story as well as storyreading. The role of story is too large a topic to cover here, but we recommend a deeper dive into the role of

Figure 9.3 Jake's chair, a twisted symbol made as a result of the story . . . an expression of his anger and tummy sensations

story in therapeutic space, especially the outdoors as outlined by Gersie and King in their book *Storytelling in Education and Therapy* (1990).

You could say that these four qualities are what create emotionally literate people.

What Jon also had on his side was that the outdoors also helped Jake work with his overwhelming anger by providing space to *move* (to exercise), resources to *make* (to create) and people to *meet* (to empathise) – the three Ms!

Heather Plett's (2016) quotation says it all:

To truly support people in their own growth, transformation, grief, etc., we can't do it by taking their power away (i.e. trying to fix their problems), shaming them (i.e. implying that they should know more than they do), or overwhelming them (i.e. giving them more information than they're ready for). We have to be prepared to step to the side so that they can make their own choices, offer them unconditional love and support, give gentle guidance when it's needed and make them feel safe even when they make mistakes.

If we decide to take a more constructivist problem-solving approach when working with young people and children, particularly more vulnerable groups, we need to be comfortable with our feeling self. This, as stated previously, speaks to our capacity for *empathy*, not the need to *rescue* and miss out on the learning and problem solving a learner can undertake. Our role is not to be sympathetic but empathetic (watch Brene Brown, 2013, via video link see resources section at the end of the chapter). Note, the previous chapter discusses the importance of mirroring and showing empathy in a natural world setting to see how empathy can aid brain and cognitive processes – especially the slower executive functioning that can help us control our actions.

As stated earlier, we are not trying to be therapists, though we do want to have the awareness and skills to normalise a 'typical' range of feelings, including distress. Regarding our own empathic feelings towards our learners, we do have to regulate our empathy – there is such a thing as 'over empathy'; we need to beware of taking on other people's feelings which would eventually paralyse us. Luckily, we have a 'super mirroring' system so we don't get overwhelmed or 'over mirror', as outlined in Chapter 7 (Banks, 2015). If it gets too much and we can't help, we need to know when to get help from colleagues or signpost children and young people to other services that can support a much higher degree of difficulty.

Often with behaviour, it is the practitioner that is being challenged, not the young person or child. We need to recognise our challenges, the feelings associated with these and where in the body these may be, what behaviour we exhibit when in distress or anxious and lastly what is the need in us that is not being met.

Porter (2003) recommends a 'guidance approach' which aims to teach thoughtful behaviour as opposed to compliance. A guidance approach involves the following eight characteristics:

- Be a leader, not a dictator! Earn respect through building a strong relationship rather than exerting control.
- Observe and respond to children's needs – showing consideration will influence them to do the same to others.
- Acknowledge when a child behaves considerately rather than giving praise – "They are not good people when they please us, and bad people when they displease us. It is not up to us to judge or label them, but we can say when we appreciate their considerate behaviour" (Porter, 2003, p. 23).
- Use negotiated guidelines rather than rules – rules are what *not* to do and usually outline punishments if not adhered to. Guidelines negotiated with children are about what *to* do, for example how far we can roam at Forest School versus "do not go beyond those two trees".
- Remember that mistakes in behaviour are part of natural development – "Just as we would not punish toddlers for falling over, so too we should not punish children for behavioural

mistakes. Mistakes are natural at all ages, and are an occasion for teaching children how to be more skillful, rather than a reason to punish" (Porter, 2003, p. 24).

- Look to resolve, not blame – demonstrate communication skills through listening and problem solving.
- Teach skills for self-control – accept that sometimes 'misbehaviour' is a result of a child being emotionally overwhelmed. Though they may know that hitting another child out of frustration is not acceptable, they are unable to act on that information because of their overwhelmingly strong feelings. Teach them self-calming methods to better control their impulses next time (deep breaths, quiet time).
- Recognise our own challenges and the importance of how we as practitioners deal with them.

All of these characteristics takes time to master. It's an ongoing process that requires us as adults to practise a lot of mindfulness and awareness to change our habits. A simple place to start is to become better at communicating *our* needs to children when they behave in our minds inconsiderately or challenge us. Instead of trying to exert control, simply tell them how their behaviour made you feel (see Jake and Jon story).

WORKING WITH ADVERSE CHILDHOOD EXPERIENCES

Chapter 8 gave some background to ACE. One of the keys to working with ACE is trying to understand what experiences learners have sometimes been through, know that behaviours are communicating this and try on, like a new cloak, that perspective.

The Forest School approach enables children (and adults) to receive natural sensory inputs and have healthy relationships and experiences. With the right support and understanding, the natural world is an ideal context, where participants can shift feelings generated by traumatic ACEs (by applying body-based, bottom-up strategies with a therapeutic approach; see online appendix). Time in nature literally releases the internal medicine cabinet as outlined in the brain/body chapter. This is prophetically described in Candace Pert's book *Molecules of Emotion* (1997). After 25 years of working on 'drugs' generated by our bodies, Pert discovered neuropeptides (the brain's emotional messenger molecules) that help the body release 'healing' molecules such as opiates and endorphins, aided by strong relational exchanges between other humans, the environment and the internal workings of our mind and body. She propounded that we can regulate without prescription, providing our own capabilities and relational intelligence were nurtured:

A sense of safety in being in the world which comes from the intuitive knowledge that you can regulate the flows and shifts of your bodily-based emotional states either by your own coping capabilities or within a relationship with caring others.

(Pert, 1997)

Adapted from Marie S. Dezelic Phd (2013)

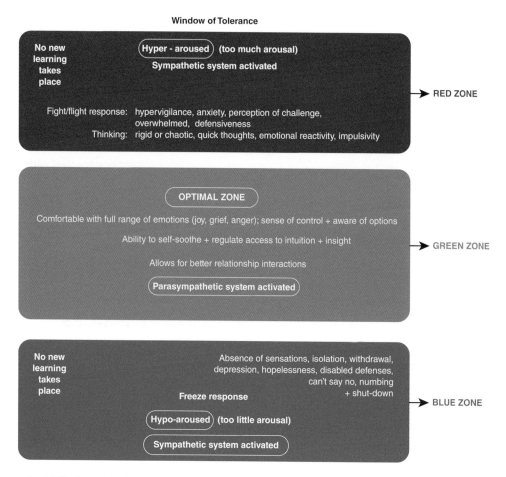

Figure 9.4 Windows of tolerance – hypo and hyper arousal states and ways of working with these states

WORKING WITH PEOPLE WHO ARE OUTSIDE THEIR 'WINDOW OF TOLERANCE' – HYPER AND HYPO AROUSED STATES

Our responses to sensory stimuli can be hyper (over) sensitive or hypo (under) responsive where equilibrium provides normal level of alertness (see Figure 9.4).

Our responses to verbal or body communication can also be oversensitive or undersensitive, where you have more or less choice in how you respond. These responses can change depending on:

- Environment
- Who the child is with

- Stress levels
- If sensory tolerance levels have been met

Remember: What is the child/person trying to tell you? What response do they most need from you? What strategies (see online appendix for suggestions) can you employ to support the young person to widen their window of tolerance? Start with yourself first! (See the useful resources section for direct training.)

Ideally, all practitioners would be trauma informed, always be an emotionally available adult, and use appropriate tone of voice and a coherent narrative.

ROLE OF ADULT:

- To keep them safe to enable learners to be brave
- To adhere to key boundaries – not 'anything goes'
- To contain your dysregulation
- To assure safety
- To not rescue or take on their emotions, not there to fix
- To listen
- To empathise
- To be a soothing presence
- To use open-ended questions

None of us are able to learn if we can't regulate. When we 'emotionally' fill up and have no release valve, our emotions spill out and we appear to lose control. Adults are quite frightening to children when we lose control, as are most older, physically stronger people. With traumatised children, their sensory systems have become so sensitised to the possibility of danger that they become 'sensory defensive', and others have sensory disorders. Children lash out from sensory overload and are punished for 'bad behaviour' when they are actually experiencing an incapacity to emotionally regulate rather than engaging in oppositional defiance or power plays. They really are doing their best.

We need to self-regulate first. Building a relationship with a young person and observing young people help us to understand their behavioural and sensory needs or profile. We become aware of our child/adult bias. Looked-after children and adopted children, for example, are more likely to present with a combination of sensory processing and attachment difficulties because of history of separation, loss, abuse and neglect. The ACE research shows how we are all vulnerable. However, if a child has sensory modulation difficulties, this can impact the ability to have successful attachment relationships, for example touch can be felt as hurt, and hypervigilance and fear of sensations may be overwhelming (e.g. too much sound, unpredictable movement). The child or young person may become overwhelmed and the adult exasperated. An understanding of this can really help practitioners with this exasperation and approach the situation with a calm, soothing empathic response, as outlined throughout this chapter. The following is an example of this approach.

Remember Gina from the previous chapter? Her 'window of tolerance' was quite narrow and often couldn't cope with noise and not being in control. Gina would demonstrate hyperarousal and scream at the top of her voice when in a state of hyperarousal and run off. On the first occasion of witnessing this state in her first Forest School session with Jon, she was by the swing with another boy who she seemingly got on well with. However, he wanted his 'go' on the swing and Gina wouldn't allow him on the swing, so he raised his voice and she started stomping and shouting, which elevated to screaming and running. The teaching assistant who had the closest relationship with her quickly nodded to other staff and told Marina she would follow and ring if she needed assistance (this group of staff had been coming to the centre for about 6 months and had a good working relationship with each other and Jon). The group had previously agreed that Laura (the TA) would keep an eye on Gina. A protocol with the centre was in place also if a learner from this group did a runner. Jon rang the centre, who alerted other group leaders on the site that Gina was on the run and shouting. Jon went to the pond in the woods – the main concern regarding hazards on the site. Laura followed Gina, trying not to run but to keep within visual distance and talk to Gina in an audible voice in between the shouting to reassure Gina it was OK and asking clearly if she could approach her. After about 5 minutes, which felt much longer, Gina allowed her to move closer. Without any judgment, she explained to Gina that she was going to come close to help her calm. Eventually she slowed down and Laura put her arm around hers and immediately this clear, calm presence was saying, "It's hard, isn't it Gina?" She brought Gina back into her 'window of tolerance'. She was still in a slight hyperaroused state but could regulate her body and verbal response. Laura asked for permission to ring Jon to reassure him that Gina was OK, and she did.

After the incident, Jon and Laura debriefed and talked to the boy who liked being with Gina and requested if Gina wasn't giving him a turn to ask quietly and try to not raise his voice so she didn't react in a heightened state (this was common at school). It worked, and after a few weeks Gina took great delight in pushing him on the swing.

WORKING WITH OTHER AGENCIES AND PROFESSIONALS

Working alongside health organisations with learners that have specific needs and experienced an adverse situation can be a gift and very effective. We can apply a range of strategies that may be helpful for those with issues and those with diagnosed emotional and behavioural difficulties, for example attachment disorders, ASD SPD etc. Do they have a 'behaviour plan', a 'sensory profile', what are their, and importantly our, 'triggers'? We do recommend that practitioners attend sessions with family workers, occupational workers or therapists working with the learners, if possible, to gain a deeper understanding of the behaviours displayed by those with specific needs, or at least dialogue with child/young people therapists. Even more effective is working alongside health professionals in the natural world (see bonus online chapter: 'The evidence and green interventions').

For many years, Marina's organisation, Circle of Life Rediscovery (CLR) CIC and East Sussex CAMHS, National Health System (NHS), have worked together to facilitate funded programmes in nature. Generically, they could be referred to as 'forest therapy' programmes. This has grown over the years to offer projects with different departments that include CAMHS (Child and Adolescent Mental Health Service), CAMHS-LD-FISS (Learning Disability-Family Intensive Support Service), ADCAMHS (adoption), dementia and early psychosis intervention (see green interventions). All the programmes work in close contact with health professional experts (clinical psychologists, family workers, occupational therapists, mental health practitioners) and nature-based experts providing regular sessions in a local woodland. These projects are entirely participatory, meaning that they are co-developed through listening to the young people, families and adults involved. There are many benefits to working in this way, the most being that in order to meet the complex needs of many of the participants and clients, you need to have significant knowledge, experience and understanding of how best to support them. The NHS provides this. A Forest School training does not provide the in-depth training needed to work with behaviours that are challenging, and it often takes a specialist to unravel what is happening and to provide the ongoing relationship outside of the woodland setting. A partnership project also provides in-kind time from the health practitioners as part of their own job description; this means that from a resource perspective fund raising is needed only for the woodland aspect. Often, the ratio of practitioner to client is 2:1 or 1:3, which is very costly, though often cheaper than other programmes. Whilst over the years we have learned from each other through regular partnership trainings and skills shares, we have very clear roles during the programme. CAMHS staff are there to support the emotional well-being, and we are there to support the woodland activities. The CLR team is responsible for all the health and safety aspects, including lost child protocol, emergency protocol, all the activities, observing the young people/family, and recording through our 'passport system' where we have key information about the family/young people (YP), sensory profiles, likes and dislikes, and comments. The programmes are co-developed so that when we next meet we are building on the past experiences. The CAMHS team may use sign language and carry visual communication aids that are used in other settings, and they have a wider overview of any current medication, challenges at school or in the home, whether the parents are struggling, and what may be really helpful to support the individuals and meet their needs. CLR makes the final decisions on health and safety relating to the land, boundaries and activities. There have been specific times where we have had to agree to differ as organisations in our approach to managing a 'runner' at a programme. From a CLR perspective, we were not able to 'manage' a young person who repeatedly went to the road and seemed in our view to put himself in danger. However, CAMHS staff felt that they were able to manage this situation, and we agreed that they would take on responsibility for first aid, making further judgments on this young person's well-being and capacity to follow instructions. It was felt from the experienced practitioner that they had a strong enough relationship with the individual to manage this distress and behaviour, where CLR staff were not comfortable. This example shows that we also need to draw a line and confirm our boundaries in partnerships as well as with individual young people and clients. As a manager who holds ultimate responsibility for her staff and the programme, it is often necessary for me to think through scenarios and do my best to make sure that high-need groups are looked after, and that as a strong and supportive partnership, we are able to hold different views, listen well to each other and provide useful strategies to hold a safe-enough space where we can all thrive.

'HELP' SCRIPTS

It is important, particularly in highly charged situations, to work as a team and to work out both a consistent way of working and how to work together, as in the case study with Gina described earlier. How to communicate within a team is key – especially if we are to *help* each other and not undermine or escalate a situation. These are help protocols previously worked out to be gentle and informal. They can be either verbal or non-verbal and in some cases to prevent escalation becoming to a 'kicking off' incident . . . it may be a gentle eye contact or a cue like "Marina, I need the toilet; are you OK to be with Jamie?" or "I'm going to make a cup of tea". All the while you need to show the learners that you are there to help if needed but have needs that the rest of the team need to know about.

When situations have been de-escalated, it is worth remembering that the important part of the process is the follow through and problem solving, as with the Gina incident and the boy she was playing with.

The TELL acronym (see Allen, 2009) is helpful and worth working through with the team:

Timing. There is no hard and fast rule, but positive listening and debriefing can only start when the learner is ready; don't force it. Also, staff need sufficient time to process. Don't rush it.

Environment. Choice of environment should be neutral – this is where the outdoors is useful, as it provides plenty of neutral space (the fire is a good one). Make sure you are on the same level and alongside the person; maintain personal space.

Listen. Listen with your eyes and body and ask non-judgmental, open questions. Listen to the feelings as well as the words. Use "I" and "we" language.

Learn. You need to describe without judgment and try to help learners understand their feelings, motivations and needs and link them to yours. Then explore requests for further working together to build positive relationships and reduce the chance of repetition. Help them learn how to manage their behaviour and ask them what I, as the practitioner, can do differently to help.

DEBRIEFING FOR THE PRACTITIONER

We would recommend that all practitioners have their own special people and even natural places to whom and to where they can go for 'debriefing', 'support' and 'release'. Jon has a mentor he goes to for support when needed. At his previous workplace, if any significant incident happened, there was a whole debriefing process with the person at work he had most trust in. Marina has regular supervision with a body psychotherapist and thorough debrief with partnership projects.

In the end, the most important person's health is our own! Without this, we cannot be effective in our work.

The next four chapters get into the nitty gritty of planning and running sessions and include some ideas around working with plants, animals and the elements.

QUESTIONS FOR PRACTITIONERS

Do you believe people are doing the best they can?

How expansive is your own window of tolerance?

Do you have the courage to engage children and young people in communication about sensitive and emotive subjects?

How do we set expectations at the start and through our programmes?

Where do we get our personal support?

USEFUL RESOURCES (SEE ONLINE APPENDIX FOR SPECIFIC RESOURCES FOR STRATEGIES)

The online appendix for Chapter 9 (www.routledge.com/9780367425616) has an essential summary of the key strategies and a toolbox for non-therapists working with 'behaviours'.

Power, Threat, Meaning Framework Overview (2018) The British Psychological Society's Division of Clinical Psychology as a Member Network publication. See www.bps.org.uk/news-and-policy/introducing-power-threat-meaning-framework

Allen B (2009) *Persuasive Scripts*. Steaming Publishing. This book is full of useful ways of working with 'scripts' and communication to promote prosocial behaviour. Bernard Allen is a world expert in working with learning disability and behaviour management.

Brene Brown on Empathy – www.youtube.com/watch?v=1Evwgu369Jw RSA

www.sensory-processing-disorder.com for identifying SPD includes excellent case studies and ways of working out 'sensory diets' and points to other excellent resources.

'The Scared Gang' by Eadaoin Bhreathnach. An excellent set of books based on the Mr Men explaining how children with SPD feel and can work with sensory modulation. Eadaoin's website (www.sensoryattachmentintervention.com) is also a good resource for understanding sensory attachment.

Forest School and Autism by Michael James – see Michael's website for further resources.

Circle of Life Rediscovery CIC Training: What Are You Trying to Tell Me? Understanding Mental Health in the Classroom and Working with Young People with Challenging Behaviours in the Outdoors: www.circleof liferediscovery.com/index.php?page=cpd-for-teachers

Phoebe Caldwell's resources: see https://phoebecaldwell.co.uk/ and http://thecaldwellautismfoundation. org.uk/index.php/responsive-communication-the-films/

Video links

https://youngminds.org.uk/resources/ A youth-based organisation that has many resources related to working with mental health issues.

www.adversechildhoodexperiences.co.uk/ This is the 'go to' site for information about ACE.

Robb, K. Emotional Wheel of Feelings: https://brotherpeteshistory.blogspot.com/2015/11/the-best-and-most-beautiful-things-in.html

Russell Brand & Brene Brown: Under the Skin Podcast (Vulnerability and Power Brene Brown & Russell Brand June 2019): www.youtube.com/watch?v=SM1ckkGwqZl

BIBLIOGRAPHY

Allen, B (2009) *Persuasive Scripts*. Steaming Publishing.

Bandura, A (1997) *Self-Efficacy: The Exercise of Control*. New York: W.H. Freeman.

Banks, A (2015) *Wired to Connect: The Surprising Link Between Brain Science and Strong, Healthy Relationships*. Penguin.

Brand, R and Brown, B (2019) *Vulnerability and Power – Under the Skin Podcast*. See www.youtube.com/watch?v=SM1ckkGwqZl.

Erikson, E (1950) *Childhood and Society*. W.W Norton & Co.

Gans, C (2019) *Forest Schooled: The Book*. See www.forestschooled.com.

Gersie, A and King, N (1990) *Storytelling in Education and Therapy*. Jessica Kingsley Publishers.

Harari, Y (2018) *Yuval Noah Harari on What the Year 2050 Has in Store for Humankind*. See www.wired.co.uk/article/yuval-noah-harari-extract-21-lessons-for-the-21st-century.

O'Toole, C (2017).

Pert, C (1997) *Molecules of Emotion: Why You Feel the Way You Feel*. Scribner.

Plett, H (2016) *What It Really Means to Hold Space for Someone* (May 8). See https://upliftconnect.com/hold-space (accessed 17/02/19).

Plotkin, B (2003) *Soulcraft: Crossing into Mysteries of Nature and Psyche*. New World Library.

Porter, L (2003) *Young Children's Behaviour* (2nd edition). London: Paul Chapman Publishing.

Power, Threat, Meaning Framework Overview (2018) *The British Psychological Society's Division of Clinical Psychology as a Member Network Publication*.

Rosenburg, M (2003) *Nonviolent Communication: A Language of Life*. Puddle Dancer Press.

Siegel, D and Bryson, T (2018) *The Yes Brain: How to Cultivate Courage, Curiosity, and Resilience in Your Child*. New York: Random House Books.

Van der Kolk, B (2015) *The Body Keeps the Score: Mind, Brain and Body in the Transformation of Trauma*. Penguin.

Wiseman, T (1996) A Concept Analysis of Empathy. *Journal of Advanced Nursing* 23: 1162–1167.

Zohar, D and Marshall, I (2012) *Spiritual Intelligence: The Ultimate Intelligence*. Bloomsbury.

10 Planning a nature-based programme

Health and safety law is often used as an excuse to stop children taking part in exciting activities, but well managed risk is good for them. It engages their imagination, helps them learn and even teaches them to manage risks for themselves in the future. They won't understand about risk if they're wrapped in cotton wool. Risk itself won't damage children, but ill managed and overprotective actions could!

(UK Health and Safety Executive)

This chapter is all about getting prepared and having everything in place, in particular the essentials that may be required by a country's legislation. It includes:

- Introduction – some principles and starting points to consider
- Health and safety policies and procedures
- Safeguarding and equality policies and procedures to consider
- Site management, reducing impact and enhancing site and learning
- Communication and working with colleagues and other stakeholders
- Session planning
- Resourcing – kit lists, management plans, sample forms (in online appendices)

INTRODUCTION – PRINCIPLES AND STARTING POINTS

Within this field of work, we need to consider where legislation and regulations might influence and impact what you do. These include working with young people, working outdoors in remote or urban places and taking young people into natural spaces with specific flora and fauna.

Nature Pedagogy is participatory. We want young people to be as involved as possible in all the processes and activities, including, for example, contributing to risk-benefit assessments and the risk management process. However, the adult 'leader' is ultimately the one who is responsible for what happens at Forest School and in a nature education session, we have a 'duty of care'. There is a lot of planning that goes on in advance of welcoming a group and running a session.

We know that there are many benefits to allowing children to play freely in local woodlands or green spaces on a frequent and regular basis.

Forest School offers learners the opportunity to take supported risks appropriate to the environment and to themselves.

Whilst we recognise the value of woodlands as an integral part of a child's learning process, we want to enable children in all settings to play outdoors.

In the UK, educationalists have been devalued over many years and many of us have been left feeling that our knowledge and expertise is not reflected in policy and the current curriculum objectives. We are part of a movement that reclaims early year's practitioners, primary school teachers, secondary school teachers as experts in their field and it is necessary to listen to what the experts are saying.

(Palmer S, 2016)

The values and principles that underpin strong reciprocal relationships between ourselves and the ecological communities we learn in combine lived knowledge of what leads to a full learning experience and should dictate our plans, policies and procedures. At the same time, we recognise that qualified and experienced teaching practitioners, for example, already have key knowledge on what constitutes healthy learner development and observation within their practice (particularly in the early years). The information in this chapter needs to be applied in a flexible and adaptive way, enabling you to fill your own gaps in knowledge and skills and clarify 'why you do this!' You are the

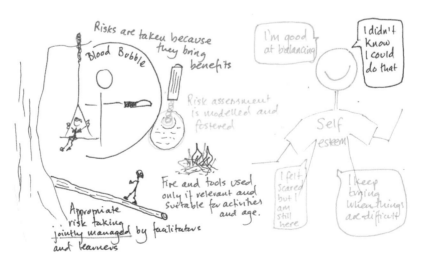

Figure 10.1 Forest School risk principle
Source: Drawing by Rivkah Cummerson

best person to do this. You need to develop your confidence and belief that you have the skills and competencies, underpinned by a set of values, to provide quality sessions.

The Forest School model is very comprehensive, yet it is not necessary to have this training in order to take children and young people outdoors. Many very practical documents (see the useful resources section) provide the key stepping stones on how to organise and safely set up sessions in the outdoors. As practitioners you can add to your skill set by additional skills training, for example in ropes, shelters and tools use, foraging etc., at a later date!

Fundamentally, you need to be able to:

- Locate a suitable green space or woodland space and take practical steps to ensure your setting is able to use it.
- Prepare, educate and inform staff in your setting, volunteers, children and parents about the nature-based visits and all the policies and procedures underpinning your practice.
- Extend children's experiences and development of playing and learning in the natural world (the Nature Pedagogy).

The approach to 'nature' visits is underpinned by the UN Convention on the Rights of the Child (in particular Articles 3, 4, 12, 28 and 31). Many terms are used to describe children playing and learning in woods or other green spaces: Woodland Learning; Nature Kindergarten (75% of time outdoors); Nature Play; Forest School; Outdoor Settings; Forest Kindergartens – all are beneficial, and it is useful to apply the four key dynamics of practitioner, place, person (child/YP/client), and resources to the experience. The best practice you can offer is to be a reflective practitioner, valuing the learner's agency and understanding what their behaviour is trying to communicate. Our aim is to embed and model the Forest School principles and good practice, such as an outdoor access code, for example the Scottish Outdoor Access Code: Countryside and Rights of Way Act, and rights and responsibilities (see the useful resources section).

To prepare for accessing the outdoors, educational settings will need to prepare a 'working set of documents' that guide practice. In a Forest School programme this is referred to as the 'Handbook' (see Chapter 10 online appendix for a simple overview – for more detail go to the Forest School Association website listed in the useful resources section). We emphasise that this is a 'working' practical document and should not be confined to the shelf. It is this that we will be referring to for the remainder of this chapter, and while specific to Forest School, it still provides a 'quality' baseline for all Nature Pedagogy.

Forest School Handbook and starting points

In the UK, if you are to run a Forest School programme, your first step in planning is to train to become a Forest School Level 3 leader – see the Forest School Association website. However, for many outdoor practices such a comprehensive qualification is not needed and shorter professional development can be located in a number of places, for example IOL, CLOTC, OWL and The Outdoor Teacher (see the useful resources section). Other organisations also offer deep nature connection training – it is worth looking around and talking to other practitioners.

The Handbook sets out clearly all your procedures and protocols that affect your Forest School practice. Creating this can often feel daunting; however, after 30 years of working outdoors with young people, we find the process and completion of creating the Handbook creates a clear guide to keep our practice safe, challenging and inspiring whilst providing the best nature and learning experience possible. It is also a good communication tool. Your experience and qualifications will give you your starting point and your comfort level with complying with local health and safety regulations, insurance, relevant ratios and assessment of any risk. The practices and procedures in the Handbook need to reflect the legislative requirements of the country the practitioners are operating in.

The Handbook, which includes the risk-benefit assessments, session plans, woodland management plans and ecological impact assessments, to name a few procedural documents, are all living documents, meaning that what is in there is part of a written ongoing reflection process of staff, volunteers, young people and assistants. It is updated and also reviewed as situations or experiences change and develop. These documents reflect what you do and can be displayed in many diverse ways.

We are providing a service for people's children and young people. Our experience with and confidence in working with a range of ages and backgrounds, including challenging groups, stem from an understanding and adherence to meaningful protocols and procedures that are built on a loving and wholesome understanding of child development and best learning practices (see Chapters 8 and 9 on behaviour). If your 'clients' or young people have more complex needs and in some cases more specific associated risks, the more it is necessary to have developed a very clear understanding amongst your team to what is expected in terms of an emergency or challenging situation.

A good starting point is to do an audit of what you feel confident in and what information and skills you may need to get and grow. See the wonky wheel in Figure 10.2, which serves as a useful audit tool (see https://kindlingplayandtraining.co.uk/forest-school/wonky-wood-cookie-wheel-reflective-practice/).

Key areas to consider when preparing policies and procedures are:

Health and Safety – risk management statement, includes risk-benefit assessments, site safety, activity procedures, meeting certain specific needs, lost child procedures, first aid, emergency plans and weather conditions, transport to and from site, other users etc.

Safeguarding – adult to student ratios, child and vulnerable people protection procedures, complaints, reporting, toileting, GDPR procedures etc.

Equality – catering for all needs – emotional, cognitive and physical.

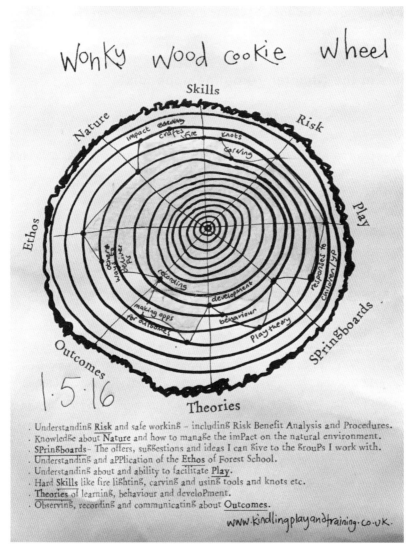

Figure 10.2 Tool for assessing own knowledge and competencies at Forest School

Source: Lily Horseman, see www.kindlingplayandtraining.co.uk

Behaviour – see Chapters 8 and 9

Ecological Impact and Site Management – ecological principles and workings of your wood, site surveys, impact statements, management plans including minimising impact and ways of enhancing the site that reflect 'earth care, people care and fair share'.

Session Plans and Pedagogy – Aims and ethos of the practice and how this looks in session plans (see also Chapter 11)

Helpful items in the Chapter 10 online appendix

- Key examples of areas you would normally include in your Handbook
- A range of example risk-benefit assessments
- Example site appraisal form (adapted from the Scottish Forestry forms, including Guidance for Landowners)
- Assessing risks and hazards
- A list of what you may want to consider before beginning
- 12 steps to making a woodland plan and management plan template
- Environmental impact template

HEALTH AND SAFETY POLICIES AND PROCEDURES

On their webpage, the HSE states:

> This is one of the oldest chestnuts around, a truly classic myth. A well-meaning head teacher decided children should wear safety goggles to play conkers. Subsequently some schools appear to have banned conkers on 'health & safety' grounds or made children wear goggles, or even padded gloves!
>
> Realistically the risk from playing conkers is incredibly low and just not worth bothering about. If kids deliberately hit each other over the head with conkers, that's a discipline issue, not health and safety.

In the UK, we are required by law (Health & Safety at Work Act 1974) to ensure that the health, safety and welfare of our employees and members of the public are looked after as far as *reasonably* practicable. In addition, when you are in charge of children, we have a common law duty of care to act as any *reasonable* parent would. Anyone working with children also needs to have a safeguarding policy in place which relates to the protection of children.

Reasonably practical means "balancing the level of risk against the measures needed to control the real risk in terms of money, time or trouble. However, you do not need to take action if it would be grossly disproportionate to the level of risk" (www.hse.gov.uk/risk/faq.htm#q8).

Our Handbook and risk-benefit assessments need to be created *before* we work directly with any groups. This creates a standard of practice, communicates to others, provides protection against litigation and is a legal requirement.

What health and safety documents need to be in place before you run your FS programme:

- Risk-benefit assessments – including the site and activity assessments for the first session; these will develop (see sample in online appendix)
- Current first aid certificate and emergency plan
- Current CRB/DBS disclosure for all adults – this is the UK police check
- Insurance – for the site (land manager needs this) and for the group and 'activities' (public liability)
- Programme outline/ideas and session plan for first session (see sample in online appendix)
- GDPR-compliant recording and data storage
- Forest School Handbook

Why do we need risk-benefit assessments (RBAs)?

In the UK we have a legal duty to assess the risks to the health and safety arising out of our work. This applies to any employees, other adults and, in our case, children and young people. There is no particular requirement to present an RBA in any form, but it needs to show a consideration of what might cause harm, and how, and who might be affected.

You should be able to show from your RBA that:

- a proper check was made
- all people who might be affected were considered
- all significant risks have been assessed
- the precautions are reasonable
- the remaining risk is acceptable
- the learning and development benefits of doing an activity are included in the judgment of whether to include an activity in your programme

You do not need to include insignificant risks. You do not need to include risks from everyday life unless your work activities increase the risk. It is down to our perceptions, own experiences and competences when deciding on how and when to help learners manage risks and whether to have a risk assessment in place. Often, for example, people see fire and tools as presenting the biggest risks in Forest School, but many would say that poisonous plants such as deadly nightshade, which can get mixed up with other berries, present higher level of risks.

'It depends' is an accurate statement with RBAs. It really will depend on the circumstances and the young person (and practitioner) in mind as to whether there is significant risk. For example, what is the risk of a child walking across a self-made dam over relatively shallow water? You may want the child to learn about risk and danger and be glad you were there as an observer. Or perhaps the child is only 2 years old, and this activity might be too risky for them.

We are not required by law to include the benefits of carrying out an activity. However, in more recent years 'nature and play' experts all recognise that it is vital we weigh up the benefits of carrying out an activity with what risks may exist – particularly as we now understand the importance of risk and risky play (see Chapter 5). In practice, this means that for our RBAs we spend time considering and documenting the benefits of what we are doing. This has multiple advantages, as it allows us to communicate a range of outcomes that may have been invisible to the untrained eye, helps us to unpack the benefits within learning, health and development, and helps us to plan and support adults to go beyond their own 'risk adverse' position.

To successfully complete an RBA, you need to understand the core definitions of and differences between a *hazard* and a *risk*. If you spend a little time identifying what they are at your site, you will avoid later confusion. In addition, RBAs often begin with describing the hazards (and to whom) and subsequent risks *before* you put in any control measures. Then the process is repeated and control measures are added, *after* which there is a reduction in the likelihood and the level of harm. Once there is a reduction in the likelihood of a significant harm, the activity is 'safe enough'. Generally, the aim is to lower the likelihood, not the severity – the first aid kit will be key in reducing the severity.

A **hazard** is something with the potential to cause harm, for example a branch at eye level, a fire.

Risk is the combined likelihood of the hazard harming someone and the likely consequences if it did occur, for example risk of getting your eye poked, risk of being burned. *Harm* and *injury* are the two key terms with risk.

Risk is often judged by levels of harm – for example by using the terms High, Medium and Low or a numerical system.

The Play Safety Forum (2008) promotes the idea of keeping children *as safe as necessary, not as safe as possible*. When we prepare our RBAs, we may want to eliminate the hazards that are not obvious to the child, for example a broken tree branch, but not eliminate all the risks, involving the child in the assessment. After weighing up the benefits of an activity with the risks, we then will decide if the activity is worth pursuing – this is, after all the control measures are in place. Quite often this means assessing long-term benefits that may prevent larger accidents in the future.

You will need to carry out the following RBAs for the FS programme:

- Site risk assessment per site – see online appendix
- Daily risk assessment for each session
- Activity RBAs – see a sample in the online appendix

It is impossible to assess or plan for every possible scenario or situation. For this we adopt a dynamic process called 'dynamic risk assessment'. This allows us to be responsive to a person, activity or environment whilst thinking through consequences of our decisions.

A recent example came up for Jon when a girl came to him to say she had found a metal stake and held it up with a smile. She wanted to make a spear and go hunting. Jon took a deep breath and thought, *Ooh I don't have an RBA for this*. But then he paused and took a typical four-step approach to dynamically and jointly assessing the risk of the said spear making and throwing:

Step 1: Oooh! Look at that, that's interesting. . .

Step 2: Am I comfortable with that?

Step 3: Shall I intervene or is it fine to carry on?

Step 4: If we do carry on, how will we do that safely?

In the end, she made a spear and had a dedicated throwing area with its own safety procedures!

Figure 10.3 shows an illustration of the process from Lily Horseman.

Emergency bag

It is good practice to have a dedicated emergency bag for use during your FS programme, the contents of which must be suitable for your site, your group and the activities you have chosen. It will likely include:

- First aid kit (should adhere to the contents recommended in your first aid training)
- Medical details of the group, including the adults
- Other emergency equipment needed for the specific group and site
- Emergency plan
- Lost child policy

See sample emergency bag content list in the online appendix.

Insurance

You will need to be insured through your own organisation or the school/group providing the children. You will need to check the extent of the insurance cover (it may not cover you for fire, tools, taking

Forest School Dynamic Risk Assessment

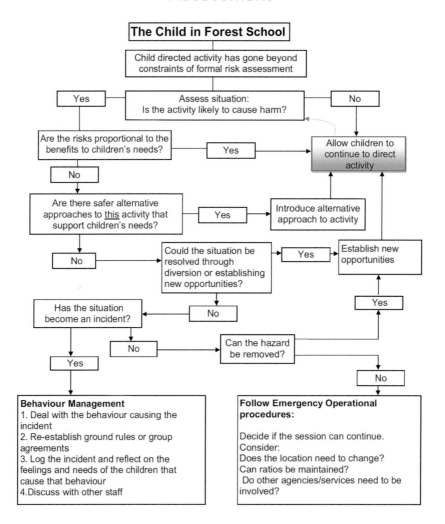

The Child in Forest School

Child directed activity has gone beyond constraints of formal risk assessment

Yes — Assess situation: Is the activity likely to cause harm? — No

Are the risks proportional to the benefits to children's needs? — Yes → Allow children to continue to direct activity

No ↓

Are there safer alternative approaches to this activity that support children's needs? — Yes → Introduce alternative approach to activity

No ↓

Could the situation be resolved through diversion or establishing new opportunities? — Yes → Establish new opportunities

No ↓

Has the situation become an incident? — No ← Can the hazard be removed? — No

Yes ↓

Behaviour Management
1. Deal with the behaviour causing the incident
2. Re-establish ground rules or group agreements
3. Log the incident and reflect on the feelings and needs of the children that cause that behaviour
4. Discuss with other staff

Follow Emergency Operational procedures:

Decide if the session can continue.
Consider:
Does the location need to change?
Can ratios be maintained?
Do other agencies/services need to be involved?

Original document by Dan Rees-Jones Playwork Partnerships 2008
Adapted by Lily Horseman and BEYCP Play Team July 2008

Adapted for Forest Schools by Kindling www.kindlingplayandtraining.co.uk 2011

Figure 10.3 Dynamic risk assessment process

Source: Lily Horseman, see www.kindlingplayandtraining.co.uk

children off site etc.) and plan your FS programme accordingly. You will also need to check that the site you are using has public liability insurance – this is the responsibility of the landowner.

Other countries have different regulations and approaches with insurance. In China, for example, individual children are often insured by their parents, not the organisation.

Remember the four key dynamics at Forest School

1 **You the practitioner**: You have to put on your own 'oxygen mask' before you save anyone else. As a practitioner be prepped and prepared, unconditionally accepting of who you are and extending this empathetic approach to those around you.

2 **The young people/children in your care/other staff**: Who are the children you are working with? They may be from a school, youth group or other organisation. You will need to get information to the children and their parents on what the FS programme is about and what they need to wear. You will need some background information on the children who are attending and what your aims for the FS programme are in order to build in some progression into your planning. You will need to have parental consent and medical details for each child attending. If you are intending on taking photographs of the children, you will need permission from their parents to do so. Finally, you need to think about where you are storing information about them; recent EU GDP Data Protection Law has clear protocols and procedures. What support and experience do your other staff or volunteers need?

3 **Your place/site and season**: You will need an outdoor site. This can be attached to the school/organisation you are working with or be a nearby woodland or green space. You will need the landowner's permission for the programme generally and for any specific activities such as fire lighting. Our ethos is to care for and enhance your site, which is where effective management of woodland or green spaces come into play (see later section on site management). See online appendix for a sample ecological impact statement and woodland management plan.

4 **Available resources**: The land will offer various 'affordances'. These represent the qualities or properties of an object, for example a tree or a stream, that define its possible uses. What is the land and season offering? Do you have a budget? Can you afford to equip yourself with some basic 'kit'? (Refer to the kit list recommended for Forest School, found later in the chapter.)

Key elements to think about in your preparation (this will be documented in your Handbook)

The children/young people/other staff (key dynamic 2):

Playing outdoors is exciting and memorable! The more you plan, the more you can relax and enjoy being outside. No manual can answer every issue or cover every eventuality! Building relationships over time with the children, your team, and your place make the day-to-day experience more fulfilling and any risks easier to manage.

There are several aspects to consider giving your attention to.

CLOTHES

How will you keep children warm when it's cold and/or keep them dry when it's wet? Are you providing extra gear for the children and staff? How are you going to dry clothes? Some Forest Schools ask parents to put their Forest School clothes in a simple plastic bag, and the muddy and wet clothes are returned home for cleaning and drying. Some nurseries or organisations supply full rain gear and boots and have space for storage and cleaning. You can start simple and if things grow, invest in more equipment and infrastructure. The children need to be involved in preparations and be given every opportunity to develop confidence and independence. Getting them to carry their own bags and key session items is all part of the learning experience.

TOILETING AND HYGIENE

What toilet facilities are you providing? How can all your participants develop and keep good hygiene practices? Where will you change nappies or provide facilities for people with extra needs, maintaining good practice manual handling procedures? When thinking about toilet provision, we need first to protect the privacy and dignity of children and adults and make sure that staff can manage comfortably. It's important that parents, landowners and any key authorities know and agree with what you are providing.

The only omission from National Trust's list of 50 things to do before you are 11 years old is to pee outside! There is a lot to be said about being comfortable and confident in our bodies and free enough to feel we can go to the toilet in nature.

There are several options (see Figure 10.5):

- Use of conventional flush toilets near your site – public or part of your organisation/school.
- Fixed compost toilet – longer term facility. Composting can use many different methods of decomposing waste (see resource links).
- Environmentally friendly chemical and portable loos with a toilet tent – need to consider how you dispose of any waste.
- Wild toileting – usually a designated area with a private barrier and a hole in the ground.

HANDWASHING AND WATER

If your site has no mains water connection, you will need to transport enough water to your site on a regular basis. This can be supported by your group rolling in barrels of water, which can be

Figure 10.4 Bucket toilet in Ireland

Figure 10.5 Various compost toilets

Figure 10.5 Continued

fun and a great learning experience. We mostly use 10-litre water containers that are easier to carry in (see kit list). We also encourage the children and young people to help set up the camps.

All water containers used need to be cleaned thoroughly and checked for any mould on a regular basis. We often use the 'milton tablets' four times per year to clean our containers.

If you are renting land that has non-mains water supply, make sure that the landowner checks and is responsible for regular testing for the quality.

It is considered good practice to provide running warm water (warm for comfort and encouragement for little ones), liquid antibacterial soap and disposable hand towels or a clean designated hand towel to encourage children to wash their hands independently and comfortably. There are containers with taps that can be filled with warm water (heated on a fire or from a thermos) that can be used for hand washing (see Figure 10.6). It is *not* recommended to share a communal bowl for washing hands. All visible cuts and abrasions should be covered with a waterproof dressing/plaster, and alcohol hand rub should be available for use by staff (if children are very young). You can also use environmentally friendly hand wipes, and then wash your hands with warm water when you are back in a building.

FOOD AND WATER

Providing food, snacks and drinking water is essential to well-being and an integral part of a caring and welcoming environment. Sharing and enjoying food together can form the foundation

Figure 10.6 Various washing methods

Figure 10.6 Continued

of a long-term healthy relationship to food. Many children bring along their own drink and lunch in a rucksack, but you are likely to provide some food, or snacks that may need cooking and hot drinks. Carrying good-quality thermoses with hot water for tea/hot juices or foraging (see Chapter 13 on plants) is a simple solution if fires are not available.

What people bring with them also impacts the other participants, particularly in relation to allergies. All this information needs to be gathered in advance of your group (see consent/medical forms) coming to Forest School, with parents having a clear understanding of what they need to provide.

Some food will need to be kept at the appropriate temperature, and food hygiene standards and food safety regulations need to be followed. You can take simple online courses on outdoor food hygiene or organise an onsite training. For many of us this is common sense, but you need to think about and prepare for how you are going to clean and store food and equipment, and provide enough containers for warm and clean water.

It's really important that children can access suitable drinking water at all times. If you're using a public facility, check that the drinking water is suitable.

Cooking on a fire and preparing and helping serve lunch and snacks in an informal and relaxed atmosphere create empowering experiences for children and young people. When cooking outdoors, you will need to consider storage and disposal of any litter. We try to separate compostable material from recycled and landfill waste and encourage children to take back their own rubbish, to avoid practitioners cleaning up after the groups, and share responsibility for our waste. Certain food needs to be stored at the correct temperature, particularly if it is outside for a number of hours. Portable freezer boxes work in warmer climates. A sample HACCP (risk assessment) for outdoor cooking is in the appendix.

We recommend gaining a food hygiene in the outdoors accreditation if you are going to be cooking on a fire; see the IOL and FSA websites for advice on this.

ADVERSE WEATHER AND CONTINGENCY PLANNING

We always aim to be outside as much as possible. As leader, you will need to check the weather forecast prior to the session and make a decision accordingly.

Figure 10.7 Food preparation and cooking in the outdoors

Figure 10.7 Continued

If a weather change happens unexpectedly, you need to think through a contingency plan. This may be ending the session, going indoors (if this is a possibility) or moving to an alternative location.

We follow the Beaufort Scale (Figure 10.8) to decide whether the session is safe to go ahead in windy conditions. We cancel all sessions if the wind is above Force 7 (32–35 miles an hour).

However, in most cases the session will not go ahead if the wind is Force 6 or above. The final decision is made by the facilitator who knows their site specifics and factors, for example age of

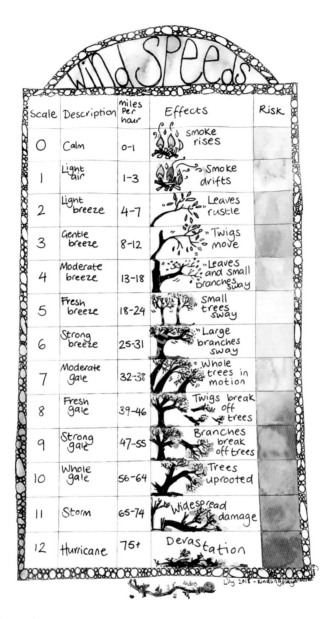

Figure 10.8 Wind speed assessment

Source: Lily Horseman, see www.kindlingplayandtraining.co.uk

Force	What it looks like	What it's called	Wind speed
0	Smoke rises straight up	Calm	0 mph
1	Smoke drifts, indicating wind direction	Light air	1–3 mph
2	Leaves rustle; weathervanes move	Light breeze	4–7 mph
3	Leaves and twigs move	Gentle breeze	8–12 mph
4	Branches move; flags flap	Moderate breeze	13–18 mph
5	Small trees sway; whitecaps on water	Fresh breeze	19–24 mph
6	Large branches move; flags beat	Strong breeze	25–31 mph
7	Whole trees move; flags extend	Near gale	32–38 mph
8	Twigs break; walking is hard	Fresh gale	39–46 mph
9	Signs blow down; slate blows off roof	Strong gale	47–54 mph
10	Trees uproot	Whole gale	55–63 mph
11	Much general damage	Storm	64–72 mph
12	Widespread destruction	Hurricane	72+ mph

Figure 10.8 Continued

trees, time of year, if trees are in leaf, if there are any overhanging branches and type of tree (e.g. horse chestnut or beech).

THUNDER AND LIGHTNING

If possible, walk to nearest vehicles or modern buildings. The following four actions can reduce your lightning risk:

- There is rarely a freak or surprise storm, so plan well and leave time to get to shelter. Sound travels a mile every 5 seconds. If the length between the lightning flash and the sound of thunder is 30 seconds or less (i.e. less than 6 miles away), you should seek shelter immediately.
- If you are exposed to the elements with nowhere to shelter, try to make yourself as small as possible by crouching down with your feet together, hands on knees and head tucked in. This keeps as much of you off the ground as possible, as lightning will not necessarily target the highest object in an area but the object providing a path with the least resistance to the ground. If you have a foam pad to stand on or a pack/sit-upon to sit on – do it. The aim is to reduce your overall footprint to the ground. Try to do this in an area that provides the best protection for you. Lying flat increases the risk of ground current.
- Move away from wide-open spaces or exposed hilltops. Wide-open ground offers high exposure to lightning.

- Do *not* stand under tall or isolated trees. It has been estimated that 25% of people struck by lightning were so as a result of taking shelter under these types of trees. Trees contain about 20% moisture content, compared with humans who have a 65% moisture content. As lightning always takes the path of least resistance, you may become that path for any lightning jumps or radial energy from a strike.

Our weather is constantly changing, and all its magnificence provides a multitude of fun, exciting and imaginative learning.

If you do need to move sites, have a contingency plan (or plans if you have different ones for different circumstances).

- Ensure the alternative location meets the requirements for providing a quality experience and be able to articulate the activities/experiences that will be on offer there.
- Consider how you intend to access the alternative site location, and consider how you will inform parents/carers about changes to location. This could be before the session or during.
- Assess the feasibility of your plans when the session has begun.
- Assess what conditions are likely to cause issues for your site. This is likely to rely on weather forecasts, so you may need to set out criteria for triggering the decision to move to an alternative location. Bear in mind, not all weather reports are accurate, so you may need to experiment until you find the one that's best for your location.

CLOTHING AND KIT – OTHER RESOURCES

Depending on your group, the season/climate and their needs, you may want to think about carrying extra clothing or sunscreen. Ideally, we want the individuals to learn to care for themselves, which begins with physical self-care. People often rise up to our expectations, so if we believe they can't, they won't. A colleague in Scotland was adamant that all her children, as young as 2, learned to get up and move if they felt cold! In the same way as we approach risk-benefit assessment, we need to intervene when a child or young person, for whatever reason, is not able to look after themselves and support them to do so.

You the practitioner – the kit

If your site is off-grid and in a more remote location, you need to consider what *electrical* equipment you need!

- Mobile phones only work where there is reception, except in emergencies where you can use 112. What3Words is the latest app to communicate to emergency services exactly where you are located. You need to know where there is mobile reception so you can make logistical and emergency calls. For more vulnerable groups, we carry walkie-talkies so that we can remain in quick and close communication if necessary. You may need to keep other digital devices such as cameras charged, so a back-up battery pack is advised. Before starting a day, we check our mobile signals and go through the daily risk assessment. All relevant phone numbers are pre-loaded and phones are fully charged.

- A list of participants, including medical conditions and allergies (do they need medication and how is it administered?).
- Storage for medicine.
- Emergency contact details and procedures.
- Bottle of water.
- Emergency snacks.
- Basic equipment to support nature play-based learning across all curriculum areas.

Basic kit list (numbers depend on size of group):

Gaffer tape (always useful to have!)
Assorted ropes and string
Tarps/sheets
Metal buckets and trowels
One pair of loppers and one pair of secateurs
Mallets and stakes
Pruning saw
Fixed blade knife
Sketching and painting kit – scrap paper, crayons, charcoal, pencils, watercolour kit
Bag of sit mats
Firelighting kit
Water carrier (10 litres)
Kettle and 'brew kit'
First aid kit appropriate to site, learners and activities
Bottle of 'sterile water'
Tissues/toilet paper
Mobile phone

Other useful supplies: Below is a list of common items that you may wish to take or trial:

- Bags for rubbish
- List of expectations that have been agreed and shared with everyone

Figure 10.9 Forest School kit

- Toilet equipment – depends on approach to toileting taken
- A whistle (check that children know the calling sound)
- High-visibility vests for adults to wear, especially if walking near roads in the dark
- A mat to sit on or a portable seat
- A few simple resources, e.g. magnifiers, field guides, white sheet, etc.
- A fully charged tablet, iPad or similar

(Adapted from the advice contained in Education Scotland document *Outdoor Learning: Practical Guidance, Ideas and Support for Teachers and Practitioners in Scotland* (2011).)

Additional example of an equipment list from a Forest School practitioner is provided in the online appendix.

Children's clothing and resources

The children need to be involved in the preparations and have every opportunity to develop confidence and independence. Each child can carry:

- Their own drink and snack. The children should put any unwanted food, drink and litter back in their backpack or bag or put it in a bin. Encourage each child to take responsibility for their rubbish.
- A portable seat – important for insulation on cold, damp ground.
- Extra clothes such as a hat, gloves, etc., if these are not being worn.
- Their own treasures that they find.

SAFEGUARDING AND EQUALITY POLICIES AND PROCEDURES TO CONSIDER

- Staff ratios, roles and responsibilities (including volunteer), including CRB/DBS checks.
- Lost or missing child procedure – what will you do if someone is lost, how long before you dial 999.
- Safeguarding – who is the safeguarding office, training for helpers, DBS, parental permission.
- Disclosure – recording and reporting.
- Confidentiality procedure – records and registers.
- Complaint procedure – issues that children/learners, parents/guardians or other adults/helpers might warrant a complaint; who to raise them with.

- Insurance – public liability for leading and for the site.
- Use of photographs.

SITE MANAGEMENT, REDUCING IMPACT AND ENHANCING SITE AND LEARNING

What factors do you need to consider when planning and caring for your site?

A good starting point and website to refer to when looking at management plans and ecological impact is https://sylva.org.uk/myforest/education-promo.

We have included an example of a site assessment and template in the online appendix along with a Forest School management plan.

Your site should have the capacity to provide a range of high-quality play-based practical learning experiences for young children which are positive, challenging, playful and enjoyable. Check for any major hazards – large water bodies may be problematic; a major dog-walking site or drug-using site might mean the site is not really appropriate – this is your initial assessment of the site.

If you feel the site has play and learning potential – with conducive 'spaces' – then the next steps are important (see site appraisal form in the appendix):

- The first port of call is, who owns it? Is there any existing management in place?
- What facilities might the site need? (At the very basic level you need to check access for the group and emergency services, toileting possibilities, seating area and, if needed, vehicle parking.)
- What level of permission do you have – can you light fires etc.?
- Drawing up an agreement with a landowner – see FSA website on guidance.
- Checking out your own insurance and the landowner's insurance for public liability.

Things to consider

- Access for families – public transport.
- Places for parking that don't impede other traffic (this can be one of the main planning issues for a change of use for sites starting to be used for education and more access).
- Boundaries, if they need maintaining, site assessment. (Chapter 10 goes into more about setting up weekly boundaries within the session.)

- What will your entrance look like? Think carefully about making your entrance inviting and exciting for children and visitors. This is your most important boundary line, and it conveys a message about your vision, values and ethos. This could be a favourite tree!
- Are there fixed boundaries that will need to be maintained?
- You can use many types of boundaries in an outdoor context. Informal features include:
  - a change of surface where the edge of a path or a line of trees visually indicate the boundary.
  - scarves, ribbons or other decorations to create a working boundary in a woodland.
  - cones, branches or markers on grass in a public park.
  - natural feature such as an outcrop of rocks or a line drawn in the sand on a beach.
- With regular practice that focuses on children's independent ability to stay within boundaries, almost all remember and meet the expectations. If a child struggles with this, consider why and decide how to positively support the child to manage it.

If your site has fixed boundaries such as walls, gates, hedges or fences, you or the landowner will need to maintain them in good condition. Planting hedges can help increase biodiversity and act as a barrier to road traffic pollutants. As an intermediate barrier, you can create a brush barrier weaving branches and other long natural materials to form a temporary barrier which can encourage brambles or other wild plants. Shrubs/small trees on the edge of the woodland and glades, such as hazel, elderberry, blackthorn, damson, and crab apple, can be useful for food and resources. It is good to follow permaculture design principles when looking at enhancing the site for humans and wildlife, and the 'edges' within and on the outside of the site are often the most exciting (see www.childreninpermaculture.com).

Actions you can follow if you have a site to care for in the long term (see sample management plan in online appendix)

- Decide on your long-term vision for the site. How would you like it to be in 3/5/10 years' time?
- Consider starting by dynamically and informally helping the whole community understand the ecological principles that relate to woodlands.
- Mapping the woodland area is a great way to get 'inside the wood'. Mark any boundaries, access points, water features and activity areas such as fire site and shelter-building area. Can the children be involved in this? Do a site survey of the trees, plants and animals – even mark what eats what or the light levels in different places. Include old decaying trees, veteran trees. Are there any rare species that need protecting or invasive species that would benefit from active management?

Figure 10.10 Surveying and mapping your site

A novel way of recording trees and plants on your site

- Ecological impact assessment. How can your children be involved?
- Check for environmental designations/restrictions.

Figure 10.11 Minibeast hotels, bird feeders and tree planting

Figure 10.11 Continued

- Ideas to improve biodiversity or habitats: bird boxes, dead hedging, habitat piles, tree planting etc. Can you plant food plants for plants and animals – and of course humans?
- Make a 3-year plan based around your ecological impact assessment.
- Consider the best time of year to do work.

Figure 10.11 Continued

- Monitor to see if what you are doing is working/sustainable – surveys/fixed point photos.
- It is advisable to have a tree safety survey done. The regularity of this will depend on the site and impact of any weather. It is recommended in most woodlands that this is done on a 3-year basis.
- Do not assume all potentially harmful plants must be removed. They are an opportunity for children to learn how to be safe. Instead, take simple measures such as strimming or mowing pathways through some areas to create access in the height of summer.
- Perhaps clear other areas to control invasive species such as Japanese knotweed.
- Store bulbs and seed packets out of reach of children.

Figure 10.12 Types of shelter and places to play, including an outdoor classroom covered area!

Figure 10.12 Continued

Shelters

What kind of **shelter** are you planning to provide? Is there existing built or natural shelter you can use or adapt? Do you have a place where you can be warmer and retreat from some of the wilder weather? Is there a place for younger children to sleep and rest? A key Forest School skill is being able to rig up a shelter when you need it. This can be done before the group arrives or with the help of a willing crew of young people. Making a home is an essential part of feeling safe and grounded.

Forest School is most well known for sheltering under a tarpaulin which is above a central fire place!

Under the shelter you will most often find tree stumps, and if you are lucky, you may have some cosy insulated mats to sit on as well!

For further ideas on woodland management plans and involving children, see https://sylva.org.uk/myforest/education and https://woodlandwildlifetoolkit.sylva.org.uk.

COMMUNICATION WITH THE MAIN STAKEHOLDERS

Prepare, educate and inform your staff, volunteers, children and parents about the nature-based visits: Despite the supportive research and increased awareness of the benefits of nature, there may be people who are worried about children in their care spending significant time out of doors. They might have heard teachers and parents concerned that other STEM (science, technology, engineering and maths) subjects may be compromised if they spend too much time 'just playing'. At the other end, some people will want their children to experience more challenge, risk and active experiential learning. We need to listen to as many voices as possible and find a way to communicate how, what and why we are advocating the outdoors as a necessary part of education, health and well-being. See online appendix for a sample parents/carer information letter and information leaflet for adult helpers.

Communication with colleagues and decision-makers: See the sample communication strategy in the online appendix.

SESSION PLANNING

In the next chapter is one example of a first session plan for an early years' group and one for a 'family' group. The first session will probably be one of the more adult-led sessions, including choice included from the start. This is mainly because the learners will not be familiar with you and the site and you will need to 'hold a safe space'. The largest part of the session planning sheet will be the observation, evaluation and possible lines of development sections. These inform the following session and are based on the learners' interests and progression of learning and development. When it comes to thinking about routines and a 'shape' of a session, here are some thoughts.

Joseph Cornell (2015), considered the grandfather of experiential nature education, spent many years observing nature and how young people behaved in nature. He developed a simple 'formula' that mapped his sessions in nature with young people. Although he didn't link it directly with the times of the day or the times of year, he understood that we all tend to follow a cycle which works best, using the following four key steps. The following four key steps or stages and the five tenets make up Cornell's theory of 'Flow Learning'. He identified, after many years of working with groups in nature, that this sequence provided 'flow'. The 'experience' step was more immersive if the first two steps were present.

- Every session should create **enthusiasm** (or inspiration) for the group.
- Then, the group would be able and willing to **focus**.
- After that, it was important to provide an experiential, sensory-based experience, which he called **experience**.
- Finally, end a session with enough time to gather and **share an inspiration**.

Joseph based his teaching on five tenets that have helped him work with energetic, lively children:

- Teach less and share more.
- Be receptive.
- Focus the children's attention without delay.
- Look and experience first.
- Talk later and ensure that a sense of joy permeates the experience.

His book *Sharing Nature with Children* (2015) offers a range of excellent activities and explains his methods more thoroughly (see Bibliography).

It is worth embracing these principles when planning sessions, especially the first one when we are trying to create both a 'safe container' and a sense of 'magic and joy'.

Jon Young et al. (2008), another leader in the field of nature-based community building, and others developed this natural observation of children's learning and drew on Lakota spiritual philosophy in order to explain (among other things) a way of organising a session in nature and how a team is organised around natural principles (see later for an example of an adapted nature-centric session).

Jon furthered Joseph Cornell's work by linking these natural processes of learning to nature's cycles, the times of the day, year and life cycle of a human see Figure 10.13). He drew on extensive traditional based knowledge of the nature-sun cycles and placed this knowledge

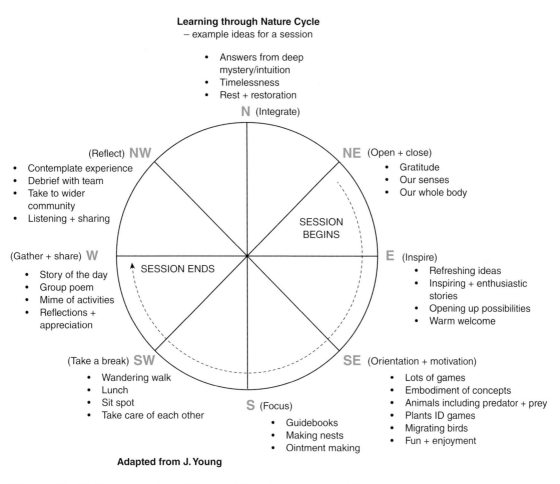

Learning through Nature Cycle
— example ideas for a session

- Answers from deep mystery/intuition
- Timelessness
- Rest + restoration

N (Integrate)

(Reflect) NW
- Contemplate experience
- Debrief with team
- Take to wider community
- Listening + sharing

NE (Open + close)
- Gratitude
- Our senses
- Our whole body

SESSION BEGINS

(Gather + share) W
- Story of the day
- Group poem
- Mime of activities
- Reflections + appreciation

SESSION ENDS

E (Inspire)
- Refreshing ideas
- Inspiring + enthusiastic stories
- Opening up possibilities
- Warm welcome

(Take a break) SW
- Wandering walk
- Lunch
- Sit spot
- Take care of each other

SE (Orientation + motivation)
- Lots of games
- Embodiment of concepts
- Animals including predator + prey
- Plants ID games
- Migrating birds
- Fun + enjoyment

S (Focus)
- Guidebooks
- Making nests
- Ointment making

Adapted from J. Young

Figure 10.13 Planning cycle and ideas to follow the seasons and directions

Source: Adapted from Jon Young's natural learning cycle in *Coyote's Guide* (2018)

into an educational framework. When planning a Forest School/nature-based session, Jon's work showed how it is useful to consider the stages: north-east (open and close) to west (gather and share), the external part of the cycle. All children benefit from eliciting enthusiasm and inspiration at the beginning, linked to movement and action, which then enables them to willingly focus, followed by a 'break' or 'free time', then gathering or sharing. The internal or west to north-east cycle in the natural learning cycle represents the reflection, processing and integration time that may occur between sessions. This model is a useful reference and planning guide, but in the end we are following the child's lead, so any formal planning may easily go out the window!

During your reflection time, it is worth reviewing if all of the previously mentioned elements were included or if any were missing. I have noticed that sometimes a session doesn't go as well because we moved too quickly into focus without providing lots of running around time and arrival and inspiration.

As well as the overall 'shape' and 'feel' of the session, it also worth considering the eight play 'themes' outlined in Chapter 6 on play when looking at components for a session plan.

- Becoming at home
- Playing hunting and gathering games
- Gaining height and prospect
- Anthropomorphising non-humans
- Constructing adventures
- Imaginative narratives
- Pathways and journeys
- Rituals and celebrations

When beginning your journey as a practitioner, trust that these natural design principles will provide endless learning, fun and opportunities to grow socially, emotionally and physically. It is necessary to put aside the adult need to fill time and direct the learning and observe what emerges through the play and time in the outdoors. Returning to the nature play cycle (Chapters 3 and 6), we have to be vigilant that our role encourages agency in the young person and to develop the necessary skill of standing back and interrupting at the 'right' time!

> By using these nature play themes, a bottom up approach that builds upon children's interests happens. For example, think about what children do with and in trees: climb them, build houses in them, read in them, hug them, make nests with their leaves, ride on their branches, play with dolls in their shade, gaze at the sky through the leaves, smell them, become friends with them. Nature play is more about the relationships that can be cultivated between children and trees in their own backyards as a precursor to saving the rainforest as they get older, when they can actually do something about it. Talking to trees and hiding in trees precedes saving trees.
>
> *This approach is more effective than an adult imposed top-down mind set, e.g. rainforests are disappearing, so let's teach children about the rainforests so they will save them.*
>
> (Juliet Robertson from http://creativestarlearning.co.uk/nature-play-learning/nature-design-principles/)

After completing the planning and running of the first session, and the nerves settle, it is imperative to deeply reflect. Then move on, diving deeper into the relationship building with the group and natural place. The action now really kicks in, which we expand on in the next three chapters.

QUESTIONS FOR PRACTICE

Where on the wonky wheel are you in regards to experience and preparations?

Do you know where to get support and advice?

Have you made a checklist of all the things you need in place before conducting your first session?

USEFUL RESOURCES

The online appendix for Chapter 10 (www.routledge.com/9780367425616) has many of the planning resources and templates including sample risk benefit assessments, site checklists, site management plans and much more.

www.owlscotland.org/ The main website and network for supporting outdoor learning in Scotland. This site has lots of useful resources on it – from policy and procedural documents to lots of useful activities and support for programmes like Forest School. For Scottish networks and 'care' guidance in the outdoors, also see www.playscotland.org/world-ourdoors/

www.outdoorlearningwales.org/ The main Outdoor Learning Wales website useful for resources and networks 'alive' in Wales.

www.lotc.org.uk/ Council for Learning Outside the Classroom. One of the main 'go to' websites for supporting schools with outdoor learning, lots of updates on government and national policy, outdoor learning resources and accreditation schemes.

www.outdoor-learning.org/ The Institute for Outdoor Learning is the UK umbrella body for all types of outdoor learning with many resources and trainings relating to outdoor learning provision.

www.theoutdoorteacher.com Marina Robb also offers Online Professional Training. Courses include in-depth practical tutorials on making fires, shelters and wood crafts, forest games, foraging and cooking with wild plants as well as a broad range of webinars and bespoke trainings.

www.circleofliferediscovery.com A community interest company offering nature-based programmes, green interventions and Forest School for education and health practitioners, specialising in working with vulnerable groups.

www.forestschoolassociation.org/forest-school-knowledge-base/ The Forest School Association provides lots of advice on establishing Forest School, including resources on the website and a provider endorsement scheme.

www.hse.gov.uk/services/education/school-trips.pdf The government body for health and safety at work, HSE provides lots of resources and information about outdoor learning, including this general document about 'myths' that relate to health and safety on outdoor school trips. A very useful website. For information on ratios and local guidance, refer to local authority guidelines and the Outdoor Education Advisors panel – see https://oeapng.info/

https://playsafetyforum.wordpress.com/resources/ The Play Safety Forum has produced many resources relating to risk management and risk-benefit assessments.

https://naturenet.net/index.php For easy-to-use and -read information on protected species and good wood-land/countryside management advice and resources.

BIBLIOGRAPHY

Ball, D, Gill, T and Spiegel, B (2008) *Managing Risk in Play Provision: An Implementation Guide*. Play Safety Forum.

Cornell, J B (2015) *Sharing Nature: Nature Awareness Activities for All Ages*. Nevada City, CA: Crystal Clarity Publishers.

Palmer, S (2016) *Upstart: The Case for Raising the School Starting Age and Providing What the Under-Sevens Really Need*. Edinburgh: Floris Books.

Sobel, D (2008) *Children and Nature-Design Principles for Educators*. Stenhouse Publishers.

Young, J, Haas, E and McGown, E (2008) *Coyote's Guide to Connecting with Nature*. Washington: Owlink Media.

11 Planning to action

There was a child went forth every day
And the first object he looked upon, that object he became,
And that object became part of him for the day or a certain part of the day,
Or for many years or stretching cycles of years.

(Walt Whitman)

It's a cold February day, and we have gotten to the woods early to light a fire to welcome the group. We thought a warm soup would be a good idea today! We set up one swing and a hammock, put out our emergency bag (with RBAs, lost child policy, emergency plan, extra first aid – see Chapter 10 online appendix), set out our fire equipment and have a pre-meeting check-in with the staff and volunteer. The group (teenagers who meet monthly who are attached to CAMHS) arrive at the gate on Park Lane in East Sussex, and we walk into our main site, a good transition from home for some of these teenagers. They are used to the routine by now – we have a check-in (gratitude/what we appreciate around the circle) and a drink, divide up into our three main 'set-up' groups to prep food, light a cooking fire, set up the net, and then play a seasonal game – like nest robbers! We let the group know what is on offer today (based on last time's reflections), and then they can choose what they want to do. This is a group with lots of emotional needs, so as staff we try to help them connect with others, whilst respecting that sometimes solo time is just what they need. Some lie on the net, others crack on with a craft project, some set up another swing and we offer something relating to the season such as making a bird feeder or willow cordage in spring. We say, "Let us know if you need anything".

Play on the net looks a little too rough. "That doesn't look like Harry is enjoying that. Harry?" What can we do when we don't like something that is happening?

A girl looks a little lost. "What can I do?' "What would you like to do?" "Don't know." "Let's think about some choices." I give some time for quiet space between us. "Can I paint something?" "Yes we have paints, what material do you want to use?" "Have you got any of that material from last time?" "The calico? Yes, here, let's go get the things." The girl then took her time to paint a design with a quote on it to take home.

Figure 11.1 Planning to action – a freely chosen art experience with support from the leader

We finished the last chapter looking at session planning and some key things to consider when planning for a first session, particularly in a Forest School programme. The story of page 267 is a typical moment in one of Marina's established programmes with its routines and community-based pedagogy in the woods. It demonstrates how the learners do become the place and the objects they are 'playing with'. This chapter aims to thread together the core routines, practices and activities that you may see across the year at a Forest School and/or nature-based programme

Figure 11.1 Continued

and look at how we deliver a Forest School/nature education programme. The subjects we will look at include

- General practices to consider
- Long-term planning – working with the seasons in different cultures and with different age groups

- Case studies – session planning at different stages in a programme and with different types of groups
- The art of observation and different ways of recording observations and evaluations
- Importance of language and communication – ways we communicate when facilitating nature education

GENERAL PRACTICES

Much of this chapter is based on a northern hemisphere's temperate climate, where we are blessed with seasons that happen across the year, or indeed in one day! All programmes reflect the key dynamics of people, place and season, practitioners and resources. Within the Forest School model, we apply good play-based and learning pedagogy, values and principles across the stages of life, and apply our experience to the individuals and groups that we are working alongside.

In Forest School and wider nature-based education, we are most commonly focused on childhood (3–18 years) up to young adulthood (18–25). The health and well-being programmes that work with specific 'targeted' groups may be offered to those of older ages, for example the programme on dementia in the woods. The focus in this chapter, however, is on young people and children.

However, it is worth noting that many programmes often are intergenerational and do involve parents, community members, adolescents and younger children. Even when the focus is on early years, for example, it is worth considering the adult helpers as an integral part of the programme and, as such, what their relationship to nature and environmental issues may be. The 'natural blueprint' model from Scandinavia is a useful reminder of these relationships (see Figure 11.2).

When delivering, planning, delivering, planning, delivering etc. (as all teachers do in the mainstream education system), it is worth reminding ourselves in a nature-based programme of what we are doing – all programmes aim to provide embodied experiences that build a multitude of relationships with humans and the non-human world. We are looking for endless opportunities for us to get to know the learner and build social relationships. All the while, we all grow and learn as part of the wider community. *At the heart of deep learning is relationship*, providing connections that are nourishing and enable well-being.

Of course, there are many challenges and difficult relationships we can benefit from, cultivating compassion for ourselves and others (Chapter 9). Before embarking on delivering a Forest School programme, we may do well to be aware of challenges that may lie ahead and the courage needed to take the plunge and *learn from any mistakes*! Maybe we wake up feeling irritable for no particular reason, or something or someone frustrates us. Try to take a moment to centre yourself and consider your well-being. Naming something you are grateful for is an easy way to acknowledge the challenges whilst finding a kinder way of behaving towards yourself. This will help you to organise yourself and offer a grounded container for contentment and well-being.

A natural blueprint

Influence society

Take a position about environmental care

Learning how man affects the nature

Understand nature

Observe the nature – and get experiences

Be in the nature – and enjoy it

Figure 11.2 The natural blueprint regarding human interaction with nature at stages of development

As practitioners, you have to have all your health and safety integrated into what you do; which is made easier when learning benefits are integrated into our health and safety procedures (through RBAs). Once you begin to meet the children or young people and the 'helpers', you can co-develop sessions and get to know the people, finding ways that best support them emotionally, physically, mentally, cognitively and spiritually. First, try to cultivate a way of working that looks after yourself and gives a moment to connect with your helpers. It's not easy to prioritise this, but keep trying – group gratitude before the day begins and an intention for the day is a nice start.

Planning ahead, getting your gear ready in advance and having a clear session outline based on the previous week are all essential and valuable nature pedagogical practice. Staff need to know expectations and any assumptions to do with their role. This is all part of creating a safe container, where the entire team feel held and know what they are doing, as well as focusing on the areas we are supporting through the practice. It is totally understandable why practitioners overplan, creating a raft of possible ideas and resources in advance. The general principle is to plan thoroughly, particularly if you are working as part of a team, and then expect to drop at least 50% of what was planned! What you do is equally important to the relationships formed.

The stage of life and development does affect the key dynamics in your sessions. Early years' practitioners are more likely to need fewer resources and base their session around self-directed play, imagination, movement and sensory immersion (e.g. mud kitchens and puddles). An older group's interests and emotional development is likely to be more complex, and you may need more resources or experience to be able to support them. This doesn't mean you have to have the answers or the expertise. Not having the answers and working things out together is great modelling and very realistic. It's very hard for a young person to show they know anything if you, as an adult, always seem to have the answers, so be generous with your 'not knowing'. This approach to education is not to give knowledge but to try to draw out their knowledge – and there is an art to this!

Weekly sessions throughout the year offer developmentally appropriate child-centred education in the outdoors. The Forest School approach developed in the UK is one of several nature-based programmes. In the UK, the training offered enables practitioners to work alongside children from the early years into young adulthood, and as we will see this is now being applied to green care and interventions. All groups plan a beginning, middle and end, much like writing a story! How you begin and the rituals you have in place are diverse and reflect the group you are with, the place you are in and what is happening at different times of year. Holding a circle, singing a song, sharing a word and preparing the food or backpacks may all be part of your beginning. Whether you start your session from the classroom, walk to your green space or meet at the woods will influence the day ahead. There is no such thing as bad weather, only bad clothing! This is a very true statement, one that is usually more troubling to the adults than the young people. Two-year-olds will move if they are cold but may need to be given permission. Temperature can affect your pleasure and safety, so having the right gear really helps – second-hand shops or a shout out from your local community can make this possible (see Chapter 10 for clothing advice). A warm welcome and friendly relationship with parents and school staff builds supportive relationships (see information for parents, carers and volunteers in Chapter 10 online appendix).

HOW LONG IS, HOW FREQUENT IS, AND HOW MANY CHILDREN ARE IN A TYPICAL FOREST SCHOOL SESSION?

Forest School is part of mainstream education in the UK. Teachers train to become a Forest School Level 3 leader, or schools employ a Forest School leader from outside the school organisation. There are different ways of training and recognising 'pedagogues' or educators in other countries. Our view is this provision should be part of every person's education and not in any way exclusive. Our aim is for every child, from early years through secondary education, to have access to high-quality outdoor play-based, person-centred education. Within the constraints of current government policy and priorities, in the UK, most Forest School is delivered as a morning or afternoon, once per week within early years' and primary schools. The early years' curriculum promotes play and movement, but does not necessarily give access to the 'natural' outdoors, and we are pushing against the digitalisation of children's lives and downward creeping academising of formal early years' education.

Typically, a Forest School session would last 2.5 hours (a morning or afternoon), have up to 16 of the same young people (conveniently half a class) and meet once a week throughout the

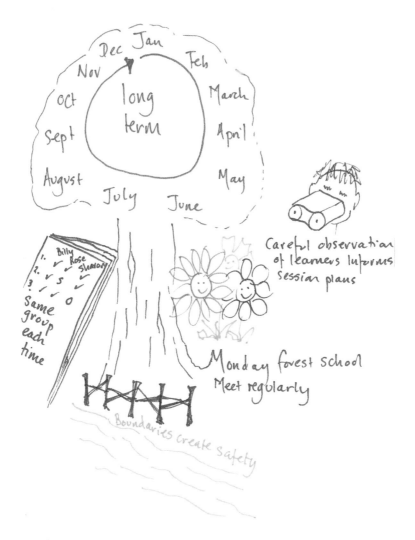

Figure 11.3 Forest School regular, long-term principle

year. This is much more likely to happen in a primary school (ages 5–11 years). Depending on your location and age of group, at a minimum you would have at least one trained Forest School leader (practitioner) and a volunteer, who may be a Forest School assistant (Level 2 trained). Of course, the higher the ratio of adults to young people, the higher the quality of relationship, which is the key switch for learning and well-being. All the key dynamics are in play and influence each other. Most countries and schools have a predefined ratio of adults to children. This needs to be followed. Using tools often requires additional staff (see Chapter 12) and is related to the risk perception of an activity.

In secondary school, Forest School is often offered to targeted groups of young people who are struggling with mainstream education and may be a whole-day session within school time or morning or afternoon. Many home-schooled children also access Forest School sessions.

Early years' Forest School and nature-based models

Beyond Forest School, especially within nature-based early years' programmes, there is much greater flexibility within the curriculum and support by national policy. In Scotland, recent changes in childcare hours have been promoted as a great opportunity to offer children greater access to the outdoors. Indeed, the Scottish equivalent of our OFSTED – 'The Care Inspectorate' – has published several documents promoting outdoor settings for the early years (see the useful resources section – My World Outdoors pdf; Out to Play pdf). The Care Inspectorate has used the term 'outdoor setting' to describe early learning organisations that have registered specifically as an outdoor early learning and childcare establishment in which children are outdoors all of the time (90%) except in extreme weather conditions.

The Forest/Nature Kindergarten movement that surfaced in 1960s in Scandinavia flourished in 1990s (Egle, 2013 – see Robertson) in Finland, Norway, Sweden, Denmark, Germany, UK, Australia and New Zealand. This is now beginning to flourish in many other countries as well, including those on the American and Asian continents (McCree, 2014), and often promote 75% of the day outdoors. The emphasis is on social-emotional development. Children in nature pre-schools, a North American–coined programme, spend 50% of the day outside supported by a progressive early years' indoors curriculum.

Scotland has developed its own Forest Kindergarten Practice and Training (supported by the Forestry Commission: Scottish Forestry – see online appendix) specifically for early years' practitioners, and the rest of the UK are currently looking to follow a similar model. Here, like Forest Schools, they offer young children frequent, regular opportunities to learn through play in a woodland (and green spaces). It involves repeated visits by the same group of children, usually weekly, to the same site, throughout the year, in almost all weather. During the sessions, the children are free to play, explore, have fun and learn. There is no specific recommendation for time spent out of doors.

In Sweden, Skogsmulle was developed by Gosta Frohm in 1957. 'Skog' means 'wood' and 'Mulle' is a fictional character who helps children learn to love and care for nature, a little like the 'Woodcraft movement', and is activity-family based. This was so successful that it was integrated into the first nursery school by Siw Linde in 1985, called "I Ur och Skur" translated as 'Rain or Shine'. This eventually became state funded. Over the course of the year, the children will spend over 80% of the time outdoors. These schools have specific structures based on age-related nature-based activities and are an ideal playground.

In reality, practitioners around the world who understand the benefits of learning in local (see Sobel's place-based education (2004)) and natural places are finding ways within their own local constraints to support children's learning, development and well-being outdoors and to apply local place-based cultures and connections within their programmes. The expertise of practitioners and the values, principles and pedagogy unite the approaches across the world.

Traditional session planning within education

Within education, there are many useful planning tools and session templates that provide a helpful way to think and reflect upon a session in advance and after each session (see the previous chapter). The reflection is really the most important aspect of our learning, where we digest what we have experienced and observed and listen to what the group or individual would most benefit from.

Many practitioners create a termly overview of place- and season-based 'offers' that the participants can choose to engage with. This is a nice way of collecting ideas that you and your clients suggest and could include cooking ideas, winter crafts or autumn foraging cordials. The recently published *The Children's Forest* (Casey et al., 2019) provides a wealth of ideas that link particularly to the eight Celtic seasonal 'markers' and celebrations. We see it as good practice to not only follow the learner but also nature and the rhythms of the year. It helps attune our senses and bodies, supporting the brain/body/heart/environment synchronicity (see later).

If this programme happens year after year, it is important to follow the place and see how things change each year, such as when buds start budding, when leaves start forming and falling, when birds come and go, and how trees and plants might change from year to year and to observe the influence of climate change (see Woodland Trust and OPAL in the useful resources section for support). Are trees being affected by diseases such as ash dieback and phytophera? You can monitor this through and over the years and contribute to some of the citizen science happening around the UK (see www.observatree.org.uk/). Much of this can contribute to our understanding of issues such as climate change that affect our woods and natural environment.

SESSION AND PROGRAMME PLANS – WOODED, GREEN AND URBAN SPACES

In the Chapter 11 online appendix, we have included a number of different programme and session plans from a variety of groups, including early years, a family group with particular needs, and an urban group of 6- to 7-year olds. You can see that the observations are indeed the key to each session and the subsequent session, as well as how much thought goes into planning. Preparation is key. This is a mindset whereby we are working with all four dynamics:

- deeply reflecting and working hard to **understand the learners'** needs, motivations and stages of development
- **resourcing** the sessions
- working with the **site and season**
- thinking about our, the **leaders and other adults**, needs and relationships to site and community

You can see from these session plans and reflections on the sessions that the reflection part of the process occupies as much, if not more, space in the planning. This relies entirely on good observation practice, which we will now examine.

Observation – the key to our practice

We need to cleanse the windows of perception.

(Aldous Huxley, 1954)

People often say to Forest School leaders, "All you do is play in the woods or stand around watching the children", and our reply is "Yes! Observation is probably the most awesome duty any educator has if we are to draw on the wisdom all learners have and help them build on this to make meaning of the world. And play is the deepest form of learning!"

We need to be able to see, hear and feel what learners are doing in order to assess the wisdom within, before deciding what is happening in any given learning situation and then deciding whether we accompany the learner or leave them be. The observation bit, however, is a real art, as shown in the online examples . . . all of us bring baggage and our own perceptions of what is going on with the learners. Someone once said, "Perception is the difference between what we think we see and what we actually see". So we really have to wipe away all our filters to observe learners with fresh new eyes, in order to observe the truth. We constantly walk around making meaning of the world – fitting it into our own frameworks and belief systems. If meanings don't fit, then we can sometimes experience discombobulation. It's amazing that we start making meanings and perceptions when we are very young – interpreting facial expressions, tones of voice, body language, words. When we get to adulthood, these are pretty well fixed, and we are all slightly different as a result of our childhood, temperaments and life experiences. As nature educators, we need to be aware of how we instantly interpret what learners are exhibiting in order to keep in check our filters. We need to know our 'baggage', judgments and prejudices – to be aware of how our values may influence. We need to stop ourselves expecting what we expect to see, that is, our own points of view! In other words, we need to be mindful – to engage in fully conscious practice when observing learners.

Let's make this concrete with a situation Jon encountered at Forest School last spring. A young adolescent, Shaun, aged 14, with a 'label' in the classroom for being disruptive and somewhat 'hyper', was attending his first session. He had a good session from Jon's perspective, engaged in many aspects of this Forest School session – from splitting wood and trying to light the fire, taking note of my instructions on safe and effective ways of working with the firesteel, to waiting for his turn on the swing. On the way back he was 'helping' push the equipment trolley, by walking alongside the trolley and holding the rail. His voice was slightly raised and he was involved in the banter of the moment. At one point he started moving quite fast with the trolley. The teacher in charge of the group – who had been talking 'at' him throughout the session, complimenting his involvement and picking up on his every movement, stopped him and pulled him to one side. She started scolding him for not being 'controlled' and threatening to not allow him to come again – there had been a split-second observation wrapped up in interpretation of what was happening. Jon had to intervene to give his observation of what had happened. From Jon's perspective, the learner was pushing the trolley enthusiastically and safely while engaging in the fast conversation he was having with Jon. From the teacher's perspective, he was being disruptive and unsafe – it was a matter of two perceptions and sets of 'baggage' shading what was actually happening in that moment. Context is everything.

Let's examine what is involved with observation and how our own perspectives and evaluations interact with the act of observing.

Take a look at Figure 11.4.

Write down what you see.

Take a break and then examine your list.

Are there any words that may be interpretive or judging, such as 'happy', 'unsure', 'teamwork'? If so, cross them out, as these words are not observations about what you see; they are about what you think you see.

If there is a smile, write 'smile' rather than 'happy'. If the children are making something together, write that children *a* and *b* are putting sticks and stumps on top of each and child *a* puts the first stump on the ground and then child *a* steps back and child *b* picks up another stump and places it on top of the first stump very slowly so it is flat on the top, rather than children *a* and *b* are cooperating and working as a team to make a stump tower.

Were you surprised at how many evaluative words were used or were you using pure observational narrative without any 'judgment' words?

From this simple example, if you really wanted to know what was going on in terms of the interactions and actions witnessed, we would need to somehow subtly find out what the learners'

Figure 11.4 Forest School scene

perspectives are while not interrupting the 'flow' (see the ludic process in Chapter 6 137 – 139). Only then can we check out our own interpretations of what we see and either clarify our own understandings and/or through the dialogue help the learners understand what might be happening for them and understand the learning through their constructs. Without this learner/practitioner dialogue turning into a typical teacher/learner interaction, that is, a 20 questions-type interaction, the checking in with the learners should be as informal and human as possible so you really get to the genuine honest 'what is going on for me' learning. Obviously, this could become overwhelming if we were to observe every little thing that is happening in a Forest School session – the practitioner would spend all their time checking their interpretations, interrupting the learning process incessantly!

So how do we observe when we really do want to know what is going on for every individual at Forest School, and what do we record to inform ourselves, the learners, 'significant others' and our organisations about the learning and development that a nature education programme is facilitating?

The observation process – what are we observing?

Our observations need to have both the child/learner and Forest School context in mind while all the time being aware of our own values that influence our interpretation of observations we do or don't see and hear.

In order to do this, the Forest School leader needs be both a good seer and a good listener. Imaginative play, such an important aspect of Forest School with early years' and primary school children, provides us with lots of opportunity to listen to child's talk, helping us get 'inside their head'.

Margaret Meek (1985, p. 49, 1) pointed out "children can say all they know, in any way they like . . . they attempt in play what they might not risk in everyday activity".

The most fundamental three questions we need to ask ourselves when looking at learning and development during the observation and planning process are summarised in Figure 11.5.

When we ask what is there to see, hear and feel, we need to be open to anything happening and at the same time be alive to what our broad reasons for having this provision for the learner regarding their own specific learning or development needs. A FS leader must observe everything, including the unforeseen and unwelcome, and include both the cognitive and emotional development of learners. This was something Jon often espoused for Forest School practitioners, but how can this happen? We can't really observe everything in everyone and enter into their worlds! The collection and selection of evidence is inevitably incomplete and partial – this is the natural condition of the human mind (Lowenfield, 1935), especially in large groups who have freedom to roam the woods! If we can't take everything on but still need to be keenly aware of everything – what do we do, what do we observe?

We literally have to wipe away our own perceptions and see things for what they are, not what we think they are, and quite often we miss the child height and child perspectives. To overcome

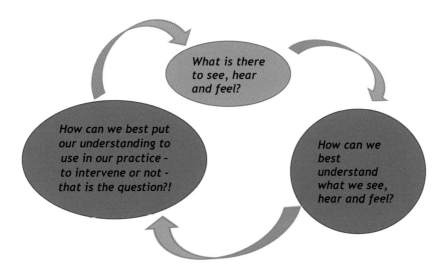

Figure 11.5 The observation process
Source: Mary Drummond, 2003

this, as practitioners we need to rediscover the joy and adventure in exploring the world with all our senses, get a magnifier out and really look at the veins in the leaf as if for the first time, delve hands into different soils and clays, balance on a branch (not too high up!), swing on a rope, lie under the trees as the leaves are budding, and listen to the heartbeat of a tree. We need to rediscover what it is like to experience this multisensory environment for the first time and be curious about how the world works. Why do many plants emerge with two big leaves to start their journey towards the sun? What makes the firesteel spark? Unless we can enter this world and shed all our own baggage, can we really see what the child and learner is experiencing and doing from their perspective? It is enough to realise the world is full of mystery and invention.

It is not necessary for the child to awaken to the sense of the strange and humorous by giving a man a luminous nose. To the child it is sufficiently strange and humorous to have a nose at all.

(G K Chesterton, 1908)

Sometimes story helps animate the wood, but quite often the curious nature of nature is all that is needed.

At the same time, we are social creatures and, as we have emphasised throughout the book, this 'community' of learning also has the all-important social aspect; observation should and can also include the many facets of how we relate to our human community.

Observation can take on many aspects of development. Are we looking for the sensory? the curious? the invention? connection and immersion in the natural world? how the learner interacts with others through their communication and language? What ways does the learner communicate feelings? What is their mood? What skills are they developing – motor skills? movement? problem solving etc.? Phew! It is a big subject. To skilfully observe, we may have some specific things we are looking at – notice we said looking *at*, not looking *for*; as soon as we look *for* things the observation process becomes narrow and reverts to a 'product-based' process rather than a 'learning-process' process.

This question of what are we observing came into sharp focus for Jon when working with the two adolescent males, Jeff and Bill, whom we talked about in Chapter 9. Jon's feedback to the setting was based on the settings' (i.e., the special school) aspirations for Jeff and Bill on improving their relationship with others in their peer group and how they interacted with the two adults and each other. Jon was also looking at the particular practical skills that may be developed in the outdoors – working with tools, fire, rope etc. However, it became very clear that what Jon was observing with Jeff, one of the learners prone to fighting in the setting, was the relationship with animals and the natural world in minute detail, as this seemed to be the place he came alive and was curious about the world. Jon and the group's TA ended up making detailed observations of Jeff's language – verbal and body and the way he was, emotionally and physically, when in the company of snakes, newts, invertebrates and bees. The centre Jon worked at kept beehives on the site, and Jeff had a couple of excursions in the bee suit with the centre's beekeeper. Jon's observations of Jeff's language are outlined in the next section on how we observe.

The key to deciding what to observe is to start by making some baseline observations on some of the broad aspects of why you are running your Forest School programme – back to the broad aims of the programme as outlined in the Session and Programme Plans section of this chapter, but don't miss the opportunity to follow the child's interests and what is happening in the natural world. You may also be channelled down the route of what the 'flavour of the day' is in education. Currently in England, OFSTED is taking more seriously health and well-being, behaviour and personal development. Indeed, in the new inspection framework for education settings in England, introduced in September 2019, 'Behaviour and Attitudes' and 'Personal Development' are two of the four priorities (one of the others is 'Quality of Education', which includes moving away from a reliance on national tests for assessment). This makes observation at Forest School all the more relevant. However, a word of caution – we, as practitioners, should still be attempting to observe what is relevant for the learner and the place. Our values impinge on this. Jon and Marina are always looking for connections to nature, as that is one of our main reasons for being involved in environmental learning, ever since we both started this vocation over 40 years ago! Values and the education climate of the day can take away from focusing on the individual needs and aspirations of the learners.

A number of 'measures' people look at when observing learners in Forest School may well dictate what you observe. These should be based on recognised pedagogies/models of learning such as those outlined in Chapter 3 in the wheels of development:

- Stages of learning and development
- Brain development
- Emotional development
- Learning styles
- Principles of holistic development
- Multiple intelligences
- Schematic development
- Early years' effective learning characteristics
- Learner talents and interests (as well as those essentials for living in this modern world)

If we are to understand learning and development, this cannot be reduced to a tick sheet; humans are far more complex. Many forms and constructs have been devised for child observation, from the current English EYFS profile with its 20 early learning goals that include six effective learning characteristics and seven areas of learning through to the PEMS+ (see ACEWILD, 2015) system for looking at young people with 'challenging behaviour'. As an observer, the question to ask is, Do these relate to a learning and development theory and actually make sense of the 'learning in action'?

In the online appendices, we have outlined a number of observation tools that relate to well-being, motivation, personal and social development and 'skills' development.

If, like us, you really want to look at deeper nature connection, you may want to ask questions such as:

What does the group do in relationship to the natural world?

What captures learners' interests?

What seems pleasurable?

What questions that relate to the natural world do learners pursue?

How do learners interact with plants, animals and the elements?

What meaning of their connections to the natural world are they making?

Do you see specific connections being made to certain plants, animals or elements?

You may want to look at their relationship to the woodland and natural world using the Human Nature Connection Indices (Lumber et al., 2017), which presents six statements relating to nature connection:

I always find **beauty** in nature.

I always **treat** nature with respect.

Being in nature makes me very **happy**.

Spending **time** in nature is very important to me.

I find **being** in nature really amazing.

I feel **part** of nature.

These are used by environmental nongovernmental organisations (NGOs) when assessing their five pathways to nature (Richardson, 2019):

Contact – The act of engaging with nature through the senses for pleasure, e.g. listening to birdsong, smelling wild flowers, watching the sunset.

Beauty – Engagement with the aesthetic qualities of nature, e.g. appreciating natural scenery or engaging with nature through the arts.

Meaning – Using nature or natural symbolism (e.g. language and metaphors) to represent an idea, thinking about the meaning of nature and signs of nature, e.g. the first swallow of summer.

Emotion – An emotional bond with and love for nature, e.g. talking about and reflecting on your feelings about nature.

Compassion – Extending the self to include nature, leading to a moral and ethical concern for nature, e.g. making ethical product choices, being concerned with animal welfare.

You may want to look at how the learners interact with one another. Questions that may arise for you to note when observing may include, How do learners talk to each other regarding requests? Do they listen to each other and take note of each other's observations?

Once we have focused on what we observe in Forest School, how do we observe?

As Jon pointed out when talking about Shaun at the start of this section, in order to get inside Shaun's head he had to get down to his level, he had to be at just the right distance to hear but not interfere. Being at the learner's level is so important; standing around with a clipboard or Post-it notes does not enable us to be with the learning and to understand where the child/learner is at in any moment in time – this upsets a playful dynamic, gives out the message that we are measuring and recording, and subliminally will affect the learning process (even if the children are used to this approach – seen in schools and settings all over the country!). Sitting at the base of a tree, dancing around the fire with the learner, enthusiastically pushing the kit trolley with Shaun helps us tune in. When observing we try to record what is being said and what the learner is 'doing' as close to what is happening as possible. Sometimes this is on our phone (don't forget to delete immediately afterwards once the observation is written up), sometimes in a very small notebook or sometimes after the session. With older students who are moving into the 'what does all this mean?' phase (see Chapter 4, Wheel 4), we may jot a few things down if there are key phrases we know we will forget, which then goes straight back in the pocket once jotted on (we don't want to appear like an inspector), but for us it is important to just be with the conversation and to write down our observations afterwards. Here is an example from Jon's small notebook:

Josh put down the saw next to the saw horse, after replacing the blade cover, he put the cover on then he saw it didn't cover all the teeth, looking at the saw for a few moments with a curled up lip and quizzical look in his eyes). Tom (teaching assistant) pointed out some teeth were showing. Josh paused, took the cover off and slowly replaced it on the blade – covering all the teeth, a small smile appeared – then put it down on the saw horse, quickly, and ran to the shelter. He went to Holly in the shelter, actually he ran, his preferred locomotion! And asked Gaynor if he could make biscuits. She replied, "Yes, ask Holly how to do it" (Holly is another pupil). Josh asked Holly, "what goes in the biscuits Holly?" She showed Josh, saying, "don't throw the flour everywhere Josh." Holly didn't say much else, just showed him. Josh waited till Holly stopped showing him. He said, "I can do that" and he took the cup and scooped flour out of the packet and poured flour into the bowl – it all went in the bowl – the start of an exacting and successful biscuit-making session lasting 45 minutes.

After the session Jon wrote in his session review:

Josh seems to be regulating his enthusiasm for everything and stayed with the biscuit making until the biscuits were made on the fire and being eaten. He also keenly watched Holly and communicated in a more measured clear way with her. He has well-developed fine motor skills and is concentrating on instructions – his actions reflect a measured safe way of doing things at Forest School – from looking after tools through to measuring out correct ingredients for cooking. I am still loving his enthusiasm for everything and impressed with increasing ability to stay focused at Forest School.

This evaluation of the session was helped by checking in with Josh during the session to find out from him what is going on for him. He communicates willingly and often over a cup of juice and, in this instance, while eating the biscuit – that is the time to get real informal 'thoughtful' chat going to find out if what Jon think he is seeing is what he is really seeing. Also a chance for Jon to bear witness and almost 'honour' his voice. He was pleased with the biscuit, which was tasty, and he said he felt calmer. Jon stated what he saw with the saw blade and he said back to Jon "that's what I learned from you . . . am I doing well here Jon?" He had showed some meta cognition, was he really wanting some praise? Jon's reply was, "Josh, I just love your enthusiasm and joy you bring to the group and I am impressed with the thoughtful way of looking after the saw. You realised, after Tom said some teeth were showing, that you needed to take the cover off and put it on again – you can look after tools." No over-the-top praise – specific recognition and a witnessing tone – as said before making this into a blessing. He smiled!

Apart from checking in with the learner to both check that what you witnessed was what you saw and then to check your understanding of what was happening for them, the other 'how' is to check out your observations and evaluations with the other adults/practitioners in the group. For us this is often on the walk back from the Forest School site or if engrossed still with the whole group to either grab a valuable few minutes before all depart or write it up immediately and check in electronically or on the phone with the other adults. In many settings the invaluable time afterwards, which may be a 15-minute tea break, really helps to crystallise the observations and evaluations and importantly to look at what the preparation for the next session might entail, regarding both resources and possible planned experiences and what questions we might ask to inform what we are observing. Are there patterns and progressions evolving? You may have behaviours, attitudes and actions that perplex or annoy you. Turn these into investigations to delight in by asking questions that start with "Why do . . . ?" "How do . . . ?" "Is this the first time . . . ?" or "What are my theories on . . . ?"

For observations to become all-round meaningful and to help us advocate for this type of learning, checking in with parents on what learners are saying and doing at home can also be invaluable. At Leigh and Sinton Forest School in Worcestershire, just putting pictures of the session up on the Forest School shed in the playground as parents came in the same day to show what was observed proved a useful tool to both get parents talking and to provide further parental support for more Forest School in the setting.

As well as writing, recording, sketching, making books and stories, taking photographs and filming are all useful observational tools. FS practitioners would do well to look at the approaches taken by Reggio Emilia (le Blanc, 2007), in northern Italy, where documentation of child development takes a variety of forms – video, art, photographs, handwritten notes etc. and is done in collaboration with other practitioners and the learners.

To help with this more creative way of observing and evaluating, it is worth incorporating into FS sessions some creative ways of reviewing and reflecting that are seen as part and parcel of the learning process, and not necessarily just the routine, and to be honest, sometimes boring sharing circle at the end of each session. See Gans (2017) for some good starters for creative integrated reviewing exercises.

To finish this section, Jon would like to share an observation of a well-practised early years practitioner, Laura, working with learners with English as an additional language on her first Forest School programme.

Laura was clearly taking a back seat but keenly observing, making herself available only when needed – she was 'on tap', observing, not 'on top'.

She started the session off asking the children to explain to us the safety aspects of Forest School and what they had done the previous weeks. She then asked them what they wanted to do; this was their fourth session. They formed their own groups and off they went, while Laura and her assistant watched the ensuing play. After approximately 10 minutes, a small person grabbed me by the hand, and here is the dialogue that ensued:

Child: "Jon, come and look at my new home!" (He had been working on a shelter the previous week.)

Jon: "Great . . . it's a bit cold in here."

Child: "Yes it's wet and drafty." (This was a cold, windy, wet West Midlands day, but I did think to myself – good language.)

Jon: "Mmmm." 15 seconds of silence (This is important – teachers on average give a maximum of 5 seconds thinking time; Kontos, 1999)

Child: "I need a door."

Jon: "Have you any door shapes in mind?"

The next exchange was, for Jon, pure child-centred learning and a perfect example of this 'on tap' approach. Laura had been listening in while sharing a mud castle being made by two of the children on one of the molehills.

At least a minute's silence, wandering around and thinking had gone on.

Laura: "Do you remember the shapes we were looking at last week in the class?"

Child: "Ahh – a rectangle. That's the one with two long and two short."

The child then went off to find two long sticks and two short. He then mused a long time and came over to me again.

Child: "Not sure how to join these."

Jon: "Would you like me to help?"

Child: "Yes."

Jon: "Do you have any ideas on how to join them?"

Child: "Mmmm," (more silence) "string!"

And lo and behold, without any prompting from either Laura or me, he asked her for string, which she asked her assistant to get from the classroom. The child ended up making a door he was very proud of (still drafty, mind!). While this may seem a small incident, for Laura, who is clearly a skilled early years' practitioner, it was symptomatic of a huge shift from being 'on top' to 'on tap'. She admitted she had to fight all her instincts to intervene and show him what he might do and just *observe*. The resulting learning from her point of view, and the child's, was far more powerful. What he had done was take ownership of the learning, invested his own thoughts into the door, and applied learning inside the classroom to a real-life situation outside the classroom, in Forest School.

What was so gratifying was watching Laura observe the interaction, staying away and realising that just one small interaction with a powerful memory jogger and being 'on tap' for the string supported the child's meaning making far more than being alongside with lots of overbearing adult dialogue. Observation truly is one of the most awesome responsibilities for educators; it informs a more effective learner-centred dialogue, which we will look at in the next section.

Language and communication at FS – The art of dialogue, a listening conversation

In Chapter 6 we talked about play helping children 'become'.

"Our words can be our jewels or weapons in either helping the learner become or to stop the meaning making and 'becoming' process." These were wise words shared with us many years ago by a very experienced early years' practitioner and manager. We need to carefully choose when and what we dialogue if we are to maintain this shared community of learning as per the learner-centred Forest School principle. This section will look at what sort of dialogue in nature is required if we are to maximise our 'jewels'.

What children and young people see and interact with has a tremendous impact on them, and this is clear at Forest School. As stated in the previous section on observation, we need to tune into where the learner 'is at' and how the natural world contact is so important to, in Walt Whitman's words, help the child 'become',

> The early lilacs became part of this child,
> And grass and white and red morning-glories, and white and red
> clover, and the song of the phoebe-bird,
> . . . These became part of that child who went forth every day, and
> who now goes, and will always go forth every day.

> (1855)

Children, at an early age, seek meaning through sensory and imaginative interactions that are not overfiltered by history, culture and showers of adult words that have no context and are 'adult agenda-led'.

If Jo hadn't taken up a strategic position playing with a small group by a tree (important for her incognito-ness!) and watching and listening to Tom, she would not have witnessed his play and passion and trials and tribulations associated with his 'becoming', and importantly would not have known when to interact and dialogue to support and join without interfering (see Julie Fisher, 2016). She was keenly aware that this was all about him directing his own learning; in this case he was definitely in the child-led section of the nature play cycle (see Chapter 6 on play). His internal dialogue was all about his own intrinsic goals for the day. Jo heard him voice his internal dialogue fairly near the start of the 'project'.

Tom: "We're going to dig down a small way and make this tunnel round so the roundish train can get through – I know, I'll be a mole with a trowel." Then he went to Jo to ask for said trowel and she obliged without any judgment.

Jo: "I heard you say you're making a railway, is that what it's for?" With a digging and tunnelling action, she went on to say, "Good luck, moley, on your special mission." He nodded and off he went back to his developing hole, smiling and returning her comment on the way.

Tom: "This will make me into a good mole!"

Jo didn't shower him with endless questions or demanding statements – all that was needed was an informal but interested acknowledgement, briefly entering his world and mirroring to check and reflect back to him what he was thinking and doing. There was a sudden realisation that in 'observing' a learner doing, thinking and feeling, she was understanding what he was doing, thinking and learning, not what *she thought* he was doing, thinking and learning. The Forest School leader, Jo, was in fact doing two things with her dialogue.

Firstly, by keenly witnessing this child 'becoming' in his difficult labour and not interfering, Jo kept her words to a minimum, only interacting to say she saw the labour in his project. With her learner-centred dialogue, she briefly entered his play, staying with the metaphor and returning his play cue with another cue – the moley mission and bodily tunnelling action. It was like a blessing – made all the more special and dare I say it 'sacred' by being in the natural world.

Towards the time for packing up and leaving the session, Jo stated: "I saw what you did with the underground, Tom. You made the overground after trying hard to get through the thick soil and make the hole big enough. Was the mole tired?"

Tom smiled and his shoulders lifted – he was honoured by her comment.

Jo continued after a pause: "And then with great thinking and creative work with your moley hands, the train track was made and you travelled the track like a supersonic train."

By witnessing and stating that she saw him labour, she was giving more than affirmation; it was like a blessing, an even greater smile appeared and he visibly 'grew' full of purpose and life.

Secondly, she was really tuning into his interests, actions, language and feelings in order to know when to turn on her interactions and dialogue with Tom to aid his learning, support his own expression, empathise with his feelings, extend his thinking (if needed) and most importantly know when to get out of his hair! Quite often the silences speak more dialogue than words – our body language and tone can account for more of the communication than words can. Words give content, but tone, body language and context give flavour and meaning. We as adults often want to fill silence with words, but it is the spaces we create with silence and absence that give space for reflection, day dreaming (so important for subconscious learning), and time to consolidate learning before the learner voices the meaning making.

One certain way of promoting a trust in the learner's own capacity and wisdom is to frame our language in a positive way. Rather than saying "CAN'T DO", for example, "Don't run out of sight", "Be careful on that log", "Watch out", "No, you can't go up that tree", or "Don't pick the nettle", rephrase and be specific by saying what is possible – "CAN DO", for example, "Go to where you can see me", "Try moving slowly on the log", "I wonder if this tree is safe. Let's see, which tree is safe to climb?", "Yes, try out touching the nettle this way so the hairs flatten and won't inject their sting."

This is all part of building a more trusting, equal relationship – right from the word go. It says we all have wisdom and can learn from a reinforcing, specific cumulative way.

If we are to take this approach to our own dialogue, there is a need to observe and evaluate what children do and how they articulate their understandings and to see things from 'their' constructs and contexts in order to enter into dialogue. What we as educators tend to do, Jon and Marina included, is to jump to interpretation in the first instance. "Oh, she is just playing at being a dog. Her language is new but as she is by herself and won't play with anyone else, she has not developed the capacity to socialise yet." With the above story about Tom, you could say he does not socialise well with his peer group; he's not really a team player. However, by keying into the 'small big moments', we can pick up on key aspects of the children's development and play – he had some effective small interactions with others in the group – adults and children alike – that served his railway project. We miss the child height and child perspectives if we can't dialogue and see things from their perspective.

This question of how we articulate what are we observing came into sharp focus for Jon when working with Jeff and Bill, the two adolescent males we talked about in Chapter 9 and at the start of the observation section in this chapter. The centre kept beehives on the site and Bill had a couple of excursions in the bee suit with the beekeeper at the centre.

By keying into Bill's passion and questions, Jon could ask questions that enticed him into exploring the topic of bee dance further. The following is Jon's observation record from the second excursion.

Jon: "Hey, let's look at the way they move" while he tried to move in the way the bees were moving outside the hive. Mark also started moving in a circle and with a wiggle between circles.

Bill: "They are going around a few times."

Jon: "Goodness – I wonder what that's about?"

Ken (the beekeeper): "The size of dance and type of waggle tells the other bees how far the best flowers are and where they are."

Bill and Jon stopped moving and Bill turned to Ken and then me.

Bill: "Wow, a bit like when I go to find the snakes? And the way you walk, Jon!"

Silence while we watch.

Bill: "But how do they know it is saying that?"

Jon: "Mmm, good question. I guess it's like how do we know that run means run . . . we, like the bees, just learn it?"

Ken: "It's all genetics!"

Bill: "What's that?"

The group ended up talking about what shapes us into who we are. Who would have known the waggle dance would have led to this?!

It is exactly this sort of informal enquiry dialogue coming from both the learner and facilitator that we strive for, with questions that demand active seeking for answers rather than the closed 20 questions many educators adopt that can be threatening to many learners. Jon could have started with, "What do you think the bees are saying with their dance, Bill?" putting him on the spot and, *importantly*, taking away the spontaneous non-threatening informality.

For us it's not the questions we ask as facilitators, even those supposedly 'open questions', so much as provoking the learners to ask their own questions and ending in a collaborative exploration of a topic/issue in the natural world. What happened in the interaction is we had created this informal democratic community of enquiry, referred to by Professor Robin Alexander of Cambridge University as 'collective dialogue'. This can really only be done through strong relationship building (see Alexander, 2017). Once we all start expressing our own needs and purposes through body and word dialogue, including the need for space, time and play in the natural world, then we are moving to a more creative dialogue that is prosocial and pro-ecological relationship building . . . this is what creating a 'community of learning' is all about.

A community of learning also means involving the learners, as much as possible, in creatively exploring what is going on for all of us, thus the more *we* will 'become' together. This is what embeds learning, "think, do, observe, review". When we look back at some of the fundamental learning theories expressed by Dewey, Kolb, Montessori and others in Chapters 1, 2, 3 and 7, reviewing and reflecting on the observations are essential for further planning in our FS programmes. This informs what we choose to plan for and how we learn *with* nature. The next two chapters look at ways of working with plants, animals, and the elements, including Pretty's third element of developing the green mind – 'crafting'.

QUESTIONS FOR PRACTICE

How do you respond to learners' interests and needs in sessions, especially when there is something you haven't planned for?

What resources do you feel are the bare minimum for taking out on sessions?

How do you brief and set expectations for helpers and other staff attending sessions?

What are the most 'sticky', challenging moments for you when you are facilitating? How do you feel and how do you 'act' in the moment?

USEFUL RESOURCES

The online appendix for Chapter 11 (www.routledge.com/9780367425616) has sample session plans, observation and evaluation tools, and descriptions of two sessions including a storytelling session.

www.acewild.eu/ A European website with a number of observation and evaluative tools from simple to quite detailed, including PEMS+, SDQ etc.

www.theoutdoorteacher.com Marina Robb also offers Online Professional Training. Courses include in-depth practical tutorials on making fires, shelters and wood crafts, forest games, foraging and cooking with wild plants as well as a broad range of webinars and bespoke trainings.

Westall, D and Walmsley, N (2018) *Forest School Adventure: Outdoor Skills and Play for Children*. GMC Publications. This is a good book for inspiration when planning sessions.

Curtis, D and Carter, M (2013) *The Art of Awareness – How Observation Can Transform Your Teaching*. Redleaf Press. An excellent book on observation with some useful exercises.

www.forestschooled.com An excellent blog about Forest School by Caylin Gans – a real deep dive into what being a reflective practitioner means with lots of examples of practice. This is now in a book.

www.kindlingplay.co.uk This is another good resource, especially Lily Horseman's blog on this site with lots of useful tips for practitioners.

www.creativestarlearning.co.uk An excellent outdoor learning resource full of thoughtful blogs and experiences covering all the curriculum.

Forest Kindergarten Resources in Scotland – www.owlscotland.org/local-options/forest-kindergarten/

OPAL: www.opalexplorenature.org/ www.observatree.org.uk For monitoring and recording information about the place useful resources can be found.

Woodland Trust: https://naturedetectives.woodlandtrust.org.uk/naturedetectives/ and https://naturescalendar.woodlandtrust.org.uk/ A useful website if delivering sessions in woodlands in the UK and tracking changes in woodlands.

Children and Nature Network: www.childrenandnature.org/

Out to Play: Practical guidance for creating outdoor play experiences in early learning and childcare

https://www.gov.scot/binaries/content/documents/govscot/publications/advice-and-guidance/2020/02/
out-play-practical-guidance-creating-outdoor-play-experiences-children/documents/out-play-practi
cal-guidance-creating-outdoor-play-experiences-early-learning-childcare/out-play-practical-guidance-creat
ing-outdoor-play-experiences-early-learning-childcare/govscot%3Adocument/out-play-practical-guid
ance-creating-outdoor-play-experiences-early-learning-childcare.pdf

My World Outdoors: Sharing good practice in how early years services can provide play wholly or partially
outdoors.

https://hub.careinspectorate.com/media/1557/my-world-outdoors-sharing-good-practice-in-how-early-
years-services-can.pdf

BIBLIOGRAPHY

ACEwild (2015) A European Project for an 'Alternative Curriculum Education out of the Wild' in Secondary
Schools. See www.acewild.eu/

Alexander, R (2017) *Towards Dialogic Teaching: Rethinking Classroom Talk*. Thirsk: Dialogos.

Athey, C (1990) *Extending Thought in Young Children*. London: Paul Chapman.

Casey, D, Richardson, A and D'Ascoli, H (2019) *The Children's Forest*. Hawthorn Press.

Chesterton, G K (2008) *Orthodoxy*. Waking Lion Press (first published 1908).

Drummond, M (2003) *Assessing Children's Learning*. London: Fulton.

Egle, A (2013) Waldkindergarten – Forest Kindergarten in Germany. See Juliet Robertson webpage https://
creativestarlearning.co.uk/early-years-outdoors/waldkindergarten-forest-kindergarten-in-germany/.

Emotional Literacy Support Assistant (ELSA) www.elsa-support.co.uk/.

EYFS Profile. See https://assets.publishing.service.gov.uk/government/uploads/system/uploads/attach
ment_data/file/790580/EYFSP_Handbook_2019.pdf.

Fisher, J (2016) *Interacting or Interfering? Improving Interactions in the Early Years*. Open University Press.

Gans, C (2017) A Practical Guide for Forest School Leaders (or anyone really!) to Facilitating Reflection in
the Outdoors. See www.forestschooled.com/resources – PDF download.

Gans, C (2019) *Forest Schooled – The Book*. Self Published.

Gibbs, G (1988) *Learning by Doing: A Guide to Teaching and Learning Methods*. Oxford: Further Education
Unit, Oxford Polytechnic.

Greenaway, R (1993a) Reviewing: What, Why and How? See http://reviewing.co.uk/_review.htm#why Also
see Greenaway's website which is full of creative ways of reviewing and thoughts on the reviewing process. http://reviewing.co.uk.

High/Scope UK see www.high-scope.org.uk (accessed 06/08).

Huxley, A (1954) *Doors of Perception*. London: Chatto and Windus.

Kolb, D A and Fry, R (1975) Toward an Applied Theory of Experiential Learning. In Cooper, C (ed.), *Theories
of Group Process*. London: John Wiley.

Kontos, S (1999) Improvisation: An Analytic Tool for Examining Teacher–Child Interactions in the Early Childhood Classroom. *Science Direct*.

Laevers, F (ed.) (2005) *Well-being and Involvement in Care Settings. A Process-Oriented Self-Evaluation
Instrument*. Leuven: Kind and Gezin. See www.kindengezin.be/Images/ZikohandleidingENG_tcm149-
50761.pdf (accessed 9/10).

LeBlanc, M (2007) Reggio Emilia – An Innovative Approach to Early Childhood Education. See www.commu nityplaythings.co.uk/learning-library/articles/reggio-emilia.

Lowenfield, M (1935) *Play in Childhood*. London: Gallancz.

Lumber, R Richardson, M and Sheffield, D (2017) Beyond Knowing Nature: Contact, Emotion, Compassion, Meaning, and Beauty Are Pathways to Nature Connection. *PLoS One* 12(5): e0177186. https://doi.org/10.1371/journal.pone.0177186.

Meek, M (1985) Play and Paradoxes: Some Considerations of Imagination and Language. In Wells, N M and Nicholls, S (eds.), *Language and Learning: An Interactional Perspective*. London: Falmer.

Mel McCree (2014) International Perspectives on Forest School: Natural Spaces to Play and Learn. *Early Years* 34(3): 318–319. doi: 10.1080/09575146.2014.936139.

PEMS+ plus other evaluative tools (European) (2015) www.acewild.eu/evaluation-toolkit.

Richardson, M (2019) Five Ways to Well-Being with Nature. See https://findingnature.org.uk/2019/01/28/5-ways-to-wellbeing-with-nature/.

Sobel, D (2004) *Place-Based Education: Connecting Classrooms and Communities*. The Orion Society.

Whitman, W (1855) *Leaves of Grass*.

Williams, E (2017) Building Learning Power at Earthlings Forest School – See www.forestschoolassociation.org/building-learning-power-earthlings-forest-school

Young, J Haas, E and McGown, E (2008) *Coyote's Guide to Connecting with Nature*. Washington, DC: Owlink Media Corporation.

Appendix

Daily Site Check Sheet

Daily site check for . . . .

(Undertake prior to each visit)

- The met office app is free, easy to read and automatically locates where you are! It provides information about average wind speed and likely gusts over the course of the day.

Hazard	Date checked by	Date checked by	Date checked by	Date checked by	Date checked by
Windspeed					
Other weather					
Ground conditions					
Plants and trees					
Low-level bush					
Canopy					
Litter					
Dog mess					
Structures					
Phone reception					
Other site users					
Other					

Comments including action taken to reduce risk   **Date and Initials**

12 Crafting – working with our hands in the natural world

'Crafting', be it crafting an object from plant, animal or mineral, crafting a fire, or crafting a meal outside to be cooked on a fire, is something very human and can really be done in a playful way. The Oxford English Dictionary definition of craft is "to use the hands to make something using skill and dexterity". This is something that is being lost in today's technological age. Research is showing that loss of craft does impact on our learning and development, in particular a certain physical dexterity which is also accompanied by 'dexterity and detail' in language development. This chapter examines why handcrafts are so important to Nature Pedagogy, in particular Forest School. We look further at the importance of working with handtools, fire and 'the elements' – in particular water, soil and clay and plants.

Topics covered include

- health and safety considerations
- legal considerations
- processes and techniques
- ways of introducing craft that are learner-centred and can be both safe and playful – importantly the learner-centred dialogue

The next chapter will expand on working with plants. A number of resources are also presented in the online appendix supporting this chapter.

> At least once in a child's life that person should have the very ancient, and very human experience of walking onto the land, seeking, harvesting and making some item they then use. This experience is critical, after being raised amidst an abundance of purchased commodities and functionless items, this may be the only experience in a person's life that provides an alternative to a non-commodity perspective of land . . . Such experiences may allow the veil to be lifted and people to recognize that all material comes from the earth and are gifts to be respected, not abused and controlled by humans.
>
> – Elizabeth MacEachren (2000)

WHY HANDCRAFTS IN A NATURE PEDAGOGY?

One of the key answers to the question 'why handcrafts?' is that it is this that makes us human and has enabled us to 'craft' civilisation and culture, and importantly feel part of rather than separate from the natural world. Twenty-first-century education has inevitably veered towards the technologies of the time – 'screen culture'. This is defined through a device, the mobile, made of highly processed materials that come from a remote location on the planet – can we in Britain really know and feel the extraction of 90% of the iPhone's precious metals, with names never mentioned in advanced chemistry, mined in China and Inner Mongolia? Feeling part of the tools we use and how we can directly craft an item with our hands and handtools profoundly enables us to feel the natural resources we are crafting, which a screen can never do. Being able to make an item from a tree that you can harvest and then use to produce something of utility, while consciously honouring this, provides access to and gives voice to the more-than-human world.

Something as simple as harvesting a stick of willow, crafting it into a toasting stick, to make a damper from flour and water with our hands, that you can also cook on a fire crafted by our hands collecting wood and arranging it for the fire, and then eat it makes such a direct connection to the natural world; a screen can never do that. If this process is consciously honoured and thanks are given to the willow – the tree that 'sallies forth', hence *salix*, thanking the fire and wood – then the 'feeling part of' the more-than-human world is more likely to follow.

Figure 12.1 Harvesting willow for crafting a toasting stick! A clear cut followed by a moment of gratitude

Handcrafts are also beneficial to our 'whole' self as shown by the mind map on page 301 (Figure 12.3). In particular we have noticed over the years that they instil a huge degree of resilience supporting a growth mindset, a craft takes practise . . . you have to put the work in. Craft is hard work but the reward is huge in terms of the returning connection to both the creative self and the 'other'. Creative connection is often subconscious but craft provides the foundation of often hard practise and experimentation which then guides the creative process. Take Jake's chair in chapter 9 on page 218, that took lots of practise and experimentation and out came something that Jake could not only use as a metaphor for his feelings and behaviour, but also a good deal of skill development and chopping and changing saw him becoming a less impatient 'I'm going to stick at this' person.

Our main 'why' is that crafting really consciously helps us interact with the natural world in a meaningful way that brings satisfaction. This is why Julian Pretty and his 'green mind', described in Chapter 7, sees crafting as key to well-being and sustainability. This is nothing new, and it is built on many traditional craft movements such as the Slöjd educational movement, started in Finland in 1865 – a handicraft education still taught throughout Scandinavia.

Many resources and trainings can be found on tool use, fire and working with 'organic materials', some of which we will point to at the end of the chapter. This chapter will cover what we see as key considerations in a nature pedagogical and Forest School framework. This particularly relates to the following Forest School principles:

- FS uses a range of learner-centred processes to create a community for being, development and learning.
- FS aims to promote the holistic development of all those involved, fostering resilient, confident, independent and creative learners.
- FS offers learners the opportunity to take supported risks appropriate to the environment and to themselves.

Handtools

Why work with handtools?

We often are asked by teachers and other educators, "Why does the Forest School training emphasise the use of handtools?" This seemingly is quite an easy one to answer, but we always stop ourselves from making a glib answer such as 'it develops our fine and gross motor skills' in a way that doing what we are doing as we write this (i.e. punching the keys on a laptop) can never do! Also, this is a perception, as Forest School is far more than 'having an emphasis on handtools' – handtools are just part of a holistic approach to human development.

First, what handtools are we talking about? In our experience the most useful tools at Forest School and nature education are the loppers, fixed blade knife, baton (piece of wood for tapping a bladed tool to split wood), pruning saw, bow saw, panel saw, hammer, hand drills (brace and bit being the most effective) and 'pegs/braddles'. Once mastered the hatchet, froe, spokeshave, crook knife, draw knife, and various chisels and gauges can be introduced. The first choice of tool depends very much on the task, material and abilities of the tool user – more about this later.

SENSORY DEVELOPMENT

Sensory and physical stimulation and development are two obvious benefits from working with handtools. Selectively and sensitively coppicing some sycamore and hazel and paying attention to making friends with the pruning saws and hatchets creates sensory connections with trees and tools. Then converting

Figure 12.2 The act of making a tree platform/house is a multisensory experience

Figure 12.2 Marina starting her treehouse in a multisensory Winter!

the poles into something of utility and play, a treehouse for 3-year-olds, brings about huge smiles and satisfaction – as one teacher put it, "pole cutting and square lashing has changed my life!"

Working with handtools is a vital part of sensory development and links to brain development. Michael Cohen's list of 54 natural senses (see Chapter 8) have been documented in much scientific work and are described in Cohen's work with ecopsychology (see www.ecopsych.com/insight53senses.html). These senses include aesthetic sense, sense of form, sense of space, sense of weight, gravity and balance, in addition to sense of touch – all of which are stimulated by working with handtools. When these senses combine with the many senses stimulated by being

Figure 12.2 Continued

in the natural world, there is a 'completeness' to human development. This combination is also known to aid holistic brain/body development – not just the prefrontal cortex that our modern industrial society is obsessed with. After all, the prefrontal cortex cannot exist without the rest of the brain, as outlined in Chapter 7.

> *What you naturally sense and feel counts. It is more intelligent, important and powerful for your life than most things that you learn.*
>
> (Cohen, 2007)

PHYSICAL SKILL DEVELOPMENT

We have noticed in our combined 20 years of Forest School training and 50 years of environmental education training that it is as if adults have increasingly malnourished handskills, struggling to tie knots, saw wood and thread needles. Kurt Hahn, one of the founders of the UK Outward Bound movement, who formulated his 'six declines of modern youth in the 1930s', said:

> *I welcome this occasion to register my indebtedness to Dr. Zimmerman to whom I owe the watchword 'training through the body, not training of the body.' He agreed with Plato "Let us build up physical fitness for the sake of the soul."*
>
> (see www.kurthahn.org/wp-content/uploads/2017/02/2017-obt1960.pdf)

LANGUAGE, EMOTIONAL, SOCIAL DEVELOPMENT

We know that *praxis* – the ability to plan and execute motor actions or behaviour – relies on movement. The part of the brain that activates handwriting and helps with recognising shapes and patterns and therefore language – 'phonics' – can be stimulated by the use of handtools (see www.childsupport.in/html/ourservices_handwritingskills.html). We have traced in our ancestry that the use of handtools is directly linked to the parts of the brain that saw development of written as well as verbal language (Wynn and Coolidge, 2010). Moreover, we know that mimicking movement, such as learning how to use a saw from watching and participating with a skilled educator, can stimulate the mirror neurons which, when firing with the rest of the brain, can help develop empathy.

We hear lots about the cotton wool generation and younger people, indeed even us older ones, being less willing to take big risks, and when we do, physical and emotional injury is more likely to happen. What better way of regulating the emotional propensity for injury through increased stress than to spend time totally in the 'flow' while crafting a stake or gouging a spoon?

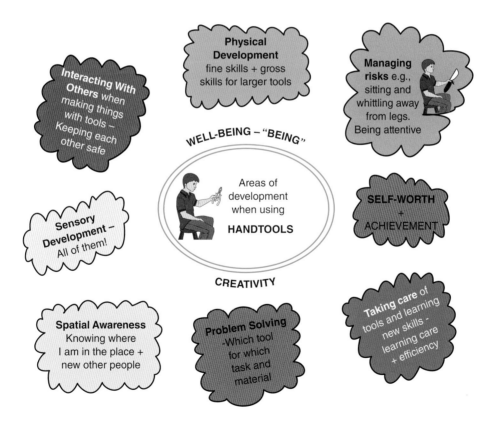

Figure 12.3 Handtools and holistic development

We haven't met one person, and we are serious about this, who hasn't felt the therapeutic effect of spending time shaping a piece of wood with a handtool. Realising that taking the risk with a spoon gouge – which is so easy to cut your thumb with – helps with our own risk management and attention to looking after ourselves. Indeed, the whole attention deficit problem, which is seemingly on the increase and can lead to more incidences of injury, can be improved upon when we have to 'attend intentionally' to keep ourselves safe while working with a handtool.

The justifications for using handtools in education are endless, as shown by the above simple mind map done by a FS practitioner.

When to introduce handtools

This is a tricky one to answer, as there are lots of variables to consider about what handtools to introduce and when; as before, there are four elements to consider for good learning (see Figure 12.4).

There are no hard and fast rules for when to introduce a tool, and one of the main pieces of advice we can give for the practitioner is to really assess where each learner is regarding their fine and gross motor skills, strength and attention to detail when it comes to materials and tool selection (see Figure 12.5 for a way of assessing tool introduction through a self-assessment exercise). It is so easy to take a formulaic approach to the use of handtools in which we introduce the whole group to making a similar item using one tool – sawing tree cookies and cutting small wooden discs from a branch come to mind! It should be a matter of assessing each learner and

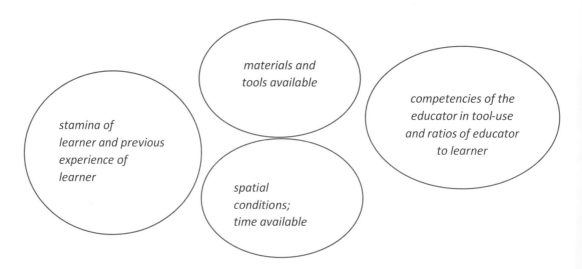

Figure 12.4 Factors affecting when to introduce a handtool

'Pre-Tool' Concept Exercises – Scorecard

Game	My Score	Group Average Score
Branch hanging (*strength & stamina*)	Seconds	Seconds
Chin-ups (*strength*)	Chin-ups	Chin-ups
Pulley weight (*stamina*)	Pulls	Pulls
Hook a creature (*dexterity & coordination*)	Points	Points
Thread the beads (*coordination*)	Seconds	Seconds
Half-hitch cordage (*dexterity*)	Knots	Knots

Rate your skill levels:

Strength:	1	2	3	4	5	6	7	8	9	10
Stamina:	1	2	3	4	5	6	7	8	9	10
Dexterity:	1	2	3	4	5	6	7	8	9	10
Coordination:	1	2	3	4	5	6	7	8	9	10

Figure 12.5 Assessing for tool use

gearing the introduction to the learner's competency, leader's competency, tools and materials available and the place *plus* (and probably most importantly) what learning you are supporting at the time and what the learner wishes to make.

How to introduce a handtool

When introducing a handtool, a practitioner may just start by making their own artefact, modelling and providing a springboard without 'teaching' the learners – just sitting and making their own thing, seeing a need or purpose, or bringing in a number of craft items that may act as stimulus/springboards of interest.

Jon was observing an FS session and watching a learner in a Year 1 group (about 6 years old) who was seemingly at a loss, wandering around a tree by himself and hardly interacting with the remainder of the group. He was knocking the tree with a stick, and at one point he picked up another stick and started rubbing them together as though he was whittling the bigger stick into a spear, spending about two minutes 'whittling' with a degree of gusto and exact hand-eye coordination.

303

He started stabbing the tree with the larger stick. The FS leader approached the learner and said, "Not sure hitting the tree is a good idea Joe, how about joining the others and make a shelter?" Joe looked at the leader and continued to stab the tree; the FS leader continued, "Joe, can you put the stick down and stop hurting the tree or maybe use the stick on the shelter?" Joe's shoulders fell, he dropped the stick and walked, kicking the ground, to the nearby grove of leylandii where there was a group of four making a shelter. Watching this incident and seeing Joe attempting to whittle the stick with another stick could well be an ideal moment to introduce the idea of using a knife to make a spear . . . a purposeful moment for a young learner who seemed to have the hand-eye coordination to really work with a knife – was he ready? This provides a challenge for the FS leader – when we witness a purposeful moment for introducing a handtool for one learner, can we realistically consider this while others need the leader on hand as a learning resource to support their play and learning? On top of this, maybe the whole group want to whittle, which isn't possible, partly due to lack of tools and partly for safety reasons. In this instance the group were all fully engaged in their own play, fully aware of the 'boundaries', and maybe it was an ideal opportunity to pull out a knife, sit down with Joe and introduce whittling. This is where observation becomes so obviously the most awesome responsibility of the educator in order to really 'see' where the learner is at and what, with appropriate intervention, can encourage their own learning and interests . . . while maintaining *their* power over their own learning. So what would have been the appropriate dialogue with Joe? As with all observations, we need to time this properly in order to not annihilate or, at worst, adulterate the play and interest of the learner (see Chapter 6). In this instance Jon had made an initial assumption/judgment that Joe was 'at a loss' . . . but was he? Maybe he was in his own play frame. Who are we to say this wasn't a form of imaginative play – the tree representing a character in a story that needed 'slaying', or it could have been socio-dramatic play – the tree representing authority and the whittled spear a defence? So how do we sensitively interact if we see a moment to introduce a handtool? Descriptive dialogue without judgment-laden words is important at this stage.

For example, saying, "Hi Joe, just noticed you rubbing those two sticks together, is the bigger one a spear?" makes no judgment and at the same time expresses interest in Joe's activity. We then have to take our lead from the learner and see what comes back; the answer may then either invite you into their world or say this is not your place to 'intervene'. If Joe engages, and we find time and again that eye contact can be the key, then it may be your opportunity to invite them to make a spear using a knife and proceed to ask if they have used a knife before to gauge if the learner has any experience of whittling. At this stage, the leader may need to scan the group and communicate with colleagues to explain that you are going to spend some time sitting with Joe in a safe place, which could be two tree stumps or a designated tool area, in order to whittle the said stick. Once sorted in terms of safe space and ensuring the remainder of the group are OK, the next move may be to check that the material and appropriate tool are chosen. This could be the first type of whittling the learner has done, in which case the wood needs to be whittlable! There is a fine line between enabling an achievable task and learning from 'not achieving'. In the observation Joe had picked an old, well-seasoned oak stick which would have been hard to whittle, so having a stick of green wood to hand, or lopping a green stick in a safe and caring way, is the way to go. If a spear is required, then hazel sunshoots or a selected willow rod are by far the best two materials to choose. These could then be compared to the oak stick Joe had

Figure 12.6 Choosing an easy material and artefact like a hazel sunshoot to turn into a spear is a good start for whittling. Whittling safely away from the legs and on to a block can be easier, as we can use our bodies more and it is safer for tool and body!

Figure 12.6 Continued

picked, and he could see the difference in how easy or hard it is to whittle the different types of material. Just whittling a point on a stick presents so many learning opportunities and chances for experimentation. We will come back to technique and see the main handtools, their applications and techniques in the Chapter 12 online appendix.

Figure 12.6 shows a number of ways to whittle; there is no one sure way. It depends on material, individual choice of most efficient and comfortable way, and feeling and keeping safe.

From the previous case study, you can see that *purpose* and *need* are two key factors that are considered when introducing a handtool.

The FS practitioner may decide to introduce an artefact that is a little more exciting into their programme and which will be useful to the setting, such as a spatula for cooking with – this may be a *springboard* to more creative learning through skill development. When working with learners, we often have a piece of craft work that is started and will bring it into the setting to work on the item at an appropriate moment – while the group are doing 'their own thing'. There are two reasons for doing this: (1) it means we can observe without seeming to interfere in 'their own thing', and (2) it may stimulate an interest in a subliminal way. If it does, then so be it – the springboard has worked, and if not, no harm done – we will have created another item to use in the programme. Quite often an interest may emerge a few weeks later, as described in the following case study.

The first time Jon introduced a bentwood chair to a group, almost 16 years ago now, he learned one of his biggest lessons in toolwork. Jon had decided to introduce chairs after the group had made some spatulas for frying bacon for bacon butties – their favourite lunchtime meal. They clearly had the dexterity and motor skills for bentwood chairmaking. Jon's plan was that he would show them the almost finished item and finish it in a session, then take this small group of five 14-year-olds through the process with the same design from Mike Abbott's classic book *Green Woodwork* (1989). This proved to be his biggest mistake. Jon had assumed this was the easiest and safest way for a group of five young males to make a chair. Pretty soon into the process – 5 minutes to be exact – three of the group wanted their own design and two showed little interest in chairs and just wanted to chop the wood to bits! Being new to teaching bentwood chairmaking to teenagers, Jon was flummoxed and didn't really know where to take this. Moving from fixed blade knife and baton work while making spatulas to the lopping, sawing, drilling and hammering required for bentwood chairs, it seemed that the only safe and successful way was through a formula. Surely there was only one way to do this – after all it says so in Mike's book! Was the spatula making just lucky or had Jon timed it right in terms of novelty – after all, they had all engaged with that task pretty well.

In the intervening week, Jon consulted with a colleague who had more experience than he had in bentwood chair making. He decided in the following week to offer a choice of design and go through the basic details needed to make the base steady and supportive – they didn't all need to be bentwood chairs! This was Jon's moment of realisation. If we are to release the creativity, they need to learn a few basic skills and techniques, but from there on we need to let go and take a more creative problem-solving approach – not a formulaic approach, and learn with the learners. Bringing in a chair almost finished had stimulated three of the group to have a go but not the other two – Jon should have seen this as a positive start and then 'let it go'. From this point the group harvested the hazel needed from different 'hazel stools' depending on design, while the two choppers made kindling for the fire (Jon had a member of staff from the school with him who had an interest in woodworking). Sawing with a panel saw on sawhorses ensued while with some of the thinner chairs (not bentwood) the heavy duty loppers were used to cut lengths. The other lesson from this was related to the preparation beforehand by having the right tools for the right job, so it is an easily achieved task – pruning saws and bow saws for coppicing, panel saws and sawhorses for easily sawing larger pieces of timber squarely and accurately, heavy-duty loppers for thinner yet still strong poles. The group were away and in the end five items were made – one bentwood chair, two upright chairs, a stool and a rustic table! Peer influence did kick in during the third day of 'chairmaking', and all five ended up making something.

Figure 12.7 Projects and artefacts that have stimulated a variety of woodworking projects – chairs, spoons and knives and a traditional rake

Figure 12.7 Continued

MATERIALS HARVESTING

Once we have timed the introduction to a handtool and engaged the learner, how do we make the task of toolwork easy, achievable and safe? Here are a few factors to guide you. It is worth saying that there are many ways to whittle a willow rod, just as there are many ways to skin a squirrel. So while this is our opinion on safe ways of working, the educator/FS practitioner needs to constantly risk assess and see what works for them, in a safe way, and assess what is working

Figure 12.7 Continued

for the learner. If the learner is really struggling, this may be due to the technique used, but it is also worth saying that you may need to review the tool, material and task – "Is this the easiest and safest way?" If the learner is struggling, then something may need adjusting, and if you feel it is unsafe then definitely make an adjustment.

If the learners have had no experience working with handtools, it is worth bearing in mind that we have all probably had experience with knives and forks and probably scissors. Build on these basic skills. When first handling a tool, encourage learners to shake hands with it – feel its weight in the hand, treat it like a friend and encourage the first-time user to consider both its friendly side and its dangerous side. Things to discuss are sharpness and/or pointiness/jaggedness of blade, where to hold safely, how to carry and store safely and safe working distance – see the online appendix for suggested procedures for a number of handtools. Once they have said hello and gotten to know the look and feel of the tool, then it will be time to harvest in a mindful and caring way. Figures 12.8 and 12.9 show how to prune to make as little damage to the parent plant and how to cut/coppice/pollard so as to cause minimal impact and allow the plant to continue to grow and even regrow – coppice or pollard. We also emphasise that when material has been cut, we leave the plant in the best condition possible and use all the material collected or leave it to become part of the soil cycle and deadwood habitat in the wood . . . and most importantly show

Figure 12.8 Coppicing – starting from the outside and working your way in, angling the cut so water flows away from the 'stool'

Figure 12.9 To cut a stick to use for a project, 'prune' the branch just above the 'collar' of the branch junction

appreciation and gratitude for the gift the plant or even animal (if creating something from bone, for example) has made.

Once you have made the choice of material, the harvesting really needs to be part and parcel of the **sustainable management** of a site/place. It may be fitting in with the coppice cycle of a site, it may be part of tree thinning, or it may be sensitive pruning as outlined earlier. You really

Figure 12.9 Continued

need to see this as part of a management plan for the site (see Chapter 9). Most cutting of wood has the least impact on the parent plant if done in the winter when the plant is almost dormant, that is, from November to February. If you need to cut material during the growing period – early spring to autumn – then this needs more serious consideration: what part of the plant to take and what impact this will have. For example, the odd sunshoot on a hazel tree – these are the very straight thin rods going straight up towards the sun – can be taken with little effect on the parent plant; the same can be said of willow. Otherwise, it is worth asking any tree surgeons, landscape gardeners or other land managers if they are doing any pruning or tree work and 'scrounge'. We have spent many a time in sawmills, woodyards and abandoned brash piles pulling out bits of wood that are ripe for whittling or construction.

BUILDING STRENGTH AND STAMINA

Two of the key things that many learners may need to build, both young and old alike, are *strength* and *stamina*. This is because we will need to use muscles and techniques not used before; we need to practice to build muscle memory. For certain tools, such as the knife, you may need to start and give confidence by having a good garden glove, preferably with leather across the back of fingers and knuckles, on the non-tooled hand. A good starting point is to work with materials that are easy to manipulate, cut and shape. If the tool blade is sharp, there should be little chance of any small cuts – see later in the chapter for tool maintenance advice. Once the memory is built through practice, take away the glove – it allows for more grip on the material being worked on, and a stronger natural world connection to boot. When looking

Figure 12.10 Working with loppers as a first tool

at woods, start with the softest and easiest to cut soft woods such as pine, if available, or the softer hardwoods such as willow, birch and hazel. Always strive for wood with few knots and as straight a grain as possible – they are so much easier to manipulate and cut. One of the first tools we will introduce is the lopper, as children as young as 3 can use these on finger-size wood such as hazel sunshoots or small willow rods.

Also, loppers and a bow saw, panel saw or Japanese pull saw can be used to cut small birch branches with smaller twig-size branches and then split to make clothes hooks/pegs, for example. The birch tree is ideal for cutting cross sections of wrist-sized branches, and once holes can be hand drilled in a jig (see techniques section), the creative possibilities are endless – from making figures with simple dowel-type joints to cars, trains and planes! (See the online appendix that illustrates some of these starting points and appropriate materials for certain items and levels of handtool work.)

HANDTOOL TECHNIQUES

There is a school of thought that whatever tool will help learners move in small stages on to the 'proper' tool, then it is all grist to our handtool elbows. For example, potato peelers are frequently used as introductions to whittling. Having visited two Scandinavian countries – Sweden and Finland, both known for their handcrafts – and seen children as young as 3 using fixed blade knives, and by the time they are 5 manipulating adult-sized tools, we are firm believers in choosing the appropriate tool for the appropriate job. Even though we now know the brain is much more plastic than we thought throughout life, we are so much quicker at building muscle memory in our early stages of life. So if we have learners who clearly have little dexterity, then maybe a good starting point would be potato peelers used for their purpose, that is, to peel a potato, carrot or cucumber while sitting comfortably, away from the danger area (i.e. the thighs), but not towards the ground where the tool could pick up grit. Then, when ready, move to a knife for whittling wood, and if a little hesitant the leader can give gentle emotional and physical support (see Figure 12.11).

Likewise, if we wish to make holes in wood and we feel the learner doesn't have the strength, then, although palm drills may seem easy to handle and can work on thin pieces of wood, we may need to introduce them to a small brace and bit and the correct technique of placing a shoulder and whole weight on to the drill in order to drill thicker pieces of wood that they may want to use for creative purposes. Also, it's important to have the setup at the right height in the right clamping device/jig for the wood being drilled.

The quicker we can assess the learner and move them on to the correct tool, correct material, appropriate environment/space/setup, and easiest and appropriately safe technique, then this becomes habit and with a little practice success will come. We have seen so many learners grow in stature when they realise they are entering the 'adult tool world', working safely and

Figure 12.11 Gentle support while allowing for independence when starting to work with tools

competently with the same tools we use, even if slightly smaller versions for those with very small hands! The table and pictures in the Chapter 12 online appendix give some tips on techniques and ways of progressing with certain tools.

For inspiration and information on whittling techniques and projects, we recommend you look at the useful resources section at the end of the chapter. Also see figures 12.12, 12.13 and 12.14 for a sample of a plethora of projects involving handtools with different stages of development.

A FINAL NOTE ABOUT HANDTOOL PROCEDURES AND RISK-BENEFIT ASSESSMENTS

All of the considerations in this section and in the appendices should be logged on a risk-benefit assessment of your tool procedures:

- benefits
- assessing when, what, where and how to introduce tools
- ways to support learners with handtool use, including some basic techniques to keep safe outlined in Figure 12.2
- transportation, storage and maintenance

Figure 12.12 Drilling using a brace and bit and palm drill. Clamp wood using a G clamp and simple jig to hold wood for safe drilling

Figure 12.13 A flying pig made by a 5-year-old at Forest School with a hand drill and saw

Figure 12.14 Projects from a Forest School group of 8- to 11-year-olds – pencil people, car, puppet and xylophone!

Fire

When I was 6 I made a discovery, which I think was prompted by my dad, it was to change my life, a moment indelibly seared into my brain and body. I was with my brother in our garden under a tree with large brown things hanging off it, on a sunny day when I held a magnifier over some brown grass and smoke appeared and when I blew on said dry grass a small flame appeared. Kazam! *I had made fire*. My brother and I felt so powerful and I was hooked. How did this work? Can I do it again? Can I make a bonfire? The questions flowed. Ever since then fire has been a constant companion, and to this day I am still amazed by fire's alchemy, beautiful waving patterns and pure calming, soothing effect.

Jon's earliest memory of firemaking

It is essential that all children experience fire. All you need is a good risk management process in place, the training for teachers and educators can be got in many ways, not necessarily just through Forest School.

This section will look at more reasons for including fire in our school system, when to introduce fire and ways of working with it.

Why fire?

We would be so bold to say that Forest School is not Forest School without a fire, not every day, but as the heart and reference point of the setting . . . it is that ingredient that pulls this learning community together. There is nothing like the calming effect of a fire at the end of a session, when everyone returns to the fire circle from a day's activity and we all just sit and stare, and often there is no need for a prompt to reflect on the day's learning – it just happens!

Fire is history, and if you are looking for curriculum application and enhancement, what better way to teach history than light a fire and tell a story? After all, that is how we learned for centuries – through storytelling around a fire. Many schools re-enact the great fire of London by making fire and burning small buildings, making the lesson so much more meaningful! Fire can be used to introduce writing, as one of our first books in the English language, *Bede's Chronicles*, was written with oak gall ink which requires the earth, air and water elements to be conjoined by fire, and – hey presto! – we have an ink (see in Chapter 13 on plants how this is done). Make a quill and we can write and at the same time study what Bede wrote 1300 years ago – the first time Christian theology was translated into the English language. During a Forest School session with a secondary school group, a 12-year-old suddenly 'dug' into this past after having crushed oak galls and made ink and quills and started writing a poem about a tree, with said ink. She exclaimed, "I can't believe I am writing as Bede did all those years ago and writing as authors have done over hundreds of years – I am Shakespeare!"

There are many other reasons for including fire in any outdoor practice. As stated at the start of this chapter, **physical development** benefits greatly. This is a fine way of developing fine motor skills from the collection, sorting and arranging of small kindling to the action of using a firesteel, flint and steel, matches or, if you are really advanced, fire drills.

Resilience

Firemaking is a great way to build **resilience**. We once had an 11-year-old who was desperate to master the bow drill; he had read about it at home and came to Forest School demanding to learn this technique of fire lighting. It is not normal to introduce the bow drill until well into a Forest School programme and only when the learner asks after it – especially at primary level (we may start with a pump drill – see later in the chapter). It took this boy 5 weeks of sheer perseverance and trying for himself to get an ember from rubbing wood on wood through the power of the 'bow'. His class teacher was amazed, as he seemed to be 'always' giving up on learning in the classroom – if he couldn't get a maths problem or a certain way of writing, first time, his pencil or pen would go flying across the classroom! This was a lesson in resilience, practice and problem solving. We have witnessed many occasions of children, especially nursery and reception, persevering with a junior firesteel to light a small fluffy bundle of tinder (thistle down previously pinched from a thistle head by small hands).

Risk management

Working with fire is such a great way of introducing **risk management**. We often get people asking, 'you don't light fire with little ones, do you?' If we learn how to manage the risks at an early age, then we won't get burnt at an older age! As we stated in the play chapter, this is one of Sandseter's risky play types, and children soon learn how to behave in a safe way around a fire, how to move, the safe way of lighting a fire and how to manage a fire (see online appendix for fire risk-benefit assessment).

There are a host of new **skills** associated with fire. Numeracy is an obvious one related to sizes of wood, shapes of fire and safe distances from fire. Cooking is another key area of skill development. Linked with cooking is the real community building and tying in with seasonal celebrations around fire, from cooking pumpkin soup at Samhain and Halloween to wild garlic pesto on bread, made on the fire, at Beltane/May Day celebrations (see the plant chapter). Identifying tree species that burn well is essential (when dead!) – especially if we are to limit the effects of fire smoke, as some burn cleaner than others. Cooking also brings in a more global and local culture – essential for community building.

The **knowledge** development associated with fire is endless. This can range from all of the things outlined earlier to looking at how fire has been key in ecosystem developments to manage habitats such as heathland. Our transport would not have developed without fire – when you show people a fire piston, suddenly they understand the workings of the internal combustion engine!

Probably the biggest benefit is the **emotional and community development** that fire can catalyse. Some of the best conversations we have had with young people over our combined 70 years of involvement in environmental education have been round a fire – from exploring the meaning of life to singing deeply meaningful songs to working through emotional well-being issues.

Ways of firemaking

There is a plethora of resources about how to make fire, both on YouTube and in other books. Some are useful and some not so (see our recommendations in the resources section at the end of this chapter).

Figure 12.15 Hackney Forest School cooking plantain on the fire

So, in this section we would like to concentrate on how fire is introduced in a learner-centred way and on some of the key safety aspects to take into consideration.

Let us tell you about Jim (not his real name).

A few years ago, Jon worked with a group of 14-year-olds from a special school in Worcester, including a youngster who was diagnosed with ADHD, Jim. His behaviour was consistent with the diagnoses; he tended to start one thing then flit to another activity, and his language could be choice as well as fairly 'audible'! Jon felt that in the first session the group and Jim were not ready for a fire, although they all expected one, since the school had been doing Forest School for a few years and fire was an expectation. Jon had to stay firm; also, he didn't bring any firekit out, so he had a good escape clause! On the third session, after having discussed with the group safe ways to 'be' around the fire, the group decided to have one – they were ready. Here is the dialogue that ensued as soon as they sat down and Jon explained that this week the group needed to boil our own water for a brew (previously it was served from a flask):

Jim saying as they all sat down: "I really want to light a fire."

Three others in the group all made the same request, and so Jon said, "Let's all go and collect some dry snappy stuff that is hanging off the trees or from the ground so we have some fuel to burn to bring the brew to a boil." Both Clare (the TA with the group) and Jon duly demonstrated exactly what was meant as he was explaining. At first all six plus the adults started collecting, then three got distracted and went off to carry on shelter building, leaving three, two of whom felt it unfair as the others weren't collecting. The session continued for a short time and Jim climbed a tree! Clare and Jon stopped and looked at each other as if to say, *Why are we doing this?* Do we stop and know that the group will get grumpy due to lack of waffle and drink (yes, this group had a penchant for waffles and jam!)? So, with some diversionary stick games with Jim, which pulled in the two learners, enough fuel was collected, in the end, for fire. Jim suddenly remembered he wanted to light a fire as soon the stick juggling started! It's all in the timing. Jim went on to successfully light the first fire of the year, dropping a spark on to some thistle down to make flame and carefully laying further kindling in the form of dry cow parsley stalks and small birch twigs on to the said flames – building this up with dead dry wood. Claire exclaimed, "I've never seen him so concentrated!"

Some key pointers to lighting a successful fire are included in the online appendix.

When it comes to **safety** round the fire, we often we see the flames as the most dangerous parts of the fire and are afraid of directly burning flesh, clothing or hair. We have found, however, that most people are pretty good at self-regulating around flames; it is often other aspects of the fire that are most important when working around fire. Table 12.1 is a grid to help take into account key considerations (see the risk-benefit assessment in the Chapter 12 online appendix).

To demonstrate the 'power of fire', we'll finish this section by going back to Jim's story.

Table 12.1 Fire risks grid

Actions	Risks	Control measures
Picking up hot objects from the fire such as kettles and frying pans	Burns or blisters → infection	Have fireproof gloves available to wear when picking up hot objects from the fire
Spilling hot food or liquids on skin	Burns or blisters → infection	Ensure containers are carried properly (by the handle) and if there is a lid ensure this is on the container if needed. Ensure the pouring of hot food and liquids is done effectively and supervised, if needed
Clothing or hair catching fire	Burns or blisters → infection	Tie back hair or loose clothing. Be aware that some clothing catches fire more easily – especially from 'plastic-based' material
Regular smoke inhalation	Respiratory damage and eye irritation	Ensure seasoned wood is being used. If regularly lighting fires, you might want to look at the most effective fire 'lay' – an upside-down lay can be more effective at burning off fumes. Do not use painted or treated wood Encourage people to move away from the smoke area to minimise smoke inhalation
Woodland and soil catching fire	Damage to the wood and potential burning of living beings, including humans	Ensure the fire is kept small and, if needed, put in a fire surround of either larger logs or rocks that do not explode when heated, e.g. granite When finished, ensure the soil is cooled, using a good dousing of water, and made safe; check the soil below the fire, especially in dry conditions

What came with fire was an interest in the alchemy of flame. In our fourth week, while making pan-cakes, Jim asked Jon, "How is it that just heating eggs made them 'solid'?". He had never asked himself that question before – how often do we take what is seen as the mundane/'everyday' for granted, and yet these daily presentations can help us grow wise. This was a type of 'enquiry'

Figure 12.16 The community of fire

question he had never really asked before, and in that moment we spotted a possible passion for cooking . . . it was so!

In December of that year Jim's home situation became more challenging, and he ended up being cared for by his grandparents. In January, the school had an OFSTED inspection. Sue, the head at the school, announced to Jim that the inspector was coming out to Forest School – would he cook something for us? There's nothing like food to persuade! Jim came up with the goods – he and the group cooked bread in a homemade oven, as well as a curry and an apple pie! When the inspector left, Jon commented that the food seemed to hit the mark! While we sat round the fire reflecting on the visit, Jim suddenly put his head on Jon's lap, and Jon admitted he panicked (Jim had made a clear connection with him). He looked up and Jon asked:

"What's going on, Jim?"

"This is like a second home, Jon."

Long pause, then Jon replied, "How so?" being mindful that the small word 'Why?' can close down conversations in our judgmental education system – ironic that OFSTED had just visited.

"The fire, cooking and I am calm here." He looked up to the tree canopy, "I don't need my meds here, do I? It calms . . . I mean the fire, trees and you guys."

Fire is truly good medicine.

MUD, SOIL AND SOUL!

Earth is an amazing material. It is the medium from which nearly all our food is fed and is therefore the mineral building block of our cells and bodies. It is probably the first material we manipulated to make containers and 'cooking' pots – we are *of the earth*. At Forest School and in nature education, there comes a time when we can't help but smear 'paint' in the form of clay or plant pigment on our faces to either camouflage ourselves or become part of a 'tribe' – we have a deep affinity to soil and earth. Indeed, in Celtic and Greek culture it is said we were born out of clay and it is part of our 'soul'.

Working with and mixing soil and water is something instinctual. To get the right balance, sieving soil to separate out the larger particles and stones, is a great exercise – we have spent many an hour with children dancing and sieving! Then combining the finer stuff with water until it becomes malleable, but not too wet, to make a 'clayey mix' and wrapping in newspaper to bake in the sun and – hey presto! – you have a mud pie. To take this further, you can use soil and clay and straw all mixed with water and tread on it while squashed between a tarp and we have cob. Tamp this down into a square form to make bricks or into a bucket to make building blocks of different shapes. You can use cob to coat surfaces and even form a wall from some fences made from hazel or willow – wattle and daub!

If your learners suddenly start getting into some serious digging and larger 'earthworks' projects, you will need to check on the following:

- Land ownership – this may sound obvious, but it's not always totally straightforward, as some landowners may be averse to you digging up their land.
- Services – any gas, electricity or water mains? Telephone or cable lines? Drainage or sewer runs?
- Check your ecological survey and management plan. Identify any flora and fauna you may be disturbing.
- Check for any previous archaeological work that may have been carried out.
- Dig trial pits to determine what you are dealing with – depth of topsoil, subsoil and possibly bedrock.
- Make soil tests to determine composition, clay/sand contents, pH etc.

In the early days of Forest School at the Bishops Wood Centre, Jon ended up sculpting a dragon and newt from the land with a group, having discovered newts on the site. This moved on to making a baby dragon cob oven with Forest School leaders from Dudley see Figure 12.7 . . . all born from a group of 9-year-olds who were mad about pizzas!

Small pots are always a 'hit' if you have a soil/subsoil that has a high clay content, anything from finger pots to larger bowls; a popular Forest School motif is the 'tree guardian' or 'blobsters'. If your site doesn't have a clay type of soil, then it is worth bringing in an air-drying clay. Combining this with natural materials such as leaves, stones, bark, juices from berries to colour said clay makes for even more creative responses to working with this very 'primal' material. Jon will never forget telling the story about the search for the 'tree with three fruits', a Welsh folk tale, where at the end the apprentice priest built a church of stone and wattle and daub around a tree that provided for bees, birds and pigs. This stimulated lots of making of small clay bees and pigs populating a clay church around a tree that one of the teaching assistants with the group got totally engrossed in. It turned out to be a real 'play frame' that the whole Forest School community engaged with. Such is the way that nature and the elements can really stimulate storymaking and pure play!

We recommend you look at the resources section at the end of the chapter to discover other possibilities, such as making mud bricks and mud kitchens.

Plant-based crafts

Once you start looking at ways of working with natural materials, the possibilities become endless! All it takes is imagination, some wood, bark, mud and some plant colour from berries or leaves, for example, and our creative juices start flowing. To see one example of ways of working with plants (to make ink), see the online appendix.

Figure 12.17 Cob making with local clay, and a cob oven made with clay and soil on site mixed with straw, which is now an oven for Forest School meals – the oven was made by Forest Schoolers from Dudley and named 'Dudley the Dragon'.

Figure 12.18 Baglan's church from the story "The Tree with Three Fruits"

If you have access to birch, willow, hazel, nettle and bramble, all of the following 'plant handicrafts' become possible, and these are just the starting point!

- Bramble and nettle cordage for tying and making bracelets, necklaces, ties. There are many YouTube clips to demonstrate how to make cordage (see resources section) – the best time of year for this is in early spring.

329

Figure 12.19 Mud combined with clay and soil and grass, squeezed by a wood form, makes a basic building block; with mud and water we have a 'mud kitchen!'

Figure 12.20 Oak gall ink on calico

- Weaving circles with thin willow or hazel sunshoots, which are the basis for all sorts of projects such as dreamcatchers, headdresses, platters, baskets.
- Weaving from willow bark to make pots and mats.
- Using birch bark with wood to make cups and pots.
- Stitching leaves together with hawthorn spines to make crowns.
- Flag making from calico/old cotton, painting on plant pigments or bashing with stones to make imprints (hapazome).

All the previously mentioned activities are starting points, and once you start playing with materials of the earth, you'll see things happen and be amazed at what learners can create. We are intrinsically creators, and it is this creativity that has always gone hand in hand with 'nature's flexible nature' and ability to be moulded and moved by the human hand, *but* only if done in a respectful, reciprocal, mindful way. We are big believers in respectfully approaching projects and will always have a feedback mechanism that either results in connection or disconnection. The next chapter will explore how we follow nature and the non-human, in particular plants and animals, in a 'connective' way.

QUESTIONS FOR PRACTICE

What materials on your site can be used for handcrafts?

Do you have the appropriate tools for working with handcrafts? Are there any adults in the local community you may be able to call on to help your learners with new handcraft skills?

How do you ensure that the ecology and respect for the materials being used help maintain an integral natural community and where possible actually minimise the impact of your 'craft' practices?

USEFUL RESOURCES

Books we would highly recommend for more projects and ways of working with wood and young people in the woods include:

Forest Craft: A Child's Guide to Whittling in the Woodland by Richard Irvine (Guild of Master Craftsman Publications, 2019). Really good for getting started on whittling projects with great pictures showing the possibilities as well as safety tips and techniques.

Making Woodland Crafts by Patrick Harrison (Hawthorn Press, 2017). Lots of well-illustrated examples of projects with wood and knots!

Green Woodwork: Working with Wood the Natural Way by Mike Abbott (Guild of Master Craftsman, 1989). This is still the go to book for an introduction to turning greenwood and making basic structures for shaving and shaping wood – good for those working with older children and young people.

Forest School Adventure – Outdoor Skills and Play for Children by N Walmsley and D Westall (GMC, 2018; see pp. 72–91).

A Year of Forest School – Outdoor Play and Skill-Building, Fun for Every Season by J Worral and P Houghton (Watkins, 2018; see p. 15).

Learning through Woodwork – Introducing Woodwork in the Early Years by Pete Moorhouse (Routledge, 2018). A very practical book encouraging creativity through woodwork – although this is very much 'workshop' based, it is full of tips and tricks for working with younger ages.

The Children's Forest; Stories & Songs, Wild Food, Crafts & Celebrations All Year Round by D Casey, A Richardson and H d'Ascoli (Hawthorn Press, 2019).

The Teachers Handbook of Slöjd by Otto Salomon (Forgotten Books, 2018). This is the Swedish classic craft teaching book, written in 1891 but just as relevant today! It delves into the philosophy and practical aspects of 'craft' teaching.

Woodland Craft by Ben Law (GMC, 2015).

Woodcraft – a Practical Celebration of the Tree by John Rhyder (Practical Nature, 2018). For any practitioner who wants the best advice that encompasses woodland management, tool use and maintenance and craft ideas, this is the one to get! An excellent comprehensive guide on the main craft topics, from harvesting, choosing tools and carving, and working with natural fibres, fire, natural glues, dyes and inks to working with plants and fungi and playing with ropes and knots.

The Art of Fire; the Joy of Spark, Tinder and Ember: A Step-by-Step Guide to Starting, Building and Handling Fires by Daniel Hume (Century, 2017). We recommend this for working with fire. It gives a good history of fire and all its uses, different ways to light fires, types of tinder and wood – an all-round excellent book for use in education.

Essential Bushcraft by Ray Meers (Hodder and Stoughton, 2003).

I Love My World: The Playful, Hands-On, Nature Connection Guidebook by Chris Holland (self-published, 2012) is on many nature educators' bookshelves. Chris weaves many crafts into storymaking and telling, in a playful way. This is also online at www.wholeland.org.uk/

For working with mud and water:

The Mud Kitchen Book by Jan White and Muddy Faces, downloadable at https://muddyfaces.co.uk/activity_tag/mud-kitchen-book/. The book includes some great ideas for working with mud and other materials, including how to make oak gall ink.

Jan White is a leading expert in all things related to playing outdoors with materials, particularly in early years. Her book *Playing and Learning Outdoors* (Routledge, 2019) is a classic, and her blog is well worth a read, particularly when wanting to play with the elements; see https://janwhitenaturalplay.wordpress.com/

For working with organic materials and all sorts of earthy pigments and creating paints and inks, look no further than Nick Neddo's book *The Organic Artist: Make Your Own Paint, Paper, Pigments and Prints and More from Nature* (Quarry Books, 2015) and *The Organic Artist for Kids: A DIY Guide for Making Your Own Eco-Friendly Art Supplies from Nature*.

For many traditional indigenous crafts worth looking at, go to Zabe MacEachren's web page. At the bottom of the publications section you will find many articles from the *Pathways* journal – worth a look at for guidance on everything from cordage to kites! See https://educ.queensu.ca/zabe-maceachren

For crafting with plants, here are some good books and a website to start with:

Natural – Simple Land Art Through The Seasons by Marc Pouyet. Francis Lincoln (2019)

Handmade Baskets; from Nature's Colourful Materials by Susan Vaughan. Search Press Ltd (2014)

Living Willow Sculpture by John Warnes. Search Press Ltd (2001)

Nature Crafts for Kids at www.naturecraftsforkids.com includes links to a number of websites and resources

BIBLIOGRAPHY

Abbot, M (1989) *Green Woodwork: Working with Wood the Natural Way*. Lewes: Guild of Master Craftsman Publications.

Cohen, M (2007) *Reconnecting with Nature: Finding Wellness through Restoring Your Bond with the Earth*. Ecopress.

MacEachren, Z (2000) Crafting as a Practice of Relating to the Natural World. *Canadian Journal of Environmental Education* 5: 186–199. See https://journals.sagepub.com/doi/abs/10.1177/105382590402600305

Wynn, T and Coolidge, F L (2010) Working Memory: Beyond Language and Symbolism. *International Journal of Evolutionary Biology* 2011: 741357.

13 Journey with plants and animals – working with the ecological

THE ECOLOGICAL

We as humans are having a profound effect on this vast cradle of life. Collectively we need to simultaneously learn to love and respect our ecological systems whilst rapidly mobilising all our knowledge to create carbon-neutral and regenerative cultures. Through science we now understand that our living systems and elements such as our oceans are the support system of our planet. Our education system can and, in our view, should support this understanding, though this needs to be underpinned by appropriate Nature Pedagogy, where learning and knowledge begin through experience in the body. This chapter focuses on the plant and animal kingdoms, part of the system that we share a closer kinship with and relate to more easily.

> Know the ways of the ones who take care of you, so that you may take care of them. Introduce yourself. Be accountable as the one who comes asking for life. Ask permission before taking. Abide by the answer. Never take the first. Never take the last. Take only what you need. Take only that which is given. Never take more than half. Leave some for others. Harvest in a way that minimizes harm. Use it respectfully. Never waste what you have taken. Share. Give thanks for what you have been given. Give a gift, in reciprocity for what you have taken. Sustain the ones who sustain you and the earth will last forever.
>
> (Robin Wall Kimmerer, *Braiding Sweetgrass: Indigenous Wisdom, Scientific Knowledge and the Teachings of Plants*, p. 183)

Perhaps we forget too easily how so much of our everyday life originates from plants and animals – we take too much for granted. This book and chapter repeatedly claim that healthy human development is directly linked to healthy ecology. It is a human and earth right to grow up in a culture where our human systems remain within the laws of nature.

> You say you love your children above everything else. And yet you are stealing their future. We cannot solve a crisis without treating it as a crisis.
>
> (Greta Thunberg, 2019)

The ecological systems are literally breaking down all over the planet, and this crisis requires us to rethink the way we connect with the ecological and provide hope and a different cultural narrative.

How do we develop connection and kinship?

In Europe, we tend to love our pets and see them as part of the family. In older traditions, attributing plants and animals and even mountains as *family* is an extension of the notion of a 'pet' as family and is based on a valued relationship. Deep connection forms when you feel safe enough and belong to a group/person and/or place. The journey through life grows ever more deeply to a belonging to place, to self and finally to the whole of life.

A journey with plants

The term Forest School evokes deep connections with our plants and woodland culture. This rich and diverse context supports the development of a relationship between the learner and the plant world. Trees provide some of the most diverse places for playing and learning. After all, the stick, according to the latest research on playthings by the University of Colorado, is still the most popular toy in the world.

Our ancestors had intimate relationships with plants and trees from which they gathered food, made fire, built shelters, made crafts, buildings and boats and harvested medicines. Nowadays we often just see 'a wall of green' without having developed the brain patterns to pick out all the details and differences that exist between the plants and their different families. Human development has evolved in partnership with the plant kingdom, which provides a perfectly suited environment to explore, experience, play and grow up in – nature or Vitamin 'N' (!) is the essential ingredient to healthy development, general well-being, spirit and survival.

> In an age of rapid environmental, economic, and social transformation, the future will belong to the nature-smart – those individuals, families, businesses, and political leaders who develop a deeper understanding of nature, and who balance the virtual with the real.
>
> (Louv, 2011)

When children are given time outdoors, they begin to listen and respond in a different way. They recover a sense of freedom that is a birth-given attribute, and all their senses begin to come alive, exploring among the plants and giant trees. Like a sponge, given the chance, the young ones absorb all the knowledge and experiences effortlessly, becoming natural botanists. Plants, unlike humans, are quiet; they create a unique atmosphere of different smells, textures, colours and responses. They are young and old, large and small, and undetected pass electrical impulses through their roots and trunks, enabling a communication network.

Plants are marvellous

Plants convert energy from sunlight into food stored as carbohydrates through a process known as photosynthesis. This is a marvel in itself. At Forest School we often tell stories about how fire was created, and we learn that by rubbing sticks from trees together, we can re-create the 'fire potential' that is already inside the plants. We like to anthropomorphise the plants, to see them like us, needing air, water, heat and earth, have different characters, and change in appearance and size over a lifetime and through the seasons.

Plants provide an important source of the oxygen that humans and animals breathe; they use carbon dioxide for photosynthesis and release oxygen into the atmosphere. When we are outdoors, we sometimes take a moment to breathe in the pure air and chemicals released from the plants. They give back our carbon dioxide, and there is a sense of everything breathing together.

The most astonishing thing about trees is how social they are. The trees in the forest care for each other, sometimes going so far as to nourish the stump of a felled tree by feeding it sugars and other nutrients . . . scientific research aimed at understanding the astonishing abilities of this partnership between fungi and plant has only just begun.

(Wohlleben, 2016)

Why are plants important in the context of FS and education?

Trees provide places to play with ropes; climb; create imaginary worlds in, on, underneath and above; to shelter under; to provide us still with fuel and fodder; to 'bathe' in; and to create and tell stories from and under. Indeed, they are places for creating learning communities that should be linking into our built communities. Through your senses, trees and plants are a feast of smell, shape, size, colour, texture, taste and sound.

Forest School recognises that developing awareness and relationships with nature necessitates the children's confident ability to recognise and interact appropriately with trees and plants. Huge benefits result from the ongoing development of these relationships. With safe and professional guidance, the children are shown some uses of the plants for food, medicine and other practical uses (see Chapter 13 online appendix). This greatly enhances their appreciation of their environment and leads to intrinsic motivation to protect it. We may gather the plants and process them together, which, as an activity, promotes teamwork, community and an appreciation for our own heritage uses of native plants. The children also

Figure 13.1 In spring: primrose (*P. vulgaris* on right) and foxglove (poisonous) leaves (*Digitalis purpurea* on left)

gain self-confidence in being able to correctly identify plants and trees and apply this knowledge practically.

Fear has been identified as one of the barriers to spending more time outdoors. By raising awareness of plants that are useful, fear will be replaced by knowledge and sense of place. Building an intimacy with plants enables us to see in a different way. For our brains to develop the ability to see, we need developed pathways that come from exposure to repeated patterns that enable us to detect complex visual patterns. If the inexperienced practitioner or young person is not exposed to different shapes, smells and colours, they may not see the difference between a 'safe' plant and an 'unsafe' plant (see Figure 13.1). In Forest School, we want to give time and space to develop a relationship to plants.

Picking blackberries is a favourite pastime. Children are often shown this berry from a young age, have tasted it and eaten crumbles and pies – so we have developed a 'pattern' in our brains to identify and recognise it. Some Forest School policies say they have a 'nil by mouth' or 'no pick no lick' policy in which case they don't consume any plant/berry ever with the children. Our approach is to start with what we call 'green light' plants (see table starting on page 352) – plants which are abundant and safe to use, and we get to know them well. We find fun ways with a young group of saying hello to the poisonous plants but not touching them. We use a host of engaging ways to help children and adults see plants in more details.

Bringing Forest School alive

It's springtime at Forest School, and the children are watching the flowers return once again.

Some children are really interested in the flowers and like to look more closely at them with magnifying glasses. What do they see? Why are there different bits growing inside? What does it smell like? What does it feel like? Are there any leaves?

Why not create your own flower from clay, sticks, string and what you find around you? (see Figure 13.3) You could go home and research what these different parts are called and what their purpose is, which all links to biology in the National Curriculum.

FS Principle 2: Forest School takes place in a woodland or natural wooded environment to support the development of a relationship between the learner and the natural world.

Observation and knowing your place

We want to make observation fun, create new long-lasting brain patterns, and co-develop a familiarity and kinship with the plants. All the while we are ensuring an increase in our knowledge about plants.

Figure 13.2 Child holding primrose

Figure 13.3 Flower made from woodland materials

We open all our senses to what is around us. We rub our noses to 'enhance the fragrance'; we rub our ears, to draw in the sounds; we feel the temperature of the air or wind; we smell the fragrance of the forest and see the multitudes of plant eye candy.

As foragers, we need to heighten our awareness of the plants, to be able to correctly identify a plant, as a mistake could significantly harm us. Following good processes enables the multitude of benefits that outweigh the risks (see risk-benefit assessment in online appendix). The use of nature awareness and sensory games ensure that we refine and develop our observation skills.

Connecting plant exercises (see the useful resources section)

- Smell pairs: if you have 10 young people in your group, prepare five pairs of different plants. Ask each person to cusp their hands to create a container. Place the plant into their hands (so they can't see it) and let them have a smell. Then they need to find the person in the group with the same smell!
- Blindfold your group and pass around some leaves, nuts, berries (depending on the season): get the YP to describe what they are feeling, the size, texture. Number each one they feel, then put the objects on a cloth and when their eyes are open, get them to point to the first one, second etc. They could then go and see if they can find it in the woods.
- Nettle, pine, bramble teas: carry a flask of hot water and add in some leaves of the nettle and bramble, or pine needles, to make some tea to share. You can do this with berries too (as long as they are 'safe').
- Sit spot: having a special place outdoors is a great way to be on your own and eventually become keen observers. It's a moment to listen, observe, think and be quiet – it is only when we are quiet in nature that the wildlife will show themselves.
- Duplication game: set out a number of natural objects on a cloth – give the YP 10 seconds to look at the objects then go and find them in the woods (make sure they are abundant and safe things!).
- Drawing from memory: take a pencil and paper and draw a plant/berry and the leaves. Then look again, notice what you have missed, add bits. Describe what you have seen to another person.
- Make a craft or medicine from a plant, for example nettle cordage or plantain cream. Knowing where things have come from creates relationship and understanding.
- Matching game: give or find leaves and ask the group to find the other people with the same/ similar leaves. You can extend this with sizes, colours etc.

Life cycle of a plant

As described in Chapter 4, let's remind ourselves of plant wheels and this cycle.

We share many similar journeys with the plants and animals (see Figure 13.4). With young people, you can use a compass to mark out where the directions are. You can ask, Where does the sun set and rise? Where does a plant or tree like to live? Where is the sun in the sky – what direction does it move in? To embed a young person's sense of place and belonging, they may explore the site in a particular direction. They may map out where things are living or where they noticed a bird singing or a fox's den.

Children love role play and drama, where the line of 'whose reality' is much thinner – the realm of the imagination. Embodying the plant cycle is one way to feel yourself as a seed growing up through the seasons of your life – we will do this like a moving guided meditation, getting the group to enact different parts. On page 343 is an example of the role play called 'plant cycle journey' (see Figure 13.5).

We all learn best by doing. In a natural environment, children will explore in their own way. As a practitioner you may refer to your knowledge on learning theories that are being expressed by their play or the behaviour you are observing. At Forest School we will often see children spinning, twirling under the trees and drawing on the ground with a stick (rotation schema); making shelters or building walls or wooden frames (enclosure schema); dropping leaves to the ground or in water, throwing sticks or rolling stumps from place to place (trajectory schema); finding lots of different natural objects and lining them up, making patterns from smallest to biggest (positioning schema). The FS practitioner continues to connect with the place, the plants and the season, to follow the young person drawing on their own experience and observation, deciding when to offer a more adult-led activity. A natural environment has so many more advantages than the indoor classroom – it's different every day, allows for a breadth of expression and exploration and provides a healthy

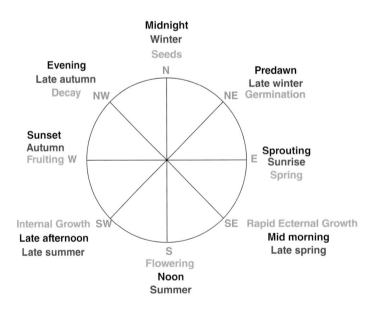

Figure 13.4 Wheel 4: plant cycle

North – Winter Solstice *(you curl up on the ground with your eyes closed.)*
- All is dark, there is immense stillness, the seed is in pitch dark, you are a little star about to be born.
- You are sleeping and dreaming of who you are and what you will become.

Northeast – Imbolc *(you begin to move and slowly a little arm may appear as the shoot.)*
- Something begins to stir within you, you are beginning to awake.
- You break free of your casing and send a small shoot down into the earth (the soil), looking for a strong foundation so that you can grow in this world.
- Now another shoot emerges, this time reaching upward. Maybe you don't know it yet, as everything is still completely dark, that you are reaching toward the sky.

East - Spring Equinox
- Pushing through the darkness and the weight of the earth, now the warmth is quickening your growth and you hear birdsong calling you on.
- You are inspired and filled with energy.
- You emerge into the light, into the world!
- You are greeted fully by the energy of fire, the great sun, giving you warmth and light, by the wind, the air giving you breath. You feel the rain fall upon your body and quench your thirst.

Southeast – Beltane
- You start to grow faster, your shape changing and getting stronger, pushing you forward and outward.
- You are full of motivation and passion for life.
- You are alive! You express yourself in your fullness.

South – Mid-summer Solstice *(you create a flower using your hands around your head; the leader buzzes around you!)*
- You are beginning to flower. There is so much work to be done. Pollen fills the air. Insects are visiting your beautiful flowers. It is time to reproduce.
- Feel the hot sun.
- Hear the insects hum and the birds sing.
- The warm earth is supporting and feeding you.

Southwest – Late-summer Lammas *(your petals are withering and you are beginning to grow a seed within you.)*
- Now there is a lull, a slowing down, a relaxation.
- Your growth is internal, not visible from the outside.
- Your fibres are hardening, you are gathering your energy.
- The beauty of youth has passed, and your petals are withered.
- You are forming seeds and fruits for the generations to come.

West–Autumn Equinox *(you are now a ripe seed, the leader may be a bird going to eat you and poo you out! Or a wind that blows you.)*
- It is time to celebrate all you have been and experienced.
- Your seeds are ripe, waiting for nature's escort. Maybe an animal or bird will eat you and deliver your seeds elsewhere, or the wind, or a hoarding squirrel to bury for later, hopefully to forget where you are.
- There is a feeling of sadness, it is all over, but also a sense of the great value of life.

Northwest – Halloween *(you fall to the ground and the leader covers you in a blanket/cloth as the autumn leaves cover you.)*
- Your seeds fall to the earth. You are covered by leaves. You are feeling tired. It is time to sleep and dream.

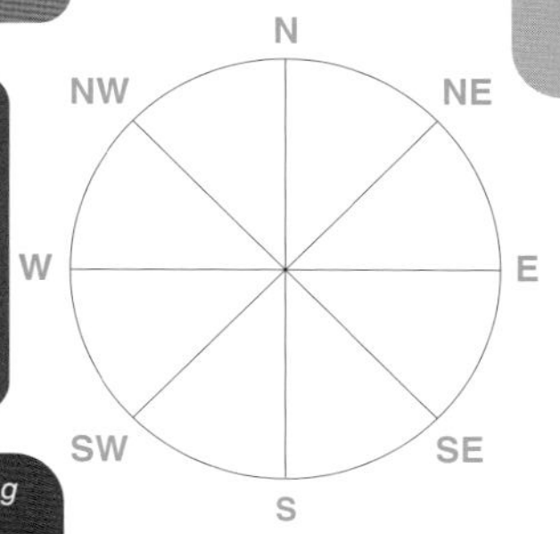

N
NE
E
SE
S
SW
W
NW

Figure 13.5 Wheel of the plant cycle journey

amount of risk and discomfort (see Chapter 6 on risky play). There is so much learning to be had from trees and woods regarding architecture, ecological complexity, community, creative and craft skills, numerical and linguistic development – the list is endless.

At Forest School, we get to know the trees over time and through the seasons – we try and build up our knowledge and get to know what the tree offers us at different times of the year. It's a great idea to keep a journal of what you do and what you all notice when you are outside. Here are some ideas around the hawthorn tree!

The common hawthorn tree (Crataegus monogyna)

The hawthorn tree was traditionally associated with love and fertility! But the hawthorn does not usually flower until May, so it is also known as the May tree.

> These thorny branches bore the May,
> So many months ago,
> That scattered petals lay,
> Like drifts of fallen snow,
> "This is the stories end" you said;
> But O, not half was told!
> For see, my haws are here instead,
> And hungry birdies shall be fed
> On these when days are cold.
>
> ("The Song of the Hawthorn Fairy" by Cicely Mary Barker,
> Flower Fairies, 1923, published 1996)

The blossom of hawthorn is worth capturing! We take our recycled jars and put some olive oil inside – then we carefully pick some flowers to make perfume! After allowing the oil to infuse for a few days, we drain the flowers out, leaving a sweet-smelling oil! We also dance around the trees with our forest instruments! If you get thirsty, you can make a tea with the flowers by adding a few flowers and hot water. As a medicine, they are particularly good for stimulating circulation. As a popular boundary hedge, they also offer a safe haven for nesting birds.

In autumn, we gather hawthorn berries to make hawthorn leather. First, we spend time exploring and looking carefully at the berries, getting to know who lives in or near the hawthorn, in the playground, the hedgerows, the field. We look through our magnifying glasses to see the little hawthorn 'star', we touch and smell the leaves, we notice the shapes of the leaves and how they grow on the stem. When we are ready, we gather some berries and give them to the adult with us (who checks we have the right berry). Back at base we count and sort the berries into little cups, removing their stems and getting them ready to make a fruit leather. We squash the berries

Figure 13.6 Hawthorn in flower

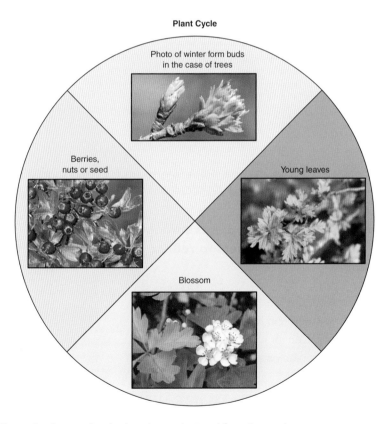

Figure 13.7 Example plant cycle: the hawthorn plant and foraging cycle

Figure 13.8 Foraging through the year: plant discoveries throughout the year – making hawthorn 'leather' in autumn

through a sieve, so we don't have the seeds (the seeds are mildly poisonous like apple seeds), then we paste the berry mush onto some baking paper or a safe leaf to dry out in the sun or at home. Sometimes we add some honey.

Other ideas for connecting to plants through the year:

You could insert your own wheel to reflect your own site and the plants and animals living there

Dec: roots and pine needle tea, pine nuts
Jan: gorse blossoming, ground ivy tea
Feb: primrose flowers, cleaver juice, dandelion
March: dandelion, larch nibbles and birch sap
April: wood sorrel, wild garlic

Foraging through the year

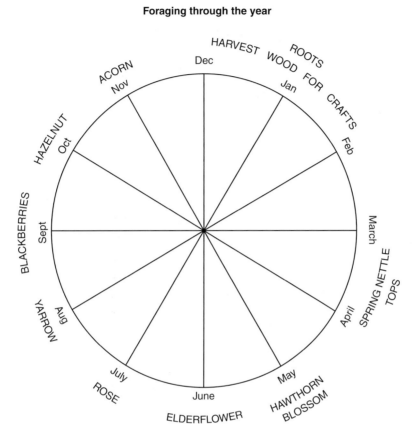

Figure 13.9 The foraging year

May: hawthorn blossom and leaves, jack by the hedge (garlic mustard)
June: elderflowers, stinging nettle leaves
July: chickweed and fat hen
Aug: meadowsweet tea, crab apples
Sept: blackberries, elderberry, rowan berry
Oct: hazelnuts, wild rose hips, beechnuts, sweet chestnut, sloes
Nov: acorns, holly tea, hawthorn berries

Figure 13.10 Dandelion – flower and 'clock' – the seed

Dandelion – elder and young one together!

Journey example session 1 with a group of reception/Year 1

Late September:

We played some nature awareness games together. We looked for signs of autumn. The children noticed leaves on the ground, the mushrooms, the smell of autumn, the spiders, acorns on the trees and so much more. We practised fox walking, and the children were amazing at being silent walking through the forest.

We sniffed the grass and the bracken and the oak tree – it was autumn! There was a light and fairly warm breeze from the east. We walked to the great woods, going into the tree groups – pines, ash, hazel, oaks and chestnuts – and had buddies so no one got lost; we thought about directions a lot. Some children wanted to carry on building their shelters – some for themselves, some for the animals of all different designs, sizes and locations. Some helped gather bracken and sticks to make a fire and others wanted to help make hawthorn tea. We sang our fire song, drank tea and shared a story.

Next session: We planted our own oak trees today. We mixed compost with soil and then put them in the pots – we had some sprout acorns like this and we planted them on their sides because the first shoot is the taproot. We then gently put the soil on the top and said good night so they can go to sleep until spring and dream of becoming oak trees.

Next session: We followed in the footsteps of our ancestors today; the forest was our home. We needed to find fire, water, shelter and food. We also looked for medicine in case we got ill.

In the meadow, we found acorn and to eat we found sorrel, chestnut and hazelnut, but we were thirsty so we used the alder tree to tell us where the water was and found it in the stream bed where we dug down. Then X led the way to find the deer – we had signals and walked in a big long line all the way to the big meadow, where we found an old ancestral lodge to live in and made a fire using a fire striker to eat our foraged apple and listen to our story around. We all took a cup of water to help put the fire out and said what we are thankful for. The wood really felt like home today!

Story of the day – on our way back, we listened to what the children noticed about nature and what they wanted to do next time.

Journey example session 5 with a group of referred young people

Time of year: mid-February and cold

The group arrive and we walk into the woods – we harvest some willow for dream catchers. We have a little taste, too – what does it taste like? Aspirin – willow is nature's aspirin.

Figure 13.11 Marina collecting cleavers for firemaking and nest-making materials

At the main camp, we pick a nature name of a local woodland bird – inspired by the amount of birds that are beginning to get their nests together.

We have remembered to bring our bird song book (where you can listen to the different bird sounds).

One of the young people prepares the main fire, while we talk about the yearly cycle and this time of year – thinking about something we may hope for or something we would like to do this year. We are going to experiment with gluten-free biscuits in the Dutch oven and try out a new frying pan pizza recipe that was discussed from the last session. Food is a big inspiration in this group!

First, we wander into the woods to gather firewood for the pizza and Dutch oven fire! We have learned that birch wood is really good for fire lighting, as well as the dry larch twigs hanging in the trees! This time we are going to use jute string and birch bark to light the fires. One young person has heard of using a bow drill to make a fire. While a group makes a fire, another group wants to put up the nets and ask for some help with knots – we check that there is no dead wood above, that the trees are strong and healthy and nothing under the net that we could land on! The fire is lit. We wait for some embers, then we make delicious pizzas (using frying pan and lid method)! All the while some are playing on the nets and ropes, one group begins to make dream

Figure 13.12 Making bread while we collect!

catchers, and another group is working on bird boxes (using planked wood). We discovered that there are many different kinds of bird boxes depending on the bird! The robin needs a bigger hole because its legs don't bend! And the woodcreeper has one more like a small bat box.

Before we end, we have a sit spot and take a moment to be quiet in nature.

We all pack up together, get everything ready, make sure all our fires (except the main camp one this time) are completely out and left with no trace and sit down for a final check in. What worked today? What do we want to do more of? Sharing some observations of each other.

One girl wants to bring her ukulele next time; a few others would like to make a big shelter, carry on with sawing and making boxes, make some nettle soup.

Appendix

COMMON PLANTS TO USE AT FOREST SCHOOL

Green-light plant table: If you are just beginning, stick to the green-light plants!

CIRCLE OF LIFE REDISCOVERY

EDIBLE GREEN-LIGHT PLANTS

Key list	Attributes/ character	Medicine	Cautions	Edible part or parts used	Poisonous look-alikes	Habitats/where they thrive
Hawthorn	Small tree often in hedgerow, tree of heart protection	To strengthen the heart, especially the berries	Do not take in conjunction with other medication for blood pressure/heart	Leaves, flowers, berries	In a hedgerow be careful of black bryony – red berries	Sun/minimal shade, very hardy. Found on moors hill, cliffs, also hedgerows
Elder	Small tree – nature's medicine chest	Many uses: Flowers – eyes, catarrh, sinus Berries – anti viral Leaves – aches and bruises	Avoid leaf, bark and roots internally unless under medical herbalist directions. Cook the elderberries	Flowers and berries can be eaten, best cooked	Flower clusters could be confused with poisonous umbeliffer plants	Sun, minimal shade throughout the land, though won't produce flowers in too much shade
Plantain	Ability to draw nutrients from compacted soil. Humble yet powerful medicine	Pulped leaves to draw out infection, insect bites, internally draw out phlegm	Seeds with husks on are laxative	Leaves and winnowed seeds	Red/white campion before flowering	Well-trodden paths. Compact soil, widespread, likes sun and shade

EDIBLE GREEN-LIGHT PLANTS

Key list	Attributes/character	Medicine	Cautions	Edible part or parts used	Poisonous look-alikes	Habitats/where they thrive
Nettles	Mineral-rich plant of nourishment and activation	Activates the body systems. Nourishes externally for rashes, stings, burns, anti-histamines	Some people are allergic/sensitive to nettle stings and eating	Leaves before flowering, seeds in small doses	Dog's mercury; annual mercury	Edge places, can tolerate shade and sun but likes both and grows in community
Bramble	Plant growth, vigorous protection and aggression	Leaves stop bleeding and diarrhoea. Fruits protect body with vitamin C	Beware of thorns	Leaf buds and very young branch tips; fruit	None known	Brambles enjoy edge places but can survive in many places
Dandelion	Plant of light and hope – cleanses the body of winter grumps	Cleanses the body – leaves and flowers for kidneys, roots for liver	Go gently with the root as it can be too much detox too quickly	Flowers, leaves, roots	Most plants in the same family are edible; be careful of Ranunculus family	Sunny positions, particularly lawns and playing fields
Daisy	Plant of resilience, poor man's arnica, bruisewort	For bruises, coughs, vitamin C and tonic	Careful if grass has been sprayed with chemicals	Flowers, stems, leaves are edible	None known	Sunny positions in playing fields, mown lawns

(Created by Marina Robb and Anna Richardson)

A journey with animals

In 1993 Robert Pyle, a lepidopterist, coined the term 'extinction of experience', writing,

"What is the extinction of the condor to a child who has never known a wren?"

The natural world is full of things that creep, crawl, climb, fly and hide. At some point in Forest School you will find yourself admiring bugs and splashing in water. If you are lucky, you will hear the sounds of birds, watch frog spawn and fish and discover the track, trails and homes of a group that is formally known as the animal kingdom. An urban green space also is full of urban-based mammals like the fox, and our skies are home to many local bird species. A child that can grow up in a world that is more than human builds an awareness of a highly complex system that provides all the food we will ever need. Whilst we are not nurturing scientists per se, the fundamental understanding of our ecology is a child's right and prepares them for a world that needs everybody, in any profession, to value and care for nature.

Shockingly there are young people at school who still think that eggs and meat come from the supermarket and not from a living chicken or a cow. There are children in the UK who have never seen a sheep. As a primary school teacher, Marina found this was very common. We forget that things we take for granted are a privilege for many young people. Our children have lost the right to roam, from 6 miles away from home in 1919 to 330 yards today (*Daily Mail* report, 2007).

Dr William Bird (2007), from his report 'Natural Thinking' says, "Studies have shown that people deprived of contact with nature were at greater risk of depression and anxiety. Children are getting less and less unsupervised time in the natural environment." 'The State of Nature Report' (2016) found that more than one in 10 of the UK's wildlife species are threatened with extinction, and the numbers of the nation's most endangered creatures have plummeted by two-thirds since 1970. Combined with historical deforestation and industrialisation, these trends have left the UK "among the most nature-depleted countries in the world". Average abundance of wildlife has fallen by 13% with the steepest losses in the last 10 years (State of Nature Report, 2019).

Sir David Attenborough, in the foreword to the report, said, "The natural world is in serious trouble and it needs our help as never before. We continue to lose the precious wildlife that enriches our lives and is essential to the health and well-being of those who live in the UK."

THE ANIMAL KINGDOM

We know that humans have had a relationship with animals for centuries, and there is evidence to suggest that wolves and humans co-existed around 400,000 years ago (Beck and Katcher, 1984).

Why are animals important in the context of FS and education?

All living animals offer us a rich awareness that is full of multisensory and emotional experience, presenting recurring patterns of sight, sound, touch, smell and movement. Interactions with the wild world stimulate new conceptual thinking, altering the child as a result of new information or new experiences. Learning is happening everywhere, all the time. We are programmed to make relationships, but the impact and benefits are underestimated and poorly researched. The feedback and communication may be different to the human world, but nevertheless it is a dynamic, mutually satisfying and mostly positive experience! How many people have shared their deepest feelings with an animal? How many toy animals have accompanied humans to bed? Once again, when we are in the outdoors we are within a field of 'intelligences' that provide feedback to us through our senses that affect our state of being and processing of information.

One key characteristic of maturity is linked to knowing that the world does not only revolve around you (refer to stages of development in Chapter 2). Interactions with animals, be it pets or wild creatures, provide a vast context that goes beyond a child's own family and are of great importance to many people. Relationships to pet animals can provide unconditional love and acceptance, and to the wilder varieties, an abundance of fascination and endless emotion! Being in the presence of animals facilitates learning on what animals need, increases awareness of needs that can be linked to our own needs, and increases empathy. Like many other aspects, the absence of wild animals from children's lives as the norm is a modern concern and prevents children from becoming much-needed ambassadors of what is left of non-domesticated land. Although it remains still rare, a dog at Forest School is often one of the most wonderful friendships available to the participants – and one that becomes even more important if they are struggling (see bonus online chapter: 'The evidence and green interventions').

CASE STUDY: TEENAGE BOYS

In Chapter 6 we looked at two teenage boys Jon worked with, whom we will now revisit. We are 2 months into working with this small group of early adolescent boys/young men with certain 'challenges' – not least our constrictive non-natural and non-wild education system. Interestingly, their attention has been captured by encounters with animals at Forest School, watching blue tits fledging, counting eight chicks in a nest box dwindling to none over a period of 3 days, catching newts, observing a grass snake refugia, looking at beetles under a microscope and opening up a beehive. This is the first time one of the youngsters, who is 12, in his education has been seen to 'stay with something' for more than 1 minute!

Why do the boys I am working with stay attentive, calm and caring when in the company of animals when they can show such 'uncaring' and destructive behaviours in a 'school' setting, to the humans around them? Why do 'animals' restore relationship and encourage the 'attention' and relationship building with the groups of youngsters I and many others work with in Forest School?

Figure 13.13 Smooth Newt and it's soothing effect

The **non-judgmental** and **accepting** aspects of animals is another factor that creates connection. When Bill started to get agitated by the presence and 'winding-up' behaviour of others in the group, he would take himself off to either the snake refugia or sit by a log where he frequently found smooth newts. After watching and handling newts, he would calm down and be ready to come back into the group. What is it about animals that helps us calm? Is it down to their complete acceptance of us and the immediate gentle watching and handling, if possible, which cannot but prompt a calming atmosphere? Animals do not judge us for our behaviours and yet can somehow 'sense' a certain presence and connection. They appear to help us self-regulate. This is certainly the case with Bill and newts . . . there had been many moments where we have not had to intervene because of the presence of newts and snakes! He wanted to be with them simply because they 'are', and it is a privilege to enter into their space. The only intervention needed from Jon is a demonstration of how to handle animals gently and when it is and isn't appropriate to handle. Can we legally handle? Are they raising young? Are they young? What parts of the body are sensitive to touch? Will touching cause us any danger etc.? Note – you may need a licence to handle certain animals; in the case of great crested newts you definitely need a licence (see www.gov.uk/guidance/wildlife-licences).

Stillness is a diminishing quality in our high-energy-input world (business-centric model, not quality-of-life model). Animals, especially wild ones, encourage us to be still and attentive. If we are not still and attentive, the animal will melt back into the woods not to be seen or even heard, yet alone talked with or touched! Sitting with Jeff watching the blue tit parents tend their young and feed them would never have happened without our 'stillness'. The ensuing learning and calm fireside conversation would never have happened if we hadn't spent the previous 20 minutes silently sitting.

Spending time donning our white suits and bee masks and gently 'smoking the hive' and sliding the frames cannot but engender **care**. When interacting with animals, we are experimenting but can't help but feel the effects of our presence. We are playing with our power and exploring vulnerability – this is the basis of empathy and finding out how to care for other living things. In most cases, squashing bugs leads to a sense of remorse . . . this is part of growing. Having some part in the complex honey-making process gives a sense of power and purpose but within the animal's domain – the hive in this case. Bill spent a whole morning with our beekeeper. The care with which he lifted the frames and smoked the bees was a complete surprise to one of his key workers, let alone the questions that he had during the session. What happens to the workers when they have finished feeding the queen? Where does the queen go in winter? How many bees does an average hive have? Do the bees help the meadow and all the grasshoppers in the meadow? (The Forest School setting is right next to a meadow that Bill loves spending time in hunting grasshoppers.)

Figure 13.14 Beekeeping suit to fit a learner

A pet is an island of sanity in what appears to be an insane world. Friendship retains its traditional values and securities in one's relationship with one's pet. Whether a dog, cat, bird, fish, turtle, or what have you, one can rely upon the fact that one's pet will always remain a faithful, intimate, non-competitive friend, regardless of the good or ill fortune life brings us.

1

DOMESTICATION AND NON-DOMESTICATION

We are witnessing today the proliferation of a single species, the human animal. Our ability to think and create means that we are able to change our ideas and adapt to new ways of positioning ourselves within nature. The Forest School movement and its philosophy supports the conscious selection of ideas that foster 'a relationship with nature through regular personal experiences in order to develop long-term, environmentally sustainable attitudes and practices in staff, learners and the wider community'.

This approach recognises our long evolution and the benefits of our 'wild' attributes as well as our more 'farmed' attributes. The quality of wildness is often underestimated – the capacity to be innovative and creative, thinking out of the box, sense of freedom, alertness, focus and independence. The opposite is being passive, captive in our safety, dependent on some external agency for direction and control. We often fear the wild, the wild animals and our own wildness. Yet if we can meet that fear with presence of mind, we are capable to explore beyond our self-imposed and culturally imposed limits.

Back in nature to our delight we often find tracks of other mammals, like deer, fox, badger, and if you know how, the tracks of mice and shrew. Nature is full of sounds, for example bird sounds, that can help us to orientate ourselves to our place in space.

An early years' group stood in a circle with their very own sticks. As they listened to the bird song they imagined themselves as conductors of the sound, swaying and moving their sticks to the music of the birds. Each one holding a special nature bird name for that season, building a relationship of connection and knowledge, invisibly entering their neural networks and memories that will last a lifetime.

In the air, we hear and see buzzards and many songbirds like the blue tit, chiff chaff and wren. Many spontaneous, unstructured observations of and interactions with wild animals persist at Forest School, at school and in our neighbourhoods. Squirrels nest in the trees, bees buzz around the flowers, earthworms wriggle in the dirt and rabbits burrow in nearby fields. The emotional impact of exposure to wild creatures is an important dimension to the child's experience, engaging the deepest feelings. Seeing a fox walking carefully is an incredible experience, as is watching a bird kill its prey or a frog hop along. The outdoors provides endless opportunities to move physically, to jump, catch, care for, hover, focus and eat! Do you remember trying to catch a frog, lizard or fly? Providing time for exploration and self-directed learning invariably teaches all the curriculum subjects!

From a Vygotskian perspective, a child's 'zone of proximal development' at Forest School is optimised when a more skilled person guides the child to wild animal encounters. Research now shows that children encouraged to direct their own learning and explore and discover places with wild animals, free from adult structure or supervision, gain more cognitive and emotional growth (Pyle, 1993).

According to Wilson's biophilia hypothesis (1984, 1993), interaction with living beings provides information-rich sources for cognitive learning. Children's attentiveness is heightened, as living organisms are multisensory, dynamic and autonomous – where did that bug go? Kindergarten children from Japan raised goldfish for a year and were able to reason more accurately about the biological properties of the fish than were 19 schoolmates without the goldfish care experience. Moreover, the children who had cared for goldfish also reasoned more accurately about unfamiliar animals, such as frogs, using analogies from their experiences with goldfish (Inagaki, 1990). Knowledge comes from a living relationship. In order to get up close to animals, there are some key skills that young people can have fun developing.

What helps us understand and connect with the value and interdependence of all life?

Empathy between the child and the natural world should be a main objective for children ages 4 to 7. As children begin their forays out into the natural world, we can encourage feelings for the creatures living there. Early childhood is characterised by a lack of differentiation between the self and the other. . . . We want to cultivate that sense of connectedness so that it can become the emotional foundation for the more abstract ecological concept that everything is connected to everything else.

(Sobel, 1996)

Playing and immersion, lying on the ground, under the bracken or in the mud, and going on bug hunts are some embodied ways that connection emerges. The more diverse your Forest School spot, the more likely you are to encounter wildlife. Nevertheless, we have found many tracks and trails in school playgrounds – a bit of snow shows up what is really living near you. Put down some sand and see if you can capture tracks! Most ground-based wild animals are masters of camouflage and stillness and can pick up vibrations from our walking from a fair distance.

Story can also help develop connection with animals. Children's instinctive feelings of continuity with nature are demonstrated by the attraction to fairy tales and myths set in nature and populated by animal characters. In the early years children often have a deeper connection with animals than other beings; they are seen as alive and have emotions and so get anthropomorphised more than plants do. Plants are often not seen as living beings to start with, as they don't move and don't have 'faces' (Driver et al., 1985). It is interesting that we now know we share more brain patterns with higher order animals than previously known – indeed the mammalian brain or human mid-brain does indeed think about feelings (Panksepp and Biven, 2012). We all know when a dog is in distress. Only yesterday the neighbour's dog refused to go out on the road, demonstrating fear . . . he showed all the common 'human' body language: curled body, stayed frigid still, turned towards the house, droopy eyes etc.

Animal-based exercises:

- Camouflage games – versions of hide and seek.
- Create a trail using some crumbs, for example bird seed, and follow them to a particular place: perhaps your favourite bear is waiting for you.
- Use plaster of paris to make moulds you find of tracks on the ground.
- Cut out tracks on cardboard and use them as a stencil to make tracks.
- Nest and robber games.
- Nest activities, making own clay eggs and painting them.

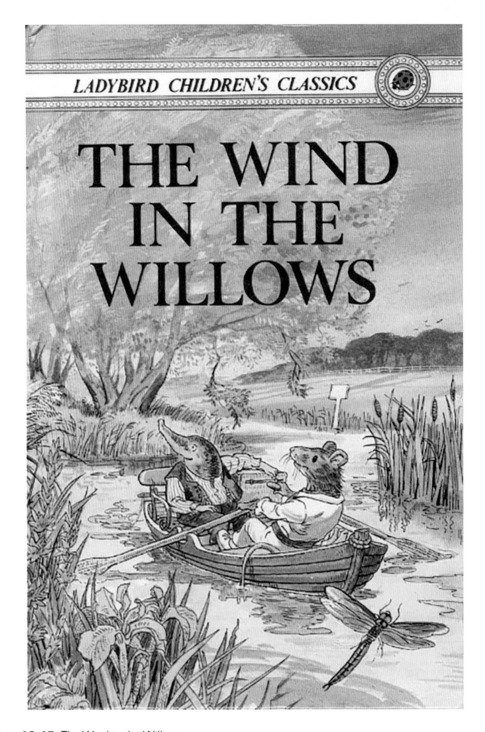

Figure 13.15 *The Wind in the Willows*

- Bird voices and games – sparrow hawk is coming!
- What are the common species in your area?
- Think of your everyday movements and list common birds, plants and trees where you live. You begin to develop the language of nature, little by little. Are any of them dangerous? The best way to find out what species are interesting to young people is to watch them play, and they all gravitate to different things!
- Ask your group to lie on the ground and close their eyes.
- Walk around and see if your group can point to where you are by feeling the vibration through their bodies of your footsteps – it really points out how noisy we are and what it will take to encounter something that is wild!
- Deer ears, owl eyes, fox walking (see *Learning with Nature* book in useful resources section).
- Bugs and hunts.
- Keeping bees at Forest School can be a powerful exercise in interrelationships and ways of sensitively being with animals. It is worth getting in touch with the local beekeeping association to get expert advice on this.
- Making bird boxes and observing bird behaviour without disturbing the birds, especially during nesting time. Putting cameras in nest boxes can be a powerful observational tool.

Wild mammals are almost impossible to see due to their highly prized invisibility. This is where learning to track comes in.

TRACKING BASICS

There are many useful resources for tracking – see the Field Studies Council (www.field-studies-council.org/) and other organizations for a list of resources.

Tracking can involve looking at the footprints, and all the 'prints' and 'signs' the animals leave.

Questions and tracking: Who – identification; What – interpretation of behaviour and habits; When – aging the tracks; Where – trailing them to their home and habitat; Why – ecological tracking and prediction; How – empathy, imagination/story telling.

Signs: Trails, runs, pushdowns, beds, lays, rubs and nicks, scratching and gnawing, droppings, feathers, bones, pellets, hairs.

Larders: Food store – what food draws what predators, or herbivores, or insects, or fish – and food chains. They tend to be seasonal, for example fresh greens, berries, nut trees, compost, leaf and woodpiles, bird feeders, hatches of insects, frogs, reptiles, amphibians, bird eggs and nestlings, fungi, newborn mammals.

Lacks: absence of lards – not just lack of food, but also cold winds, shady places or warm places, drier places if it's been raining a lot, certain nutrients.

Heritage species – aquatic species: salmon, whales, bears, wolves and large cats.

Figure 13.16 Track signs to help follow animals and read their pattern of behaviour

Figure 13.17 Small creatures like snails attract instant attention and curiosity from small humans as shown in this long interaction between adult, child and snail

TRACKABLE CREATURES

- Woodpeckers – cavities in trees, patterns in bark, stores of acorns.
- Earthworms – piles of their castings, 'poo', mark their territory – what do they eat?
- Slugs and snails – slime trail, how far can you follow it?

Telling a little story about your animal encounter is an ideal way to create interest in local wildlife.

We all go silent as someone points to a deer in the trees. Her ears prick up and we can see her looking directly at us! She is on alert. We stay impossibly still until . . . a crack beneath our feet and she is off, bouncing with speed into the undergrowth. How long was she there watching us? I need to be really quiet to see her again, says G! Where does she sleep? Let's go follow her? Off we go. . . .

Children still see the living world as alive. Their sense and sensitivity of what is 'real' is extended to most things outside themselves. They experience an encounter with a wild animal as a social encounter.

A child's encounter with a wild animal presents an opportunity for the child to recognise and respect the capabilities of the animal. What happens when we encounter a child pulling the legs off an insect, persisting with disturbing an animal, stamping on a minibeast? Here is an example of an account of such an encounter Jon had with another Forest School leader during the training process running her programme for an early years' group.

Child: "Ooh look this one is squishy." The woodlice is crushed by the child.
FS leader: "Ahhh, that woodlice looks like he has had a hard time, is he moving?"
Child: "No, he's squished. I squished him and he's dead."
FS leader: "Mmm, that's a shame. I wonder if the woodlice had any children?"
Child: "Don't think so."
FS leader: "Mmmmm, maybe we should see if they do have children."
Child: "I'm going to play with Amy."

The child ran off. Jon wondered if there had been a different way of working with this situation or if the FS leader had done as much as could have been done.

This is a tricky ethical dilemma. Clearly, the child was experimenting and wondering what would happen if she squished a woodlice. The FS leader had started probing a little to see what the response might be if she could see the consequences of killing the woodlice. Woodlice don't really care for their children; they lay the eggs and that's the job done. How far should we anthropomorphise in order to encourage a respect of all creatures and plants, and see them as of equal value, if that is our 'value base'?

Animals cannot fail to stimulate our curiosity, especially the wild ones – where does the grass snake go on warm days? what is it eating? how does it move so quick without legs? What does the newt do the rest of the year? are just some of the questions Bill has asked. While the injury and sometimes killing of an animal (mostly the accidental killing of very small creatures like spiders and small insects) is sometimes anathema to the very education those in FS are engaged with, we cannot deny the instinctual urge and fascination in us all to see how an animal responds to our presence, prodding and probing.

All these aspects of being with animals – story, acceptance, stillness, hunting and care – make essential elements to include in any nature-based learning programmes, including Forest School. For us the magic is in the emotional connection and resulting behavioural changes that wild and domestic animal contact gives. This is especially important if we are to reconnect with land. There is a somewhat worsening state as we lose more 'intact' landscapes with 'memory' of ecological relationships, which include deep human connections with animals as well as plants and all the elements that are part of the balance. Forest School is one of the beacons of connection that can help reinstate that landscape intactness. It is not just the larger remote wild landscapes where FS can take place. The 'cultural' ecological landscapes that we find in urban areas, be they small pockets of urban woodland

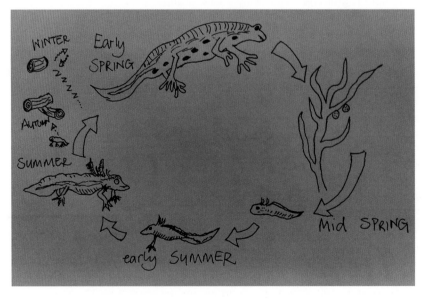

Figure 13.18 Animal cycle and seasons – the newt cycle

or 'emerging woodland' on the edge of an allotment that is home to fox, wren, blue tit, nuthatch, wood mouse and even great crested newt can provide an antidote to the 'extinction of experience'.

We need to open up the conversation about how we relate to, and value, the non-human, even at the tender age of 4. Having regular contact with plants and animals is key to building a relationship with the non-human, and if we, as leaders, show an empathic and caring approach to plants and animals, our hope is that a respect for and valuing of them will follow. In the next chapter we will explore, in more detail, some of the research into the value of contact and connection with the non-human.

QUESTIONS FOR PRACTICE

How much time do you spend observing through your senses the plants and animals that exist in the places you conduct your nature education? Do you drop all the linear thinking – thinking in names and numbers – and really try to get to the essence and heart of the non-human?

When you are drawn to a plant or animal, do you first get to know it and then go to a 'knowledge' source to increase your understanding of the 'being' you were drawn to?

How much do you know about the ecology of your place and how will you increase this understanding?

How do you respond to a learner demonstrating a perceived negative ecological impact on a site or 'being'?

USEFUL RESOURCES

The online appendix for Chapter 13 (www.routledge.com/9780367425616) has information on plant law, poisonous plants, benefits of interacting with plants, and sample risk assessments.

The Secret Teachings of Plants: The Intelligence of the Heart in Direct Experience of Nature by Stephen Buhner (Bear and Company, 2004) provides a good read and a challenging yet really informative view on plants and their importance to our hearts and minds.

http://childreninpermaculture.com/resources/ Lots of resources for working with plants in particular.

Learning with Nature by M Robb, A Richardson and V Mew (Green Books, 2015). Packed with games and activities with plants and animals.

The Children's Forest by D Casey, A Richardson and H d'Ascoli (Hawthorn Press, 2019). An excellent book packed with craft, story and seasonal practices with plants and animals.

www.eatweeds.co.uk/ This is one of the most comprehensive foraging websites around, and Robin Harford writes easily and poetically about the plant kingdom.

Track and Sign: A Guide to the Field Signs of Mammals and Birds of the UK by John Rhyder (The History Press, 2021). An excellent field guide helping us to look for patterns in the land and getting into the 'habits' and 'patterning' of animals.

BIBLIOGRAPHY

Beck, A M and Katcher, A H (1984, February 15) A New Look at Pet-Facilitated Therapy. *Journal of the American Veterinary Medical Association* 184(4): 414–421.

Bird, W Natural Thinking (2007) *Investigating the Links Between the Natural Environment, Biodiversity and Mental Health*. See http://ww2.rspb.org.uk/Images/naturalthinking_tcm9-161856.pdf.

Capra, F and Luisi, P (2014) *The Systems View of Life – A Unifying Vision*. Cambridge University Press.

Chawla, L (2012) *The Importance of Access to Nature for Young Children*. Early Childhood Matters (June). See http://earlychildhoodmagazine.org/wp-content/uploads/2012/07/ECM118_11_The-importance-of-access-to-nature_Louise-Chawla.pdf.

Cilek, V (2015) *To Breathe with Birds: A Book of Landscapes*. Philadelphia, PA: University of Pennsylvania Press.

Driver, R Guesne, E and Tiberghien, A (1985) Some Features of Children's Ideas and Their Implications for Teaching. In Driver, R Guesne, E and Tiberghien, A (eds.), *Children's Ideas in Science* (pp. 193–201). Philadelphia, PA: Open University Press.

Inagaki, K (1990) The Effects of Raising Animals on Children's Biological Knowledge. *British Journal of Developmental Psychology* 8: 119–129.

Levinson, B (1978) *Pets and Personality Development*. Sage Journals.

Livingston, J A (1995) *Rogue Primate: An Exploration of Human Domestication*. Roberts Rinehart Publishing.

Louv, R (2006) *Last Child in the Woods: Saving Our Children from Nature-Deficit Disorder*. Chapel Hill, NC: Algonquin Books of Chapel Hill.

Louv, R (2011) *The Nature Principle: Human Restoration and the End of Nature-Deficit Disorder*. Algonquin Books of Chapel Hill.

Maturana, H and Varela, F (1990) *Autopoiesis: The Organization of the Living*. Dordecht: D Reidel.

Maturana, H and Varela, F (1998) *Tree of Knowledge – The Biological Roots of Understanding*. Boston: Shambhala.

Melson, G F (2013) Children and Wild Animals. In Kahn, Jr. P H, Hasbach, P and Ruckert, J (eds.), *The Rediscovery of the Wild* (pp. 93–118). Cambridge, MA: MIT Press.

Panksepp, J and Biven, L (2012) *The Archaeology of the Mind: Neuroevolutionary Origins of Human Emotions*. New York: W.W Norton & Co.

Pyle, R M (1993) *The Thunder Tree: Lessons from an Urban Wildland*. Boston: Houghton Mifflin.

Sobel, D (1996) *Beyond Ecophobia: Reclaiming the Heart in Nature Education*. Orion.

State of Nature Partnerships (2019) *State of Nature 2019 Report*. See https://nbn.org.uk/wp-content/uploads/2019/09/State-of-Nature-2019-UK-full-report.pdf.

Thunberg, G (2019) Speech to the UN Climate Summit in September 2019, see https://www.theguardian.com/environment/2019/sep/23/greta-thunberg-speech-un-2019-address

Van Matre, S (1990) *Earth Education – A New Beginning*. Institute for Earth Education.

Wohlleben, P (2017) *The Hidden Life of Trees: What They Feel, How They Communicate – Discoveries from a Secret World*. London: William Collins Books.

Wilson, E O (1984) *Biophilia*. Cambridge, MA: Harvard University Press.

Wilson, E O (1993) Biophilia and the Conservation Ethic. In Kellert, S and Wilson, E O (eds.), *The Biophilia Hypothesis*. Washington, DC: Island Press.

14 Nature Pedagogy's place in the world – teaching within a nature-centric worldview

OUR GOALS REVISITED

Educators are the most important mentors and leaders we have. We believe education holds a major key to bringing about the personal and societal changes needed today and that access to nature during the school years, indeed throughout life, is an essential ingredient. This book has set out to frame key areas of learning which enable educators and facilitators to work with an approach that fosters healthy and purposeful adults. This is a journey from dependence to independence and autonomy, where we remain inextricably part of a community, that is, interdependence. We need a new paradigm where nature is part and parcel of our education and health systems, providing a 'human wholeness' and ecological responsibility.

> The more clearly we can focus our attention on the wonders and realities of the universe about us, the less taste we shall have for destruction.
>
> (Carson, 1962)

Our intention is not to be prescriptive and leave you with the idea that one model fits all – a 'how to'. Human development is not outcome-based, where we produce a particular kind of product. Rather, this long human life experience, with all its tensions, is the process of developing relationships and providing sustenance for us to thrive, value 'the other' and feel valued. A core goal is to realise that we are part and parcel of the natural world and to help repair relationships so that we are able to live more harmoniously with each other and the natural world, to walk and act alongside each other and nature.

Like the natural world, education is about change – evolution and constant adaptation. This book has been about shifting the way we relate to the world, our worldview, how we tune into the natural world and its rhythms, while respecting and understanding our own development and stage of life. It is also about recognising the benefits of partnering with nature, promoting health behind

Figure 14.1 How we are connected into the ecological world.

Source: From 'A Day in the Life of a Tree' by M R O'Connor, August 27, 2019, *The New Yorker* – illustration by Christelle Enault

all systems and participating in a regenerative culture. People have commented, "Isn't what you are proposing something old, *not relevant* to this world?" On the contrary, we see the huge learning potential and deep satisfaction that can be found when we experience life as connected and as one system of integrated relationships. It doesn't have to be so complicated. What we are saying is that crafts and skills, time to play and be in 'flow' in nature is immensely valuable. This is exactly what this book has been postulating – we have not been saying that technology and modern society is all bad, but that we need to reclaim some of the human/nature centred practices. This means being free to experience the deep wisdom, awe and wonder that the other-than-human world inspires . . . it is this that feeds our soul and brings about true maturation and a common ground to bring the human race together.

OUR HUMAN NATURE: WHAT HAPPENED TO US?

We need to begin with ourselves – the educators. To acknowledge what has happened to us and how this influences our behaviour and choices. This is empowering and directly increases our capacity to understand our own and our learners' vulnerability. There is a reason that 'Know thyself' was inscribed at the Temple of Apollo at Delphi in Greece.

We are asking you for a moment to contemplate an initial question: "What has happened to you?" This question provides us with a tool for agency (a sense of self-control and power) in the world. It moves us away from the idea of what is 'wrong' with us, freeing us to be less judgmental and self-depreciating, and more accepting and self-loving. Thus, it locates problems within the whole system rather than the individual and promotes self-respect and dignity. It means being empathic and compassionate with ourselves so we can build empathy with the learning community we operate within as well as the wider society and natural world. Even though many of us may not have had a good educational experience or upbringing, we can learn to do things differently.

Sociology professor Arlie Russell Hochschild, in her 1983 book *The Managed Heart*, first named "emotional labour": managing one's own feelings and relationships, in order to assist others in managing theirs. It is work that is often invisible and almost always undercompensated in the education and health worlds – and it's also really hard, but it brings about a rewarding life. It has to be done to uphold and rebuild a society working on courageous relationships which operate within our ecological limits. All of us can do it, often with support.

Any human being living a fully satisfying life is immersed in such social connections. And this is not only a philosophical truth about human beings, but one that is deeply rooted in our very biology.

(Gopnik, 2017)

When we greet our 'nature learners' off the minibus, we are faced with 10 learners bringing a range of emotions and 'happenings' associated with these emotions. In order to guide these learners, we need to adopt both a calm tone and energetic resonance (see Chapter 7 on the brain and Amy Banks) in order to give learners their capacity to take control of their own learning. If we are to do this, we need to have undergone our own emotional journey and ask what we have undergone . . . it is 'emotional labour'! Let's make this concrete.

One morning Jon had a run-in with his line manager about not meeting a target regarding a booking process and 'charging deadlines', a familiar theme in education! He had to meet his group of 'special needs' learners that morning and was feeling tight in the chest and slightly off balance and knotty in the stomach after the altercation with his line manager. Luckily, he had prepared earlier and was ready in the car park about 5 minutes before the group arrived. He managed to clock how he was feeling, took some deep breaths (great calming strategy) and said to himself, "I am going to put this to one side, tackle it later in the afternoon and concentrate on the group – in particular Dan's journey to the site" (there had been real challenges in getting Dan down to the site). He had talked through, with himself, what had happened to him, and then set it aside for the learners in front of him, who come in with their own stories.

This is one of the most difficult paradoxes in education: our profession elicits strong emotional reactions from its practitioners and learners, often more 'present' in the natural world, as we start to feel more accepted and unjudged. For the sake of the learners' well-being – not to mention the decidedly unappealing prospect of an out-of-control group – Jon had to develop an illusion of unflappable calmness and prosocial and ecological control. On that day, Jon talked to Dan's support worker and they came up with a new strategy to get him down to the site – they felt Dan's need was to get there before everyone else. Dan set off secretly with his support and – hey presto! – he got there.

Only by going through his own emotional 'labour' could Jon concentrate on the emotions and needs of the group.

Once we tune into ourselves and what has happened, we can self-soothe and self-empathise, which increases our own agency, as in the above case with Jon. If we are to have agency, then we need to know and love ourselves, not in a narcissistic way, but to find acceptance and belonging in our own skin. True belonging is not something we achieve or accomplish with others, but others can help; ultimately, it's something we carry in our own hearts. Once we belong thoroughly in ourselves, true belonging is ours. Belonging to ourselves means being called to stand alone – to brave the wilderness of uncertainty, vulnerability and criticism (Brown, 2017). In this place we rediscover our natural birthright of this deep connection and attachment to all the natural beings. With the world feeling like a political and ideological combat zone, this is remarkably tough. We seem to have forgotten that even when we are utterly alone, we are connected to one another by something greater than group membership, politics and ideology – that we are connected by love and the human spirit. No matter how separated we think and believe ourselves to be, we are part of the same spiritual story.

Love doesn't have goals or benchmarks or blueprints, but it does have a purpose. The purpose is not to change the people we love, but to give them what they need to thrive. Love's purpose is not to shape our beloved's destiny, but to help them shape their own. It isn't to show them the way, but to help them find a path for themselves, even if the path they take isn't one we would choose ourselves, or even one we would choose for them.

(ibid)

It is this empathic practice that really brings about change, which we will now explore further regarding system change.

HOMO EMPATHICUS: AN EMPATHIC CIVILISATION

Nature Pedagogy is necessarily about emotional intelligence and a shift in the way we think about ourselves, our relationships with each other and with life as a whole. Nature, with its stress-reducing and restorative qualities, has a significant part to play in providing the spaces where we can learn and heal. What the natural world does so well is encourage a sense of 'present centredness' that enables us to 'dig in' to our feelings and what has happened to us. Long-term nature programmes, held by competent practitioners, enable and strengthen our system 1 (instant, instinctual and present biased) while our system 2 is given time to reflect and think through problems, providing this calmness that Brown (2018) defines as "creating perspective and mindfulness while managing emotional reactivity".

Jeremy Rifkin (2009) has framed what has happened to the world's society over the ages. He propounded that we evolved from early hunters when our ties were with our 'blood family', then to a bigger 'religious family' (and some would say we are still stuck in this family), to the 'nation-state family' (which, by the way, is a 'fiction' in biological terms). He goes on to state that through developing technology we *could* evolve empathy for the entire human race within the biosphere. Take the many global tragedies, for example earthquakes, where there are hundreds of thousands of Twitter hits with empathic messages – we can all 'express feelings across the planet'. Ironically, this very technology could see the family becoming a 'corporate family' if we are not careful, our ties becoming stronger towards the likes of Google and Facebook.

Rifkin states that we could become '*Homo empathicus*' with the aid of the massive 'neural interweb network' whereby we can broaden our sense of identity to include humans and non-humans as fellow sojourners, without losing blood, religious and cultural ties but to feel a 'part of the whole world'. To do this we need to bring out our core nature and feelings that accompany this empathic way of being and doing. What Rifkin has done for many of us, in a nutshell, is describe what has happened to us humans in time and space regarding traditional 'powerplay', and he has helped create a narrative of what has happened to us in our lives. This resonates with the Power Threat Meaning Framework (PTMF, 2018) produced by the British Psychological Society, which shifts the emphasis from what is wrong with the individual to the question – what has happened to you?

Figure 14.2 Evolution of the human

The language of feelings and nature

Very recently, a friend of Jon's relayed the following story, which illustrates how important it is to get in touch with our own feelings around topics that may come up when we are facilitating sessions, before we dive into the actual topic. This can really help us understand the implications of our words and impact on the learning community – our agency as nature educators.

Lou's daughter, who is aged 7, had come home from school in a traumatised state, which manifested itself as inconsolable crying and grief. In class that day they had been looking at the increasing number of fires (that have been) blazing in the Amazon in 2019. The teacher (admittedly a young, inexperienced teacher in her first job) had explained that smoke from the fires, visible by satellite imagery, darkened the city of São Paulo, even after the dry season, at the end of August. São Paulo is thousands of miles from the Amazon. At this time, it was reported there was a 77% increase in fires across all of the Amazon rainforest in Brazil, Bolivia, Paraguay and Peru, endangering biodiversity and indigenous people (906,000 hectares had been lost just this year). It released large amounts of carbon dioxide and monoxide within the biome; in addition, it had a large impact on global climate. Lou's daughter came home with the message that the *planet's lungs were burning* – she was beside herself. Lou had to spend the whole evening trying to calm her daughter and tap into her own feelings of fear and despair. The following morning the conversation continued, and Lou went into school to talk to the teacher and explain the impact this had had on her daughter – her daughter was over-empathising with the Amazon but also feared for herself and the rest of the planet's life. That weekend Lou spent time talking with her daughter about the Amazon experience at school, and her daughter decided to research the ecology of trees and their role in the world. Within two weeks the daughter had collected acorns and other tree seeds, and then contacted the Woodland Trust to order trees to plant and presented to the class a project for tree planting in 2020. She also studied the effects on the relationships to the forest that indigenous people have – making a presentation at school on the values and practices of the Amazonian indigenous peoples.

The language of feelings and nature are something that all teachers and educators need to be equipped with when exploring 'nature education'. Out of the despair had come empowerment, and Lou's daughter felt like she had some agency in the world in the face of such a massive 'nature catastrophe'. This hope and action we are sure is in large part down to an empathic, ecologically literate parent who also feels deeply and cares for people and planet. Lou would probably deny this and say it was largely down to a passionate, caring 'alive' daughter, however the learner has a sensitive, 'holding', significant other, whose support helped her take positive action.

WHAT DOES THE CASE STUDY TELL US?

The learning from this case study is enormous. As educators we need to be nurtured and trained in ecological and emotional literacy and learn to demonstrate empathy with the nature topics/subjects we teach. Some would say we need to be objective if we are to encourage critical independent thinking. However, these topics and Nature Pedagogy are not emotionally neutral. We cannot objectify an emotional subject – our lives do depend on healthy ecological systems. If we are to support thoughtful, emotionally literate talk and exploration of subjects such as the state of rainforests and the UK's own forests and woods (the UK has one of the lowest percentages of woodland landcover in Europe!), we need to be honest about our own values as nature pedagogues. Often in situations like the one mentioned earlier we need to say less and 'hold' more, we need to 'be with' the feeling.

We have talked a lot about the importance of our feeling self. We have placed more emphasis on feelings because most Western thinking arises from an educational system that favours the rational thinking above the body. It teaches that real work happens indoors and diminishes the value of play, creativity and imagination. Feelings have been so repressed and restricted within our culture. Yet just as we need our somatic (body-based) intelligence, so we need our focused thought that serves our heart, as our heart serves our mind, as explained in Chapter 7. Developing our thinking and expanding our window of tolerance is part of development where we learn to appropriately utilise our feelings alongside our rational selves. There are of course many occasions where we benefit from humans being more rational. The evidence and green interventions bonus online chapter onlines some of the key recent research into the benefits of green/nature interventions and nature educations, using rationale research paradigms, and we as educators can tap into this 'evidence' to advocate for our practices. We also have the law. Laws exist to maintain certain norms and standards and to protect our fundamental rights. It is to this aspect that we now turn our attention, with a view to reminding ourselves that as educators we have laws that back our own agency.

International law: a tool for positive change

The 1948 Universal Declaration of Human Rights became law. Member States are bound by these international laws. As educators and educational establishments, we are bound by the UN Convention on the Rights of the Child (under 18s) Articles 28 and 29, that deal with education (1990).

These articles give us clear guidance for our practice with children and young people. This includes not humiliating or shaming children when their behaviour is not what we would like. In classrooms, there are many casualties. "85% of the men and women interviewed (13,000 pieces of data) can recall a time in school that was so shaming that it forever changed how they saw

Figure 14.3 Children's rights!

themselves as learners" (O'Toole, 2019). These 'rights' can equip us (if we feel we need) to challenge practices within the institutions where we work. It is easy to forget these fundamental principles when we get so wrapped up in the minutiae of guidance coming from government, senior leadership, colleagues and ourselves.

Article 29 states:

1   Parties agree that the education of the child shall be directed to:

(a) The development of the child's personality, talents and mental and physical abilities to their fullest potential

(b) The development of respect for human rights and fundamental freedoms, and for the principles enshrined in the Charter of the United Nations (right to learn, for safety and respect)

(c) The development of respect for the child's parents, his or her own cultural identity, language and values, for the national values of the country in which the child is living, the country from which he or she may originate, and for civilizations different from his or her own

(d) The preparation of the child for responsible life in a free society, in the spirit of understanding, peace, tolerance, equality of sexes, and friendship among all peoples, ethnic, national and religious groups and persons of indigenous origin

(e) The development of respect for the natural environment.

Article 28 states:

2   Parties shall take all appropriate measures to ensure that school discipline is administered in a manner consistent with the child's human dignity and in conformity with the present Convention.
3   Parties shall promote and encourage international cooperation in matters relating to education, in particular with a view to contributing to the elimination of ignorance and illiteracy throughout the world and facilitating access to scientific and technical knowledge and modern teaching methods. In this regard, particular account shall be taken of the needs of developing countries.

LEARNING FROM HISTORY: EARTH RIGHTS, THE FUTURE AND THE LAW

Nature Pedagogy recognises a person as *part of* the ecosystem and no more inherently important than any other lifeform or element. We are not separate from or superior to the other-than-human world. We have gotten to this point in time where we have to make a radical shift and take on board people's rights, earth rights and multiple ways of knowing. The Nature Pedagogy we are advocating requires an empathic view of humans and non-humans. Today, we are still grappling with what kind of society we want to be, with what values and morals. We look forward to a change in the law and our way of thinking towards the land. As nature pedagogues, Polly Higgins' work (see https://ecocidelaw.com/) is something we all need to be familiar with. Polly, who sadly died of cancer in April 2019, led the way in a movement that is trying to establish an international law that would protect the earth – giving us earth rights, in the form of 'an international crime of ecocide'. Ecocide is "serious loss, damage or destruction of ecosystems", and includes climate or cultural damage as well as direct ecological damage. Under earth rights, we all benefit when we look after and respect each other, our beloved men, women, children of all beings and the earth.

Earth rights embrace the importance of the rights of indigenous communities, and while this subject is beyond the scope of our book, we feel this needs to be embraced. After all, we have based much of our thinking on Nature Pedagogy in this book on indigenous spirit and knowledge. After over 30 plus years of working in nature, it is impossible for us as authors to not hold a deep and humbling respect for peoples (around the world) who have deep land-based knowledge – the real experts with an intimate familial relationship with the earth, those who can identify a tree's type by the sound of wind on the leaves or track animals through the way they move. If we can show kinship with the belief systems of our ancestors and indigenous communities – through song, story and skills in nature, there is a mutual understanding and solidarity that can emerge, which can be both commensurate and compensatory in a technological society.

Where does this leave us regarding Nature Pedagogy's place in the world and how this education becomes more embedded in our current systems and not just be something seen as fringe?

REGENERATIVE MODELS IN THE WORLD

We return again to the understanding that we are holistic beings and that we are moving beyond the idea of sustainability and into the regenerative systems. In Chapter 2, we gave a history of nature education with examples of inspiration from various countries. Today we can take inspiration from the fact that the term Forest School seems to be mainstreaming in the UK, and nature education is witnessing a growth around the world (see the now global Children and Nature Network). Green prescriptions and interventions (see bonus online chapter) are increasingly being recognised in the UK, individual school academies are seeing this as an important integral part of a child's education, and various organisations are seeking a more holistic 'radical' approach. There are some projects happening at the local level that are trying to integrate the pedagogy we have outlined. The case studies we have described give a glimpse into this. Given the state of our ecological crisis, this needs to be scaled up and needs to be more holistic at a societal level – a shift from an 'ego'-based system which relies on individual identity and competition to one that is more cooperative and reciprocal. What we are proposing is almost a clarion call for all the agencies to come together and share their commonalities. As the late Jo Cox, Labour MP who was murdered in 2018, said, "we are far more united and have far more in common with each other than things that divide us" (Cox, 2016).

Table 14.1 South Korea's Forest Welfare Policy – The Green Welfare 7; "from cradle to grave, life with forests"

G1	Birth – prenatal education in the forest
G2	Early Childhood – children's forest playground – Forest Kindergarten
G3	Childhood to Adolescence – education in the forest – provision of Forest Education Centers
G4	Early Adulthood – forest trail and mountain leisure sports
G5	Midlife to Mature Adulthood – recreational forest
G6	Late Adulthood – forest healing – national forest healing centres
G7	After Death – eco-funeral 'tree burial forest'

Figure 14.4 Forest Kindergarten in Seoul, South Korea – sharing a mandala that represents feelings about the season, a universal symbol of connection

Individuals and institutions need to really start recognising this, otherwise we will end up with even more broken systems that won't regenerate. We need to see the commonalities at all levels of society.

> *The strength of the social hierarchy and the importance of status serve as indicators of how far a society departs from equality. The further the departure from mutuality, reciprocity and sharing, the stronger the basic message that we will each have to fend for ourselves.*
>
> (K. Pickett & R. Wilkinson)

We would do well to look towards South Korea (see Table 14.1), a country that is, ironically, one of the most technologically advanced nations and had its fair share of dramatic ecological impacts but is trying to embed a more holistic way of harmonising with the natural world at a policy level. The country has developed the policy of forest welfare therapy, which could inform wider practice around the world across the whole of society. This inspiring model creates invitations for all the stages of life, linking people to nature. The forest welfare system provides vouchers to enable access to the nature experiences.

(See Forest Welfare for Life Cycle Service: Forest Therapy Conference Finland 2019: Professor Dr Bum-Jin Park, Department of Forest Environment and Resources at Chungnam National University in Korea.)

Governments can take policy measures to revitalise our forests and land and we can collectively, regardless of political positioning, get behind change and reap the benefits of healthy green spaces.

Meanwhile, our institutions and NGOs would do well to heed this call for a holistic way of working where egos are put to one side. We have networks and bodies trying to work to a similar end, and the more we find commonalities the more effective the agency will be and institutions don't just stay in the 'blessed unrest' state (Hawken, 2008). This can, we believe, change the world and our systems. As practitioners, let's welcome more talking and working together with other organisations that we are not part of but have similar goals, from the numerous environmental organisations, Black and minority ethnic organisations through to health organisations such as local mental health teams. When we see ourselves ultimately as citizens of the earth, we are more likely to reach out in our own small ways.

It is these ways that build strong relational communities that include the human and more-than-human. The educator and, indeed, all the learners should strive to be empathic and curious while maintaining playful accepting relationships, in the face of the challenges of disconnection and fear. After all, this Nature Pedagogy that we have tried to outline in the book is about walking alongside each other in a serious yet playful way which can provide hope in our changing world.

NATURE AS KITH AND KIN – OUR FINAL WORD

Respect is at the heart of kith. Kith means the territory, the attachment to place, that emerges alongside an affinity for one's family, or people/kin. Very few people we meet in the woods question the benefits of nature anymore. In fact, there is a deep thirst for being outdoors and how it feels to be among the trees, the wind and the rain and to breathe deeply. The most important and life-saving relationship for us as authors, outside of our families, has been nature. It has been our haven. We have talked out loud to many trees, we have cried and not felt alone, we have had the most wild and 'big thoughts' about life and death, clarity and resolutions and the bitter sweetness of time passing and always been immensely grateful for some more time and that we got to enjoy the trees, the blossoms, the mountains and the sea in this lifetime. We have found a deep-seated and comforting relationship with the natural world that is not based on knowledge/facts but rather a fondness of animals, birds, plants and insects and a gladness for their company. Our current social and economic systems have forgotten something essential and vital for a good life, and that is a priority to return to caring for and loving the land we need.

Like John Muir, we have spent days on our own in the wild, feeling the wildness of our own spirit and a communion with an unknowable force/s, an unexplainable and helpful source of comfort and friendship. We feel deeply moved by the intense beauty that our senses perceive and cannot imagine a future where our grandchildren won't have the choice to have this relationship. Even our own children 'feel' this, and despite their oft-voiced admonishments of our generation for allowing the current disconnected state of our schooling and ecological systems, they still feel that sense of community in wild places.

Long ago, the ancients say this land was free and we shared it all with the mountains and the sea, the birds and the trees, we lived in peace, long ago before the others came and built fences by cutting the trees, dug mines, by cutting the earth, removed her blood, the oil that lies within, formed long ago like us, who lived in peace. The birds sang less, without the trees, the land became dry without the birds to plant the flowers, and we too became quiet watching our mountain die, listening for the birds, that no longer flew – but we still lived in peace. What sustained us through all those years? The nights of silence and the songs of the frogs for we know as the ancients said this land will again be free and we will again share it all with the mountains and the sea, the birds and the trees for we still live in peace, and we wish you the same, for we are all one.

– Harriet Kofalk, inspired by the Bribri, indigenous Costa Ricans
(*Earth Prayers*, from around the world edited by
Elizabeth Roberts and Elias Amidon)

QUESTIONS FOR PRACTICE

How can we balance our love of our own children within a broader politics of child-rearing?
What would this mean for public policy?
How do we repair and heal from the past?
How do we co-participate, listen to all the voices and move towards 'true belonging'?
How do we challenge ourselves to rethink our assumptions and build reciprocal relationships, addressing power inequalities?

USEFUL RESOURCES

Indigenous Ally Tool Kit: http://reseaumtlnetwork.com/wp-content/uploads/2019/04/Ally_March.pdf
Self Compassion, Dr Kristin Neff, https://self-compassion.org/the-three-elements-of-self-compassion-2/
Robin Wall Kimmerer and her books, especially *Braiding Sweetgrass: Indigenous Wisdom, Scientific Knowledge and the Teachings of Plants*; see www.humansandnature.org/robin-wall-kimmerer

BIBLIOGRAPHY

Akwesasne Notes (1978, 1981, 2005) *Basic Call to Consciousness*. Rooseveltown, NY: Mohawk.

Bragg, R and Atkins, G (2016) A Review of Nature-Based Interventions for Mental Health Care. Natural England Commissioned Reports, Number 204.

British Psychological Society (2018) The Power Threat Meaning Framework Overview. See www.bps.org.uk/sites/www.bps.org.uk/files/Policy/Policy%20-%20Files/PTM%20Overview.pdf.

Brown, B (2017) *Braving the Wilderness: The Quest for True Belonging and the Courage to Stand Alone*. London: Vermillion.

Brown, B (2018) *Dare to Lead. Brave Work. Tough Conversations. Whole Hearts*. London: Vermillion.

Burton, R (2008) *On Being Certain: Believing You Are Right Even When You're Not*. New York: Martin's Press.

Burton, R (2013) Where Science and Story Meet: We Make Sense of the World Through Stories; A Deep Need Rooted in Our Brains (April 22). See http://nautil.us/issue/0/the-story-of-nautilus/where-science-and-story-meet

Carson, R (1962) *Silent Spring*. Middlesex: Penguin.

Children's Commissioner (2018) *Playing Out: A Children's Commissioner Report on the Importance to Children of Play and Physical Activity*. See www.childrenscommissioner.gov.uk/wp-content/uploads/2018/08/Play-final- report.pdf (accessed 11/5/19).

Cox, J (2016) Jo Cox's Maiden Speech To Parliament: 'We Are Far More United Than the Things That Divide Us'. See https://www.bbc.co.uk/news/av/uk-36560418.

Department of Education (2017) *Statutory Framework for the Early Years Foundation Stage: Setting the Standards for Learning, Development and Care for Children Age Birth to Five*. See www.foundation-years.org.uk/files/2017/03/EYFS_ST ATUTORY_FRAMEWORK_ 2017.pdf (accessed 10/5/19).

Dominelli, L (2012) *Green Social Work*. Cambridge, UK: Polity Press.

Gopnik, A (2017) *The Gardener and the Carpenter: What the New Science of Child Development Tells Us About the Relationship Between Parents and Children*. Penguin.

Hawken, P (2008) *Blessed Unrest: How the Largest Social Movement in History is Restoring Grace, Justice and Beauty to the World*. Penguin.

Hochschild, A (2012) *The Managed Heart: The Commercialisation of Human Feelings*. University of California Press.

Iacoboni, M (2009) *Mirroring People: The Science of Empathy and Connecting with Others*. St Martin's Press.

Mind (2018) Nature and Mental Health. See www.mind.org.uk/media/23671047/nature-and-mental-health-2018.pdf

O'Toole, C (2019) Time to Teach the Politics of Mental Health: Implications of the Power Threat Meaning Framework for Teacher Education. *Clinical Psychology Forum* 313 (January).

Pickett, K and Wilkinson, R (2019, January/February) Inequality Is Making Us Ill and Destroying the Planet, but We Can Redress the Balance. *Resurgence and Ecologist* (312).

Rifkin, J (2009) *The Empathic Civilisation: The Race to Global Consciousness in a World in Crisis*. Polity Press.

UNICEF (2018) *Learning Through Play: Strengthening Learning Through Play in Early Childhood. Education Programmes*. New York: UNICEF.

UNICEF (2019) *A World Ready to Learn: Prioritizing Quality Early Childhood Education*. Global Report. New York: UNICEF.

United Nations (1990) Convention on the Rights of the Child. See https://downloads.unicef.org.uk/wp- con tent/uploads/2010/05/UNCRC_united_nations_convention_on_the_rights_of_the_child.pdf?_ ga=2.188103723.2074022203.1557401864–855043956.1557401864.

United Nations Children's Fund (2015) Unless We Act Now: The Impact of Climate Change on Children. See www.unicef.org/publications/files/Unless_we_act_now_The_impact_of_climate_change_on_children.pdf

World Health Organisation (2016) Urban Green Space and Health: Intervention Impacts and Effectiveness. Report of a Meeting, Bonn, Germany, 20–21 September.

Index

Note: Page numbers in *italics* indicate figures and page numbers in **bold** indicate tables on the corresponding page.